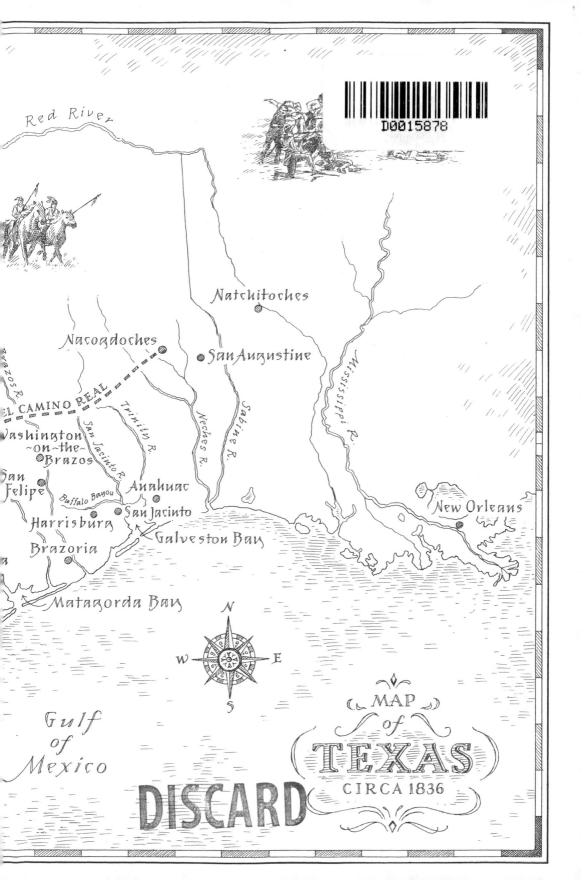

Red River

Natchitoches

Nacogdoches

San Augustine

EL CAMINO REAL

Washington
~on~the~
Brazos

San
Felipe

Brazos R.

Trinity R.

San Jacinto R.

Neches R.

Sabine R.

Mississippi R.

New Orleans

Buffalo Bayou

Anahuac

San Jacinto

Harrisburg

Galveston Bay

Brazoria

Matagorda Bay

N
W   E
S

Gulf
of
Mexico

DISCARD

MAP
of
TEXAS
CIRCA 1836

LONE STAR NATION

Other Books by H. W. Brands

★

The Age of Gold

The First American

T. R.

The Reckless Decade

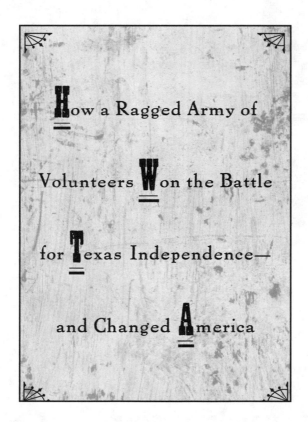

How a Ragged Army of

Volunteers Won the Battle

for Texas Independence—

and Changed America

Doubleday

New York Toronto London Auckland Sydney

LONE STAR NATION

H. W. Brands

PUBLISHED BY DOUBLEDAY
a division of Random House, Inc.

DOUBLEDAY and the portrayal of an anchor with a dolphin are
registered trademarks of Random House, Inc.

Book design by Donna Sinisgalli
Endpaper map by John Burgoyne

Library of Congress Cataloging-in-Publication Data
Brands, H. W.
Lone star nation : how a ragged army of volunteers won the battle for Texas
independence—and changed America / H. W. Brands.—1st ed.
p.   cm.
Includes bibliographical references and index.
1. Texas—History—Revolution, 1835–1836.   2. Texas—History—To 1846.   3.
Texas—History—1846–1850.   I. Title.
F390.B833 2004
976.4'03—dc22   2003061921

ISBN 0-385-50737-2

PRINTED IN THE UNITED STATES OF AMERICA

March 2004
First Edition

1   3   5   7   9   10   8   6   4   2

Contents

Part Four: Lone Star and Union (1836–1865)

LONE
STAR
NATION

PART ONE

The Banks of the Brazos

(to 1828)

The Promised Land

The land was enough to excite any man's lust, and perhaps emotions more deadly. Geology and climate had shaped the region of Texas between the Gulf of Mexico and the Balcones Escarpment almost as if they had human settlement in mind. Like most of the North American continent, this land formed beneath the sea, from sediment drifting down through tepid waters inhabited by prehistoric crustaceans and bony fish. The bones and shells mixed with mud to form the chalky limestone that would characterize much of Texas when it surfaced. Eventually the sea bottom rose, as it did all across proto—North America, but where in other parts of the continent the rising was rapid and disruptive, producing the jagged highlands of the Rocky Mountains and Sierra Nevada, in Texas it was measured and calm. A handful of minor volcanoes spread lava across the landscape, but for the most part the emergence involved little more than a gentle tilting of the seafloor, with the northwest rising slightly more than the southeast.

The placid nature of this process, and its undramatic outcome, had two important results. First, it left Texas with no dominant river—nothing like the Mississippi or the Ohio or even the Delaware or the Hudson. Instead, Texas had (and has) several more or less equal rivers, all relatively small, running roughly parallel from northwest to southeast. In the age before motorized land travel, rivers were the key to crossing continents; with no large rivers, Texas held the key to nothing besides itself. To find Texas, one had to be looking for it; consequently Texas remained off the beaten track for many decades after neighboring regions were explored and settled.

Second, the gentle gradient and modest flow of the Texas rivers meant that their valleys retained most of what their waters eroded. Unlike such large, powerful rivers as the Missouri, which transports its silt hundreds of miles before depositing it in the delta of the Mississippi, the slow, small rivers of Texas drop their burden along their own banks, in bottomlands of wonderful fertility. In the early nineteenth century, when farming formed the mainstay of the American economy (and the economies of nearly every other country), fertile land was money in the bank; it was the pride of the present and the hope of the future; it was what separated the haves from the have-nots; it was what made democracy possible and America different from Europe. Many immigrants to Texas came from Tennessee, where the stony ridges and thin soil tested the patience of even the Jobs among the plowmen; at first feel of the deep black earth along the Brazos and Colorado and Guadalupe, these liberated toilers fell in love.

Love wasn't what drew the Austin family to Texas. Moses Austin and his son Stephen responded to emotions more mercenary. Neither was a husbandman; they came not to plant but to extract. Yet they were happy to exploit the land lust of their contemporaries—indeed, their plans depended on such passion.

In another respect, though, Moses Austin was typical of the Americans who settled Texas in the 1820s and 1830s, even archetypal. Failure in the States drove many to this border province of Mexico, and no one's failure was more spectacular than Moses'.

He was born in Connecticut in 1761, when Texas was part of the Spanish empire and Connecticut part of the British empire. He came of age amid the American Revolution, a conflict that left him an orphan with an inheritance of seventy pounds sterling, which he invested in the dry-goods trade. He practiced briefly in Connecticut before relocating to Philadelphia; the commercial (and recurrently political) capital of the new republic, where he partnered with his elder brother Stephen (for whom Moses' son would be named). But Philadelphia was a tough market to crack, and Stephen a hard man to live with, and Moses soon continued south to Richmond, the new capital of Virginia. The young city showed promise, between its location at the head of navigation on the James River and the construction that must accompany the establishment of a seat of government. Unfortunately, the promise remained unfulfilled during Moses' first years there. "As to business," he lamented in the summer of 1787, "nothing can equal it for badness."

Moses didn't discourage easily, and at twenty-six he was willing to seek new outlets for his ambitions. A principal item of inventory for any eighteenth-century dealer in dry goods was lead. In later generations this humble metal would be superseded for many purposes by substances more durable and less toxic, but in Moses Austin's time (as for the preceding couple of millennia), lead seemed a marvel of nature. It was used in plumbing (the Latin for lead was *plumbus*), in painting (as an ingredient in various pigments), in printing (type was cast in lead), in hunting and war (for lead bullets and shot), in ceramics (pigments again), in tableware and buttons (as a constituent of pewter), in construction (as roofing material and in windows), and in dozens of other ways. Thomas Jefferson praised lead in his *Notes on the State of Virginia* and pointed to a large deposit on the upper reaches of the Great Kanawha River near Virginia's border with North Carolina. "The metal is mixed, sometimes with earth, and sometimes with rock, which requires the force of gunpowder to open it," Jefferson observed. But despite the difficulties of extracting the metal, Jefferson suggested that money could be made, and American society benefited by the exploitation of this deposit.

After talking brother Stephen into joining him in the venture, Moses persuaded the Virginia legislature to lease the Kanawha mine to the two of them. In 1789, just as George Washington was taking the oath of office as the first president of the republic established under the new federal constitution, Moses Austin embarked on a career as a frontier industrialist. Whether by design or afterthought, this coincidence became part of Austin's business plan. Explaining how essential lead was to American security and independence, the Austin brothers lobbied the federal government to provide tariff protection for domestic lead against imports. Jefferson, now secretary of state, disapproved of protective tariffs on the principle that they taxed the many to enrich the few, but Treasury Secretary Alexander Hamilton, Jefferson's arch-foe and the apostle of assistance to industry, endorsed the Austins' argument. President Washington sided with Hamilton, and when Congress joined the president and the Treasury secretary, the Austin brothers got the duty they desired.

A knack for working the border between the public and private sectors would become an Austin family trademark. For now it gave Moses and Stephen the confidence to invest heavily in their new venture. The brothers borrowed to lure laborers to the mines, including some English experts who commanded premium salaries. They built a town—Austinville—to house the workers and provide the services they required. They aggressively hawked their product line—sheet lead, rolled lead, powdered lead, lead ingots, lead shot—in nearly every state, in the belief that while the American market should be shielded from foreign competition, that market ought to belong to the Austins.

In 1785 Moses wedded Mary Brown of Philadelphia. Two years later Maria, as Moses called her, bore a daughter who lived barely a month. In 1790 the couple had another daughter, who died after a half year. Perhaps they thought Richmond was jinxed, for they moved to Austinville, where in 1793 Maria gave birth to a son, Stephen Fuller Austin. This child encountered the usual infant maladies but clung to life. A sister, Emily, similarly resilient, arrived two years later.

By then the restless Moses was looking farther west. The price of lead rose and fell on rumors of war with Britain or France, which had renewed their ancestral struggle and appeared bent on entangling the United States. The commercial turmoil bankrupted the Austins' customers, leaving the brothers holding worthless notes and having to ask their own creditors for grace. Stephen traveled to England to try to unload the mine, only to be imprisoned for debt.

Moses sought salvation in the opposite direction. In the same passage of his *Notes on Virginia* that praised the mines of southwestern Virginia, Jefferson had mentioned still richer mines "on the Spanish side of the Mississippi, opposite to Kaskaskia." Moses had felt the influence of the Spanish mines in the competition their lead afforded his own for the growing market of Kentucky and Tennessee. During the late autumn of 1796, as cold weather and snow brought operations at Austinville to their winter's halt, he set out to visit the Spanish mines and see how rich they really were.

The route west was called the Wilderness Road, and though few travelers disputed the first part of that label, many questioned the second. The road—a trail, actually, as often as not—crossed the Cumberland Gap, the natural gateway between the uplands of Virginia, where rivers flow to the east, and the Ohio and Mississippi Valleys, where streams run west and south. White travelers first found the gap in the middle of the eighteenth century; Daniel Boone went through in 1769 and spent the next two years roaming Kentucky. He subsequently returned with his family and other prospective settlers, but the party was ambushed by Indians at the gap and forced to turn back. Yet Boone persisted and subsequently laid the route for Boone's Trace, the path that became the Wilderness Road.

By the time Moses Austin embarked on his journey, Kentucky was a state. During the milder seasons of the year, travel along the road wasn't especially arduous, even if long stretches remained sparsely inhabited. But during the winter, the going was difficult to the point of dangerous. Moses left Austinville in the second week of December, accompanied by Joseph Bell, an employee at the mine. Despite severe cold and heavy snow, the pair made rapid progress, as much as thirty-five miles a day. The harsh weather kept them from camping out—although some nights Austin and Bell wished they *had* stayed out of doors. Austin characterized conditions in one hut where they took refuge as "abominably bad." Seventeen travelers crammed into a space a mere twelve feet square, forcing all to jostle and jab for elbow and knee room.

Moses' journey that winter opened his eyes to something he had generally sensed but never fully appreciated: the lengths to which his contemporaries would go to acquire land. "I cannot omit noticing the many distressed families I passed in the wilderness," he recorded in his journal.

Nor can anything be more distressing to a man of feeling than to see women and children in the month of December traveling a wilderness through ice and snow, passing large rivers and creeks without shoe or stocking, and barely as many rags as covers their nakedness, without money or provisions except what the wilderness affords. . . .

Ask these pilgrims what they expect when they get to Kentucky; the answer is Land. Have you any? [Austin inquired.] No, but I expect I can get it. Have you anything to pay for land? No. Did you ever see the country? No, but everybody says it's good land.

Can anything be more absurd than the conduct of man? Here is hundreds, traveling hundreds of miles, they know not what for nor whither, except it's to Kentucky, passing land almost as good and easy obtained, the proprietors of which would gladly give on any terms. But it will not do. It's not Kentucky. It's not the Promised Land. It's not the goodly inheritance, the Land of Milk and Honey.

The desperate search for land was astonishing to behold, and Austin, though not a farmer himself, couldn't help being moved by its power. Perhaps unconsciously, he filed a mental note.

A heavy snow fell on the second day of 1797, trapping Austin and Bell at Vincennes on the Wabash River. For forty-eight hours they waited, with Austin chatting up townsfolk and fellow travelers. But his patience ran out, and, despite warnings that he would lose his way among the drifts and be frozen, Austin decided to press on. He hired a guide, a weathered Frenchman named Basidon, and the trio plunged into the storm.

The first two days went well enough, although the nights—spent in the open, huddled around large fires that required constant stoking and sank slowly in the snow—were uncomfortable. On the third day out, they lost the road beneath the drifts. Then the weather warmed and, paradoxically, their situation grew more dangerous. The moisture that had been falling as snow turned to rain, which soaked the travelers and their mounts and coated the bushes with ice, preventing the horses from browsing the leaves. Basidon and Bell began to wonder what Austin had gotten them into, but Austin cheered them by saying that if the worst came, they could eat the horses and mule. And if they kept moving west, they couldn't miss the Mississippi. Yet even Austin had his worried moments, and when they finally stumbled upon a small village not far from the great river, he was most relieved. "None but those who have been in a similar condition can have an idea of our feelings," he wrote. "Had the everlasting trumpet sounded our eternal happiness I do not think it would have been more agreeable."

In 1797 the Mississippi formed the boundary between the United States and Spanish Louisiana. The Mississippi Valley had been explored and claimed by the French in the seventeenth century, and it was one of the prizes of the subsequent wars among the Europeans and their American kin. When the French lost the French and Indian War (also called the Seven Years' War, despite lasting nine years), Britain took the eastern half of the valley and Spain got the western half. When the British lost the American Revolutionary War, the United States acquired the eastern half, with Spain keeping the west. Yet French interest hadn't vanished, nor had French influence. The French language was still commonly spoken along the Mississippi, and many officials of the government of Spanish Louisiana, headquartered at St. Louis, were in fact French.

St. Louis, founded a century earlier by Robert Cavelier de La

Salle, showed the benefits of location in commanding the trade of the Missouri, Illinois, and Mississippi Rivers. "It is fast improving and will soon be a large place," Austin wrote upon arrival. The prospect piqued his desire to see the mines he had come so far to examine. François Valle, the commandant of the district, was at Ste. Genevieve, on the river a day's ride south; Austin went there and made such a good case for himself that Valle provided fresh horses for the final forty miles.

Knowing the mining trade, Austin could see almost at a glance that the tales he had heard of Spanish lead deposits weren't exaggerated. "I found the mines equal to my expectation in every respect." The ore was close to the surface and was of "better quality than any I have ever seen." The deposit was called Mine à Breton, after its discoverer, a French soldier named Breton who was said to have chased a deer into the district, fallen over a rock, and detected a remarkable resemblance between the rock and his ammunition. Austin was more impressed by the recent history of the place, starting with the production just that last summer of four hundred thousand pounds of lead, and by the inefficiency of the miners' techniques, which meant that the deposits would be even more productive in the hands of someone who knew what he was doing. Observation and brief experiment convinced Austin that he could triple the mines' output.

Returning to Ste. Genevieve, Austin presented a plan to Valle whereby Spain would grant Austin land and mineral rights in exchange for his commitment to develop the mines and furnish Spain with the lead shot and sheets its army and navy required. With Spain enmeshed in the wars of the French Revolution, Austin guessed that this strategic angle would appeal to Valle. It did—almost as much as Austin's offer to cut Valle in as a partner. Valle endorsed Austin's plan and sent it south to his superiors in New Spain.

Austin returned to Virginia to await the verdict of the Spanish government. Six months later it arrived. Austin was awarded less land than he had asked for—one league instead of sixteen—but, given that he had requested far more land than he needed, he was happy to accept Spain's terms.

In the summer of 1798 Moses Austin led his family and followers out of Virginia and into the mountains of Tennessee. The family consisted of Maria, five-year-old Stephen, three-year-old Emily, and Austin's sister and her husband and two sons; the followers were some thirty free workers and slaves from Austinville. They went to establish a mining operation at Mine à Breton, but also a colony, since nothing in the way of a settled community existed there. Moses Austin would be employer, political leader, and patriarch.

The journey lasted three harrowing months. Austin's sister died of disease, as did one of her sons. The other son drowned in the Ohio. All the travelers were gravely weakened by the bad food, bad weather, and bad luck of the trip; when the party landed on the western, Spanish bank of the Mississippi, several could hardly walk.

Spanish officials were scarce in Upper Louisiana, and Austin, after renouncing his American allegiance and declaring himself a subject of the Spanish crown, was essentially free to govern his colony as he chose. This brought him no more than the usual conflicts with family and his own workers, but the handful of seasonal French miners who had previously worked the Mine à Breton objected. They hadn't entirely accepted the notion of Spanish rule, and now to find themselves confronted by this American—whatever nationality he currently claimed—sat even less well.

More troublesome than the Frenchmen were the local Indians,

who hadn't accepted *any* of the whites. The Osages and their neighbors didn't entirely resist the white presence, for they valued the trade goods the whites provided: the knives, cooking pots, firearms, beads, and other items that made aboriginal life easier or more pleasant. But where the French and Spanish had come primarily to trade, these Americans were coming to settle. The effect on the neighborhood could only be disruptive.

The Osages attacked in 1799, then again the next year, and the year after that. The most serious assault occurred in May 1802. Stephen Austin was eight years old at the time, and the experience stuck in his memory. "In 1802," he wrote later, "the village of Mine à Breton was attacked by a large party of Indians, their chief object being to plunder my father's house and store, and to kill the Americans, or Bostonians, as they called them." Stephen Austin continued: "He had, however, taken the precaution to provide himself, in addition to other arms, with a three-pounder [a cannon that fired three-pound balls], and being fully prepared for a defense, the Indians failed in their efforts and were driven back."

Against the Indians and the French, Moses had his hands full defending his colony. Yet he had never expected the frontier to be for the faint-hearted, and he proceeded to develop the lead mine according to his initial blueprint. He poured all of his own money into the works and borrowed many thousands of dollars from others. He built high-efficiency furnaces, which recovered far more metal from each ton of ore than his predecessors had managed (and allowed him to profitably mine the tailings of previous operations on the site). So efficient was Austin's operation that other miners in the region brought him their ore to smelt; even after he took his 50 percent cut, they came out ahead. He built a tall tower for the production of shot (molten lead was allowed to dribble from trays at the top of the tower, and in the weightlessness of free fall congealed into spherical beads that were collected at the bottom). Within several years his operation achieved an annual production of eight hundred thousand pounds, making Austin a very wealthy man. In 1810 he estimated his net value at $190,000.

But nothing stayed the same for long on the frontier—not even the location of the frontier. Within a half decade of his arrival, Austin found himself once more on American soil. In 1800 France's ambitious new ruler, Napoleon Bonaparte, extorted Louisiana back from Spain, and in 1803, after a sudden change of plans, he sold it to the United States. Moses Austin, having abandoned the country of his birth and sworn fealty to Spain, found himself living again on American territory. Had Austin been more patriotic, he might have celebrated this unexpected reunion; but had he been more patriotic he might never have left American soil. In fact, Austin's loyalty was as fluid as that of many frontiersmen, who acted like Americans on the American side of the border, like Spanish on the Spanish side, and even like Indians among the Indians.

In at least one sense, American sovereignty posed a threat to Austin's position—a threat worse than that of the Indians or the French. His control of Mine à Breton rested on Spanish authority; whether the Americans, who were notorious for ignoring titles granted under predecessor regimes, would accept his control was an open question. Some did; others didn't. The latter included a Tennesseean named John Smith, who had a murderous temper and the ear of James Wilkinson, the newly appointed governor of Upper Louisiana. Wilkinson had been a general in the Revolutionary War, a land speculator and merchant afterward, and an intriguer all his life. During the 1790s he engaged the Spanish authorities of Louisiana in negotiations that seemed at least faintly treasonous to his many American enemies, but influential friends in the American government deemed his local knowledge essential for a territorial governor and won him the job.

Between them, Smith and Wilkinson made Austin's life a trial. Smith stirred the French miners against Austin, challenged the validity of Austin's title, and apparently attempted to provoke Austin to a duel. "What have I done to this *monster* in society?" Austin moaned to a friend. Austin declined to duel, but he had no effective answer to the campaign of sabotage and character assassination Smith mounted against him, with Wilkinson's help.

Austin's deeper problems derived from the tumultuous state of the American economy, which in turn reflected the unsettled condition of American diplomacy. During Thomas Jefferson's second term as president the serial fighting between Britain and France became a battle to the death; in their extremity both sides preyed on American shipping, with Britain seizing American vessels bound for France and France waylaying American ships headed for Britain. Jefferson judged that American security required keeping clear of Europe's wars, and he persuaded Congress to embargo trade with Europe. The embargo proved an economic disaster, plunging American seaports into depression and generating shock waves that spread up American rivers as far as St. Louis. The lead market collapsed, leaving Moses Austin with tons of metal he couldn't unload and stacks of bonds he couldn't redeem.

His prospects improved when a chastened Jefferson and Congress rescinded the embargo, but the War of 1812 (against Britain), after briefly driving prices up, produced another collapse. British warships strangled American trade, and men and money fled Upper Louisiana for the theaters and markets of the war. Moses Austin tried to solve his manpower shortage by leasing a small regiment of slaves, and to augment the local money supply by helping establish a St. Louis bank. Yet the slaves required more upkeep than he had reckoned, and his bank ran into liquidity troubles. The result was that Austin's debt simply grew deeper. By 1818 he was compelled to put the Mine à Breton up for sale. "Would to God my business was closed," he lamented. "I would leave this country in a week."

Potential buyers, however, guessed that if Moses Austin couldn't make lead pay, neither could they, and the mine went begging. Austin's debts continued to grow even as his ability to repay them diminished. The end—or what certainly seemed the end—came in March 1820 when the sheriff arrested and jailed him for nonpayment. Once the greatest man in the district, Austin now shared quarters with drunks and common criminals. The fall would have broken the spirit of most men, and it came close to breaking Austin's. He pleaded with his daughter's husband to hasten to his rescue lest the sheriff auction the lead works to pay down the debts. His plea failed, and the richest mine in the North American heartland was hammered away for pennies on Austin's dollars.

Austin won his freedom, but it held no pleasure for him. He refused to live a pauper where he had been a prince. "To remain in a country where I had enjoyed wealth, in a state of poverty, I could not submit to," he recalled. Two decades earlier, Moses Austin had started a new life in a new country; he was convinced he must do so again.

Yet there was a difference to the moving this time. The trek to Spanish Louisiana had been a hopeful journey by a young man in the prime of confidence and energy; this move was the desperate act of a man drowning in failure and debt, a fifty-eight-year-old with no margin for further failure and nothing to fall back on should this last scheme go awry.

★

The region to which he pinned his hopes was Texas. Moses Austin knew little of Texas beyond that it was Spanish—a fact crucial to his plans. A treaty concluded just several months earlier had apparently marked the end of a decade and a half of bickering between the United States and Spain over the border between their respective territories. Jefferson had asserted that the southwestern boundary of America's Louisiana Purchase was the Rio Grande, but he did little to defend this interpretation, having his hands full with the British and the French on the high seas. His successor, James Madison, had even more trouble with the British, culminating in the War of 1812 (which didn't end before the redcoats chased the president from the White House and burned the mansion and the Capitol). Meanwhile, American friction with Spain focused on Florida, which General Andrew Jackson of Tennessee, the military hero of the war and a rising political force in the West, and many others demanded be added to the American domain. By 1819 Secretary of State John Quincy Adams was willing to surrender whatever claim the United States might have had to Texas in exchange for a tidying up of the Florida question (in America's favor) and other details between the United States and Spain.

Moses Austin was that rare American west of the Mississippi who wanted Spain to keep Texas. By this time it was becoming an item of the American gospel—at least as that gospel was preached in the West—that American sovereignty must chase the setting sun. Westerners denounced the abandonment of Texas to Spain as a sellout of their region by New England (Adams was from Massachusetts), an ignoble surrender of territory honestly acquired by purchase from France.

Moses Austin dissented from the gospel. Whether or not he consciously thought himself so, he was a man of the border, an expert in the arbitrage of political and cultural differences. His successful start in Spanish Louisiana had resulted from his ability to broker between the Spanish on the west bank and the Americans on the east; his prospects declined when both banks became American. Others were more adept at business, at straightforward buying and selling, than he; what Austin required was the added complication of a frontier, a political border.

And so he was pleased to learn that the border between Texas and the United States had been preserved, and he prepared to exploit it. He would travel to Spanish Texas, as he had traveled to Spanish Louisiana two decades earlier, and he would present a plan for developing the country. He assumed that the same incentives applied now as had applied then: that the Spanish authorities, eager to increase the population and prosperity of their district, would welcome the immigration of responsible, productive individuals and families. For his part in arranging this boon, he hoped to be compensated in land, of which Texas had far more than the Spanish could ever use themselves.

He set off in the spring of 1820, traveling south to Little Rock, Arkansas, where his son Stephen, now an adult, was living, and where Moses contracted malaria. He spent the summer and part of the autumn regaining his strength. Not till November did he resume his journey, riding a horse borrowed from Stephen, carrying fifty dollars from Stephen, and accompanied by one of Stephen's slaves, a young man named Richmond, who rode a borrowed mule.

Moses and Richmond proceeded south to Natchitoches, on the Red River in the state of Louisiana. For more than a century the hundred miles between Natchitoches and Nacogdoches, the first town on the Texas side of the Sabine, had been a no-man's-land, inhabited by individuals who preferred the uncertainty and lawlessness of border regions. Although the Louisiana bank of the Sabine had calmed down somewhat, the Texas side remained desolate and wild, as Austin discovered on crossing over. Indeed, the entire five hundred miles to San Antonio de Béxar, the capital of Texas, was nearly deserted.

Austin's reception at Béxar, as the inhabitants called the town of two thousand, made him regret he had come. The governor, Antonio Martínez, refused to listen to his proposal. Texas had been plagued by American filibusters (from "free-booter" in the language of the Dutch, who had made a business of the piracy the term connoted), and Martínez had orders to allow no more Americans to enter Texas. If Austin had not been carrying the Spanish passport he had acquired twenty-three years earlier, Martínez might well have thrown him into prison; as it was, the governor told Austin to turn around and go home.

With nothing at home to go back to, Austin refused to let the conversation end so quickly. He spoke no Spanish and Martínez no English, but both spoke French, and in French Austin tried to warm the governor up. Martínez still wouldn't listen. His superior, Commandant Joaquín de Arredondo, had made it clear that no aid whatsoever was to be extended to any Americans, and Martínez was loath to cross Arredondo, a man of terrifying reputation. Merely talking to Austin risked trouble. Consequently, the more Austin tried to crack Martínez' reserve, the more anxious and angry Martínez became.

Finally, denying Austin even the hospitality of one night in town, he ordered him to leave Béxar immediately.

Austin had no choice; the town was small enough that his every move was public knowledge. He found Richmond and told him to water, feed, and saddle the horse and mule for departure by dusk.

But then occurred something so unlikely that many contemporaries and even some later historians refused to believe it was a coincidence. Walking across the plaza of Béxar that waning afternoon in December 1820, Austin encountered a person he had met many years before in New Orleans. Philip Nering Bögel was a Dutchman born in the Netherlands' South American colony of Guiana and raised, for the most part, in Holland. As a young man, he joined the Dutch army and later became a tax collector. Evidently he collected more than he remitted to his superiors, for he suddenly fled Holland back to the New World, leaving behind a wife and children and a prosecutor waving a reward of one thousand gold ducats for his arrest.

By the time he resurfaced in Spanish Louisiana—shortly before Moses Austin's first visit—he was passing himself off as the Baron de Bastrop. Promotions of this nature weren't uncommon on the frontier, and the title stuck. He applied for and received permission to plant a colony in the Ouachita Valley and to engage in trade. He remained in Louisiana through the reversion of that territory to France, but when the United States acquired the country he crossed into Texas. He applied at San Antonio de Béxar for permission to found another colony, northeast of the town. Though his application was granted, the colony never amounted to much. Bastrop took up residence in Béxar, where he dabbled in business and served as assistant alcalde (the alcalde was an appointed mayor-cum-sheriff), as an unofficial one-man chamber of commerce, and as host to the strangers who periodically wandered through.

This was the man Austin encountered in December 1820 in the Béxar plaza, and he listened as Austin told his story. Austin explained that he hoped to bring three hundred American families to Texas and to be rewarded in land for doing so. Confident of his persuasiveness if he could only get a hearing with Governor Martínez, he asked Bastrop for help.

Bastrop arranged for Austin to stay in San Antonio over Christmas, just two days away. During that time the American convinced the Dutchman that his colonization scheme made sense. For several generations the Spanish government had tried to populate Texas in order to keep interlopers and Indians at bay and to lend credibility to Spanish claims of possession. But the efforts had always fallen short. Texas was far from the inhabited regions of Mexico, and it held few attractions that couldn't be matched by neighborhoods less remote. In part as a result—as Moses Austin had observed on his way south and west—large stretches of Texas were uninhabited. Yet they wouldn't remain so: already land-hungry Americans were crossing the Sabine illegally and seizing unoccupied tracts. By 1820 the question wasn't whether the Americans would come; the question was whether they would come with Spain's blessing and under some measure of Spanish control, or unblessed and uncontrolled.

Austin's arguments echoed some Bastrop had made on behalf of his own colonizing efforts. Moreover, as a businessman, if not a very dedicated or successful one, Bastrop appreciated the cardinal requirement of any business: customers. Whatever they might do for Spain, American settlers would help business in Béxar.

The day after Christmas, Bastrop took Austin back to see Governor Martínez. Precisely what Austin said to the governor has been lost to history, but doubtless it paralleled the petition he laid before Martínez (which Bastrop helped translate). In his proposal Austin

spoke of the obvious intention of the Spanish king that Texas prosper, and he presented himself as "the agent of three hundred families who, with the same purpose in view, are desirous of seeing the
intention of his Majesty fulfilled." Austin's three hundred families
were, at this point, merely notional, but he contended that they would
be exemplary colonists. "All of them, or the greater part of them, have
property. Those without it are industrious. As soon as they are settled, they bind themselves by oath to take up their arms in defense of
the Spanish government against either the Indians, filibusters, or
any other enemy that may plan hostilities—coming upon call and
obeying the orders given them."

Just why Martínez now found Austin's argument persuasive is
hard to say. Certainly Bastrop's endorsement helped change his
mind. Nor did it hurt that Martínez shared Austin's (and Bastrop's)
views about the value of immigrants, and the governor couldn't fore-
see immigrants arriving under circumstances more favorable than
those Austin outlined. "The proposal which he is making," Martínez
declared in a letter forwarding Austin's petition to Commandant
Arredondo, "is, in my opinion, the only one which is bound to provide for the increase and prosperity in his settlement and even others in this Province. . . . Otherwise I look upon the appearance of
such a favorable development as quite remote."

With his petition in the hands of the Spanish bureaucracy, Austin
headed for home to await the verdict. He left Béxar in company with
a man named Kirkham, who called himself a commercial traveler but
whose principal stock was stolen horses. Kirkham robbed Austin and
Richmond in the middle of the night, taking their mounts and provi-

sions and leaving them stranded in the wilderness. January temperatures on the broken prairies northeast of San Antonio rarely remain below freezing for long, but travelers caught out in the rain, as Austin and Richmond were, risk hypothermia nonetheless. When the travelers lack food, the cold and damp become doubly dangerous. Austin and Richmond struggled east but grew weaker by the mile. They contracted colds and then pneumonia—"flux," they called it—which got worse with each creek and river forded or swum. By the time they collapsed in the doorway of one Hugh McGuffin, west of Natchitoches, Austin seemed, in words retold from a traveler who greeted them there, "a mere skeleton on the verge of death by starvation."

Yet the skeleton housed a heart that quickened to think of what lay ahead. Recuperating at McGuffin's, Austin wrote a letter to Bastrop depicting the bright future of Texas upon the planting of the American colony. To encourage Bastrop's continued support, Austin invited him to invest, avowing "full confidence" that the project would return "thousands of dollars" to those who got in early. He said he would travel north to gather his belongings before coming back to Texas in the spring. "I shall, life and health admitting, most undoubtedly return from the upper country by May next, when I wish to remove with all my property to the Colorado."

Unfortunately for Austin, life and health didn't admit. He began the journey north before he was ready, and relapsed en route. When he could travel again, he was well enough only to proceed by boat: down the Red River to the Mississippi, and up the Mississippi to home. Maria Austin, shocked at her husband's condition, ordered him at once to bed.

But he wouldn't stay in bed, sick though he was. He had been back less than a week when a messenger from Texas brought word that his petition had been approved. As Austin's luck would have it,

the government of Spain had recently decided to encourage immigration to its American empire; Austin's petition provided an early
opportunity to try out the new approach. In February 1821 Governor
Martínez dispatched an envoy named Erasmo Seguín to find Austin
and tell him that he might start signing up colonists.

Austin was overjoyed. "I returned from St. Antonio in the
province of Texas five days since, after undergoing everything but
death," he wrote his younger son, James. "For these sufferings I have
been fully paid by obtaining a grant for myself and family of land and
also for 300 families. I shall settle on the Colorado within 2 miles of
the sea and three days' sail from the Mississippi, where I shall lay off
a town under the protection of the Spanish Government."

During the next several weeks, with the promised land looming
ever larger in his mind's eye, he devoted every waking minute and
most of his dreams to this redemption of his life's work. He allowed
almost no time to eat and scarcely more to sleep. For a while his excitement carried him forward, but then his body gave way. On June 8
Maria wrote Stephen regarding Moses' condition, saying that a doctor had been summoned and had blistered and bled the patient. The
treatment worked, briefly. "I flattered myself he was much better.
But, oh, my son, I greatly fear it was only a delusion. . . . His fever
has returned this day with great violence. He breathes with much
difficulty and seems in great distress both in body and mind."

The end came before dawn a few days later. "His fever was
higher on that night than it had been," Maria related. "At four in the
morning I discovered the St. Anthony fire was all over his face, and
he had great difficulty in breathing." She wanted to recall the doctor,
but Moses demurred. "After a considerable exertion to speak, he
drew me down to him and told me it was too late, that he was going,
that he should not live 24 hours." Summoning all his strength,
Moses uttered a final message: "Tell dear Stephen that it is his dying

father's last request to prosecute the enterprise that he had commenced."

With this he slipped back into his fevered dreams of the land
that would erase his failures and make everything right, and shortly
expired.

Chapter 2

El Camino Real

For much of the three hundred years that Europeans and their descendants had known of Texas, the land seemed cursed—by fate, by human folly, and by its very allure. In the early sixteenth century the mainland of North America was still largely unknown to the Spanish, the only Europeans in the region. Spanish conquistadors had landed in Mexico and in Florida, but what lay between was a mystery. Pánfilo de Narváez, a one-eyed veteran of the Mexican conquest, aimed to diminish the mystery—and claim a victory comparable to that of Hernán Cortés—by leading an expedition to the northern shore of the Gulf of Mexico. Narváez landed in Florida in 1528 and promptly demonstrated that he was no Cortés and Florida no Mexico. He lost touch with his supply ships and floundered about the peninsula; his troops grew hungry and sick and fell victim to Indian ambushes. Upon discovering neither gold nor other reason to stay, Narváez prepared to abandon the place. Showing considerable ingenuity but little real skill, the dwindling company constructed five makeshift boats, in which they set out to the west. None in the group could navigate, so they stayed within sight of the shore, passing Mobile Bay (as it would be called) and the Mississippi River (yet to be discovered), before encountering a heavy storm. The tempest drove the flotilla apart, with two of the boats wrecking on the beach and the others sinking at sea. The survivors initially numbered about eighty, but between exposure (it was November), hunger, disease, and hostility on the part of the local Indians, these four score were reduced to four, including Álvar Núñez Cabeza de Vaca, the treasurer of the Narváez expedition, and an African slave named Estevánico.

Whether or not these were the first non-Americans to set foot in what would become Texas, they were the first to record their visit, and what they recorded hardly inclined others to follow. Cabeza de Vaca (whose name commemorated a thirteenth-century battle in which an ancestor facilitated victory by pointing a bovine skull—"head of cow"—in the direction of a strategic pass) described an ordeal almost unbelievable in its rigors. The shipwreck left them with nary a stitch of clothing; they spent the next several years mostly naked and variously shivering, scratched, sunburned, and bleeding. They were almost constantly hungry. When nuts were in season, they lived on nuts for weeks at a time. When the prickly pear cactus yielded its fruit, this provided their sole sustenance. Captured by the Indians and enslaved, Cabeza de Vaca was required to dig with his bare hands for roots among the river cane. "From this employment I had my fingers so worn that did a straw but touch them they would bleed," he wrote later. Nor were the roots any prize. "The food is poor and gripes the persons who eat it. The roots require roasting two days; many are very bitter and withal difficult to be dug." And yet they formed a local staple.

They are sought the distance of two or three leagues, and so great is the want these people experience that they can-

not get through the year without them. Occasionally they
kill deer, and at times take fish; but the quantity is so small
and the famine so great, that they eat spiders and the eggs
of ants, worms, lizards, salamanders, snakes, and vipers
that kill whom they strike; and they eat earth and wood,
and all that there is, the dung of deer, and other things that
I omit to mention; and I honestly believe that were there
stones in that land they would eat them. They save the
bones of the fishes they consume, of snakes and other animals, that they may afterward beat them together and eat
the powder.

Poverty did not in any way ennoble the natives. "The majority of
the people are great thieves; for though they are free to divide with
each other, on turning the head even a son or a father will take what
he can. They are great liars, and also great drunkards, which they become from the use of a certain liquor."

In light of his ordeal, Cabeza de Vaca had reason to be biased
against the Indians, and readers of his account might have been justified in applying the appropriate discount. Yet, oddly, he developed
an affection for those among whom he suffered, realizing the duress
under which they lived, for having shared it. "They are a merry people, considering the hunger they suffer; for they never cease,
notwithstanding, to observe their festivities and areytos. To them the
happiest part of the year is the season of eating prickly pears; they
have hunger then no longer, pass all the time in dancing, and eat day
and night." The mere thought of the prickly pears carried them
through the other seasons, and they sought to hearten Cabeza de Vaca
and his comrades similarly. "It occurred to us many times while we
were among this people and there was no food, to be three or four

days without eating, when they, to revive our spirits, would tell us not to be sad, that soon there would be prickly pears when we should eat a plenty and drink of the juice, when our bellies would be very big and we should be content and joyful, having no hunger."

Eventually the Spaniards' condition improved. As an exotic, Cabeza de Vaca was assumed to have peculiar powers, including the ability to heal; when some early patients fortuitously improved, he won a reputation and a following. This afforded him greater freedom to move about unsupervised, yet it also increased the reluctance of his hosts to let him go. Finally, however, he and the other three broke away. They traveled south and west along the Texas coast, then north and west up the Rio Grande, then south and west again until they reached the Pacific Ocean—some eight years after their shipwreck.

Although the emergence—or resurrection, as it seemed—of these last survivors of the Narváez expedition appeared little short of miraculous, the account they gave of their experience did nothing to encourage further expeditions toward Texas. The lesson of Narváez and Cabeza de Vaca—a lesson that gained a wider audience after 1542, when Cabeza de Vaca's account was published—was that Texas was a worthless land best left alone.

Yet the author wasn't quite so discouraging about other parts of the territory north of Mexico. In his description of the upper Rio Grande, Cabeza de Vaca dropped intriguing hints of mineral wealth. "Throughout this region, wheresoever the mountains extend, we saw clear traces of gold and lead, iron, copper, and other metals," he wrote.

This was what the Spanish wanted to hear, and Cabeza de Vaca's words were sufficient to set in train a great expedition to the mountains of Arizona and New Mexico. The leader of the expedition was Francisco Vázquez de Coronado, who headed north to find the asserted treasure. The Coronado expedition was a triumph of logistics, endurance, cruelty, and avarice. Coronado moved a thousand-man army and herds of horses, mules, cattle, and sheep across some of the most barren stretches of North America. His soldiers conquered several villages and terrorized many others. The expedition ran into the Grand Canyon of the Colorado River and crossed the windswept plains and struggling streams of the Texas panhandle, Oklahoma, and Kansas. On the plains the Spaniards saw buffalo and prairie dogs, and noted the natives' ingenious strategy for navigating the featureless tablelands. "Early in the morning they watched where the sun rose," explained Pedro de Castañeda, the expedition's chronicler. "Then, going in the direction they wanted to take, they shot an arrow, and before coming to it they shot another over it, and in this manner they traveled the whole day."

But they found no riches. Referring to an author who had enthusiastically elaborated upon the report of Cabeza de Vaca, a weary Coronado wrote Antonio de Mendoza, the viceroy of New Spain: "I can assure you that he has not told the truth in a single thing that he said, but everything is the opposite of what he related." Coronado realized that Mendoza would be disappointed, and he said that he was, too. "God knows that I wish I had better news to write to your Lordship, but I must tell you the truth. . . . You may be assured that if all the riches and treasures of the world had been here, I could not have done more in his Majesty's service and in that of your Lordship."

The failure of Coronado to find gold cooled the ardor of the Spanish regarding the northern frontiers of Mexico. To the extent they maintained interest at all, it was directed toward the pueblos of the upper Rio Grande. Texas languished in the Spanish imagination and was all but ignored in Spanish policy. Spanish soldiers and travelers occasionally wandered across portions of Texas, accidentally or driven by circumstances beyond their control; a 1680 revolt in New Mexico scattered missionaries, soldiers, and civilian refugees down the Rio Grande to the vicinity of modern El Paso.

But as long as Spain had the hemisphere more or less to itself—and to the indigenes—it ignored Texas in favor of regions better blessed with removable wealth. The planting of English colonies on the eastern coast of North America in the seventeenth century lifted the Spanish gaze above Mexico, but the prophylactic efforts it inspired were directed primarily at Florida, closer to the site of the Protestant infection. The French—fellow Catholics yet rival imperialists—with their settlements in far Canada, registered hardly at all upon the viceroys and other overseers of New Spain.

The situation changed in the late seventeenth century, when the intrepid but unbalanced French explorer and entrepreneur La Salle sledded and canoed from Canada to the Mississippi River, and down the great river to its mouth. Following the custom of the day, he claimed for King Louis XIV the valley of the Mississippi and all its tributaries, and christened it Louisiana.

Such a feat would have satisfied most men, but La Salle burned with ambition augmented by financial ruin, brought on by unwise investments in the fur trade and by La Salle's general lack of business savvy. He prepared to plant a colony near the mouth of the Mississippi, which would win him royal favor and allow him to corner the commerce of Louisiana. With a fleet of four ships and 280 sailors and colonists he left France in the summer of 1684. One of the craft was captured by the Spanish (with whom the French had recently been at war and who failed to receive, or simply ignored, the news that the war had ended), but the other three penetrated far into the Gulf of Mexico, till then a Spanish lake. Perhaps puzzlingly to a later generation, finding the largest river of North America posed a genuine challenge. The details of determining longitude still defied the best explorers and navigators (and would do so till the invention of accurate chronometers almost a century hence), with the consequence that La Salle did not know where either he or the river was. Complicating matters further, in its lower reaches the big river split into a number of smaller streams, no one of which was irrefutably impressive.

As a result, La Salle erred badly in picking a spot for landing. He entered Matagorda Bay—six degrees of longitude and four hundred miles west of the Mississippi—thinking he was *east* of his goal. The landing itself was a fiasco. One of his ships foundered in the shallow channel; most of its stores were lost. Indians captured several of the colonists, commencing a chain of hostilities that sapped the numbers and morale of the colonists. Provisions dwindled, but when the captain of La Salle's fleet volunteered to sail to the West Indies for relief, La Salle rejected the offer, telling him to depart and not return. After the captain left, taking some disaffected colonists with him, La Salle's last vessel was blown ashore and wrecked, stranding the colonists.

They planted crops, which succumbed to drought. Water ran short; scurvy set gums bleeding. Dysentery and other infectious diseases decimated the ranks of the men, women, and children. A rattlesnake claimed the life of one colonist; another man drowned setting a fishnet. An alligator ate yet another. "It seemed as if there was a curse upon our labors," recalled one of the survivors.

Yet the worst of the colony's troubles was La Salle himself. He acted as judge, jury, and executioner—literally, when he convicted and hanged an attempted deserter. "No one tells him anything," remarked an expedition engineer. "This is a man who has lost his mind."

Imprudently but unavoidably, La Salle left the settlement for months at a time, trying to figure out where he was. He traveled far to the west, perhaps reaching the Rio Grande. He traveled east, to the land of the Hasinai, or Tejas, Indians (who subsequently gave their name—rendered in English as Texas—to the region). Eventually he discovered his navigational mistake and struck out overland for the fort—St. Louis—he had previously established near the confluence of the Illinois and Mississippi Rivers. En route several of his men, exasperated beyond endurance by his despotic behavior, murdered him and his few remaining loyalists.

Those left at La Salle's settlement tried to make peace with the local Karankawa Indians. But after the natives realized that La Salle wasn't coming back, they descended on the fort and killed everyone there, except five children who were taken captive and forcibly adopted into the tribe.

★

The adoption, as it turned out, was temporary, for when the Spanish learned that La Salle had penetrated their private sea, they commenced a manhunt for the French explorer. He proved to be even harder for them to find than the mouth of the Mississippi had been for him; six overland expeditions and five seaborne searches canvassed the Gulf coast before the last uncovered the ruins of the French settlement (and redeemed the captive children, who had mixed emotions about being torn from their new families and hauled off to live among the Spanish in Mexico).

Besides prompting this fresh wave of exploration, La Salle's doomed experiment inspired the Spanish to fortify Texas as a buffer against further foreign incursions. They began establishing missions along a route—*el camino real,* or "the king's highway"—stretching from the Rio Grande to East Texas (and briefly beyond the Sabine River into Louisiana). The most important and durable of the missions were clustered about the upper San Antonio River. The mission of San Antonio de Valero, senior among the cluster, was founded in 1718 with seventy men, women, and children and nearly two thousand sheep, cattle, horses, and oxen. The adjacent presidio, or fort, of San Antonio de Béxar was established at the same time. Competition among the missions—and especially among the missionaries—hampered the growth of the community, but reinforcements arrived in 1731 in the persons of fifty immigrants from the Spanish Canary Islands. Gradually the community coalesced into a regular, if not exactly thriving, town. By the 1770s, when it became the capital of Spanish Texas, it had a population of about two thousand.

The Franciscan order staffed the missions, which, like all Spanish missions, received the dual mandate of spreading the gospel of the Lord and the power of the Spanish crown. The soldiers attached to the missions similarly doubled up, protecting the friars and others at the missions from hostile Indians (and from any Frenchmen who might appear) and encouraging the less bellicose natives to heed the words of the friars.

The missions were expensive and only intermittently successful. Some of the Indians who accepted baptism were evidently sincere in their adopted faith; others simply preferred their prospects under the Spanish to the depredations of Apache and Comanche raiders. Troubles between church and state in both old Spain and New Spain spilled over onto the frontier, and the commitment of the government to the missions rose and fell on the fall and rise in relations with France: when France seemed a threat, Texas appeared important; when France was friendly, Texas diminished. After France ceded Louisiana to Spain in 1762 (lest it be taken by the British, to whom the French were losing the Seven Years' War), the Texas missions lost nearly all their strategic value. The more distant ones, in East Texas, were abandoned and their personnel withdrawn along the Camino Real to San Antonio de Béxar and points south.

★

During the half century after 1770, Spain felt peculiarly vulnerable to foreign incursion. The war that began in Boston in 1775 between Britain and her North American colonies spread by the end of the decade to include France (allied directly to the Americans) and Spain (allied to France). The American-French-Spanish side won, but the victory was a mixed blessing for the Americans' European partners. Spain found itself confronting the Americans as neighbors across the Mississippi. More threatening, the success of the American Revolution set the spirit of republicanism loose upon the world. Every throne of Europe felt the ground rumble beneath its feet; within a decade of the war's end, the most glorious throne—that occupied by the Sun King of France and his heirs—was swallowed by the earthquake the Americans started.

In the wake of the revolution in France, Napoleon Bonaparte erected a new empire on the rubble of the *ancien régime*. Bonaparte's empire briefly reached to North America, after the Corsican wrested what was left of Louisiana—that is, the part of Louisiana that didn't belong to the United States—back from Spain. Napoleon envisioned reopening the American front in France's centuries-old struggle against Britain, but after he lost an army to yellow fever in St. Domingue (Haiti), he reconsidered and in 1803 sold Louisiana to the surprised Thomas Jefferson, who had sent envoys to Paris to purchase merely New Orleans. At the time, the confusion that had started with La Salle still surrounded the southwestern border of Louisiana, and neither Napoleon nor his foreign minister, Talleyrand, did anything to dispel it. "If an obscurity did not already exist," Napoleon remarked to an aide, "it would perhaps be good policy to put one there." Talleyrand enigmatically congratulated his American interlocutors: "You have made a noble bargain for yourselves, and I suppose you will make the most of it."

In fact, the American government made less of the Louisiana bargain, as it touched Texas, than did certain Americans acting on their own. Aaron Burr, already notorious for killing Alexander Hamilton in a duel on the New Jersey shore, compounded his notoriety by fleeing west and conniving to become master of some portion of the land between the Mississippi and the Rio Grande. Over whiskey and maps, Burr and James Wilkinson, Moses Austin's bête noire, evidently discussed detaching portions of Louisiana and Texas from the United States and Mexico to create an empire of the Southwest. Burr had little difficulty finding followers among the land-hungry, Indian-fighting populations of the Ohio and Mississippi Valleys, where Hamilton's death was generally applauded. Andrew Jackson, a veteran duelist himself, contributed cash and moral support to the Burr cause; men of lesser means signed on for the prospect of winning farms and plantations in Louisiana and Texas.

During the summer of 1806 the West bubbled with Burr's plotting. Volunteers mustered along the Ohio; boats were secured and supplies purchased for the journey to the front. But the plotting got away from Burr. Newspapers picked up the story and circulated it east. Federalists demanded that Jefferson act to suppress the patent separatism; a Federalist prosecutor in Kentucky charged Burr with treason. He dodged this charge but in the process lost whatever cover his conspiracy had retained. He was arrested by federal agents in Mississippi territory, then jumped bail and fled toward Spanish Florida. He was rearrested in Alabama territory and dispatched to Virginia for trial.

The case became a landmark in American legal history when Supreme Court chief justice John Marshall defied Jefferson and held the court to the strict constitutional standard of proof of treasonous acts, and Burr was acquitted. But the enthusiasm with which American frontiersmen had embraced the idea of invading Texas and making it their own augured ill for the tranquillity of New Spain's northeastern province.

What augured worse was the continuing weakness of Spain itself, which was the reason the Spanish had lost Louisiana to the French in the first place. Historically an ally of France, Spain became Napoleon's pawn in the wars that convulsed Europe during the first fifteen years of the nineteenth century. The wars bled Spain financially, and as part of their effort to raise money, Spanish authorities extorted loans from landholders in New Spain. The loans forced the sale of holdings among elites who had been a mainstay of loyalty to the Spanish crown; many of these elites, observing the prosperity of the United States after thirty years of independence, pondered whether independence might suit them too.

Dissatisfaction grew after the French invasion of Spain in 1808, which led to the deposing of King Ferdinand VII in favor of Napoleon's brother Joseph Bonaparte. As Spain rose in rebellion against the usurper and demanded restoration of the lawful monarch, Spanish America did likewise, although the sentiment *against* France

was stronger than sentiment *for* Ferdinand. In 1810 a priest in the Ba-
jío district northwest of Mexico City, Miguel Hidalgo y Costilla, a creole (American-born) son of Spanish parents, raised the cry—or
grito—of revolt in the village of Dolores. A large crowd responded,
seizing Spanish officials, releasing prisoners from jail, and for the
first time taking power into their own hands.

The revolt in Dolores ignited similar passions elsewhere in
Mexico and gravely upset the status quo. A bitter and bloody three-
way struggle developed among royalists, who adhered to the existing
government of Spain; conservative nationalists, who advocated independence short of revolution; and revolutionaries, who intended for
independence to yield a thorough restructuring of Mexican society
and politics. Resentments that had accrued over centuries among Indians and their mestizo (mixed-race) offspring gave rise to demands
for land and to mass killings of those who opposed them. Fear among
the European-born and their creole children fueled reprisals that
matched in ferocity the attacks of the rebels.

The advocates of independence sought help, with many looking
to the United States. The Americans' successful struggle for freedom
provided a tested philosophy of republicanism that appeared adapt-
able to Mexico's case, and the American people and government
might reasonably be expected to support a similar struggle by their
hemispheric neighbors—especially if that struggle had the effect of
weakening imperial Spain. More concretely, American markets at
New Orleans and elsewhere were the logical places for the Mexican
rebels to seek the weapons they needed to offset Spain's advantage in
arms. Hidalgo dispatched an envoy toward Washington to negotiate
treaties of alliance and commerce akin to those the fledgling United
States had signed with France in the 1770s; he also sent an agent
north bearing silver seized from the royalists, which was to be used to

underwrite the arsenal of freedom. The envoy, however, was arrested by the royalists before reaching the Gulf coast, and the agent was captured at San Antonio de Béxar.

But another rebel, José Bernardo Gutiérrez de Lara, carrying more silver, did manage to make his way across Texas to Natchitoches, where, among the marginal and often criminal elements that frequented the Neutral Ground (as the border region was designated prior to the 1819 treaty), he recruited an insurgent army, before continuing to Washington to solicit aid from the Madison administration. Gutiérrez got nothing formal from Madison, who was on the verge of asking Congress for a declaration of war against Britain, but Madison's secretary of state, James Monroe, offered moral support and apparently some money, and intimations of further assistance should the rebels' efforts prosper.

Returning to Louisiana, Gutiérrez enlisted Augustus Magee, a clever young American military officer (third in his class at West Point) who had grown disaffected after being passed over for promotion. Gutiérrez and Magee led a band of a hundred men against Nacogdoches, which quickly fell. As news of the victory traveled back to Louisiana and beyond, it inspired more enlistments. "The business of volunteering for New Spain has become a perfect mania," wrote William Shaler, an American merchant who tripled as an agent for the Madison administration and a political adviser to Magee and Gutiérrez. "I hear of parties proceeding thither from all quarters, and they are constantly passing through this village from Natchez. . . . I suppose the volunteer force cannot now be rated under 600 Americans, generally good soldiers, and there is every appearance of its becoming very respectable in a short time, equal even to the entire conquest of the Province of Texas." In Shaler's mind, and presumably in the minds of these recruits, more than Mexican independence was

at stake. "The volunteer expedition, from the most insignificant beginning, is growing into an irresistible torrent that will sweep away
the crazy remains of Spanish Government from the Internal
Provinces [Texas and its neighbors], and open Mexico to the political
influence of the U.S. and to the talents and enterprise of our citizens."

The expeditionary force rolled toward San Antonio, picking up
additional volunteers among the Tejanos (Mexican Texans) and even
various Indian tribes. It captured La Bahía in November 1812 without
a struggle—which disappointed the bellicose Magee. "They are a rascally set of treacherous cowards," he said of the Spanish soldiers. Although Magee fell ill and died, the invasion continued under
Gutiérrez and Samuel Kemper, a Virginia carpenter who had come
west in search of adventure and booty. The royalist forces counterat-
tacked outside San Antonio, but the rebels soon put them to flight.
Gutiérrez and the others camped outside the Alamo—a mission compound that had been converted to a fortress—while several hundred
officers and men of the royalist army switched sides and joined them.
On April 6, 1813, the victors, claiming to speak for "the People of the
Province of Texas," declared that "the chains which bound us under
the domination of European Spain are forever dissolved. . . . We are
free and independent."

Born of the Mexican revolution, the fighting in Texas reflected
the ferocity of that larger upheaval. After the conquest of San Antonio, several captured Spanish officers were executed, apparently
with the approval of Gutiérrez. This offended and alarmed some of
the Americans, who headed back to Louisiana. It also provoked
quarreling among the remaining rebels, many of whom objected to
the high-handedness of Gutiérrez in making himself "governor"
and then "president protector" of the nascent Texas republic. More

of his soldiers drifted away, leaving the rest unready to defend themselves against a fresh royalist army under General Joaquín Arredondo.

At the battle of the Medina River, south of San Antonio, Arredondo and the royalists crushed the rebels in the bloodiest battle ever fought in Texas. Of perhaps fourteen hundred rebels, including Americans, Tejanos, and various Indians, fewer than a hundred survived the battle and its aftermath. No quarter was given by the royalists; rebels captured were summarily executed, and those who fled were hunted down and likewise dispatched. The bodies of the vanquished were left unburied on the field as a lesson to any who might be tempted toward independence in the future.

Taking note of Arredondo's strategy was a slight young lieutenant of the royalist army, a nineteen-year-old with soft but penetrating brown eyes, curly dark hair, a rather sallow complexion for one who spent so much time out of doors, and a resigned, melancholic expression at odds with the martial career he had chosen. It was this last aspect that made Antonio López de Santa Anna irresistible to nearly all the women and many of the men he met—"decidedly the best looking and most interesting figure of the group," said a later female visitor who singled him out of a crowd. This visitor, benefiting from some history, went on to say, "It is strange, and a fact worthy of notice in natural history, how frequently this expression of philosophic resignation, of placid sadness, is to be remarked on the countenances of the most cunning, the deepest, most ambitious, most designing and most dangerous statesmen."

Santa Anna's cunning would take years to perfect, but his ambition was evident early. A creole from Veracruz province, the young man ached to achieve distinction beyond his family's modest station; to this end he joined the army, that traditional vehicle of advancement for those not born to privilege. His infantry regiment, commanded by Arredondo, fought Indians on the northern frontier until the revolution broke out, whereupon it turned to fighting the rebels. Santa Anna was undeniably brave; wounded in action against the Indians, he further distinguished himself for valor and vigor against the rebels in the battle of the Medina. Arredondo decorated the young man and marked him as one after his own heart.

Yet Santa Anna's ambition, besides spurring him to feats of arms, manifested itself in a compulsion to gamble. In time all of Mexico—including Texas—would be his casino; for now the gaming table was his venue, and his downfall. When he couldn't pay a gambling debt, he forged the signature of Arredondo to access army funds. The fraud came to light and Santa Anna was bankrupted and publicly humiliated.

The setback was temporary. Displaying the resilience that was the crucial complement to his ambition, Santa Anna redoubled his devotion to the royalist cause. He helped suppress a rebel invasion of Mexico launched by Francisco Mina from Galveston, on the Texas coast—which disposed him, beyond his experience at the Medina, to think of Texas as a breeding ground for brigands and pirates. (In fact the pirate brothers Jean and Pierre Laffite, operating out of Galveston, did abet and equip the Mina expedition and generally had a hand in most of the attacks against Texas during this period.) Santa Anna's actions were noted by the viceroy of New Spain, who tendered the thanks of the Spanish crown.

Returning to Veracruz province, Santa Anna directed the relocation of refugees from the revolutionary fighting there. The work went well, and he was happy to report the settlement of hundreds of displaced families. "All this is due to my activity, zeal, and hard work," he said, displaying another trait—patriotic egotism—that would characterize his whole career. "I did not spare myself work, fatigue, or danger, however great, provided only that I could be useful to my country."

Chapter 3

The People of the Horse

During the eighteenth and early nineteenth centuries, while the Spanish were approaching Texas from the south and the Americans and French from the east, another people, more formidable than either the Europeans or the Americans, entered Texas from the north. The Comanches were a young tribe, an offshoot of the Shoshones of the western slope of the Rocky Mountains. Why the tribes separated is shrouded in myth. By one Comanche tradition a group of hunters quarreled over the carcass of a bear they had killed; unable to reconcile, the group divided, with each side taking its dependents: the Shoshones to the north, the Comanches to the west and south. Another version, handed down orally to the twentieth century, explained the split differently:

> Two bands were living together in a large camp. One band was on the east side; the other was on the west. Each had its own chief. Every night the young boys were out playing games—racing, and so forth. They were having a kicking game; they kicked each other. One boy kicked another over the stomach so hard that he died from it. That boy

who was killed was from the West camp. He was the son of
a chief.

The father of the dead boy demanded vengeance, and both sides
girded for battle. At the last moment, though, one of the tribe's old
men talked the tempers down, and the western chief was persuaded
to accept horses and other gifts in mitigation of his son's death. But
he couldn't continue to live beside the easterners.

> The chief had his announcer tell the people it was time to
> move camp. "We have had bad luck here. There has been
> hard feeling." While they were still there, smallpox broke
> out. Then they broke up. One group went north; those are
> the Shoshones. The other group went west.

Whatever the occasion of the parting, the cause was deeper, as
the mention of smallpox and bad luck at the end of this story suggests.
In the late seventeenth century the effects of European settlement
farther east were rippling out across the plains and mountains of the
American West. Smallpox was one effect, and could be devastating.
With mortality rates of two-thirds or more, the disease depopulated
large tracts of Texas (as Moses Austin noticed in 1820, without understanding the cause) and of the surrounding area.

Firearms were another consequence of European contact, and
likewise destructive of existing population patterns. French fur
traders introduced guns to the Blackfeet and Crows, who had long
been rivals of the Shoshones. With the weapons the Blackfeet and
Crows drove the Shoshones from their old territory, pushing some
north and others—the Comanches—down from the mountains onto
the southern plains.

But the land the Comanches entered already had inhabitants,

and, as with most peoples moving about the continent, the newcomers had to fight to carve a niche for themselves. It was at this point that the Comanches acquired their name. Like many tribes, they referred to themselves as simply "the People." To their new Ute neighbors, however, they were "anyone who wants to fight me all the time"; rendered into Spanish, the Ute word became "Comanche."

The Comanches were fierce fighters, and grew even fiercer when they acquired horses. Like firearms, horses were a European introduction to North America, and, at least on the plains west of the Mississippi River, they were even more revolutionary. Before the advent of the horse, the tribes of the plains hunted buffalo but rarely traveled far to do so. Most were semi-sedentary, planting crops—corn, beans, squashes—in sheltered valleys and at the edges of the plains. The first horses reached the plains with Coronado in the sixteenth century; some may have escaped then, or been stolen. But not for another century were there enough horses to prompt a change of life among the plains Indians.

It was about the time the horses achieved this critical mass that the Comanches emerged from the mountains. The Comanches may have been driven from the mountains by better-armed enemies, but they were simultaneously pulled onto the plains by the promise of horses. Horses made almost everything about Comanche life easier and more rewarding. Before horses, the only beast of burden the Comanches employed was the dog, which, needless to say, could carry far less than the horse. The horse made the Comanches true nomads, freed from any particular place, roaming the plains from season to season.

Their new nomadism, in turn, allowed them to exploit the buffalo more fully than before; as the great herds migrated, so could the Comanches. The buffalo provided nearly everything the Comanches required: meat, marrow, and internal organs for food (and blood, in a pinch, for drink); hides for clothing and tenting; sinews for bow-strings and fasteners; hoofs and horns for glue and utensils; dung for fuel. And there was no end to the buffalo, which numbered in the scores of millions. In their mountain days as Shoshones, the Co-manches—like most aboriginals (including those who captured Cabeza de Vaca)—were distressingly familiar with hunger; after they mastered the horse and emerged among the buffalo of the southern plains, they almost forgot the feeling.

But if the buffalo was the sustenance of the Comanches, the horse was their pride and joy. Comanche children—girls as well as boys—were raised to ride. They started out on their mothers' mares but by four or five years of age had ponies of their own. They raced one another across the plains and practiced shooting arrows from horseback, throwing lassos, and plucking objects from the ground at a gallop. (This last skill was especially valued in battle, for the Co-manches refused to leave comrades on the field and frequently tore into the thickest part of a fight to scoop up their dead and wounded.) The horsemanship of the Comanche warrior was the envy of every rider he encountered. "He makes but an awkward figure enough on foot," recorded one nineteenth-century observer, "though he is no sooner mounted than he is transformed, and with no other aid than that of the rein and heavy whip he makes his horse perform the most incredible feats." Another, more literary witness described the Co-manche cavalryman as "the model of the fabled Thessalian centaur, half horse, half man, so closely joined and so dexterously managed that it appears but one animal, fleet and furious."

As well they might have, the Comanches loved their horses and valued them above all else. Horses constituted Comanche wealth and conferred Comanche status. A single warrior might own two hundred horses (of which he would actually ride but several and dote on a few). A chief could own a couple of thousand; a band of Comanches, several thousand.

No less than other forms of conspicuous consumption, the maintenance of such large herds came at a cost. The Comanches were nomadic not simply in pursuit of the buffalo but also in search of fresh grass for their horses. In addition, the desire to expand their herds continually tempted the Comanches to intrude upon territory claimed by their neighbors. Sometimes these intrusions resulted in roundups of mustangs—the feral descendants of Spanish escapees. But even for the Comanches, capturing and breaking the mustangs was a challenge; the same spirit, stamina, and wariness that made the mustangs such valuable horses to own and ride made them diffi-cult to catch and break. (By credible accounts, Comanche horses were trained to be lookouts when their riders were busy butchering buffalo they had killed. The horses would twitch their ears alter-nately upon the approach of a wolf or other animal, together upon the approach of a human. "Thus many lives were saved," said one Comanche.)

More to the point, there was little glory in catching wild horses. Their mastery of the horse left the Comanches with substantial spare time, which they learned to fill by raiding their neighbors. Raids were exciting; they were also a way for young men to earn distinction within the band. As brilliant as they were at riding horses, the Co-manches demonstrated even greater virtuosity at stealing them. The most adept of the Comanches could creep into a well-guarded corral or stable, cut the ropes or hobbles securing the finest mounts, and be miles away before anyone noticed. For the Comanches, horse steal-ing was a form of coup: the stroke of bravery that marked the best men of the tribe.

Equally often, the Comanches resorted to violence and intimi-
dation in their quest for horses. Starting in the mid-eighteenth century and continuing for a hundred years, Comanche raiders swooped
south to the Rio Grande and beyond, terrorizing the inhabitants and
seizing anything that could trot, canter, or gallop. As late as the
1840s, a traveler heading north from Mexico City toward the upper
Rio Grande wrote, "For days together, I traversed a country completely deserted on this account, passing through ruined villages un-
trodden for years by the foot of man." Referring to the previous
twelve-month period, this same traveler asserted, "Upward of ten
thousand head of horses and mules have already been carried off, and
scarcely has a hacienda or rancho on the frontier been unvisited, and
everywhere the people have been killed or captured."

The Spanish first heard of the Comanches at the beginning of the
eighteenth century, when reports of attacks on Apaches reached New
Mexico. As the Apaches were regular enemies of the Spanish, the
news that the Apaches had enemies of their own elicited considerable
interest. For the next few decades intelligence regarding the Comanches remained indirect and irregular; a Spanish army officer investigating the 1720 destruction of a Spanish patrol near the Platte
River wrote:

> Each year at a certain time, there comes to this province a
> nation of Indians very barbarous and warlike. Their name
> is Comanche. They never number less than 1,500. Their
> origin is unknown, because they are always wandering in
> battle formation, for they make war on all the nations.

They halt at whichever stopping place and set up their
campaign tents, which are of buffalo hide. . . . After they
finish the commerce which brought them there, which
consists of tanned skins, buffalo hides, and those young
Indians which they capture (because they kill the older
ones), they retire, continuing their wandering until another time.

By midcentury the Comanches had reached Texas. In 1743 three
Comanches passed through San Antonio de Béxar looking for
Apaches. The visit evoked curiosity among the Spanish but terror
among the Apaches, who by now knew the Comanches all too well. Indeed, so frightened by the invaders from the north were the Apaches
that they took the singular step of asking for Spanish protection. The
Franciscans interpreted the request as an answer to their prayers, as
God employing the Comanches to bring the Apaches to the gospel.
Fray Benito Fernández de Santa Anna, a leader among the Franciscans in Texas, urged the secular authorities to honor the Apache request, noting the "copious number of souls who, through the
merciful intervention of Our Lord, may be converted to our holy
faith."

Those secular authorities, however, were skeptical. Some
doubted the conversion of the Apaches. Others preferred keeping the
Apaches as official enemies, for as enemies they might be captured
and employed as free labor—slaves, in effect—at San Antonio and the
other settlements. But Fray Benito and the Franciscans persisted, as
did the Apaches, till finally the authorities gave in.

A mission was founded in the spring of 1757 on the San Sabá
River, about 180 miles northwest of San Antonio. The Spanish had
high hopes for the endeavor, which appeared to open a new chapter
in the development of the Texas frontier. But troubles vexed the San

Sabá mission from the start. The Franciscans fought among themselves, not least since the soldiers sent to guard the new outpost were taken from other missions, which now felt themselves neglected and vulnerable. But the most ominous—and puzzling—aspect of the situation involved the Apaches. After their initial enthusiasm for the mission, they cooled to the idea. For months they stayed away from the mission; when a large group of Apaches finally did arrive, its leaders made clear they were just passing through, on the way to a buffalo hunt.

In time the reason for the Apaches' reluctance grew evident. As the winter of 1757–58 approached, its north winds brought rumors of a major campaign by the *norteños,* as the Comanches and their allies were called, against the Apaches. Assessing the balance of forces on the northern frontier, the Apaches decided that the Spanish, with only several dozen soldiers in the presidio that accompanied the San Sabá mission, were no match for the Comanches, and they declined to make themselves more vulnerable by settling down at the mission.

The wisdom of this decision became evident in 1758. On the morning of March 16 a large group of Indians—at least a thousand—appeared at the mission, firing muskets and shouting contempt for the European interlopers. The leader of the missionaries and a Spanish officer tried to appease the war party but succeeded only in revealing how few the defenders were at the mission. Without warning the two were shot. "And then began a cruel attack against all," recorded Fray Miguel de Molina, one of the survivors.

The destruction of the mission was appallingly thorough. Its nature and extent were described by a Spanish officer subsequently sent to examine the carnage:

When we reached the Mission we found near the entrance to the stockade the corpse of the Reverend Father Presi-

dent. Farther inside we found, burned to cinders, the bodies of Lázaro de Ayalas and a son of Juan Antonio Gutiérrez. We recognized the former by his head and the latter by
a leg, which the flames had not completely consumed. We
buried the bodies in the cemetery near the church. The
ground was strewn with smoldering debris from its ruins.
We moved onward to inspect the other buildings, only to
find them all destroyed and the wreckage still
burning. . . . As we continued our search, we came upon
the corpse of Juan Antonio Gutiérrez, without eyes or
scalp, for it is the custom of the barbarous Indians, when
celebrating a triumph, to take the scalps of their victims.
We buried this corpse also. Then we went on with our exploration and found 18 dead oxen, and even the cats were
dead also.

The debacle on the San Sabá cured the Spanish of any desire to tangle with the Comanches. The Texas frontier retreated to the line of
the Camino Real, which became the de facto southern boundary of
the Comanchería, or Comanche lands. Not that the Comanches respected that boundary, or any other: they continued to raid, more or
less at will, to the Rio Grande and beyond. Their warriors would visit
San Antonio and saunter about the streets of the town, frightening
the inhabitants and seizing whatever caught their eye. So cowed
were the Spanish that the Comanches, despite a new and especially
devastating outbreak of smallpox, were able to win a treaty from the
Spanish in 1785 that specified large payments of tribute in the form
of trade goods. The treaty didn't preserve the Spanish settlements

from horse raids, but it did buy some protection for human life and limb.

The lopsided peace lasted till the end of the century, when the diplomacy of the Atlantic world delivered Louisiana to the United States and made the Americans near neighbors of the Comanches. Thomas Jefferson, amateur scientist as well as professional politician, was interested in the Comanches as much for their anthropological characteristics as for their military prowess, and he directed American explorers in the vicinity of the Comanchería and American officers and agents around its borders to report to him what they observed of the tribe. John Sibley, a Louisiana-based army surgeon and Indian agent, in 1808 licensed a trader, Anthony Glass, to deal in Comanche horses. Glass traveled to Texas, keeping a journal along the way. On the Trinity River he encountered a Comanche camp. "We found about twenty tents," he wrote. "They are made of different sizes of buffalo skins and supported with poles made of red cedar, light and neat which they carry with them. Their tents are round like a wheatstack, and they carry their tents always with them." On the upper Colorado River, Glass and the group he was traveling with were overtaken by a large party of Comanches—he called them "Hietans," after the Wichita word for the Comanches—who had learned that he was in the area and who wanted to do business. By day the Comanches bartered; after sunset they played. "They amused themselves at night by a kind of gambling at which a great number of horses and mules were lost and won. The game was very simple and called Hiding the Bullet; and the adverse party guesses which hand it was in. They were very dexterous at this kind of gaming."

With each day, more Comanches appeared. "We have with us now ten chiefs and near six hundred men with a large portion of women and children," Glass wrote. "I meet with them every day and we hold long conversations together. They profess great friendship for the Americans, or Anglos as they call us." Some of the Comanches had visited Sibley at Natchitoches the previous year and had appreciated his friendliness. "They are very desirous of trading with us but say Nackitosh [the prevailing pronunciation for Natchitoches] is too far off."

This last comment explained the Comanches' friendliness—and also explained something that struck Glass more than once on this trip. "Here I found myself at the distance of many hundred miles from any white settlement, surrounded by thousands of Indians, with nearly two thousand dollars worth of merchandise and a large drove of horses and mules fatting away in flesh, and no assistance but Young and Lucas [his two partners]." Why didn't the Indians simply kill him and take his goods and horses? Glass knew the answer, though he often wondered if it would keep him whole till his return to civilization. The Comanches and other Indians suffered Glass—and traders like him—to enter Texas because they wanted the merchandise the traders brought; if they killed the traders, they'd have to travel to Louisiana themselves. They preferred to have their purchases delivered.

Yet Glass discovered something else about the Comanches that constantly vexed relations between them and the whites. A group of Comanches stole two dozen of Glass's horses. Several weeks later he received some of the lost animals back, courtesy of the chiefs he had met earlier. "The principal chief told me he was truly sorry but that there were bad men in all nations, and amongst them they have no laws to punish stealing." In fact the Comanches had no laws to punish much of anything, for they had next to nothing in the way of government. The separate bands of Comanches were laws unto themselves, and what one band pledged—with respect to the whites, for instance—often had no effect on the actions of other bands. Nor, for that matter, did commitments made by the chief of a band neces-sarily bind the other members of that band, who followed whom they wanted when it struck their fancy. Natural anarchists, the Comanches recognized very little in the way of human authority, either among themselves or with regard to those other invaders who vied with them for control of Texas.

Don Estevan

In certain respects Stephen Austin could not have been less like his father. Moses was innately audacious, a gambler who crossed half a continent to build a business empire in the wilderness, who rode the western boom to become the richest man in the district, only to ride the bust into bankruptcy and disgrace, and then turned to Texas to try it all again. Stephen, on the other hand, was cautious, diffident, self-doubting. His caution owed much to his father's failure, but his diffidence and doubting were his own. He never possessed the can-do optimism that characterized his father (and the frontier generally); he constantly questioned himself and his actions. His appearance suggested a poet rather than a pioneer. Five feet eight inches tall and slight of build, he had brown ringlets for hair, an aquiline nose, hazel eyes, and skin that burned far too easily for a trailblazer and colonizer. Where the Texas project came naturally to Moses, Stephen, left to himself, would never have dreamed of anything so bold. If not for his father's deathbed request, he likely would have pursued a career of solid innocuousness. He would have become a lawyer, perhaps a state judge, and spent his life pondering the perplexities of human nature, his own included.

After his Virginia birth and the harrowing trek across the Mississippi, Stephen Austin grew up among the Frenchmen, Spaniards, Indians, and African slaves that inhabited the neighborhood of Mine à Breton. Moses and Maria educated Stephen as best they could, but Moses insisted, as the lad approached eleven, that he be sent east to receive real schooling. A suitable place was found at an academy for young men in Connecticut. Stephen suffered the homesickness that has tested boarding-schoolers since parents first shipped their children away; he also received the traditional remonstrances from home. "I hope and pray you will improve every moment of time to the utmost advantage and that I shall have the satisfaction of seeing that my expectations are not disappointed," Moses wrote. "Remember, my dear son, that the present is the moment to lay the foundation for your future greatness in life, that much money must be expended before your education is finished, and that time lost can never be recalled." On Stephen would rest responsibility for the family. "I hope to God I shall be spared until I see you arrive at an age to give protection to your dear mother and sister and little brother Elijah Brown. Remember that to you they will look for protection should it so happen that my life should be shortened. Keep in mind that this may happen."

What the eleven-year-old made of this counsel is difficult to know; that he saved the letter suggests he took it at least partly to heart. And when, after three years, his tutors declared him ready for college, he accepted his father's decision for him to attend Transylvania University in Kentucky, rather than Yale, as his mother desired. The cash flow from the lead mines was diminishing, and the college in Lexington was cheaper than Yale. At Transylvania Stephen handled himself in an "exemplary and praiseworthy manner," according to his preceptors. But his higher education was cut short after a year and a half. The lead business had gone from bad to worse, and the mine needed new investors. Moses had to travel east to find them; Stephen must come home and manage the operation in Moses' absence.

Sixteen was hardly too young to start a career in those days, although it wasn't the career Stephen had envisioned. He wanted to be a lawyer and hoped to apprentice for the profession. But for now the lead mines—that is, Moses—called, and Stephen couldn't refuse. He worked at headquarters until, during the summer of 1811, Moses consigned him a cargo of lead to float to New Orleans. Troubles delayed the departure: Stephen contracted malaria, and then a large portion of the downstream population caught yellow fever. Winter brought the yellow fever under control, as it usually did, but that winter also brought something quite extraordinary for the Mississippi Valley: a series of very large earthquakes. The tremors were centered southwest of New Madrid in southern Missouri, yet were so strong they rang church bells in Boston. They also rerouted the Mississippi River and threw river traffic into a horrible tangle.

By the time Stephen got away, in April 1812, the river was spring full and the ride daunting. "This is one of the worst eddies in the river and ought carefully to be guarded against by hugging the left shore very close," Stephen wrote of a stretch above Cape Girardeau, in a journal he kept of the voyage. He managed to escape the eddies and guide his barge nearly to New Orleans, only to strike a sandbank almost within sight of the Crescent City. The barge started taking on water and, predictably for a box filled with lead, sank.

It might have remained on the river bottom had Congress not recently declared war against Britain. The local price for lead plunged as cargoes backed up on the docks, but Stephen guessed that the war would push the price higher. "Sheet lead will sell well, and also shot," he told Moses. Accordingly he returned upriver to the site of the sinking and, after considerable effort, raised most of the lead.

The trouble and expense went to naught. Stephen's prediction about the demand for lead proved wrong, and after several weeks in New Orleans without finding a buyer, he turned north for home.

The nineteen-year-old was a likely candidate for military service against the British and their Indian allies, and he enlisted. On account of his business experience—and perhaps, too, on account of his comparatively delicate appearance—he was made quartermaster of his regiment in the territorial volunteers. He learned what moving men and animals through unsettled country required: how an army marches on its stomach but sleeps on its back, how volunteers can be cajoled but less effectively ordered, how horses are faster than mules but mules more reliable. He also learned about the evanescent nature of militia service. When his regiment encountered insufficient fighting to keep the men interested, it melted away as they returned to their civilian occupations. Stephen Austin soon followed their example.

The end of the war raised lead prices but not enough to rescue the Austin business. Moses, discouraged and distracted, leased the operation to Stephen, who accepted the transfer with ambivalence. "I have taken possession of the mines and the whole establishment here," he wrote his brother-in-law, James Bryan, "and commenced business under the style of S. F. Austin & Co., and am flattering myself with the pleasing hope of being able by the end of this year to free the family from every embarrassment." Yet the task would require all his energy and wit. "I shall literally bury myself this spring and summer in the mines."

He nonetheless found time to enter public service, gaining election to the territorial legislature. With many—perhaps most—of the members, he saw public service as a complement to his private enterprises. He drafted a petition to Congress to raise the duty on imported lead, arguing that encouragement of the lead industry would "add another most important item to the prosperity and independence of the Nation." It went without his saying that a higher tariff would also contribute to the prosperity and independence of the Austin family.

But neither Stephen's work in the mines nor his appeal to Congress brought relief to the business. The gloom that already afflicted Moses descended on Stephen. "My opinion of mankind has, unfortunately perhaps, been as bad as it could be for some years," he told James Bryan, "but the longer I live the worse it grows." His father's debts, which had become his own, weighed upon him—yet, paradoxically, gave him a reason to carry on. "As for myself, I believe I am nearly indifferent what becomes of me, or whether I live or die, unless I am to be of use to my family by living." Usefulness took one form above all: paying off the family debt. "When the day arrives that the whole family are out of debt I mean to *celebrate it* as my *wedding day*—which never will come until then."

In marrying Moses' debt, Stephen bound himself—without realizing it—to Moses' Texas venture. While Moses was dreaming of Texas and what a man might accomplish there, Stephen attempted a fresh start in Arkansas. He acquired an interest in properties that showed promise as town sites, including one on the Arkansas River at Little Rock. But though the town flourished, other men were quicker and shrewder than he at extracting the profits. He won appointment to be circuit court judge, only to have his court closed by the territorial legislature almost before he robed up.

He moved farther south, to New Orleans, where the elder brother of a college classmate took him in as an apprentice lawyer.

Austin's sponsor, Joseph Hawkins, was an attorney with standing in the community. "He is not rich," Stephen explained to his mother, "but he has a most generous heart. He has made me this offer: if I will remain with him, he will board me, permit me the use of his books, and money for clothes, give me all the instruction in his power until I am well fitted to commence the practice of law in this country; for my board and the use of his books he will charge nothing, and for the money he advances he will wait until I make enough by my profession to repay him." Having failed at business, Stephen saw the law as a means to make good what Moses had lost. "If I am left alone a few years I may get up and pay all off."

Yet he was not left alone. At the very moment that Stephen was launching his career as a lawyer, Moses was winning approval for his Texas scheme, and catching pneumonia. In May 1821 Moses wrote to Stephen from his sickbed, relating his success with the Spanish government and urging his son to join him in what would be a crowning achievement. "I now can go forward with confidence," Moses said, "and I hope and pray you will discharge your doubts as to the enterprise and, if any means can be commanded, use your utmost to have every thing brought into motion. . . . Times are changing. A new chance presents itself. Nothing is wanting but concert and firmness." Less than a month after receiving this letter, Stephen learned that Moses had died, in the letter in which Maria related Moses' final request.

Whether filial obligation alone would have deflected Stephen from his path toward law is hard to say; in any event, Joseph Hawkins seconded Moses' advice about looking to Texas for salvation. Hawkins seems to have had the best interests of his protégé at heart— "our intercourse has resulted in mutually warm and I trust lasting attachment," Hawkins assured Maria—but like nearly everyone else in the West, he couldn't resist a promising speculation in land. Moses had cut Hawkins in on the deal, and though Hawkins disliked losing a bright young assistant, he essentially pushed Stephen out the door toward Texas. He also put up the cash for the first stage of the colonization. "I have advanced Stephen all the funds he desired for the expedition," Hawkins wrote Maria, "and have promised to furnish more as he requires them."

A more forceful person might have resisted the pressure impelling him west, but not Stephen Austin. His legal career cut short, his family in debt, his father giving orders from beyond the grave, he put down his books and headed for Texas.

Austin's timing in launching the Texas venture could hardly have been better. In the aftermath of the War of 1812 with Britain and the 1819 treaty with Spain, American affairs relating to the West were at once settled and uncertain. The British war had demonstrated that the United States was not going to acquire Canada, having tried and failed three times to do so during the course of that conflict. The Spanish treaty gave the United States Florida, rounding out American holdings east of the Mississippi. It also declared Texas definitively part of New Spain.

Yet mere declarations could never be definitive in the face of America's hunger for land. The Canada question had been settled by force of British arms, the Florida question by force of American arms. And the settlement of those two questions channeled American expansionist energies toward Texas, where neither Spanish arms nor American—nor Comanche, for that matter—had established a decisive advantage. It didn't take much imagination to guess that Texas would be fought over before its fate was settled.

But the fighting developed differently than most imagined. The critical event of the second decade of the nineteenth century for the future of Texas was not the war with Britain nor the treaty with Spain, but the implosion of the American economy. Stephen Austin, sitting impatiently with his cargo of lead in New Orleans in 1812, might have been forgiven for thinking wars the principal cause of financial distress in the United States. In fact, peace was often harder on the economy. American money in those days consisted primarily of paper notes issued by scores of banks scattered across the several states, and because these banks, like all banks, owed more (to depositors) than they kept in their vaults, the slightest financial disturbance could set off a chain of failures, which might result in a strangling contraction of the money supply. Such a series of events produced the Panic of 1819, with prices plunging, debtors defaulting, mortgage holders foreclosing, and thousands of families losing their land. The effect was most dramatic in the West, where the entire economy was premised on rising—not falling—prices for land. The panic and its aftermath set an army on the march: an army not of soldiers but of farmers and their dependents, men and women and children akin to those bedraggled pilgrims Moses Austin had seen in 1796 looking for their promised land in Kentucky. The growth in population since then had pushed the promised land farther west, to the American territories of the upper Louisiana Purchase—and, as things developed, to the Spanish territory of Texas.

While financial developments made emigration to Texas appealing, technological developments made it possible. The greatest inventions of the era were the cotton gin and the steamboat. Eli Whitney's 1793 invention of a mechanical technique for separating seeds from fibers of the short-staple cotton that flourished on the Gulf Coastal plain opened whole new territories to settlement. Whitney's gin reduced costs of cotton goods, putting manufactured textiles within the reach, and on the backs, of millions who previously wore homespun. Cotton had been a crop; now it became an industry, and a very profitable one for those who acquired land inexpensively. Within a generation the territories of Alabama and Mississippi filled up with cotton planters and their slaves. Some plantations were large, sophisticated enterprises, with hundreds of slaves toiling under the supervision of hired managers and overseers. Other plantations were mere farms, with the owners toiling beside their slaves. But large or small, the cotton operations required land, and the cheaper the better.

Robert Fulton's steamboat was no less decisive for the development of the West. Observers laughed when Fulton guided his belching, banging contraption up the Hudson River in 1807, but as the revolutionary nature of his antigravity device—a boat that could travel *up*-stream, under its own power—became apparent, its commercial and hence demographic promise silenced the laughter. Never in American history had the self-sufficient farm been more than a myth; farmers required access to markets. Before Fulton, access had often been slow and subject to the uncertainties of weather and river currents (like those that sank Stephen Austin's barge). Fulton weakened the tyranny of nature by letting boats climb against the current and keep to more or less regular schedules. The first steamboats were ungainly and subject to spontaneous explosion, but as the technology developed they became (relatively) safe and able to navigate even the most modest watercourses. Every river promised to be a highway, along whose banks farmers could grow crops for sale; every estuary became a potential port of entry, the hub of a thriving community upstream.

"The land lies on the Colorado and Brazos rivers and includes a situation on the Bay of St. Bernard, suitable for a sea-port, at which place a port of entry is ordered to be established," Stephen Austin wrote in July 1821, in a public notice regarding the Texas venture. "This concession to my father is granted by Don Joaquin de Arredondo, the governor of the Internal Provinces, and is duly confirmed by the Supreme Council of those Provinces. . . . It contains a permission to settle three hundred families on the lands, to each of whom a tract of land is to be given and to whom most liberal privileges are secured, both in regard to commercial interests and civil rights."

Austin's notice, printed in several western papers, had an immediate effect. "This part of the country is all alive and nothing spoken of but the province of Texas since your publications in the papers have appeared," Maria Austin wrote from Missouri. "And I have no doubt but one-third of the population of Missouri will move in the course of another year."

There was much to do before the settlers arrived—starting with a visit by Austin to the territory he had suddenly begun promoting. He traveled by steamboat up the Mississippi from New Orleans to the Red River, and up the Red River to Natchitoches. There he met Erasmo Seguín, the emissary who had brought the news from San Antonio de Béxar that Moses Austin's proposal had been approved. Accepting Stephen in place of his father, Seguín led Austin west.

Austin kept a log of the journey; on July 16, 1821, he described his first impression of the land to which he had linked his fate.

> Started from Camp Ripley [on the Sabine River] and entered the Province of Texas. . . . The first 4 miles fine timber and poor land. We then suddenly came to an open rolling country thinly timbered, soil about the color of Spanish brown, and in some places redder. This land is very productive and is covered with the most luxuriant growth of grass I ever beheld in any country; almost any of

it would produce as much hay as the best meadows. The country so far is well watered.

A few days farther on he noted:

> The general face of the country from within 5 miles of the Sabine to Nacogdoches is gently rolling. . . . The grass is more abundant and of a ranker and more luxuriant growth than I have ever seen before in any country and is indicative of a strong rich soil. . . . The creeks are numerous and water very pure and limpid.

For one who came late to the idea of colonizing Texas, Austin caught on quickly. The two months of this first visit were a continuous search for the richest soil, the lushest grass, the sturdiest timber, the purest streams, the most promising town sites, and the most navigable waterways. His journal recorded his rising excitement at a project he initially considered dubious but which now seemed inspired. "Large rich bottoms on the banks and good pasturage on the upland," he wrote of a creek just west of Nacogdoches. On July 31 he reached the Brazos River and described the land along its banks as "very good: rolling prairie, black soil." West of the Brazos was the Colorado, which flowed between high banks on which a town might be located safely above the flood line. The soil on either side of the stream was obviously rich: "Grapes in immense quantities on low vines, red, large and well flavored, good for red wine." Fish crowded the river and buffalo and deer its banks. "I killed a fat buck," he recorded on August 5.

The landscape grew still more inviting as Austin and Seguín angled south toward San Antonio. Of the valley of the San Marcos River,

Austin observed, "Country beautifully rolling, soil very black and rich." The San Marcos was striking in that it arose abruptly from three springs and immediately crashed down a waterfall "fine for mills." The valley of the Guadalupe River was even more delectable. "Country the most beautiful I ever saw—rolling prairies, soil very black and deep." Mesquite trees, which could supply lumber, grew along the creeks that fed the Guadalupe; dazzling white limestone, ideal for building, lay all about.

As fortunate as Austin's timing was with regard to events in America, it was most *un*fortunate with respect to developments in Mexico. Or so it seemed on his approach to San Antonio de Béxar, when three scouts Seguín sent ahead returned with news that Mexico, after more than a decade of revolution, had finally won its independence from Spain. Austin's companions were delighted. "The Spaniards," he wrote (apparently without noting the irony of this characterization of Seguín and the others), "hailed this news with acclamations of 'Viva independencia' and every other demonstration of joy."

Austin took part in the celebration even while wondering what the change of governments meant for the Texas project. The charter he had inherited from his father bore the seal of Spanish authorities, now ousted. Whether their Mexican successors would view the American colonization of Texas in the same light was anyone's guess.

Austin carried on as though the charter still held. Seguín introduced him to Governor Martínez, explaining that the young man had come to carry out the commitment given by his father and to see Texas for himself. The Baron de Bastrop again acted as interpreter and go-between. Austin was encouraged upon hearing that Martínez still supported the colonization project, and, at the governor's invitation, Austin submitted a more specific plan for allotting land to settlers. Splitting the difference between American custom, which had evolved in relatively rainy country where crops were the primary concern, and Mexican practice, suited to arid country devoted to livestock, Austin proposed to give each family 320 acres of crop land and 640 acres of grazing land. Additional amounts would be awarded depending on the number of people in the families.

Martínez had no quibble with the size of the plots. Considering the immensity of Texas, he probably would have accepted parcels ten times that large. What mattered more to Martínez was the conduct of the colonists. As director—*empresario*, in Spanish usage—of the project, Austin would be answerable for the behavior of those he brought in. "They must be governed by and be subordinate to you," Martínez insisted. Austin said they would be.

After a week in Béxar, Austin resumed his reconnaissance. Following the San Antonio River southeast toward the Gulf, he continued to be thrilled by the country. "The land adjoining the river is very rich and lays beautifully," he wrote. After a week he reached La Bahía, where a small village clustered about the Franciscan mission. "This place is beautifully situated on an eminence, immediately on the bank of the St. Antonio River. The surrounding country is rolling prairie, land rather sandy but produces well; might all be watered from the river."

Austin carried letters of introduction from Governor Martínez. The alcalde of La Bahía wasn't impressed; when Austin asked for guides to conduct him on the next stage of his journey, the official said he couldn't release anyone without another letter specifically directing him to do so. The local curé, however—"a very gentlemanly and liberal minded man and a great friend of the Americans," Austin noted—saw in the empresario a ticket out of a dismal post. "He expressed a wish to be appointed the curé of my new settlement."

On this eastward leg of the journey, Austin encountered several groups of Indians. He had heard of the Tonkawas, a powerful tribe that intimidated its enemies by, among other methods, eating them. Consequently he was surprised to meet some Tonkawas along the San Antonio River who seemed as happy as the friars to learn of his project. The leader of the Tonkawa band, which comprised eight men and ten women, approached Austin in a friendly manner. "I had a talk with him, smoked and gave him some tobacco, informed him of my intended settlement, which pleased him, and he sent on two of his sons next day with me to his town to inform his nation who we were and our objects."

A run-in with some other indigenes caused Austin greater concern. On the lower Colorado he heard an "Indian war whoop." A native approached Austin's party and signaled for them to stop. His mien wasn't especially threatening, but he was backed by more than a dozen warriors. Austin, telling his companions to be on their guard, went forward to engage the Indian. This fellow wanted Austin and the others to come to his camp. Austin asked who they were, and was told they were Cocos, whom Austin knew to be a branch of the Karankawas. In light of the Karankawas' bad reputation—they, too, practiced cannibalism, and were considered treacherous by the Spanish—Austin declined the invitation, "until one of the chiefs laid down his arms and five squaws and a boy came up to me from their camp. This satisfied me they believed us to be too strong for them and therefore that they would not attack us (of their disposition to do so I had no doubt, if they thought they could have succeeded)."

Austin found his hosts worthy of note, for good and ill.

These Indians were well formed and apparently very active and athletic men. Their bows were about 5¼ to 6 feet long, their arrows 2 to 3, well pointed with iron or steel. Some of the young squaws were handsome and one of them quite pretty. They had panther skins around their waist, painted, which extended down to the knee and calf of the leg. Above the waist, though they were naked, their breasts were marked or tattooed in circles of black beginning with a small circle at the nipple and enlarging as the breast swelled.

These Indians and the Karankawas may be called universal enemies to man. They killed of all nations that came in their power, and frequently feast on the bodies of their victims. . . . An American population will be the signal of their extermination for there will be no way of subduing them but extermination.

At this point Austin's assessment of the character of the Karankawas relied on the hearsay of their enemies (who indeed included most of their neighbors, not least the Spanish). His forecast, of course, was simply a guess, but it hardly boded well for relations between this native people and the colonists Austin aimed to bring in.

Austin's Karankawa problem—or the Karankawas' Austin problem—was aggravated by their location: near the coast, where Austin hoped to establish the port of entry for his colony. He scouted the head of San Antonio Bay, at the mouth of the Guadalupe River, and though he pronounced the site "a beautiful situation for a town," the remains of a large recent encampment of Karankawas worried him. He would have examined the mouth of the Colorado but a group of Karankawas blocked the way.

Skirting the Indians, Austin and his companions crossed over to the Brazos. The area teemed with wildlife, native and introduced. One of Austin's fellows killed what Austin called "the fattest buck" he had ever seen. Feral horses roamed the prairie. "Saw three gangs of mustangs, in one of which was 2 mules." Wild cattle were "abundant." The country was enough to make any farmer cry for joy. "Land all the richest kind of soil, very deep. . . . Prairies of the richest kind of black sandy land, intersected by branches and creeks of excellent water, heavily timbered, beautifully rolling."

The colony would need a headquarters, a town that formed its center. Throughout the trip Austin had been looking for a suitable site; now he found it on the Brazos. "The prairie comes bluff to the river just below the Tuscasite [Atascosito] Road, and affords a most beautiful situation for a town or settlement. The bluff is about 60 feet high. The country back of this place and below for about 15 miles (as far as we went) is as good in every respect as a man could wish for. Land all first rate, plenty of timber, fine water, beautifully rolling."

Austin's introduction to Texas erased his doubts regarding his father's project. He was no son of the soil, but even he couldn't help lusting after the gorgeous country he traversed that summer of 1821. And when he returned to Louisiana in early October, he learned that the same lust was spreading rapidly among people who had visited Texas only in imagination. "On my arrival here I found near one hundred letters from the neighborhood of where I formerly lived in upper Louisiana (now called Missouri) and many from Kentucky and other places requesting information relative to settling in the province of Texas," he informed Governor Martínez. "And I am convinced that I could take on fifteen hundred families as easily as three hundred if permitted to do so."

Austin realized he had to move quickly. He traveled downstream to New Orleans, which he had chosen as the staging point for the initial emigration to Texas. He consulted with Joseph Hawkins and formalized their partnership, arranged additional funding, and purchased a schooner, the *Lively*, to carry the first colonists by river and sea to the Texas coast. He also selected, from among the many applicants, fourteen men to sail on the *Lively* and establish a beachhead at the mouth of the Colorado. "They are to assist in building cabins and a stockade, should one be deemed necessary," Austin and the fourteen agreed, "and to clear fence, and cultivate at least five acres of corn each of prairie or untimbered land, and to gather the crop into corn houses." The idea was to make ready for the larger emigration that would follow. In exchange for the services of the fourteen (who bound themselves for a year), Austin would provide tools, draft animals, seeds, and foodstuffs, in addition to transport on the *Lively*. At the end of their year of service, these pioneers would each receive 640 acres of farm land and a town lot.

The *Lively* set out from New Orleans during the last weeks of 1821. Austin left the city about the same time. While the boat went east and south, down the Mississippi to the Gulf, he went west and north, up the river toward Natchitoches. Traveling overland again, he would scout more of the country and meet the boat at the mouth of the Colorado in January 1822.

But the hazards of the sea befell the *Lively*. A strong west wind blew her many leagues off course, and navigational error—and the undifferentiated character of the Texas coast—led to a landing at the mouth of the Brazos rather than the Colorado. Austin arrived on the Colorado expecting to find the fourteen hard at work, but they were nowhere to be seen. Equally alarming from the standpoint of Austin's finances, neither was the boat or its cargo.

What he found instead were other immigrants who had come to

Texas on their own. Having heard and read the praises of Texas, they discerned no compelling reason to wait for permission to enter the province, and so, after the fashion of Americans for two centuries, simply settled on land that looked empty. With each week that Austin awaited the *Lively*, more squatters arrived.

Austin couldn't decide whether their arrival was a good thing or bad. The squatters' presence spoke well for the attractiveness of Texas, and it provided additional evidence that he would have no difficulty filling his quota of three hundred families. On the other hand, these first arrivals naturally sought the best locations, appropriating acreage that Austin already had come to think of as his own—his own, at least, to allot to colonists who signed up with him.

To clarify his status vis-à-vis the squatters, Austin traveled once more to San Antonio. Governor Martínez added to the confusion by explaining that events surrounding Mexican independence had thrown government attitudes and policy regarding the Texas settlements—and regarding Texas officials, including the Spanish-born Martínez—into chaos. The governor no longer spoke with confidence. "He was an European," Austin explained afterward, "and did not know at what moment he might be removed from office or how the revolution would terminate, in consequence of which he had determined not to transact any public business except such as could not be postponed." If Austin wanted reassurance, he must seek it in Mexico City.

The last thing Austin wished to do at this point was to undertake the long journey to the Mexican capital. The *Lively* and its passengers were still missing; the squatters were filling up the valleys of the Colorado and Brazos (Austin estimated fifty settlers on the Brazos and one hundred on the Colorado as of March 1822). To find the first group and fend off the second would require his best efforts here in Texas; to leave the province would be to cast his project to the whim of wayward chance and aggressive frontiersmen. The governor's advice cut against Austin's every instinct.

Yet he saw no alternative. "One night's deliberation determined me to accept of this advice," he wrote. On the ides of March, Austin headed south from San Antonio for Mexico City.

★

Just across the Nueces River—the southern border of Texas in the administration of New Spain and Mexico—Austin met his first Comanches. "Fifty Comanches charged upon us a little before sunrise," he wrote in his journal. Austin's two companions were fetching the horses, and he was alone in the camp. "They surrounded me in an instant and took possession of every article we had." Resistance was futile, and became more so when other Comanches arrived escorting Austin's companions at gunpoint.

Austin tried a rhetorical sally. "I then expostulated with them for treating their friends the Americans in such a manner." The Comanches encountered Americans as traders and generally tolerated them; these Indians had mistaken Austin and the others for Spaniards. Austin's approach worked. "When they found there were no Spaniards with me, they gave us back our saddle bags, saddles, and everything else except four blankets, a bridle, my grammar and several other little things and all our provisions." Austin may have heard something about the decentralized nature of Comanche politics, or perhaps he was just operating on his understanding of erratic human nature when he added, from the safety of Laredo, on the Rio Grande: "As the next party might not be so polite I have waited for the company that is going on tomorrow."

Why the Indians kept Austin's "grammar"—his Spanish-language primer—is impossible to tell, but its loss dealt him a blow.

From the moment he committed to the Texas project, he threw himself into the study of the language that governed Texas. He knew some French, having grown up in colonial Louisiana, and he also knew how fluency in the tongue of the locals was essential to acceptance in any community. His French aided his acquisition of Spanish, although not as much as the effort he devoted to Spanish study. The grammar he had packed in his saddlebags was supposed to help him practice during the long journey south. In its absence he would have to rely on his ear and such assistance as those he met along the way could render.

The journey was wearing. "The country from the River Medina to this place is the poorest I ever saw in my life," he wrote at Laredo. "It is generally nothing but sand, entirely void of timber, covered with scrubby thorn bushes and prickly pear." And it got little better the closer he approached to Mexico City.

Yet the Mexican capital made up for the journey. Austin registered wonder at finding himself at "the fountain head of a *new born nation*." Almost simultaneous with his arrival came word that Mexico's independence had been recognized by the United States—"an event exciting the most lively sensations here," he recorded, "and fraught, I hope, with solid and lasting benefits to both nations." The Mexican government was finding its feet, hesitantly but nonetheless hopefully. "The Congress here do business in good order and with great deliberation, though rather slow; and the most perfect harmony prevails."

Austin often erred in analyzing Mexican politics. Hope chronically clouded his judgment, as it did in this case. He expected to spend a few weeks, or at most a few months, confirming his authority to colonize Texas. In fact he spent nearly a year in Mexico City, applying to committees, bureaus, offices, and individuals regarding the need to plant settlers in Texas before the illegal immigrants and the untamable Indians made legal settlement and Mexican control impossible.

At the time of Austin's arrival, Mexican politics centered on Agustín de Iturbide, a general whose defection from the royalists to the rebels had allowed the victory of the latter and the end of Spanish rule. Iturbide was a Mexican nationalist—after his defection—but he was no republican, and he soon established himself as emperor of independent Mexico.

Austin, like nearly all Americans of his day, didn't think much of emperors. But the interests of his Texas project prompted him to keep his disapproval to himself. "I make a tender of my services, my loyalty, and my fidelity to the Constitutional Emperor of Mexico," he wrote Iturbide, "a tender which I am ready to verify by an oath of allegiance to the Empire." To underscore his point, Austin added, "This solemn act cuts me off from all protection or dependence on my former government. My property, my prospects, my future hopes of happiness, for myself and family, and for the families I have brought with me, are centered here. This is our adopted nation."

He should have saved his breath. Before Iturbide could reconfirm the Texas project, he was overthrown. Austin first got a hint of the change in December 1822. "There has been and still is much difficulty in the province of Veracruz," he wrote to his brother, James, on Christmas Day. "A General Santana has proclaimed a Republic, but he met with a defeat on the night of 20 and morning of the 21 at Xalapa, which it is expected will soon force him to leave the country or yield."

Austin discovered before long that this General "Santana" was Santa Anna, and that the defeat at Jalapa was hardly conclusive. Iturbide's defection to the rebels had caught the royalist Santa Anna flat-footed, and for some time thereafter he continued to defend the Spanish monarchy. In March 1821 a group of rebels at Orizaba invited him to follow Iturbide and switch sides; he answered with an armed attack.

Yet when the attack faltered and the rebels surrounded him, Santa Anna experienced a sudden conversion to Mexican nationalism. The rebels' offer of a battlefield promotion made the conversion that much easier.

At a time when bigger names than Santa Anna were switching sides, his coat-turning occasioned no unusual notice. Yet his efforts on behalf of independence soon won him acclaim among the now-dominant party. He marched toward Veracruz at the head of a rebel army, taking several towns along the way. At his hacienda of El Encero he issued a proclamation in the grandiloquent tone for which he would become famous.

> Comrades! You are going to put an end to the great work of reconquering our liberty. You are going to plant the eagle of the Mexican empire, humiliated [by Cortés] three centuries ago on the plains of the valley of Otumba, on the banks of the humble Tenoya, where the Castillian flag was first unfurled. The soul of Quauhpopoca, burned alive in the great square of Mexico City, because he avenged the iniquitous act of Juan Escalante, pleads for justice; and the victims of the horrible massacre of Cholula, whose cries have startled two worlds, filling both with horror, will not be satisfied unless you restore to your oppressed native land the liberty which they lost.

Fighting in his native province against officers and men with whom he had lately been allied, Santa Anna aroused predictably bitter feelings. The reputation he had acquired as a royalist scourge didn't enhance his popularity. One observer noted that assassins lay in ambush, wishing to "avenge themselves for the many cruelties that he had committed." The assassins missed their chance, but the royalist troops did better, forcing Santa Anna's rebels back. He responded with a verbal barrage:

> Veracruz! the cry for your extermination will be from this time on the watchword of our men going into battle. In all juntas and senates the demand for your ruin will be added to all deliberations. The memory of Carthage, from whose grandeur you are as far removed as the humble grass from the stately oak, should make you tremble. Mexicans! Carthage never offended Rome as Veracruz has Mexico. . . . God help you.

Santa Anna's warning didn't endear him to the inhabitants of Veracruz, nor did it cause the city's surrender. The Spanish commandant vowed he would never yield to such a despicable character.

Eventually he did surrender, but to another officer sent out by Iturbide. Swallowing his pride, Santa Anna rode into Veracruz with the conquering colonel, Manuel Rincón, and joined Rincón in urging all in the city to put past differences behind them.

He then headed toward Mexico City, where Iturbide was consolidating his power. Upon hearing that the general had made himself emperor, Santa Anna applauded the coup. "I cannot restrain my excessive joy, for this step is the most suitable possible to bring about the prosperity of all," he told Iturbide. "It is the thing we sighed for and longed for, and although it may be necessary to exterminate some discordant and disturbing elements which do not possess the true virtues of citizens, let us hope that we can hasten to proclaim and take an oath to support the immortal Iturbide as emperor." Carrying the flattery to an extreme, the dashing twenty-eight-year-old colonel conspicuously paid suit to Iturbide's sister, a not unhandsome lady but one who, at sixty, wasn't surrounded by beaus.

Perhaps the wooing was excessive, or Santa Anna's ambition too obvious; in either case a chill descended upon relations between the emperor and the general (as Santa Anna became after another promotion). The coolness acquired an edge when Iturbide abruptly transferred Santa Anna to the capital, the better to keep an eye on him. Santa Anna objected to the move, which, he said, the emperor ordered "without extending to me the mere vestiges of courtesy." In retrospect he added, "Such a crushing blow offended my dignity as a soldier and further awakened me to the true nature of absolutism. I immediately resolved to fight against it at every turn and to restore to my nation its freedom."

He discovered allies among the early revolutionaries, who resented Iturbide's hijacking of their struggle. And in their name, in Veracruz in December 1822, Santa Anna declared the republic of which Stephen Austin wrote that Christmas Day. The improbability of the onetime royalist and recent imperial courtier experiencing another conversion, to republicanism, was overlooked in the excitement of an hour that promised to fulfill the revolutionary dreams for Mexico.

The fulfillment was delayed when Santa Anna's attempt to spread the republican gospel to his hometown of Jalapa encountered the combined hostility of Iturbide's conservative supporters and Santa Anna's personal enemies; in the aftermath of his defeat there—the one Stephen Austin also remarked upon that Christmas Day—Santa Anna lost his nerve and prepared to flee the country for the

United States. But one of the original rebels, Guadalupe Victoria, urged a steady course. "Go and put Veracruz in a state of defense," the guerrilla leader told Santa Anna. "You can set sail when they show you my head."

Santa Anna remained in Mexico, and the republican reaction to Iturbide acquired momentum. Many of those who joined were as opportunistic as Santa Anna, but the weight of their influence, if not of their convictions, drove the emperor from power. In March 1823 Iturbide abdicated, and shortly he, rather than Santa Anna, was the one leaving the country.

Santa Anna hoped to be the beneficiary of Iturbide's demise; reportedly he hired enthusiasts to parade about calling "Long live Anthony the First!" But Victoria and the other veterans of the revolution hadn't survived for years in the mountains without developing a knack for self-preservation, and they maneuvered Santa Anna off to Yucatán.

Stephen Austin observed the fall of Iturbide with ambivalence. On one hand, he cheered the emergence of a more representative form of government for Mexico. A Mexican by choice, he remained an American by birth, with all the congenital preference for republican government Americans after 1776 exhibited. And he couldn't help feeling the warm glow from what he called "the spark of liberty" that was struck by Santa Anna at Veracruz and which "soon kindled into a bright flame and spread with astonishing rapidity over the whole Empire." On the other hand, Austin had invested many months and much effort cultivating Iturbide on behalf of the Texas project—time and effort that now came to naught.

Wearily Austin resumed his petitioning, this time of the republican successors to Iturbide. Finally, after eleven months in the Mexican capital, he received the requisite seals and signatures, granting authority over colonization on the Brazos River in Texas to "Don Estevan F. Austin." He left Mexico City, he informed his brother, "with all my business finished to my complete satisfaction." On the way out he surveyed the political landscape and declared, "The revolution is complete. . . . All is quiet." Yet he added, significantly, "I will not vouch for its being permanent."

Chapter 5

The Three Hundred

William Dewees found his way to Texas as many others among Austin's original colonists did: by accident following setback succeeding disappointment. Dewees was not quite twenty-one when the Panic of 1819 swept through Tennessee, propelling him west with hundreds of others from the Cumberland Valley. He boarded a boat that drifted down the Cumberland to the Ohio, the Ohio to the Mississippi, and the Mississippi toward the Gulf. The prospects appeared no better along the great water highway than back home. "On this river there are but few inhabitants," Dewees wrote. "Most of them were pale-faced, sickly looking people, apparently fishermen and wood-choppers." Natchez stood out on the river's left bank, and in the mind of this innocent young man. "I have often heard of dissipation, but I never saw it in its nakedness till I came to this place. It would fill you with perfect horror were I to describe to you the fighting which is carried on between the boatmen and the citizens of 'Natchez under the hill.' . . . Here you might see men, women, and children mingling together in every species of vice and dissipation, the very thought of which is enough to sicken the heart." Below Natchez, Dewees's boat entered the plantation country of the Mississippi delta. The scenery was "truly delightful," but all the land was owned by rich white planters and all the work was done by black slaves, leaving little room for the poor white boy who floated past.

Hearing good things about Arkansas, Dewees ascended the Red River to that territory—only to be disheartened for a different reason. "I saw for the first time a person shaking with the ague [malaria]. I supposed the person to be dying, but was told it was nothing but the ague." Dewees himself fell ill a short while later, and was incapacitated for six months. After his health improved, he joined a party of buffalo hunters heading northwest toward the Great Plains. On the hunt he narrowly escaped ambush by Osage Indians, hypothermia from the rain and sleet of winter, and accidental violence at the hands of drunken fellow hunters. At the end of the hunting season he was nearly destitute and thoroughly ready for something else.

When a friend in similar straits suggested, in early 1821, a visit to Texas, Dewees eagerly assented. Nacogdoches was their first stop. "The buildings consist of a large stone church, another large stone building with eight or ten apartments in it. . . . The remainder of the buildings are adobes, except a few which are made of wood." About a hundred people lived there, including the Mexican commandant, who had to deal with all manner of mundane and extraordinary occurrences. During Dewees's visit a distraught traveler from Mexico presented himself to the commandant and demanded to be hanged. The commandant thought he was mad and told him to go away. But the traveler insisted that he deserved death: he had murdered his partner on the road and sunk the body in the Angelina River. So importunate was he that the commandant finally agreed to send a party to the Angelina, where the murderer produced the corpse, weighted down by rocks. Upon the group's return to Nacogdoches, the conscience-stricken man got his wish. "The Commandant called a few persons together to witness the solemn scene, took the man out behind the old stone building and there, according to the man's request, hung him on a tree till he was dead."

In Nacogdoches, Dewees learned of the Austins' Texas colony and decided to give it a try. He returned to Arkansas to conclude some personal affairs, and discovered that the news of Texas was traveling fast. "When we arrived at this place [Pecan Point, Arkansas, on the Red River] we found several families had heard of this enterprise of Austin's, and they are now making preparations to join the colony." Dewees was happy to have his judgment confirmed, and he looked forward to the company on the trail. He also looked forward to sinking roots in Texas. "If I like the country I intend to remain there, as I am tired of this wandering mode of life."

By the time he reached the Austin colony, Dewees was even wearier of wandering. "We were several months in getting here," he wrote, "there being several families in company, among whom were quite a number of women and children. A part of the time we were detained by the sickness of one or another of the company. Besides this, we lost several horses on the way, and in fact we seemed to meet with a great many misfortunes. We carried our luggage entirely upon packhorses, the roads being perfectly impassable for a vehicle of any description."

Dewees and a few other families pitched camp in January 1822 where the Camino Real crossed the Brazos, a short distance above the mouth of the Little Brazos. Two families had preceded them to the spot and were busy building cabins with timber from the riverbank. "We were, all of us, well pleased with the situation of the place and decided to remain here for the present. The settlement now consisted of seven families; there is no other settlement within fifty miles. About the time of our arrival here, a few families settled below us on this river, near the old La Bahia crossing."

The pioneers' lot was hard at first, especially for the women and children. Their flour and meal ran out, and though they had planted some corn, lack of rain stunted its growth. Yet there was no risk of anyone starving. "The country is literally alive with all kinds of game. We have only to go out for a few miles into a swamp between the Big and Little Brazos, to find as many wild cattle as one could wish." These escapees from Spanish herds had multiplied along the Gulf coastal plain; their only competition came from the buffalo that wandered in from the north, and which also supplied the settlers' wants. "If we desire buffalo meat, we are able to go out, load our horses, and return the same day." The hunters worked communally and shared their take equally, with the exception of the tongues, which went to the men who felled the beasts. Dewees's companion on one hunt upstream was a "yankee preacher." Dewees called him a preacher because the man so identified himself upon hearing the other hunters habitually swear. As for the "yankee": "My reason for calling him a yankee . . . is on account of the way he managed to get our buffalo tongues. About the time we got our canoe loaded with meat ready to start home, he proposed a plan to break us from swearing, to which we all very readily agreed. The first one who used an oath was to give whoever reminded him one of his dried buffalo tongues. Oaths being so common with us, we, of course, did not notice them, and in less than three days the minister was possessor of all our dried tongues."

After some months on the Brazos, Dewees crossed over southwest to the Colorado. The allure of the land amazed him. "Around all was wild, all was silent. Before us flowed the beautiful Colorado, while around us lay the prairies, green and lovely." Dewees's party camped for the evening and was readying its dinner of deer meat when some of the members heard a dog barking, across the river and upstream. "Not knowing whether it was the dog of an Indian or a white man, we shouldered our rifles and went up opposite the place from whence the sound proceeded. There we were delighted by the sight of a small log cabin, on the west bank of the river." The river was too deep to ford, so they shouted across and raised the cabin's occupants: "two old adventurers by the names of Buckner and Powell." The pair shouted back, explaining that a dozen miles downstream on the east bank lay a small settlement of a few families. The next morning Dewees's party found the settlement, which included a friend of his from Arkansas. Having arrived only a short while before Dewees's group, the six families were busy building cabins and otherwise making themselves at home. Dewees joined them, hunting, reconnoitering the country, and doing whatever he could to be useful.

Before long a traveler from downriver brought word that a boat had landed at the mouth of the Colorado with cargo and passengers for the Austin colony. Finding no one there, the passengers and crew had headed upstream, leaving a single guard with the vessel. Karankawas had set upon the boat, killed the guard, and stolen the cargo. As their own fate depended on keeping the Indians under control, Dewees and the other settlers prepared a response. "We immediately collected all the men we could up the river; these amounted to about twenty-five. We elected Robert Kirkendall, Captain, and took up our line of march for the mouth of the river." En route the posse found a few more families along the west bank of the river, and three men from Arkansas who had an unusual quantity of provisions for some who had come so far overland.

About twenty-five miles above the mouth of the river, the posse discovered a cabin where the passengers from a previous boat had stored their provisions. These had recently been rifled, apparently by the same band of Karankawas. But a few barrels of whisky had been spared. Liquor being rare on this frontier, "we began of course to feel a little desirous to know what kind of whisky the barrels contained; we removed the bung from one of them, drew some of the whisky, and each of us took a sip." Sentinels had been posted at the edge of the camp; a gourd was filled and delivered to them. "The sentinels shortly became very brave and courageous, refused to stand guard any longer, and came into camp. The captain being fond of a wee bit of drink himself, had kissed the gourd quite often, and finally decided that we were smart enough to whip all the Indians in that part of the country, that there was no need of sentinels, and we could stay at the guard fire all night. We kept up the frolic till nearly morning, some of the company now and then exclaiming that they wished the Indians would attack us, that we might show them how the Americans could fight." Fortunately no Indians appeared, and the only injuries the revelers sustained were splitting headaches the next morning.

Upon reaching the plundered boat, the posse discovered no sign of the murdered man. "We could find nothing of the body . . . and came to the conclusion that the Indians, who were cannibals, must have devoured it." But they did find something curious: the track of a sled or litter that had been drawn from the boat into a cane-brake nearby. Investigating, they stumbled upon a cache consisting of part of the craft's cargo. "Knowing that this was not done after the manner of the Indians, our suspicions naturally fell upon those men from Arkansas, whom we had discovered with such large supplies of provisions." Returning upriver, the posse questioned the Arkansans, who denied everything. "Being unable to obtain from them any satis-factory answer, we continued our journey home."

But their suspicions regarding the Arkansans rankled. Crime was crime, whether committed by Indians or whites, and frontier security depended on punishing criminals to deter others. Several members of Dewees's party decided to investigate further. "They formed a court by electing a magistrate, a sheriff, and other necessary officers. The sheriff was sent down to take the men prisoners." One of the men, named Parks, agreed to turn state's evidence (or the equivalent, in the absence of any formal authority) against his fellows. He explained that he and the other two—named Wilson and Moss—had learned that the Indians had already stolen part of the boat's cargo, and decided to take the rest themselves, guessing that the second theft would also be charged against the Indians. For cooperating, Parks was released, while Wilson and Moss were sentenced to hard time.

This raised a problem that vexed all frontier societies: how to jail criminals where no jail existed. The tribunal in the Wilson-Moss case solved the problem in a manner that educated Dewees to the ways of the world. The prisoners were to be escorted to San Antonio de Béxar, where the Mexican authorities could imprison them; but before being taken away, Moss was allowed to visit his cabin, accompanied by the sheriff. Soon after, the sheriff returned without Moss. The prisoner, he said, had escaped. All the sheriff had to show for his efforts was a gold watch, which he said Moss had entrusted to him for safekeeping; now that Moss was gone, apparently back to the States, the sheriff guessed he would indeed keep the watch.

Dewees and two other men were chosen to take Wilson to San Antonio. While they were there, a large party of Comanches arrived. The Indians' purpose was peaceful: "They brought in dried buffalo meat, deer skins, and buffalo robes, which they wished to exchange for sugar, beads, &c." Yet the issue of peace or war appeared to be at the Comanches' discretion. "These Indians are very friendly with the Mexicans"—or at least they were on this visit—"but friendly as they are, they seem to have the Mexicans rather under their control."

Dewees and his fellow deputies left Wilson at San Antonio and returned to the Colorado. They applied to the informal court there for compensation for their time and effort on behalf of the public weal. "To our sad disappointment we found that the property of Wilson had been divided among the officers during our absence, and there was nothing left us, after the other expenses had been paid." Completing Dewees's education in frontier justice was a report received about then that Wilson, like Moss, had escaped custody and fled back to the United States.

★

"I have just had the pleasure of spending a few days in the company of Stephen F. Austin," Dewees wrote under the date August 29, 1823. "He was on this river"—the Colorado—"with a surveyor, having lots laid off from a tract of land that he had just located for the purpose of building a town, about eight miles above the crossing of the old Atas-cocito road. But he has since abandoned it, and located his town, which he calls San Felipe de Austin, on the Brazos River."

In planting his Texas colony, Stephen Austin had to feel his way along a dark and unfamiliar road. Nothing in his own experience had prepared him for this, and almost nothing in American experience provided a model for what he was trying to accomplish. His father's establishment of the settlement at Mine à Breton, and the struggles Moses had with French squatters, Indians, Spanish officials, and American frontiersmen, suggested some of what Stephen was up against. But the Texas project was far more ambitious, involving many more people, vastly more land, and convoluted politics that made Spanish Louisiana look like a New England town meeting.

In theory the job of an empresario was straightforward. Within the boundaries assigned him by the government of Mexico, he allotted land to settlers. He then registered the allotments with the government, which conferred titles to the settlers. These made the land the settlers' own, to improve, bequeath, sell, or otherwise dispose of.

Between theory and practice, however, loomed a considerable gap. Before the land could be allotted, it had to be surveyed. In contrast to the situation in the United States, where (following the Land Ordinance of 1785) a rectangular grid existed, from which new surveys might be extended, in Texas there existed no such framework or template for surveying. And the scale in Texas was much larger than in the United States. Americans thought in terms of the quarter section—160 acres, or a quarter of a square mile—which in the well-watered country east of the Mississippi sufficed to support a family. In Texas the unit was the league—4,428 acres. This reflected Spanish and Mexican practice, which in turn reflected the scantier rainfall in those countries, as well as the fact that land ownership there wasn't intended for the masses but was largely reserved to the gentry. It also reflected the fact that land was something Texas had lots of. A league, while huge by American standards of agriculture, was lost in the vastness of Texas.

The surveys were only the start of the empresario's task. Austin had to make settlement easy and attractive. He had to provide facilities for landing those colonists who came by sea, for importing the goods they required, and for exporting the goods they produced. Settlers and their families expected to be able to purchase pots and pans and glass and nails and lead and powder and guns and knives and cloth and sugar and tea and coffee and books and musical instruments and the other items that distinguished civilized people, as Americans interpreted such things, from savages. They didn't expect all of this at once, but they wanted to see progress in that direction. And to pay for what they purchased, they had to be able to sell what they produced. Every farmer was an entrepreneur; without access to markets, even Texas, bounteous Texas, wasn't worth the gamble. This was so obvious that a novice like Austin knew it, which was why in his initial advertising for Texas he had emphasized the colony's prospective port of entry and why he had sent his first colonists by boat.

Internally, too, the colony required markets, where farmers could buy and sell locally. The markets would be located at conveniently spaced towns, of which the most prominent could serve double duty as a headquarters for the colony. New arrivals needed a place where they could meet the empresario, register for their land, reprovision after the journey from the States, and receive advice from those who had gone before. All the colonists would want a place to gather, to find spouses for themselves and their children, to educate the young ones, to muster against Indian attack, to sue one another in court.

Austin had a personal reason as well for wanting to establish a headquarters, a capital for his colony. Far down the dim road along which he was groping, he could see the outlines of what would become his guiding vision. The Texas of his dreams was not a collection of isolated homesteads but a community of cooperating individuals and families. A college man, reasonably cultured and comparatively well read, Austin had no desire to live on the frontier any longer than necessary. He had come to Texas to pay the family's debts, but Texas was evolving in his mind from a means into an end. And the Texas of that end would be filled with economically independent yet socially supportive individuals and families, centered about his capital.

"Since my return from Mexico I have been trying to induce the people to move nearer together on the Colorado," Austin wrote in September 1823, regarding the initial town-building efforts Dewees described. "I could not effect this object." So he crossed over to the Brazos, to the site that had favorably impressed him on his first visit to Texas. What came to be called San Felipe de Austin consisted, at the outset, of scores of empty town lots arranged in a grid on the high west bank of the Brazos. Just beyond the town were dozens of one-*labor* (177-acre) lots, each to be paired with a one-league tract located up or down the river. Austin envisioned that the arriving families would live on their smaller lots close to town, lending a sense of security and community to the settlement. The colonists, however, had other notions, preferring to reside on their leagues away from the town. As a result, San Felipe grew slowly, and Austin, who built himself two cabins there—one for living quarters, one for the colony's land office—had little company at first.

Yet the colony as a whole grew rapidly during the last months of 1823 and all of 1824. The news of Texas was out, and immigrants streamed into Austin's colony, eager to take up the offer of free land. The absolute number was still small—several hundred by the end of 1824—but in relative terms the growth was remarkable.

The rapid growth caused problems. San Felipe initially lacked the infrastructure of supply to reprovision the immigrants, and a drought during the summer of 1823 withered the first corn crop (which had been sown by the stone-age method of burning, slashing, and digging holes with sticks). The drought also drove away much of the game, leaving the immigrants additionally afflicted. They grew hungry, then famished. "There have been a great many new settlers come on this fall," William Dewees wrote in a letter dated December 1, 1823, "and those who have not been accustomed to hunting in the woods for support are obliged to suffer. Were it not for a few of us boys who have no families, their wives and children would suffer much more than they now do; in fact I fear some of them would starve."

Dewees accounted himself an able hunter, but even he often felt discouraged—which was nothing next to what those who relied on him felt.

> Game is now so scarce that we often hunt all day for a deer or a turkey, and return at night empty handed. It would make your heart sick, to see the poor little half-naked children, who have eaten nothing during the day, watch for the return of the hunters at night. As soon as they catch the first glimpse of them, they eagerly run to meet them, and learn if they have been successful in their hunt. If the hunters return with a deer or a turkey, the children are almost wild with delight, while on the other hand, they suddenly stop in their course, their countenances fall, the deep bitter tears well up in their eyes and roll down their pale cheeks.

Hunger was the most pressing problem, and indeed it drove many of the emigrants back to the United States. But it wasn't the most deadly problem. During its first few years the Austin colony encountered persistent violence from Indians. The Karankawas posed the principal danger. "They are an exceedingly fierce and warlike tribe, and also perfect cannibals," Dewees observed. "They can shoot with their bows and arrows one hundred yards with as great accuracy as an American can with his rifle, and with an equally deadly aim." Their rate of fire, moreover, was greater than that of the Americans with rifles. Dewees reported galloping along a riverbank almost an eighth of a mile from some Karankawas and barely escaping a hail of nearly a hundred arrows launched within a matter of seconds. (The arrows stuck in the bank, so he later had a chance to count them.)

The Karankawa attacks prompted the colonists to counterattack. One day a man named Brotherton staggered into a cluster of cabins with an arrow in his back and news that two other settlers had been killed and one wounded. "We immediately raised a force of fourteen men . . . ," Dewees recounted, "and at midnight we arrived at the place where Brotherton had been wounded. We there dismounted, and five of us went to search out the encampment of the Indians." Upon its discovery in a canebrake, the scouts reported back to the main body, which moved carefully forward. "As silently as possible, we crawled into a thicket about ten steps behind the camps, placing ourselves about four or five steps apart, in a sort of half-circle, and completely cutting off their retreat from the swamp." Dewees and the others maintained their silent siege till dawn.

> When the light was sufficient for us to see clear, we could not see anything of the Indians. We now commenced talking, in order to draw them from their wigwams; in this we succeeded. They rushed out as if greatly alarmed. We fired upon them and killed nine upon the spot. The rest attempted to escape, but having no way to run, except into the open prairie, we rushed upon them, and killed all but two, who had made their escape, though wounded, after the first fire. The number killed, nineteen.

It was indicative of the kill-or-be-killed attitude of the colonists toward the Karankawas that no effort was made to single out those Indians responsible for the attack on the settlers. Dewees's only reservation about the reprisal was that two of the Karankawas had escaped death. So swept up in the savagery of the moment was he that for "the only time in my life . . . I undertook to scalp an Indian." Like all children of the trans-Appalachian frontier, Dewees had heard numerous stories of Indians scalping whites, including women and children. "Moved somewhat by a spirit of retaliation, I concluded I would take the scalp of an Indian home as a trophy from battle." But after starting in on one of the dead Indians, his nerve failed, leaving him with no trophy but a gruesome mental image. "The skin of his head was so thick, and the sight so ghastly, that the very thought of it almost makes the blood curdle in my veins."

Stephen Austin was more discriminating in dealing with the Indians, but hardly less decisive. Responsibility for Texas brought out the steel in Austin; whatever threatened his colony became a personal affront and challenge, and he responded accordingly. In December 1823, following a series of Karankawa attacks along the lower Colorado, Austin summoned "all the settlers able to bear arms" to join a militia against the Indians. The militiamen should elect a lieutenant, whom Austin deputized "to make war against the Karankawa Indians and to raise men within his command and attack or pursue any party of said Indians that may appear on the coast or on the river."

The initial efforts of the militia failed, and the following summer Austin himself assumed the command. Leading a group of more than sixty armed men, he conducted a sweep down both sides of the Colorado. The militia met no Karankawas but did discover where they had been—and what they had been doing. "Found at this encampment the bones of two men which had been cut up and boiled," Austin noted in his campaign diary for September 5. "Buried them, and called the creek Cannibal Creek." Evidently the news of the militia traveled faster than the militia itself, for Austin and the settler-soldiers traveled all the way to La Bahía before overtaking any Karankawas. The Indians had sought refuge at the mission there, and the missionaries and town fathers urged Austin to honor the sanctuary. He agreed after the Karankawas promised to keep west of the San Antonio River for a year. As he explained to the Bahíans, "It is not our wish to deprive the Indians of their hunting or fishing grounds"; the settlers' only goal was "to guarantee a secure and permanent peace." The year of the agreement would allow relations between settlers and Indians to heal. "I sincerely hope with all my heart that before that period, confidence will be mutually established between us and the Indians so that we may mix with each other without suspicion on either part."

Austin was dissimulating here. He knew perfectly well that his colony intruded on the Karankawas' hunting grounds. And the subtext of his statement—doubtless appreciated by both the Indians and the settlers—was that in a year the settlers' position would be substantially stronger than at present, and the Indians' commensurately weaker. Time was on the settlers' side, and the Karankawas couldn't do much about it.

Other tribes fared little better at Austin's hands. After a group of Tonkawas stole some horses and extorted corn and other provisions from colonists on the Brazos, Austin mounted a punitive raid. "To prevent such outrages hereafter, and to recover the stolen horses," he reported to Governor Luciano García, "I resolved to march against them, which I did. I surprised their camp . . . and compelled the captain to deliver to me all the stolen animals, and to inflict with his own hands in my presence a severe lashing of the marauders. I ordered them also to leave this river and the Colorado at once, with a warning that if they again attempted to steal cattle, or to molest the settlers on these rivers, I would not be satisfied with lashes only, but would cause the delinquents to be shot." Not to the

Indians but to the governor, Austin confided that this last recourse was "an extremity to which I do not wish to be compelled to resort."

But if he was so compelled, better later than sooner. Some Indians couldn't be intimidated, at least not yet. These included a band of Wacos who lived along the upper Brazos and were allied with the Comanches. Like the Comanches—and unlike the Karankawas—they had no desire to drive the colonists out of Texas, for they saw the settlers as a convenient source of horses, which they regularly stole, and trade goods. The Wacos' numbers and their allies prevented Austin from retaliating, but not from calculating that he someday might. "We must be vigilant," he told an associate. "I wish if possible to avoid an open rupture with them for six months longer at least. By that time we shall have more strength. . . . If they commit any more depredations, the only alternative will be an expedition to destroy their village, but this I wish to avoid until next year if possible."

Time might have been on Austin's side in dealing with the Indians, but it wasn't his ally with the Mexican government. This was no reflection on Austin, who employed every opportunity to demonstrate his devotion to Mexico. "I expect to spend my life in this nation," he wrote to Lucas Alamán, the Mexican minister of exterior and interior relations, at the beginning of 1824.

Austin took his obligations as a Mexican citizen quite seriously. In the wake of Iturbide's abdication, Mexican thinkers and political figures pondered a new frame of government for their country; Austin contributed to the discussion by drafting a plan specifying a federal structure. Iturbide's rule had cured most Mexicans of their nostalgia for empire; with his downfall and departure, republicanism carried the day. But differences developed between advocates of a strong central government and proponents of distributed federalism. Austin backed the federalists. Noting the example of the United States, whose "happy experience of many years" demonstrated the advantages of a federal system, he sent his draft to Miguel Ramos Arizpe, the leading light among Mexican federalists. Austin later remarked that his plan "had much influence in giving unity of intention and direction to the Federal party." Here he was too generous to himself—he was by no means the only one in Mexico who had studied the American constitution—but for a newcomer striving to make Mexico home, his heart was in the right place. And when Mexico adopted a new, federal constitution in 1824, he had reason to feel he had contributed to a change for the better.

Austin had reasons beyond those of the other federalists to welcome the triumph of their cause. As a son of the American South, he found it easy to assume that states' rights constituted the bedrock of any reliable republicanism. And the same considerations that recommended a distributed form of government for the United States— starting with regional differences but especially including long distances and slowness of communication—applied even more to Mexico. Austin had spent months on the road to and from Mexico City, which alone argued for as much regional autonomy as possible.

Austin also had reasons more specific to Texas for his federalist sentiments. The closer authority resided to Texas, the easier it would be for him to manage his colony. During his eighteen months away, the colony had nearly collapsed. Uncertainty surrounding land titles, combined with the Indian troubles and the failure of rain, had sorely tested the hopes the colonists carried to Texas. "On my arrival in the colony, which I had commenced nearly two years before," Austin reported to Alamán, "I found that most of the emigrants, discouraged by my long absence and the uncertainty in which they had been for such a length of time, had returned to the United States, and that the few who remained, hard-pressed and harassed on every side by hostile Indians, and threatened with the horrors of famine in consequence of the drought, were on the eve of breaking up and leaving the province." Another such absence—which, under a centralized form of government, might be required for even minor matters—could spell the ruin of the Texas project.

Austin daily encountered the difficulties of managing a colony so far from the seat of government. His charter directed him to administer justice and preserve order in his colony, pending the establishment of institutions more permanent. This was no small charge, he explained to Alamán. "The situation I am placed in near the frontiers of two nations, and surrounded on every side by hostile Indians and exposed to their attacks and to the no less vexatious pilfering and robbing of those tribes who profess friendship but steal whenever an occasion presents, renders my task peculiarly laborious and difficult and requires a most severe and efficient police to keep out and punish fugitives and vagabonds from both nations." Catching the miscreants was hard enough; punishing them was almost impossible. Current regulations required that those convicted be sentenced to hard labor on public projects, but there were neither public projects in the colony nor the personnel to supervise the labor. "We are from 40 to 50 leagues from Bexar, and have no jail, no troops to guard prisoners. . . . A condemnation to hard labor without an adequate guard to enforce the decree is only to exasperate a criminal, make him laugh at the laws and civil authorities, and turn him loose on society to commit new depredations. . . . Nothing has a more disorganizing effect than a weak and inefficient administration of the laws, as it discourages and disgusts the good and well disposed, and emboldens evil men and renders them arrogant and audacious." The solution Austin recommended to Alamán was enhanced local authority: permission to administer corporal punishment upon the settlers and to banish intruders. "I think it would greatly tend to the harmony and good order of this part of the Province."

In fact Austin already was imposing stripes on evildoers; he simply wanted official sanction for his policy. Yet he realized that punishment was a poor substitute for prevention of crime in the first place. And prevention started with keeping criminal types out of the colony. Austin instructed Josiah Bell, a friend from Missouri whom he named the colony's first justice of the peace, on what to look for in applicants for admission—and what to do when the applicants fell short. "The most unequivocal evidence of character must be produced in the first place, and those who come without any recommendation and who are unknown in this country must be informed that I gave Garner ten lashes for coming here without proper recommendations, and that unless they immediately depart and quit the country, they will be punished." Whatever the principles of republicanism or the common law might dictate elsewhere, Austin refused to assume innocence pending proof of guilt. An unsavory reputation sufficed to provoke punishment. "Should a man of notorious bad character come in, I hereby fully authorize you to whip him not exceeding fifty lashes, and seize sufficient of his property to pay a guard to conduct him beyond the Trinity River." Austin assumed that the word would get out. "One example of this kind is wanting badly, and after that we shall not be troubled more." In a sentence that summarized his policy on immigration, as well as the attitude he was developing toward those who did get in, he stressed: *"Let us have no black sheep in our flock."*

Yet even some of the white sheep grew restive, especially when Austin began charging them for land the Mexican government gave him for free. He had his reasons, starting with the fact that planting a colony cost far more than he had reckoned. He was constantly spending money; traveling to and from Mexico City and supporting himself there for twelve months had been a sizable drain in itself. Through much of this period, he relied on the funds Joseph Hawkins contributed; but Hawkins died in early 1824, cutting off that source. As empresario, Austin was entitled to a great deal of land upon the completion of his contract with the Mexican government—that is, when the three hundred families were fairly settled—but even then he might be cash-poor, for with Mexico giving away land, there wouldn't be many people willing to pay for it. Consequently, Austin had to devise a scheme for coaxing money out of his immigrants.

His empresario agreement allowed him to charge a reasonable fee for the services—surveying, allotting, registering—he provided the immigrants. He decided to set the fee at twelve and a half cents per acre. Although this was a bargain in per-acre terms, it nonetheless required the typical family to come up with more than five hundred dollars for its league—a substantial sum for that time, place, and clientele. Austin was willing to accept goods in lieu of cash, and he offered installment plans for those who couldn't pay at once. "I will receive any kind of property that will not be a dead loss to me, such as horses, mules, cattle, hogs, peltry, furs, bees' wax, home-made cloth, dressed deer skins, etc.," he announced. "Only a small part will be required in hand; for the balance I will wait one, two, and three years, according to the capacity of the persons to pay."

Despite Austin's flexibility, many of the immigrants felt badly used. They knew that Austin was paying the Mexican government nothing for the land for which he was charging them hundreds of dollars, and though the acre price in Austin's colony was lower than anything they could find in the States, they resented his middleman's cut. Some suspected him of partiality in distributing the lands, of reserving the best parcels for friends and family. The small number of

Americans whose presence in Texas preceded Austin's included several who wondered what right this newcomer had to pronounce on their actions. Aylett Buckner, with a farm on the Colorado, was a veteran of the Gutiérrez expedition. "I was one of the first men who built a cabin on this river, the first man who had a plough stuck in the field," he wrote Austin. Buckner recounted the costs he had incurred making things easier for those who came after. "I have never asked the first cent for a man eating under my roof and have fed as many and I believe more people than any man in this colony. . . . I have lost as much and I believe more property by the depredations of Indians than every other man on this river." Yet others were now benefiting unfairly from his hardships. "Some men get half a league and don't pay a cent because the other half is transferred to you or your brother. I know that lands are unequally divided. I do not consider myself a perfect simpleton, neither am I blind. My eyes are open and I look and watch with vigilance." If Austin refused to deliver justice, Buckner would seek it elsewhere. "If you refuse granting me that which I think the Government will generously bestow on me, I shall apply to that authority."

Other warnings were more dire. Jacob Betts traveled to Texas with the first Austin colonists. "I came to this colony with every assurance that I would be governed by one of our countrymen, whom I had anticipated the greatest satisfaction of spending the remainder of my days with. . . . I have spent the three last years of my life in poverty and misery, looking forward for better times, part of the time fed with soft words and fair promises." Now Betts discovered that late arrivals were being offered better farms than he had received, thereby "reaping the rewards of my labor." Betts didn't try to hide his anger. "I have to say, all confidence is lost. . . . I therefore consider myself a free man and an injured one." Betts asserted that if he received justice, even belatedly, "you will find me disposed to render my services for the benefit of the colony as fair as is in my power." But if not: "You will find I can do you or the colony as much injury as any other man."

The complaints against Austin reached the Mexican authorities. José Antonio Saucedo was the political chief (*jefe*) of Texas, stationed in San Antonio de Béxar and responsible to Mexico City for order and welfare in Texas. Hearing the carping from the Colorado and Brazos, Saucedo initially defended Austin against his detractors. "You should listen with attention and confidence to your immediate chief (Colonel Austin) whose authority is from the supreme powers of the nation to which you now voluntarily belong," Saucedo urged Austin's colonists. "You should disregard and despise all those idle slanders and vague stories which are put in circulation by the enemies of good order for the sole purpose of creating confusion and discontent."

The grumblers, however, weren't any more inclined to heed Saucedo than to follow Austin, and as the level of dissatisfaction rose, the political chief felt obliged to take stronger action. In May 1824 Saucedo suspended Austin's fee schedule and introduced a schedule of his own. The fee for a league was reduced to $192, with $127 going to the land commissioner (the Baron de Bastrop), $27 to the surveyor, and $38 to the government. Austin was left in the cold.

Now it was Austin's turn to feel aggrieved, and he took his case to the colonists. Detailing his efforts to secure their titles to the land they occupied, he said, "Look at the difficulties I have had to surmount, the risks of property, of life, of all, which I have exposed myself to; consider the advantages which you will receive from my labors; and then

let your unbiased judgment decide upon my motives and say whether
I have been right or wrong in the measures which I have adopted." He
reminded the settlers that he had been forthright from the beginning
about the terms of settlement, including the twelve-and-a-half-cent
fee they would be charged. He pointed out that although Texas was
welcoming enough now, it hadn't been so at the time his father applied for permission to establish the colony. "Let it be remembered
that at that time this Province, with the exception of San Antonio and
La Bahía, was a desert, that it was interdicted to the American
settler. . . . Until this permission was obtained by my father, those
who emigrated here did so, as it were, by stealth and without any other
security for their property or lives than the caprice of the comman-
dants who governed." He conceded that the Texas project had originated as a speculation, but once the settlers began arriving it became
something else to him. "Success was now no longer considered by me
so much a matter of speculation as a point of honor to redeem my
pledged word to the settlers." He rebutted the allegations that he
stood to make a fortune from the acreage fee, citing the high cost of
surveys (which averaged, he said, seventy dollars per league, or more
than twice the twenty-seven dollars Saucedo allowed), the taxes due
the government, and the discount that had to be applied to the in-
kind payments he accepted. "I appeal to you all to say whether I would
now get, either here or anywhere else, 40, 50, or 60 dollars for horses
which I have received at 100, 120, or 150 dollars."

The appropriate standard for judging whether his fee scheme
was reasonable, Austin said, could be summarized in a single question: "*Was it not worth it?*" Could the settlers have obtained their land
less expensively in any other way? Nor did this question apply merely
to the past. If the settlers considered the original contract dissolved,
then so might Austin.

Why have I not the same privilege to consider myself also
free from all obligation to procure titles for their lands,
and say to those who refuse to comply with the original
terms stipulated with them: Attend to your business; go
elsewhere to procure your titles; I will have nothing more
to do with the business—a thing which I might in justice
do, if the original contract was disregarded, and which I
certainly would do were I to be governed solely by motives
of self-interest.

In fact, Austin wasn't about to walk away from the colony, as the
settlers must have realized. This doubtless contributed to their complaints: appreciating his emotional investment, they reckoned that
he wouldn't abandon them—which would have been disastrous, with
many surveys uncompleted and titles imperfect—no matter how
much they complained.

Yet it was hard for Austin not to be discouraged. He continued to
hear that his Texas project was being described to the world in the
most unflattering terms. "A report has been in circulation here for
some days . . . ," wrote a correspondent from New Orleans, "that *all*
your settlers have raised the standard of rebellion and refuse obedience to law or any authority whatever." The son of Joseph Hawkins,
who naturally wanted the colony to succeed, not least that he might
recapture his father's investment, wrote from Missouri, "I have done
everything in my power to cause the people to emigrate to that country, but so many false reports come from there that if a man has not
been there he is too apt to believe such reports and decline going."
An associate from Austin's time in Mexico City, Arthur Wavell, wrote
from the Mexican capital, "I am sorry to hear such very unfavorable
reports of the state of your settlement."

Austin soldiered on as best he could. He arranged a deal with Bastrop—who realized even more than the colonists that Austin was indispensable—by which Austin would receive a third of the commissioner's fee. Although this forty-two dollars per league wouldn't cover Austin's costs, it kept the cash flowing temporarily.

The longer term looked bleak. "You ask how I am getting on," Austin wrote Wavell. "To which I answer, not very well. And I assure you I am heartily sick of the whole business and shall gain nothing by it but losses and fatigue. . . . I have spent more in this damned affair than it will ever be worth."

The most serious of Austin's settler troubles originated outside his colony. Austin wasn't the only empresario seeking to bring immigrants to Texas; his competitors included several men he had met in Mexico City. James Wilkinson—Aaron Burr's co-conspirator—was characteristically brash and simultaneously secretive about his plans. Robert Leftwich represented a group of Tennessee investors, including a rising young politician named Sam Houston, calling themselves the Texas Company. Haden Edwards had speculated successfully in Mississippi and hoped to repeat his good fortune in Texas.

Austin was more persistent than the others, or perhaps just better at persuading the right people, and his was the first project to get government approval and actually put settlers on the ground. But in the reorganization of the Mexican government in 1824, the Mexican congress approved a law allowing the states of the Mexican union to set the conditions of colonization within their own borders. The state of Coahuila y Texas (which embraced Texas and its neighbor to the southwest) authorized several empresarios, including Leftwich and

Edwards, to bring settlers to Texas on terms similar to those granted Austin.

The Edwards tract lay to the northeast of Austin's colony, near Nacogdoches. For this reason Edwards (and his brother Benjamin, who eventually shouldered more of the administration of the project) encountered problems Austin was spared. All the empresarios were required to honor existing claims, and though these were comparatively few along the Brazos and Colorado, they were many more around Nacogdoches. Often accompanying the earlier claims were the earlier claimants—the squatters, drifters, smugglers, debtors, and felons who frolicked in the old Neutral Ground and still found little reason to adapt their habits to those expected of settled societies. In particular they saw little reason to comply with Edwards's demand, posted at street corners in Nacogdoches and at crossroads in the vicinity during the autumn of 1825, that they show proof of the validity of their claims. "If they do not do this," Edwards's notice warned, "the said lands will be sold, without distinction, to the first person who occupies them."

A formula more likely to pit newcomers against old-timers could hardly have been imagined. The rift became evident within months, in an election for alcalde. Edwards put up a candidate, Chichester Chaplin, who was suspect in the minds of the old settlers not simply for his Christian name—Chichester?—but for the maiden name of his wife, who was Edwards's daughter. Against Chaplin the old settlers ran a candidate of their own, Sam Norris. Chaplin won, partly because Edwards counted the votes, which prompted the Norris side to dispute the election to *jefe* Saucedo at San Antonio. Upon investigating, Saucedo overturned the election and ordered Chaplin to give up the office. Edwards took the decision as a personal affront and objected loudly, causing Norris and the old-timers to threaten to seize the office by force. Edwards eventually yielded, but he and brother Benjamin vilified Saucedo and the state government so insultingly that the government canceled the Edwards grant.

Now the new settlers were outraged. Very few of them had perfected title to the lands Edwards assigned them; as a result the cancellation of his grant left them with nothing to show for their investment of time and resources since coming to Texas. Many flatly refused to accept the state's decree. In November 1826 a band of three dozen of the newcomers, organized militia fashion, arrested Norris and supporter José Sepúlveda. They arrested Edwards also, but only, as it turned out, to mask their intentions, for he was soon released while Norris and Sepúlveda were "tried" for crimes against the people, convicted, and sentenced to death—a sentence that was magnanimously commuted to disbarment from public office. The Edwards crowd, led by Benjamin Edwards, who pranced on horseback through Nacogdoches waving a flag inscribed "Independence, Liberty, and Justice," thereupon seized the government building in the town and proclaimed the "Republic of Fredonia." "The Americans in this end of the Province have at length resolved to throw off the yoke of despotism and to be free men," Edwards declared. He added: "The flag of Liberty now floats in triumph in the soil of Texas, and the Americans are daily rallying around it, with a determination to support their rights or die in their defense."

To Mexican officials this was treason pure and simple. Saucedo and the Mexican commandant at San Antonio, Colonel Mateo Ahumada, marched toward Nacogdoches with a regiment of troops.

The news of the Mexican approach caused the outnumbered Fredonians to seek an alliance with neighboring Indians. Some years earlier a band of Cherokees, concluding after chronic mistreatment in the American South that they'd never be safe on American soil, sought permission from the Spanish government of Mexico to settle along the Sabine River above Nacogdoches. Their request met various delays—which didn't stop the Cherokees from moving in—and was still pending (with the government of independent Mexico) at the time of the Fredonian rebellion. Edwards guessed that in their frustration at the Mexican bureaucracy the Cherokees might be willing to join the secession. Why they should feel safer under a government of Americans than they did under the government of Mexico was unclear to many observers (and to more than a few Cherokees), but the very thought that the Fredonians were trying to unleash the Indians sent shudders along the frontier.

Stephen Austin had no difficulty determining where his allegiance lay between Mexico and the rebels. "I am a Mexican citizen and officer and *I will sacrifice my life before I will violate my duty and oath of office*," he declared. Duty and oath aside, Austin's interests were all with Mexico. After its stumbling start, his colony was getting on its feet, and it did so under the aegis of the Mexican government. Austin's settlers held title to their land and lived in as much peace and order as they had any right to expect so far from real civilization. Independence couldn't improve their condition or his; on the contrary, it was likely to throw everything into turmoil. He didn't wish it for his own colony, and he wouldn't tolerate it for his neighbors.

Austin denounced the rebels to Saucedo. One of their leaders was a man named Burrell Thompson, whom Austin had earlier assisted and who now presumed on that assistance to link Austin to the insurgency. "When I knew him in Missouri," Austin told Saucedo, by way of disclaimer, "he bore a good character." But he had since gone bad—and apparently mad. "I have nothing to say in his behalf, further than that he has turned crazy and is surrounded by crazy people."

Austin spoke even more bluntly to Thompson and the rebels. He damned them for calling on the Cherokees for help. "Great God," he said, "can it be possible that Americans, high-minded, free born, and honorable themselves, will so far forget the country of their birth, so far forget themselves as to league with barbarians and join a band of savages in a war of murder, massacre, and desolation?" Anyway, the rebels deluded themselves to think they could defeat the Mexican army, or to believe that other settlers would come to their aid. "They can send 3000 men to Nacogdoches if it should be necessary," Austin said of the Mexican army. "And there is not a man in this colony who would not join them."

To the Cherokees, Austin issued a counsel of patience—wrapped in a warning. Even a tactical alliance with the rebels, he said, in the hopes of obtaining a land grant from the Mexican government, was fraught with the gravest peril. Speaking from his own experience in Mexico City, Austin wrote to John Hunter, one of the Indian leaders aligned with the Fredonians: "I know that the Cherokees can get their lands if the legal steps are adopted, *and if they take the wrong course they are lost. . . . Before the sword is drawn the Government will yield a little to the Cherokees to keep it in its scabbard, but once drawn and stained with blood they will never yield one hair's breadth and nothing short of extermination or expulsion of that nation will satisfy them.*"

To add weight to his arguments, Austin mustered a militia of his own settlers, to defend Mexico against the rebels. "It is a duty," he declared, "which every good man owes to himself, to his family, and to his country to prepare himself in time and hold himself in readiness to take up arms and march under the banners of their adopted country against them, should they still persist in their mad schemes of independence."

After Austin registered such vehement opposition, the rebels

did not, in fact, persist in their schemes, which came to appear mad-
der each day. The only hope of the Fredonians had been to bring the
Austin colony on board; with Austin choosing Mexico—so decisively—
the leaders of the rebellion abandoned their quest for independence
and retreated into Louisiana.

By early March 1827 Austin was able to report with satisfaction
that "tranquility is fully and firmly established." Assessing conditions in Texas at large, he added, "The whole country in general are
gratified, and the Mexican character stands higher here now than it
ever did before."

PART TWO

Ravenous Democracy (1828–1834)

Chapter 6

Love and War

On the morning of August 30, 1813, a band of Creek Indians quietly approached the fortified home and trading post of Samuel Mims in the part of Mississippi Territory that would become the state of Alabama. The Creeks were led by a chief named Red Eagle, and they called themselves Red Sticks, for the bloody color they painted their war clubs. Red Eagle was an ally of Tecumseh, the Shawnee leader who was organizing tribes along the American frontier against white settlers. Tecumseh's message of defiance had split the Creeks, with some advocating cooperation with the whites, and others, including the Red Sticks, favoring war. Red Eagle intended to force the issue by attacking Samuel Mims, who besides being a trader and a proponent of peace between whites and Indians was part Creek.

On that sultry morning, men and women—white, Indian, black, and mixed-race—wandered in and out of the open gates at Mims's fort, while children shouted and chased their balls and one another across the square inside the enclosure. The tension among the Creeks and between the Creeks and their neighbors had put the territorial government on alert, and a company of militia had been sent to Mims's place. But no one had seen anything worrisome lately, and the soldiers expected no trouble this day. They lounged and dozed until a drum beat the noontime signal for dinner, when they shook off their lethargy and headed for the mess hall.

In the thick air, the drum's rhythm carried beyond the fort, to the woods where the Red Sticks were hiding, just past the fields that had been cleared as a buffer around the stockade. The Indians' battle plan made the dinner drum the signal for the attack on the fort, and now the Red Sticks raised a war cry that startled those in the stockade who had never heard it and chilled the blood of those who had. The attackers poured across the open space between the trees and the fort, shouting the louder as they went. The militia commander tried to close the gate, but several of the swiftest Red Sticks got there before he secured it. They held the gate open for their fellows, who surged into the fort.

Within seconds it became apparent that this was no attempt to capture the fort or seize its supplies, but a deliberate massacre intended to sow terror among the settlers. The Red Sticks methodically killed soldiers and noncombatants alike, some in the most brutal fashion. The brains of young children were bashed out upon the logs of the fort walls; the bellies of pregnant women were knifed open and their unborn children beaten to death before their eyes. Then the scalpers went to work, seizing bloody trophies from the dead and dying. Nearly 250 persons were killed; the only appreciable group of survivors were blacks taken off as slaves to the attackers.

News of the Fort Mims massacre carried quickly along the frontier and across the West. At Nashville, General Andrew Jackson heard the news and vowed revenge. Jackson commanded the Tennessee militia and considered himself personally responsible for the security of the frontier. Jackson knew all about Tecumseh and the crusade he was preaching against the whites; apart from Jackson's righteous anger at the massacre of innocents, the militia general was convinced that letting this outrage go unpunished would encourage other atrocities.

Righteous anger was the prevailing motif of Jackson's life. As a youth he had fought in the American Revolution, and the experience scarred him literally and figuratively. He was captured after the battle of Hanging Rock, in the Carolina hill country that saw some of the fiercest partisan fighting of the war, and was ordered by a British officer to blacken his boots. Jackson—who grew up without a father, deceased before the boy's birth, and almost without a mother, burdened by the care of several of Jackson's cousins—had always been quicker to sass than to obey, and his impertinent reply provoked the officer to strike at him with a sword. Jackson deflected the blow, but it left an ugly scar behind his ear and a permanent hatred of the British.

Jackson carried his wound and his hatred west after the war, to Tennessee, where he practiced law (being, by all accounts, more forceful in argument than learned in precedent), raced horses (for stakes that alternately enriched and ruined him), and fought duels (for his own honor and the reputation of the great love of his life, Rachel Donelson Jackson). One man died by Jackson's hand; Jackson himself absorbed bullets from various duels. The chronic pain from the bullets that couldn't be dug out did nothing to improve his disposition or alter his philosophy of life, which centered on the conviction that human existence was a struggle and that those who struggled hardest and best deserved the spoils of their victories.

Jackson entered politics in Tennessee, eventually representing his state in the House of Representatives and the Senate. But the office he valued most was command of the militia, and it was to Major

General Jackson that the news of the Fort Mims massacre was delivered in September 1813. Jackson laid plans for a reprisal, and prepared his troops.

★

Among those troops was a young giant—tall, powerfully muscled, physically self-assured—named Sam Houston. Only later would anyone note the parallels, but Houston had been born in the same year (1793) as Stephen Austin, and in the same state (Virginia). Like Austin, Houston went west at an early age. In Houston's case this meant Tennessee, to which he traveled with his widowed mother. Again like the young Austin, Houston attended a private academy, although Houston's academy was in backwoods Blount County, East Tennessee, rather than in well-settled Connecticut. While lacking many educational tools, Houston's academy possessed a copy of the *Iliad*, which filled the boy's head with dreams of romance and battle. He resisted the farm work that occupied his five brothers, and when the elder ones tried to force his hand to the plow, he fled into the forest, to the lands reserved for the Cherokees. Two of his brothers followed him, tracking the runaway to an island in the Tennessee River at the foot of the Great Smoky Mountains. The island was the home of Chief Oolooteka, the local Cherokee leader; by the chief's house the brothers discovered young Sam sprawled beneath a tree, reading Homer. They urged him to return to civilization, but he refused, saying (according to his later recollection) that he liked "the wild liberty of the Red Men better than the tyranny of his own brothers."

For three years Houston dwelt among the Cherokees. Oolooteka called himself John Jolly among whites, and the adopted surname suited his character. He was far more genial than Houston's brothers, and the teenage boy found in him a refreshing relief from them, and a substitute for his missing father. As a name for himself, Houston took Colonneh, or Raven, a bird that symbolized good luck and also wanderlust. Houston learned the Cherokee language and the arts and crafts and lore of the tribe. He learned to hunt like a Cherokee, dance and sing like a Cherokee, and commune with the Cherokee spirits and gods.

He returned to white civilization in time for the War of 1812. And when he heard that the U.S. Army was recruiting in Tennessee— and paying cash bonuses—for service against the British and their Indian allies (including the followers of Tecumseh), he enlisted. A lieutenant colonel in his regiment was Thomas Hart Benton, a Missourian bound for greater things, including a central role in America's westward expansion. Benton's chief contribution at this point consisted of noting the martial prospects of the twenty-year-old Houston, who had grown to his adult six feet two inches and was showing some of the charisma of leadership that would characterize his career. Benton brought Houston to the attention of Andrew Jackson, then preparing to march against the Red Sticks. If Houston, as an adopted Indian, had any reservations about striking the Creeks, those reservations were allayed by the cooperation of the Cherokees— and some other Creeks—against Red Eagle's army.

By the time Jackson was ready to attack Red Eagle, he commanded regular U.S. infantry troops, including Houston, as well as Tennessee militiamen. The former had received some training and learned some discipline; the militia were innocent of both. Previous campaigns with the militia had taught Jackson that indiscipline meant death to soldiers and failure to campaigns, and he was determined to teach all his men discipline, regardless of cost.

His determination was tested as his army approached Red Eagle's base on the Tallapoosa River. A militiaman—or militia boy, for he was still in his teens—named John Woods belonged to a company notorious for its resistance to military order. On sentry duty one chill February morning, Woods received permission from an officer to retire early to his tent for breakfast. Another officer, encountering him there, upbraided him for leaving his post before his watch ended. Harsh words ensued, prompting the emotional—and exhausted—Woods to seize a gun and threaten to kill anyone who tried to make him obey the second officer's order. Upon this, shouts of "Mutiny!" rang about the camp, and to Jackson's tent. The general leaped up and called for honest soldiers to help him put down the rebellion. "Shoot him! Shoot him!" he ordered. "Blow ten balls through the damned villain's body!"

Woods surrendered his weapon before matters came to that, and the various onlookers sighed in relief that no one had been killed. But Jackson refused to let the incident pass. He convened a court-martial, which charged Woods with mutiny. The verdict was guilty and the sentence death. Many in camp thought Jackson, having made his point, would grant a reprieve. Yet Jackson stood firm and insisted that the sentence be carried out. He gathered the whole army, and in their presence had a firing squad execute the unfortunate boy.

What Sam Houston made of the execution is hard to say. Years later he would have his own troubles with military indiscipline; perhaps then he longed for Jackson's ability to strike exemplary fear into the hearts of his soldiers. But for now he respected Jackson's resolve and sought to earn the general's approval.

When Jackson's scouts reached the Red Stick stronghold at the Horseshoe Bend of the Tallapoosa, they were impressed and daunted by what they saw. The Indians had built a fort in the bend of the river, surrounded on three sides by water and on the fourth by a breastwork of thick logs laid horizontally. The breastwork left gun holes for outbound fire, and it was curved concavely to allow the riflemen inside the fort to cover every inch of the wall. A single gate afforded the only entrance. Jackson appreciated what he was up against. "It is impossible to conceive a situation more eligible for defense than the one they had chosen," he recorded. "And the skill which they manifested in their breast work was really astonishing."

Yet Jackson refused to be deterred. He opened fire with two small cannons, whose balls bounced futilely off the heavy logs. Reconsidering, he sent a squad of swimmers to the rear of the Red Stick position, where they lit fires to distract the defenders. As some of the latter turned to fight the flames, Jackson ordered an assault against the breastworks.

Sam Houston was among the first to respond. He braved bullets in racing across the open area in front of the fort, and he scrambled to the top of the wall, where an arrow impaled him in the upper thigh. He fought on, with the arrow protruding from below his belt, and inspired his comrades in the murderous clash that followed. The Indians thrust their rifles through the gun holes and blasted the attackers, who jammed their own guns in the holes and fired back. The fighting was so close and hot, one survivor explained, that "many of the enemy's balls were welded to the bayonets of our muskets." In time the attackers drove the defenders away from the wall and into the interior of the fort.

At this point Houston accosted a fellow fighter and asked him to pull out the arrow. The missile was barbed and resisted withdrawal; Houston's impromptu surgeon quailed at the damage it would do if he continued to pull. Houston insisted that he try again, and threatened violence if he declined. The man gave a mighty heave, bringing out the shaft, barbed head, and a sizable chunk of Houston's flesh. Houston, correctly fearing that he'd bleed to death, retired from the fray and sought a real surgeon.

He was catching his breath when Jackson rode by. Pleased by what he had heard and now saw of Houston, the general ordered him to remain in the rear for the duration of the battle. But when the Red Sticks dug in, and Jackson called for volunteers for a final assault, Houston hobbled to the fore. He charged the Indian position against their desperate fire, stopping only when one bullet hit his right arm and another shattered his right shoulder. In pain and shock, in the gathering darkness, he staggered and fell to the ground.

The battle continued to a bloody, brutal finish. The outnumbered Red Sticks refused to surrender, which suited Jackson and his vengeful men. A body count the next day showed some nine hundred enemy Indians killed, against twenty-six of Jackson's soldiers and twenty-three of his Indian allies.

Houston almost joined the dead. His condition was so dire that the army surgeons, after an initial examination, triaged him in favor of those with a better chance of surviving. He fainted from shock and loss of blood and lay that night like a corpse on the clammy ground. To the surgeons' surprise and probably his own, he awoke the next morning. At this point his wounds received more thorough attention, and he gradually began to mend.

★

The Battle of Horseshoe Bend made Houston a Jackson man, and Jackson an Army man. Jackson's victory earned him a generalship in the regular Army, and when British forces, augmented by the veterans who had lately beaten Napoleon in Europe, approached New Orleans, Jackson was ordered to defend the city. He did so with the determination that friends and enemies had come to expect of him, and with a finesse of which almost no one thought him capable. Lacking the regular forces to repel the redcoats, he cobbled together an unlikely coalition of Cajun bayoumen, free and slave Negroes, New Orleans gentry, and delta-based pirates. The disciplined British assaulted the ragtag American lines once, twice, thrice, but each time fell back before the Americans' lethal rifle fire. Finally, with three of their generals dead, the British abandoned the field.

The victory at New Orleans elevated Jackson to status as a national hero, the only general to beat the British in an otherwise frustrating war. It didn't take long for anti-administration politicos to sense that Jackson might be just the man to break the Virginia chain of Jefferson, Madison, and now James Monroe. But Jackson admired Monroe and had no desire to oppose him. Jackson's boosters bided their time, looking toward 1824.

Jackson put the intervening years to vigorous use. The Seminole Indians were a comparative novelty among American tribes, having existed as a distinct group only since the middle of the eighteenth century, when war, famine, and disease depopulated northern Florida. Spanish officials there (like Spanish officials in Texas sixty years later) hoped to defend this frontier region by planting colonies in the border marches. They invited groups of Creeks to relocate south from Georgia, which the Creeks did. They brought their black slaves with them, and also accepted into their community runaway slaves from English and then American plantations. In time a people of mixed race emerged, called Seminoles—from the Spanish for "runaway"—by their neighbors.

As did the Comanches farther west, the Seminoles engaged in raids against the established communities of the border region, in their case crossing back over into Georgia and Alabama. A particular series of raids inspired the underemployed Jackson to retaliate. Jackson led a contingent of battle-hardened frontiersmen into Florida against the Seminole settlements. After smiting the Seminoles, he attacked the Spanish town of Pensacola, partly for abetting the Indians and partly because Spain was Britain's ally. To make the expedition further worthwhile he arrested and executed two British traders for arming the Indians and otherwise acting in an unneighborly manner.

Spain was outraged but impotent, as Jackson, who noted the unfolding revolution in Mexico and the continuing turmoil in Iberia, guessed it would be. Britain wasn't impotent, but neither was it genuinely outraged over the fate of two questionable characters; after filing a protest, London let the matter drop. Monroe and most of his cabinet recoiled at the controversy and distanced themselves from Jackson. His sole supporter was John Quincy Adams, who appreciated how the Tennesseean's impetuosity revealed the hollowness of Spanish power. The secretary of state exploited Jackson's coup and, in the treaty of 1819, ejected Spain from Florida.

The Florida affair made Jackson more famous than ever. Ordinary westerners embraced him as the beau ideal of their region, the model of courage, will, ambition, and success. He wasn't exactly one of them, being a comparative aristocrat on his plantation, the Hermitage, outside Nashville; but, having risen from the humblest circumstances, he was something they all could hope to become. Easterners adopted a less favorable view of Jackson. To them he appeared uneducated (he *was* uneducated, in a formal sense, but not entirely unread), uncouth (by eastern standards, but not by those of the West, which exhibited greater tolerance for drinking, gambling, and dueling), and unprincipled (lacking, in particular, due respect for the prerogatives of business and finance). Moreover, with his prow of a forehead and his peninsular jaw, burning blue eyes, and wild white hair, he looked downright frightening—not a Hebrew prophet, perhaps, but an American equivalent.

And indeed Jackson was a prophet: of an approaching democracy. In Jackson's youth, the founders of the American republic had attempted to build a wall against excessive popular participation in government. The people's house was the House of Representatives, but it was balanced in Congress by the Senate, whose members were chosen not by the people but by the state legislatures. And against Congress were set the executive, whose chief was chosen by the electoral college, and the Supreme Court, with members even more insulated from popular passions. The franchise was very far from universal. Only adult white males voted, in most cases only those who owned property. Beyond the institutional safeguards against democracy—a term of opprobrium at the time of the Revolution—was the habit of deference that had long caused Englishmen to select their representatives from among their betters, and which was expected to inspire Americans to do the same.

Yet the Revolution, or rather the revolutionary spirit of which the revolt against King George was the most obvious manifestation, was corrosive of many old habits. By declaring all men equal, for the purpose of justifying the revolt, Jefferson and the Continental Congress made Americans feel equal for other purposes as well. And if "no taxation without representation" applied to Parliament, why shouldn't it apply to Congress and the state governments? The genie was out of the jar; having made a revolution in the name of the people's right to govern themselves, Americans had an ever harder time justifying that some people could vote and others not. And as the population expanded and moved west, away from the citadels of eastern privilege, and as other countries—France, Mexico, and most of Spanish America—took up the revolutionary cry and echoed it back to America, the logic of broader suffrage became overwhelming. Women and most blacks still stood beyond the pale, but by the mid-1820s nearly all white men in America could vote.

And the person they voted for most enthusiastically was Andrew Jackson. The 1824 race to succeed Monroe matched Jackson against Quincy Adams, among others, and was the most competitive in a generation. For the first time a westerner challenged the tidewater East; for the first time the West felt a compelling interest in the outcome. As far away as Texas, even expatriate Stephen Austin followed the campaign. "Our candidates for President are J. Q. Adams, W. H. Crawford, H. Clay and General Jackson," Austin learned in a letter from John Sibley at Natchitoches. Sibley added, "Clay or Jackson will feel more interested for Mexico and of course will be our choice."

Jackson proved to be the choice of the West, and of more American voters than any of the other three. But the four-way voting split precluded any candidate's getting a majority of electors, and the decision devolved to the House of Representatives. The last time this had happened—in 1800—the bitterness hadn't dissipated before Alexander Hamilton lay dead on the Hudson bank, the victim of Aaron Burr's bullet. Jackson intimated that his dueling days were over, but one could never be too sure about the volcanic old soldier. Henry Clay, however, hated Jackson more than he feared him, perhaps because "Harry of the West"—of Kentucky, to be precise—resented his eclipse at Jackson's hands, and he threw his support to Adams. A short while later, in what gave every appearance of being the back end of a bargain, Adams named Clay secretary of state. In those days the secretary of state was the heir presumptive to the presidency: in every election from 1800 to 1824 the winning candidate had apprenticed as secretary of state. Consequently Clay and the country had reason to believe he had traded his short ticket in the 1824 drawing for a winning ticket later on.

The Jacksonians grew apoplectic as the dimensions of what they called the "corrupt bargain" became evident. Jackson himself had expected no better. "So you see the *Judas* of the West has closed the contract and will receive the thirty pieces of silver," he muttered grimly. "His end will be the same. Was there ever witnessed such bare faced corruption?"

The campaign of 1828 began at once, energized by the Jacksonian anger and amplified by the continued democratization of American politics. Until the 1820s voters typically did not choose presidential electors; state legislatures did. By 1828, however, that practice had largely vanished (only two states still let their legislatures choose electors), with the result that presidential contests became popular referendums. And in a popular referendum, Jackson was unbeatable. He polled 140,000 more votes than Adams (of 1.2 million cast), and swept into the presidency, the first candidate clearly the choice of the American people.

Jackson's inauguration was a brawl. The army of westerners who came to see the swearing-in of Old Hickory (the name he acquired in the campaign against the Creeks, and the first popular honorific applied to a president) surged up Pennsylvania Avenue from the Capitol to the White House, where they swarmed through the doors and windows, soiled the carpets, tore the drapes, broke the furniture, and smashed the china in the drunken glory of the victory they considered their own as much as Jackson's. "I never saw such a mixture," declared an astonished Joseph Story, an associate justice of the Supreme Court. "The reign of King Mob seemed triumphant." Senator James Hamilton accounted the affair "a regular Saturnalia . . . The mob broke in, in thousands—spirits black, yellow, and grey, poured in in one uninterrupted stream of mud and filth, among the throngs many fit subjects for the penitentiary." One of the city's most proper hostesses rendered similar judgment: "What a scene did we witness! The *Majesty of the People* had disappeared, and a rabble, a mob, of boys, negroes, women, children, scrambling, fighting, romping. What a pity, what a pity."

The riot finally ended, and the people went home to sleep off their victory. The mud on the carpets and furniture was allowed to dry and cake before being brushed away. The drapes were mended and the china replaced. But the spirit of *demos* that sacked the White House was abroad in the land. It swamped the vestiges of elitism in American politics; after Jackson, even candidates favored by birth and circumstance represented themselves as sons of the soil, born in log cabins and reared in the school of rough experience.

More tellingly, the new ethos of popular power fueled and justified the landed expansion that marked the age of Jackson. As the symbol of democracy, the proud old general embodied the principle that the will of the people is as close to the will of God as humans can hope to get. And when the will of the American people drove them to assuage their hunger for land by reaching across the Sabine River to Texas, the spirit of Jackson—the spirit of democracy—drove them on.

★

Sam Houston observed Jackson's rise with intense interest, and, seeing in the general most of what he wanted to be, the fatherless young man supported Jackson whenever he could. Houston's wounds from

Horseshoe Bend healed slowly; the army, embarrassed by its initial neglect, ordered Houston to Washington for further treatment. This first visit to the nation's capital opened the westerner's eyes to the grand prospects of a country that could dream of carving a great city from the wilderness; it also opened his eyes to the continuing vulnerability of a country whose Capitol and White House could be destroyed with impunity by British forces. Houston was still in the East when the news of Jackson's victory at New Orleans arrived; even more than most of those with whom he heard the news, Houston thrilled to Jackson's feat of arms, and admired his hero more than ever.

The end of the war meant that Houston must look for other work, as the army was certain to shrink with the peace. He applied to be a federal agent to the Cherokees; not surprisingly, considering his intimate knowledge of the tribe, he won the job. Almost immediately, however, the post put him in a quandary. An 1816 treaty between the federal government and a rump group of Cherokees afforded the Monroe administration a pretext for removing all the Cherokees beyond the Mississippi River. Houston recognized that the removal was unfair, and he weighed whether he could honorably carry out its provisions against Oolooteka and other Cherokees he had come to know and love. Yet he reasoned—with himself, and with Oolooteka—that the treaty would be enforced in any event, and better for the Cherokees that it be enforced by one of the few who cared for them and might soften the terms somewhat, than by those who would simply treat it as an excuse for further exploitation.

Many of the Cherokees opposed relocation, even against the arguments of their brother Raven that they had no choice. They insisted on traveling to Washington to make their case to the government. Houston accompanied them, dressed, out of respect, in the blanket and breechclout he had worn while living as one of them. Secretary of War John Calhoun greeted the delegation at the War Department and expressed his appreciation that they had traveled so far; then he sent them to meet President Monroe. But he held Houston back and delivered a verbal thrashing. Houston—somewhat to his surprise—had managed to hold on to his commission in the U.S. Army; the war secretary demanded to know what possessed an American officer to appear at the capital in the costume of a savage.

Houston bridled at this aspersion on his judgment and integrity. He held his tongue but conceived a dislike for Calhoun that lasted their whole lives. When Calhoun added to the insult by repeating spurious allegations circulated by persons who wanted Houston's job that he had been involved in slave smuggling, Houston angrily resigned his officer's commission and, a short time later, his Indian agency.

Now he really did need work, and as he returned to Tennessee he pondered his options. He had corresponded with Jackson since the war, and he knew that the general had begun adult life as a lawyer. Better educated and more widely read than Jackson (which wasn't saying much), Houston decided to become a lawyer, too. He sped through an eighteen-month course of study in six months, and commenced practice in Lebanon, a day's ride east of Nashville. To mark his new start, he acquired a new set of clothes: a frock coat of purplish hue, assorted waistcoats and cravats, fitted breeches, gleaming boots, and a tall beaver hat.

When his work took him to Nashville—as he ensured that it did—he stopped at the Hermitage to pay his respects to Jackson. The general had no natural children, and he began to look upon the younger man as a son. Jackson employed his influence to help Houston gain an appointment as adjutant general of the Tennessee militia. He subsequently endorsed Houston, again successfully, for chief prosecutor of the Nashville district. Jackson's imprimatur carried even greater weight in a contest by Houston for commander of the Tennessee militia—Jackson's old post—and Houston soon felt the decided pleasure of hearing himself addressed, like his mentor, as "General."

The least Houston could do was return Jackson's support, which he did with gusto. "The canker worms have been (already too long) gnawing at the very core and vitals of our government, and corruption stalks abroad, without obstruction or reprehension," he wrote Jackson in August 1822, by way of encouraging the elder general to run for president. "You are now before the eyes of the nation. You have nothing to fear, but everything to expect. The hopes of men in Washington will be *frost bitten* by the bare mention of your name! . . . You have been your country's Great Sentinel, at a time when her watchmen had been caught slumbering on post, her capital had been reduced to ashes. You have been her faithful guardian, her well-tried servant! . . . Will not the nation look to you again?"

Jackson didn't need Houston's encouragement to run for the presidency, but he appreciated his protégé's enthusiasm. And, perhaps guessing that the contest would be close, and might even go to the House of Representatives, he encouraged Houston to make a race for Congress. Houston did and won.

★

Houston could have been forgiven for feeling proud on returning to Washington. The boy who had fled home to live with the Indians was now a general, a congressman, and the surrogate son of the likely next president of the United States. His imposing height, his bold swinging strides, and his brash good looks marked him as a man with prospects.

Houston observed rather than spoke during much of his first term in Congress, but in January 1824 he couldn't resist taking the floor in support of a cause fraught with meaning for his own future and that of every people desiring to govern themselves. Greek nationalists had risen up against the Ottoman yoke; Houston argued that the United States must recognize Greek independence and thereby help the fighters of Hellas become free. "The Greeks are struggling for their liberty," he explained. "Let us, then, as far as we can, consistently with our relations with foreign nations, hail them as brethren and cheer them in their struggle." Critics claimed that the Greek struggle was no business of America's. Houston derided such diffidence. The Greek struggle was the struggle of free people everywhere, he held, and American recognition of Greek independence would enhance freedom everywhere. "It would be an advantage to show them that they are not an isolated people. . . . It will be encouraging them to stand like freemen, and to fall, if they must fall, like men."

The Monroe administration refused to aid the Greeks, which simply intensified Houston's desire to make Jackson president. Following the 1824 deadlock in the electoral college, Houston had every hope that the House of Representatives would choose Jackson. "My own confident opinion is that Jackson will succeed and be our next President!" he wrote in January 1825. When the forces of Clay swung to the side of Adams and gave the latter the victory, Houston shared the outrage of all Jacksonians. "The individual who was manifestly the choice of the majority of the people was not elevated to that distinguished situation for which his qualifications so preeminently fitted him, and to which the important services he had rendered to his country so richly entitled him," Houston told his Tennessee constituents. "This is a subject of serious consideration for the citizens of the United States, and it will be for them to say, on some subsequent occasion, whether their voices shall be heard and their rights respected, or whether they will tamely yield those inestimable rights to the unhallowed dictation of politicians, who may choose to barter them for their own individual aggrandizement."

The occasion of which Houston spoke, of course, was the 1828 election, toward which he began working at once. He apparently authored an unsigned biography of Jackson, a campaign tract of no historical or literary value but of some political influence; Jackson called Houston and a couple of other writers his "literary bureau" for their value in filling newspapers with Jacksonian fact and opinion. Houston promoted Jackson in the halls of Congress at every opportunity. "I am charged, for the purpose of producing political effect, I presume, with being the organ of General Jackson upon this floor," he told the House. "I am also charged with being his personal and political friend. I will inform the gentleman that General Jackson's public acts are his best organ, and his sentiments a sure passport to the affections and confidence of his countrymen." He sent hickory canes to potential Jackson supporters and the latest political intelligence to Jackson himself. "Your friends here are confident, and your enemies are decreasing in number!" he wrote in January 1827. A short while later he added, "I have not in my life seen a cause rise so fast as that of the people . . . nor one sinking faster than the cause of a wicked and corrupt coalition!"

Jackson's enemies became Houston's enemies. One Jackson-hater challenged Houston to a duel; that the challenger was a known sharpshooter diminished Houston's devotion to Jackson not in the slightest. "My firm and undeviating attachment to General Jackson has caused me all the enemies I have, and I glory in the firmness of my attachment," he wrote. "I will die proud in the assurance that I deserve, and possess, his perfect confidence." In fact this duel fizzled, but another didn't. The second challenger, William White, was a weak shot, yet Houston—who, as the challenged, had choice of weapons—selected pistols at fifteen feet, to give White a fair chance. Jackson, the experienced duelist, offered Houston the advice to bite a bullet; this would steady his hand in case he got hit while shooting. As things happened, Houston didn't need the ballast and, while escaping injury himself, hit White in the abdomen.

"General, you have killed me," White said.

"I am very sorry," Houston answered. "But you know it was forced upon me."

"I know, and forgive you," White rejoined.

To Houston's relief and probably (although not certainly, such being the curious code of the duel) White's, White didn't die. Dueling had fallen into legal limbo in Tennessee by this time—unlawful yet still popular—and so Houston, although indicted, was never arrested. On the contrary, he was feted among the many who still considered pistols an appropriate form of argument. Houston was becomingly modest about the affray. "Thank God my adversary was injured no worse," he said.

In 1827, as the Jackson juggernaut rolled toward the White House, Houston entered the race for Tennessee governor. William Carroll, Jackson's lieutenant at New Orleans, was stepping down after three terms, as the Tennessee constitution required; he endorsed Houston as a placeholder, one who would keep the office warm until he could run again, in two years. Houston accepted the favor without embracing the condition, and made a canvass of Tennessee that revealed him to be nearly as charismatic as Old Hickory himself. "Houston stood six feet six inches in his socks," recounted one observer (noting the emotional impact of the man rather than his strict stature), "was of fine contour, a remarkably well proportioned man, and of a commanding and elegant bearing; had a large, long head and face, and his fine features were lit up by large eagle-looking eyes; possessed of a wonderful recollection of persons and names, a fine address and courtly manners and a magnetism approaching that of General Andrew Jackson." Houston's wardrobe was as striking as before, yet with a different theme. He retained the beaver hat but instead of the purple coat wore a Cherokee hunting shirt, bound by a beaded red sash with an armorlike buckle. The dazzled electorate gave him a comfortable victory.

When Jackson won the presidency the following year—at the age of sixty-one, making him the oldest man thus far to assume the nation's highest office—the political classes at once began speculating as to his successor in the White House. Tennessee appeared the obvious place to look, and among Tennesseeans none had more courage, more presence, more dash, more of everything that made Jackson popular than Sam Houston. The one thing missing from the Houston resumé was a wife. His interest in the fair sex was not in question, nor that of the fair sex in him. His presence at parties and receptions drew regular throngs of young ladies. But like Stephen Austin, he wanted to establish himself before he took a spouse. "I will not court any of the dear girls before I make a fortune," he declared in 1815, "and if I come to no better speed than I have done heretofore, it will be some time." For a decade ambition outpaced romance. "I am making myself less frequent in the lady world than I have been," he wrote in 1826. "I must keep up my dignity, or rather I must attend more to politics and less to love." But after he became governor, attending to politics seemed to require attending to love, and he began looking for a wife.

He found one in Eliza Allen, the daughter of Colonel and Mrs. John Allen of Gallatin, Tennessee. The match seemed ideal on both sides. Nineteen-year-old Eliza had blond hair, blue eyes, and a figure that turned heads and broke hearts throughout the Cumberland Valley; the handsome Governor Houston had a past to boast of and a future to bank on. The wedding was the social event of the season; the newlyweds' progress to Nashville was reported in all the papers; the state rejoiced to claim such a glamorous First Couple. Sam Houston's star had never shone brighter, nor seemed more certain to climb still higher.

And then, with a suddenness that stunned the city of Nashville, shocked the state of Tennessee, and amazed that appreciable part of America that had been following the Houston story, the marriage and the governor's life fell spectacularly apart. Word circulated that Eliza, after less than three months of marriage, had left Houston and returned to her parents' house. This was no sooner confirmed than Houston sent the speaker of the Tennessee senate a letter announcing his resignation from the office of governor. The only explanation he offered was a reference to being "overwhelmed by sudden calamities," which he declined to detail. Nor did he ever detail them publicly as long as he lived.

His silence, of course, gave rise to rumors of every sort. Most involved the wedding night and what one or the other spouse had discovered then. From such conjectures to aspersions on Eliza's virtue was an easy step for the gossips. Houston, obviously suffering, broke his silence only long enough to direct a delegation of visitors to "publish in the Nashville papers that if any wretch ever dares to utter a word against the purity of Mrs. Houston I will come back and write the libel in his heart's blood."

The most probable explanation of what happened is that Eliza loved not Houston but another, whom her family considered a less desirable match. Against her inclination she acceded to parental pressure and married Houston, only to experience wedding-night remorse. She couldn't, or wouldn't, hide her feelings any longer, and she thereby put Houston in the position of the spurned lover—except that he was married to the one who spurned him. A Houston friend asserted, years later, that this was essentially the story Houston told him, in confidence. "About one o'clock in the morning I was waiting and smoking as he staggered into the room," the friend declared. "His face was rigid. His eyes had a strange stare. He looked like some magnificent ruin. He sat upright in his chair finally, and running his fingers through his hair said, 'It was so infamous, so cruel, so vile. . . . Cursed be the human fiends who force a woman to live with a man whom she does not love. Just think of it, the unending torture. . . . She has never loved me; her parents forced her to marry me. She loved another from the first.' "

Houston might have insisted that Eliza remain with him; she was hardly the first to marry other than for love. And he did implore her to consider whether her feelings might change. But once he was convinced he would never have her heart—and by her coldness she made this clear enough—he agreed to let her go. From some combination of honor and self-pride he refused to make any public explanation beyond his vow to kill whoever breathed a word against her. And from a similar welter of emotions, he decided he couldn't carry on as Tennessee governor. Heartbroken and humiliated, he threw over everything he had worked so hard to obtain.

And in April 1829, as Andrew Jackson was settling into the White House at Washington, Sam Houston fled Nashville on a Cumberland steamer and disappeared into the West.

Chapter 7

To Defend the Revolution

Antonio López de Santa Anna married for much the same reason Sam Houston did. The governor of Yucatán had reached the age—he was just several months younger than Houston and Stephen Austin—where the lack of a wife was becoming a political liability. Moreover, matrimony provided a means of forging ties with influential individuals who could further the general's career. Doña Inés García was no beauty, being tall and thin in a time and place when those attributes weren't generally welcomed, but she brought to the marriage a handsome dowry: some six thousand pesos in real estate. And, unlike Eliza Allen Houston, she accepted her role as wife and mother, eventually bearing Santa Anna five children.

Yet if his marriage turned out better than Houston's, Santa Anna's career was no less tumultuous. Upon assuming the governorship of Yucatán in the spring of 1824, he discovered that the merchants of that peninsular province—reachable, to all intents and purposes, from the rest of Mexico only by sea—identified commercially and politically with Cuba, which remained attached to Spain. The Yucatán merchants wished to undo the Mexican revolution as it applied to them and either rejoin the Spanish empire or fashion an independent but effectively pro-Cuban, pro-Spanish republic.

Sizing up the situation, Santa Anna conceived an audacious answer to Yucatecan separatism: a filibustering expedition against Cuba. By springing Cuba from Spanish rule—to become independent or part of the Mexican republic—he would permit the merchants to continue their Cuban trade without jeopardizing Mexican integrity or independence. In the process, Santa Anna would become a hero: of Cuba or Mexico or both.

The government in Mexico City learned of Santa Anna's project and allowed him to proceed with the plans. A political struggle had broken out in Mexico over the remnants of Spanish rule; the leading government ministers believed that a blow against Spain in Cuba might simultaneously weaken the pro-Spanish elements in Mexico. During the summer of 1824 Santa Anna gathered an invading force of some five hundred soldiers and readied them to sail.

At the last moment, however, Mexico City flinched. The government had come under diplomatic pressure from Britain and the United States to avoid disrupting the status quo in the Caribbean. The two English-speaking powers reached this common conclusion by separate routes: the United States believed that a non-Spanish Cuba ought to become American, while the British believed that it should not but probably would. Lest they have to fight over the island, Washington and London preferred to leave it as it was.

The Mexican government thereupon ordered Santa Anna to stand down and disavowed foreknowledge of the invasion plans. "General Santa Anna acted without instructions or orders whatever and strictly upon his own authority," the foreign ministry explained to the American government. Santa Anna was relieved of his command of military forces in Yucatán and was ordered to appear before a court-martial. But the scapegoating went only so far: the court never convened, and Santa Anna was allowed to resign the governorship of Yucatán without sanction.

The period after his resignation was a convenient time to be out of Mexican politics. The 1824 constitution had been a victory for Mexican federalists—who tended to be liberal, secular, and anti-elitist—but only an interim one, as the centralists—chiefly conservative, religious elitists—soon fought back. The contest took place in the columns of Mexican newspapers, in the chambers of the Mexican congress, and, after a disputed election in 1828, on the field of battle.

Santa Anna reentered the fray by siding with Vicente Guerrero, an old rebel who lost the 1828 election to the conservative candidate but engineered a coup that made him president. "My beloved friend and companion," Santa Anna wrote Guerrero, "what thing can be asked of me in the name of my country and by my worthy friend, the patriot Vicente Guerrero, that I will not do?"

Guerrero appreciated the sentiment but distrusted its author. Knowing Santa Anna's history, Guerrero preferred that he remain in retirement. Yet when Santa Anna made clear that retirement no longer suited him, and that he would take up arms either for Guerrero or against him, the president appointed him governor of Veracruz.

This appointment proved inspired, if accidentally so, for it placed Mexico's most able officer at what turned out to be the country's point of greatest danger. During the summer of 1829 the Spanish launched a long-anticipated attempt to reconquer Mexico. From Cuba they embarked three thousand troops for the Mexican coast; these landed at Cabo Rojo, south of Tampico, and marched overland toward that city.

The Spanish invasion of Mexico bore striking similarities to the British invasion of the United States during the War of 1812. In each case a vengeful imperial power tried to reclaim its erstwhile territory.

And Santa Anna's defense of Tampico was remarkably akin to Andrew Jackson's defense of New Orleans. Santa Anna raced to Tampico, where by force of charm and will he prepared the city for the attack. He commandeered every useful vessel in the harbor (including some British and American craft) and compelled the merchants of the city to lend him money to mount his defense. Santa Anna exceeded his authority in much of this, risking reprimand but guessing that victory would absolve him.

The fighting lasted three weeks, beginning with a sharp attack by Santa Anna's troops on August 21, which stunned the Spaniards with its energy and coherence, and ending with a nighttime battle on September 10, which killed nine hundred Spaniards and persuaded the Spanish commander to sue for peace. Santa Anna took the Spaniards' arms and provisions and let them leave the country for Cuba.

The victory had much the same electrifying effect in Mexico that Jackson's victory had in America. All of Mexico hailed Santa Anna as the vindicator of the republic and the savior of the revolution. The skeptical Guerrero was compelled to acknowledge his rival's greatness. "I am going to send him this general's belt which I am wearing, in order that he shall put it on with all solemnity as a just reward in his camp and before his soldiers," Guerrero said. The city of Tampico renamed itself Santa Anna de Tamaulipas in honor of its defender; the city of Veracruz threw a weeklong party for the province's favorite son.

The brilliance of Santa Anna's triumph was so dazzling that many in Mexico didn't notice the officer at his side during the defense of Tampico. General Manuel de Mier y Terán was one of the most accomplished men in Mexico, having fought in the revolution beside the original nationalists and served as a member of congress and in assorted ministries. He was also a trained scientist and engineer, and had recently headed an exhaustive survey of the Texas frontier. As it happened, Terán was returning from Texas when he learned of the Spanish landing below Tampico; rushing to the scene, he directed the artillery bombardment that sealed Santa Anna's triumph. Yet unlike Santa Anna, Terán had no taste for fame, and he was content to let his superior bask in the glory of the moment. Besides, as gratified as he was that the Spaniards were beaten, he couldn't escape the feeling that their invasion was less significant and threatening than an invasion that was taking place farther north, in Texas.

The group Terán had led to Texas was called the Comisión de Límites, or Boundary Commission, and it was charged with surveying and marking the northeastern border of Mexico. That border had been specified in the 1819 treaty between the United States and Spain, but it had never been fixed on the ground. The Terán expedition was to do so.

Yet the expedition had a deeper, less public purpose. In the wake of the Fredonian rebellion, the Mexican government desired to investigate the circumstances that had spawned the revolt. Texas had always been far from the center of Mexican affairs, and in the decade and a half since the outbreak of the revolution it had grown even further. Governments in Mexico City had more pressing matters closer to home—armed uprisings, military coups, foreign invasion—with the result that even when the Mexican imagination turned to Texas, as it infrequently did, Mexican intelligence regarding that distant province was spotty and confused. To remedy the deficiency the government organized the Terán expedition. Terán was to assess the situation in Texas: the size, strength, and attitudes of the settler colonies; the condition and prospects of the Indians; the extent and value of the natural resources. And he was to recommend measures to keep Texas Mexican.

★

Terán's expedition left Mexico City in November 1827. Besides the engineers who would do the actual surveying, it included a draftsman and artist, José María Sánchez y Tapia; a biologist, Jean-Louis Berlandier (a French national); and a military escort. The group moved slowly north, reaching the Rio Grande at Laredo in February 1828 and San Antonio de Béxar in March.

Mexico's Texas problems were apparent even at Béxar, which presented a shabby face to the world. "The buildings, though many are of stone, show no beauty, nor do they have any conveniences," Sánchez reported. "There are two squares, almost joined together, being divided merely by the space occupied by the parochial church, but neither one is worthy of notice." Berlandier said that "Ciudad de Béxar resembles a large village more than the municipal seat of a department."

The sad state of the town seemed the result of neglect, both personal and public. Sánchez might have been expected to feel a certain sympathy for his countrymen, but in fact residents of central Mexico, especially Mexico City, often felt as little kinship for their frontier compatriots as the residents of Boston or Philadelphia did for the backwoodsmen of Kentucky or the Cajuns of Louisiana. Sánchez observed wryly, "The character of the people is care-free; they are enthusiastic dancers, very fond of luxury, and the worst punishment that can be inflicted upon them is work."

The prevailing distaste toward work wasn't entirely a deficiency of character; circumstances conspired to prevent work from being rewarded. Most of the families at Béxar were connected to the army, and their military obligations precluded regular farming. Other deterrents to agriculture were hostile Indians, who threatened anyone venturing far from the town, and the lack of reliable rain, which made cultivation chancy—even as the Indian threat made digging irrigation ditches unacceptably dangerous.

But the main reason Béxar failed to thrive, Sánchez and Berlandier agreed, was that maladministration and corruption had demoralized the inhabitants. "For months, and even years at times," Sánchez said, "these troops have gone without salary or supplies, constantly in active service against the Indians, dependent for their subsistence on buffalo meat, deer, and other game they may be able to secure with great difficulty. . . . If any money arrives, it disappears instantly, for infamous hands are not lacking to take it and give the poor soldiers goods at double their normal value in exchange for what they have earned, suffering the inclemencies of the weather while these inhuman tyrants slept peacefully in their beds." Berlandier condemned the local administration and wished Mexico City would, too. "I have witnessed actions," he said, "which, under a well-regulated government, ought to lead their perpetrators to the gallows."

From San Antonio de Béxar the expedition headed east toward Stephen Austin's colony. Terán was as impressed as Austin had been by the appearance of the land. "The beauty of this country surpasses all description," Terán wrote. Yet only the Americans, and not the Mexicans, were taking advantage of what the country offered. Terán almost felt he was in a foreign nation by the time he crossed the Guadalupe. "On the eastern bank of this river there are six wooden cabins, whose construction shows that those who live in them are not Mexicans." The cabins were of the American frontier style, but modified for the Texas weather. "Though the house is a single piece, it has two rooms, a high one and a low one. In the latter is found the storeroom and kitchen, whose chimney sticks up on the outside, and in the higher part are the bedroom and living room." Not only were the Americans' houses different from those of the Mexicans; so were their attitudes. The afternoon was hot—25 degrees by the Reamur scale Terán carried, or 89 degrees Fahrenheit—and Terán was tired from the day's journey. "I approached a cabin in hopes that its owner might offer me shelter, but it was in vain. I learned later that the North Americans are not used to making such invitations. One arrives quite naturally, sure of being well received. But if one stops at the door, no one encourages him to come inside."

The expedition crossed the Colorado River on a ferry operated by an American named Benjamin Beeson. "He is quite urbane, his family very honorable," Terán remarked, pleasantly surprised. "Their services were very helpful to us." Beeson and his family had been abducted by Waco Indians, who had also captured some San Antonians. The latter, more familiar than the newcomers with the ways of the natives, managed to obtain the freedom of them all. Mrs. Beeson had learned sufficient Spanish to converse easily with Terán and the other visitors, as had the couple's eldest daughter (whom William Dewees would marry). "Aside from their possessions"—a cabin, its furnishings, a herd of cattle—"Madame says they have 1,200 pesos in savings. They have been on this land for five years, and they speak with great satisfaction of its fertility and good climate. In a word, they seem happy."

On April 27 the expedition reached Austin's colony. The empresario himself was away from San Felipe, but Samuel Williams,

Austin's assistant, greeted Terán and the others and showed them to a house that had been prepared for them. Terán had heard about the industry of the Americans, yet he was amazed at what he saw. He calculated the colony's annual corn crop at the equivalent of 64,000 bushels, and the cotton crop at 240,000 pounds. In addition, the colonists were raising mules for export to the British and French islands of the West Indies. Obviously, this was no subsistence project but, for most of the colonists, a venture in commercial agriculture. If the Americans' self-confidence—which equaled their industry—was any guide, the success of the venture seemed certain.

Terán queried the colonists on various topics, including why they had come to Texas. "The reason for the emigration of the North Americans to Mexican territory, according to the colonists themselves, is the better climate," Terán wrote.

> To the north the freezing temperatures and snows create obstacles to their work for several months and force them to labor harder. In Texas they work year-round and therefore in greater moderation. In winter they clear and prepare the land that they will plant in the spring. They repair the roads for wheels, because the vehicle called wagüin [wagon] is their only means of transportation. . . .
>
> The second reason they mention for emigration is that in the north agricultural production outstrips demand, and the prices are exceedingly low. The colonists hope for greater appreciation in the ports and on the coast of Mexico. . . . They hope to take over the supply of flour, grains, and meats in the ports.

Considering how well they had already done in Texas, Terán didn't doubt that they could achieve their goal, probably before long.

Whether that would tighten their attachment to Mexico or merely increase their self-reliance, Terán couldn't say.

★

Téran would return to Austin's colony, which was the center of American activity in Texas and therefore the focus of Terán's intelligence
gathering. But his Boundary Commission had to examine the boundary, and so he pushed the group on east. The humidity thickened the
farther they went, and with it the mosquitoes. "I will remember for a
long time the suffering I endured," Terán wrote after one bad night.
Two weeks more of torment caused him to moan: "The insects have
wreaked great havoc on me. My ears and most of my face are missing
skin and continuously oozing lymph."

This land of mosquitoes was obviously less desirable than the
region to the west, and its inhabitants were clearly less well off. After
crossing the Neches, the expedition entered an opening in the pine
forest. "There is a crudely built cabin, where we found two naked and
very pallid North American children. We learned that they were living there alone because their mother had gone to Nacogdoches. This
family seems to have been reduced to the utmost misery."

The poverty of the border region was lamentable, but its lawlessness was shocking. "A great number of the foreigners who have
entered the frontier are vicious and wild men with evil ways," Terán
wrote. "Some of them are fugitive criminals from the neighboring
republic; within our borders they create disturbances and even criminal acts. . . . Since the laws do not allow for any claims by one republic against the other"—that is, by Mexico against the United States
or vice versa—"the inhabitants take advantage of their friends and
companions to attack and to defend themselves and cross from one
side to the other in order to escape punishment."

At Nacogdoches Terán reflected on what he had seen crossing Texas, and what it meant. "As one travels from Béxar to this town, Mexican influence diminishes, so much so that it becomes clear that in this town that influence is almost nonexistent. But where could such influence come from? Not from the population, because the ratio of the Mexican population to the foreign is one to ten; nor from its quality, because the population is precisely the contrary: the Mexicans of this town consist of what people everywhere call the abject class, the poorest and most ignorant." The Americans in Nacogdoches operated an English-language school for their children. "The poor Mexicans neither have the resources to create schools, nor is there anyone to think about improving their institutions and their abject condition."

Terán's visit to the border made him appreciate what Stephen Austin had accomplished in his colony. On his outward journey Terán had been inclined to consider the success of the Austin colony a potential threat to Mexican rule; now he deemed it a bulwark against the rabble of the frontier. Terán characterized Austin's colony as "the only one where they try to understand and obey the laws of the country and where, as a result of the enlightenment and integrity of its empresario, they have a notion of our republic and its government."

Yet one couldn't be too sure. Terán could accept the sincerity of Austin's attachment to Mexico and still wonder if he had set something in motion that neither he nor Mexico could control. Traveling down the Trinity River to Atascocito, Terán discovered a thriving settlement of fifty-eight North American families engaged in raising cattle and sugar. "It should be pointed out that this colony has been created without the authorities' knowledge," Terán observed dryly. There seemed to be no stemming the American tide. Returning up the Trinity, Terán encountered a small but telling bit of evidence as to what the Mexican government was up against. "Traveling ahead of us—on foot, with neither provisions nor weapons—is a North American who has come from the state of Mississippi to visit the country, with the idea of settling there. He has gone as far as the Guadalupe River and says that he is heading back to bring his family."

Terán couldn't avoid the conclusion that there was something about the North Americans that simply made them better colonizers than the Mexicans. Visiting Austin's colony again, he stopped at the plantation of James Groce, the wealthiest of the Americans. Groce's land produced huge crops of cotton; Terán guessed that he currently had 30,000 pounds ready to ship to New Orleans. Groce had his own cotton gin and grist mill, and more than a hundred slaves. (Though slavery became illegal in Mexico following independence from Spain, the ban went unenforced in the American settlements in Texas.) The fields already under cultivation were fenced by wooden rails; other fields were being cleared to expand the operation. Groce could easily have afforded luxuries—and had he been Mexican, Terán thought, he probably would have indulged himself. But he didn't. "This settler, despite the vast assets he enjoys, seeks very few comforts for himself. He lives with a young man, his son, and another white man among the huts of the negroes." Terán thought it telling that even Groce's slaves seemed to prosper. "The latter appear well dressed, with indications that they enjoy abundance."

This made the contrast with another settlement all the more striking. From Austin's colony Terán proceeded west and south; on the banks of the Guadalupe he encountered a colony of Mexicans from the state of Tamaulipas, planted by the empresario Martin de

León. These settlers seemed a sober, responsible bunch—"well-behaved people from the decent laboring class who have brought livestock of every kind to the new settlement." But the energy and acquisitiveness that distinguished the Austin colony were conspicuous by their absence.

> Since they have no notion of internal or external commerce, they do not aim their efforts at cotton, sugar, or other exportable products that have begun to appear in the Austin colony. They limit themselves to raising many cattle and tilling good fields. They also have little knowledge of the economy and settlement system of the North Americans. They lack the variety of industries which the latter usually have and which makes it so easy for them to establish themselves with no more help than what they bring with them. Among the North Americans who live in the countryside, it is rare not to find carpenters, locksmiths, blacksmiths, and bloodletters. Even in a gathering of a few families, artisans of this type are hardly ever lacking. In the Mexican colony . . . all this is missing.

A minor feature of life in the Mexican colony, contrasting to that in the North American colony, revealed a major difference. "The Mexicans escape from the solitude of the country and instead devote themselves to forming a populated body, rather than establishing themselves independently on the lands they cultivate. In the Austin colony, with more than 300 families, no more than 15 or 20 are found in the town, while in the Guadalupe colony all those who constitute it are in a rectangle around a plaza." This contributed to social cohesion and perhaps communal happiness, but it diminished the colonists' productivity. "The fields are 4 and 5 leagues away, which means that a great deal of time is spent traveling." At Austin's colony Terán had predicted that steamboats would soon be running on the Brazos to transport the colonists' produce more efficiently to market; Terán saw no steamboats in the future of the Guadalupe.

★

So what was to be done? How could Texas be defended against the invasion of the Americans?

This was a hard problem, not least on account of the invaders' infuriating smugness regarding land. "Nature tells them that the land is theirs," Terán wrote, "because, in effect, everyone can appropriate what does not belong to anyone or what is not claimed by anyone. When the occasion arises, they will claim the irrefutable rights of first possession." Terán conceded a distinction between the legal colonists of empresarios like Austin and the illegal immigrants who arrived without permission and settled where they would. The former followed the laws of Texas and Mexico, such as the laws were; the latter followed no laws but their own desires. Yet Terán wondered whether much, in the end, would really distinguish the lawless Anglos from the law-abiding. "I must say in all frankness that everyone I have talked to here who is aware of the state of the country and devoted to its preservation is convinced, and has convinced me, that these colonies, whose industriousness and economy receive such praise, will be the cause for the Mexican federation to lose Texas unless measures are taken soon."

So what did Terán recommend? First, the Mexican army's presence in Texas must be increased. "On the frontier there are intrigues," Terán wrote; and the way to prevent intrigues from becoming rebellions was to have troops at the ready. The garrison at Béxar should be expanded and one or more military colonies established, starting along the Medina River below Béxar. Second, immigration of North Americans should be suspended. Existing American colonies, most notably Austin's, should be left alone. Indeed, it was in Mexico's interest that the faithful, law-abiding Austin prosper, so that his colony could inoculate Texas against the lawless elements. But no further American colonies should be allowed, and certainly no more independent American settlements.

The most important measure the Mexican government could adopt, and the one without which the others would be but temporary solutions, was to make Texas truly Mexican. "The land of Texas, or at least its eastern part where its principal rivers begin to be navigable, should be reserved for Mexican settlers," Terán declared. He granted that this recommendation came late, as the Americans already occupied most of the best land in Texas. And he acknowledged the deficiencies of Mexicans as colonists. Even so, the government must do whatever it could to populate Texas with Mexicans. This was "absolutely necessary . . . in order to counterbalance foreign ways." Terán proposed that the government transplant five thousand Mexicans along the Trinity River as a barrier to further American encroachment. Terán allowed that such a project would be costly. "The national treasury will have to spend a hundred thousand pesos or a bit more." But he saw no other choice. "In our country nothing is done if the government does not do it." If the government did take the lead, there was cause for optimism. "The way for Mexicans to become industrious entrepreneurs is for them to be encouraged once, twice, or even three times. If they are spurred, we can rely on their perseverance, and we should expect that if they are infused with the colonizing spirit, colonization will become popular. They will be filled with this frenzy for the north country and will populate its wilderness in just a few years."

★

Here Terán was trying to persuade himself as much as his political superiors. He hoped Mexicans would fill Texas and thereby secure it for Mexico, but the evidence suggested otherwise. After helping Santa Anna defeat the Spanish at Tampico, Terán received command of the northeastern states of the Mexican federation (Tamaulipas, Nuevo León, and Coahuila y Texas). From his headquarters at Mata-moros he monitored the continuing immigration to Texas, and he continued to try to stop it. "The department of Texas is contiguous to the most avid nation in the world," he wrote to the Mexican war de-partment in late 1829. "The North Americans have conquered what-ever territory adjoins them. In less than half a century, they have become masters of extensive colonies which formerly belonged to Spain and France, and of even more spacious territories from which have disappeared the former owners, the Indian tribes. There is no power like that to the north, which by silent means has made con-quests of momentous importance. Such dexterity, such constancy in their designs, such uniformity of means of execution which always are completely successful, arouses admiration."

It also aroused alarm, or ought to. Terán declared that Mexico was about to lose Texas, not to American soldiers but to American im-migrants and the ideas they brought with them. "Instead of armies, battles, or invasions—which make a great noise and for the most part are unsuccessful—these men lay hand on means that, if considered one by one, would be rejected as slow, ineffective, and at times pal-pably absurd. They begin by assuming rights, as in Texas, which it is impossible to sustain in a serious discussion, making ridiculous pretensions based on historical incidents which no one admits—such as the voyage of La Salle, which was an absurd fiasco but serves as a basis for their claim to Texas." The extravagant claims were echoed in the American press, creating a popular demand for their vindication. Enterprising Americans acted on this demand, often disingenuously. "The territory against which these machinations are directed, and which has usually remained unsettled, begins to be visited by adventurers and empresarios; some of these take up their residence in the country, pretending that their location has no bearing upon the question of their government's claim or the boundary disputes." Terán was willing to grant that certain of these disclaimants—he was thinking especially of Austin—were sincere in their denials. But sincere or facetious, they introduced a political dynamic that was ineluctable. "Shortly, some of these forerunners develop an interest which complicates the political administration of the coveted territory; complaints, even threats, begin to be heard, working on the loyalty of the legitimate settlers, discrediting the efficiency of the existing authority and administration."

This was the current condition of Texas, Terán said, and it would only worsen. The government of the United States would be drawn in, from professed concern for the rights of its nationals. Diplomatic pressure would increase, and Mexico would find itself dispossessed of Texas in much the way that Spain had lost Florida and France Louisiana.

Terán didn't weep for Spain or France or mourn their colonial losses. After all, Mexico owed its independence to its success in dispossessing Spain. But for Mexico to lose Texas would be a different matter altogether. Texas wasn't an ocean away from Mexico, as North America was from France and Spain. Texas was part of Mexico itself, a strategically vital part. For Mexico to lose Texas would threaten the security of the republic. "How can it be expected to cut itself off from its own soil, give up to a rival power territory advantageously placed in the extremity of its states, which joins some of them and serves as a buffer to all? How can it be expected to alienate two hundred and fifty leagues of coast, leaving on them vast resources for the construction of boats, the shortest channels for commerce and navigation, the most fertile lands, and the most copious elements for providing means of attack and defense?" In a deeper sense, yielding Texas to the Americans would undermine everything Mexican patriots like Terán had fought for since the start of the revolution. "If Mexico should consent to this base act, it would degenerate from the most elevated class of American powers to that of a contemptible mediocrity, reduced to the necessity of buying a precarious existence at the cost of many humiliations."

What Will Become of Texas?

Terán's warnings gave rise to a radical change in Mexican policy toward Texas. In the spring of 1830, Foreign Minister Lucas Alamán shaped Terán's advice into a bill the Mexican congress duly adopted. The law—known by the date of its enactment, April 6—authorized the construction and manning of military posts on the Texas frontier and encouraged colonization of the province by Mexican nationals. It prohibited further immigration to Texas from the United States. It suspended empresario contracts not already completed, and it banned the introduction of additional slaves.

"A more impolitic measure could not have been adopted by this Government," Stephen Austin declared upon learning of the April 6 law. Austin had sensed that change was afoot; the uneasiness of Terán during his tour of Texas wasn't a secret. But Austin had hoped for something less drastic, something that wouldn't rekindle the anger that had given rise to the Fredonian rebellion. The April 6 law singled out Americans in its ban on immigration to Texas, and by fastening new garrisons on the settlers, it treated them as traitors-in-waiting. In so doing, Austin feared, the law might make rebels out of peaceful men. "They were becoming sincerely attached to this Government and they always have been faithful and always would be," he said of his colonists. But the suspicions that inspired the new law threatened to alter everything. "They are well calculated to create discontent and disgust where it has never existed."

The heart of the colonists' complaint was that Mexico City was arbitrarily changing the rules upon which they had made life plans. The ban on immigration meant that Texas would remain a frontier society indefinitely. Very few Americans, even among westerners, loved the frontier for its own sake. They migrated to the unsettled regions because they could afford land there, but no sooner did they purchase their plots than they wanted the frontier to look like the settled regions back east. They wanted the markets and services and stability of settled life; many also wanted their land to appreciate in value so that they could sell it at a profit (and perhaps repeat the cycle farther west). Nearly all the Americans in Texas had assumed that more of their compatriots would follow them there, and that the Texas frontier would fill with towns and eventually cities and the rising standard of living towns and cities entailed. By outlawing immigration, the Mexican government overthrew this assumption, and with it the plans of the settlers.

The embargo against slaves threatened less havoc but enough to warrant concern. Austin, like many Americans of his day, was of two minds regarding slavery: he didn't like it, but he couldn't figure out how to do without it. (In time much southern rhetoric would celebrate slavery, but in the 1820s this was still a minority view.) Austin accepted slavery as necessary for the development of Texas: most of his colonists were southerners, and many wouldn't come without their slaves. But he shuddered at the thought that Texas—*his* Texas—

might someday be as slave-ridden as large parts of the American Gulf Coast. "The idea of seeing such a country as this overrun by a slave population almost makes me weep," he wrote an acquaintance. He had tried to make others share his fear, by raising the specter of a slave rebellion, but without success. "It is in vain to tell a North American that the white population will be destroyed some fifty or eighty years hence by the negroes, and that his daughters will be violated and butchered by them." As for arguing the morality of slavery with the determined supporters of the institution, that was a hopeless cause. "To say any thing to them as to the justice of slavery, or its demoralizing effects on society, is only to draw down ridicule upon the person who attempts it." For himself, Austin was happy that the Mexican congress had barred further import of slaves. "Slavery is now most positively prohibited by our Constitution and by a number of laws," he wrote in June 1830, "and I do hope it may always be so." All the same, he couldn't deny that the ban on slavery would complicate the settling of Texas.

On its face, the April 6 law was a disaster for Austin. But he had discovered in nearly a decade in Mexico that laws were only as effective as their enforcement, and he set about ensuring that the enforcement of this law didn't undo his decade's work. General Terán, besides being commander for the northeastern states, had been appointed commissioner to implement the new settlement regime in Texas; Austin lobbied the general furiously. He complained that the April 6 law impugned his motives as an empresario, not to mention his loyalty as a citizen of Mexico. "My objects in coming to Texas were sound and pure, the purest," he told Terán. "I have worked in good faith. My highest ambition has been to win this country from the desert; and to add by this means to the prosperity, wealth, and physical and moral strength of the republic which I have adopted for my own, my rule has been fidelity and gratitude to Mexico." His colonists stood shoulder to shoulder, heart to heart, with him in this regard. And what was the reward to their labors? "To be destroyed!!!"

Austin's protests bore fruit. Terán interpreted the law to allow Austin to fulfill his pledges to immigrants on the road to Texas. And he winked as Austin stretched the road to Texas far back into the United States—and into the minds of persons he had neither met nor communicated with. Perhaps Terán was persuaded by Austin's arguments; more likely he reckoned that he needed Austin's help if he hoped to stem the tide of illegal immigration into Texas. Whatever the reason, he essentially waived the anti-immigrant provision of the April 6 law as it applied to Austin.

Austin was tremendously relieved. In a letter sent east for publication, he explained that the pertinent article of the April 6 law exempted his colony from its strictures against immigration. "No embarrassments can be legally interposed to the immigration of honest and good men of families who are comprehended in my contracts." Interpreting the statute for the benefit of American readers, he added, "The main object of the law of 6th of April is to keep out turbulent and bad men, vagabonds and slaves, and the true prosperity and happiness of this country requires that all those classes should be forever kept out. The honest and industrious farmer who brings his family has nothing to fear and will be well received and obtain more benefits and privileges than have ever been granted by any government on earth."

Yet in private moments Austin appreciated that damage had been done. Not all the settlers had the same confidence in the Mexican government he did, and although Terán was construing the law casually for now, he might change his mind—or be replaced. Besides, the mere fact that the Mexican government could overturn established policy on immigration raised serious doubts regarding the future of Texas. Only with difficulty had Austin managed to convince many of his colonists of the good faith of the government in Mexico City; with the April law, the convincing became much harder.

And there was a deeper problem: Austin's own confidence in Mexico had been shaken. "I will die sooner than violate my duty to this government, and if it would let me work I would make Texas the best state that belongs to this nation," he wrote a friend. "But, my dear sir, the truth is that the Mexicans cannot sustain a republic. The present form must fall, and what is then to become of Texas? We are too weak to set up for ourselves, unless under the protection of our powerful neighbor; and the protection which the strong affords the weak is much to be feared."

Yet Austin wanted to believe that the situation would improve. The critical issues were numbers and time. "If we had population, our course would be a very plain one. . . . I am in hopes the federal system may stand a few years longer, and that by that time we shall get in some thousands of Swiss, Germans, etc., and North Americans." In the short term there was definite cause for optimism. "The emigration is still uninterrupted to my colony, and there will be a great accession of strength this fall."

Had Austin known everyone who was coming that season, he might have thought differently. William Barret Travis was a generation younger than Austin (and Sam Houston and Santa Anna), having been born in 1809. But the South Carolina native found enough trouble in twenty years to fill forty, including bad luck in love that matched the woes of Houston. Travis grew up in frontier Alabama and taught school briefly—just long enough to meet the pupil who became his wife and to discover that he couldn't survive on a teacher's pay. An attorney in Claiborne, on the Alabama River, agreed to tutor him, and within a year Travis was ready to practice on his own. To supplement his income he acquired a newspaper, the weekly *Claiborne Herald*. In an era when papers were often the organs of political parties, Travis's *Herald* asserted its independence on its masthead: "Thou Shalt Not Muzzle The Ox That Treadeth Out The Corn."

This ox was hungry, though, and before long Travis had trouble feeding it. (In the process he discovered why papers were attached to parties: the parties provided reliable business.) The *Herald*'s circulation lagged, and the poor circulation discouraged the advertising nearly every newspaper needs to cover costs.

To make matters worse, the paper distracted him from his law practice. Sundry civil suits and the odd criminal case brought him modest but irregular fees, and although he took his practice on the road to adjacent counties, his neighbors weren't sufficiently litigious or criminal to keep him busy. The law practice broke about even financially, but with the paper losing money Travis fell further behind each month.

This did nothing good for his marriage, which like many teenage matches suffered growing pains. Rosanna Cato was barely sixteen—and Travis only nineteen—when they wed. This wasn't unusual in that era, when the de facto alternative to early marriage was often illegitimate children, but neither did it make for blissful unions. As Travis and Rosanna grew up, they grew apart, despite—or perhaps because of—the son who arrived only several months after the wedding. Travis's ambition didn't help matters, especially as it remained frustrated, and his debts compounded his frustration and the tension building at home. The expected arrival of a second child aggravated the situation further, leaving both parties feeling overburdened and underappreciated. Suspicions of infidelity arose, reflecting, besides youthful passion and marital grief, the time Travis was spending on the road. Village busybodies whispered that the child Rosanna was carrying was another man's.

By the beginning of 1831, Travis's predicament had grown insupportable. His creditors were hounding him; the walls of the home he shared with Rosanna were closing in on him; her baby—and his? or some other man's?—would be arriving shortly. Travis's moment of truth came in March, when he failed to fend off the combined legal assault of several creditors. With the sheriff on the way and debtors' prison looming, Travis fled Claiborne, abandoning Rosanna (who apparently wasn't brokenhearted to see him go), their small son, her unborn child, his law practice, his newspaper, and his debts, and headed west.

Like everyone else in Alabama, Travis had heard of Texas—heard how easy it was to start a new life there and how hard it was for American creditors and sheriffs to follow deadbeats and criminals across the Sabine. And so to Texas he turned his face, traversing the Alabama River, the Mississippi, and the Sabine before reaching San Felipe in April or May. He promptly applied to Austin for a grant of land. As befit one who wished to shed an embarrassing past, he lied about his age and marital status, saying he was twenty-two (he was twenty-one) and single. He didn't have to lie about his intentions regarding the quarter league Austin awarded him (for a down payment of ten dollars), for although Austin much preferred actual farmers, so many speculators had taken up his offer of cheap land that one more rated scant notice on that account.

Travis did rate notice for his ambition. Despite his failure at the bar back home, he intended to practice law in Texas and make the name for himself he had failed to earn in Claiborne. San Felipe had more attorneys than it needed, so Travis headed south to Anahuac, near the mouth of the Trinity River at the head of Galveston Bay. Formerly Perry's Point, the town had been rechristened when the Mexican government, following the recommendation of General Terán, established a garrison there. The function of the garrison was to prevent illegal immigration from the United States, to ensure collection of the customs duties owed on imports, and to remind inhabitants and visitors that Texas belonged to Mexico. Customs houses generate work for lawyers, as merchants and collectors haggle over what is subject to tariffs and at what rates; Travis thought he could break into the Texas bar at Anahuac.

He had bigger plans as well. Hardly had he discovered a place to live in Anahuac than he decided he wanted to be the American consul there. As this required support from influential politicians in Washington, Travis asked Austin to recommend him to Thomas Hart Benton, Sam Houston's old friend and now a senator from Missouri. Austin had to confess to Benton that "my personal acquaintance with Mr. T. is very short and limited," but Travis seemed a capable fellow. "He has been recommended to me by persons of respectability, and I can with full confidence say that he has acquired the esteem and respect of the better part of the people in the section of the country where he resides. . . . I have my self no hesitation in recommending him."

But before Benton and the American Congress could act on Austin's recommendation, Travis was distracted by local politics. As the sharpest point of contact between the Mexican government and the immigrants to Texas, Anahuac became a focus of immigrant discontent. Austin's original grant had exempted his colony from customs duties for seven years; during that period the Texans grew used to a customs-less life, and many expected their exemption to be made permanent. The Mexican government had other ideas, especially in the mood that produced the April 6 law, and it insisted on payment after the exemption ran out. The colonists, and the merchants who supplied their wants, responded with the age-old tactic of customs resisters: smuggling. This raised the stakes for both sides, as government agents seized ships and cargoes, and the smugglers bribed and occasionally shot their way past the revenuers.

To instill respect for Mexican authority, the government appointed Colonel Juan Bradburn to head the garrison at Anahuac. There was logic to the appointment, as Bradburn was an American (born John Bradburn in Virginia) who had become even more Mexicanized than Stephen Austin. Bradburn fought during the Mexican war of independence on the side of the rebels; when the rebels won he joined the Mexican army and married a Mexican heiress. In 1831 he remained a devoted Mexican patriot. This was what annoyed the Americans with whom he had to deal at Anahuac—this and the fact that he was an intemperate, belligerent man. (The Mexican patriotism of Austin bothered many of the Americans, too, but Austin had compensating gifts of tact and patience, besides being the one who distributed the land.) When Bradburn showed that he would be even tougher on the Americans than Mexican-born officers like Terán, trouble developed.

Travis was in the thick of it. One of his first clients was a Louisiana slaveholder named Logan, two of whose slaves had escaped to Texas. Logan hired Travis to recover them. In the 1850s the question of escaped slaves would be a rock on which the American union broke; in the 1830s the same question commenced the fracturing of the Mexican federation. Though slavery was illegal in Mexico, the state and federal governments tolerated a subterfuge by which immigrants from the United States, before entering Texas, compelled their slaves to sign long-term indentures. The affected blacks—many of whom had no idea what they were signing, or even that the laws in Mexico were different from those in the United States—were technically not slaves but in practice were as bound as ever. The fact that Mexico City was far away abetted the Texas slaveholders in their fraud, as did the fact that, in this form, the bound service of blacks didn't differ much from the bound service of Mexico's many (largely Indian) peons. The result was a flourishing slave system in everything but name—and often even in name. A traveler to Texas in 1831 was surprised at how openly slavery was practiced. Describing visits to various houses between Brazoria and San Felipe, he wrote, "At some of these houses, as in many of those in Texas generally, we found one or more negroes, held as slaves, although the laws of Mexico forbid it. The blacks are ignorant; the whites are generally in favor of slavery and ready to sustain the master in his usurped authority; the province is so distant from the capital, and had been for some time so little attended to by the government, that the laws on this subject were ineffectual. Negroes are even publicly sold."

Juan Bradburn, despite his Virginia roots, took the Mexican ban on slavery seriously and attempted to enforce it. But what the ban meant for runaways from the United States was uncertain, which was why Logan had engaged Travis. Travis applied to Bradburn to recover the two slaves, claiming they were contraband to whom the Mexican law didn't apply. Bradburn rejected the application. The runaways, he said, weren't contraband but free men. Besides, he added, they had joined the Mexican army and requested Mexican citizenship.

Had Bradburn been more diplomatic, he might not have provoked the reaction he did. But had he been more diplomatic, he wouldn't have been commanding a hardship post on a lonely frontier. His troops didn't want to be there, either; many were convicts sent to Texas to serve out their time. When they behaved the way convicts, not to mention conscripts generally, often do—they became drunk, insulted civilians, started fights, and reportedly raped at least one woman—Bradburn refused to rein them in, adopting the attitude that the Americans got no worse than they deserved. Needless to say, the Americans detested him all the more.

Travis caught on to how unpopular Bradburn was, and he pushed the bounds of legal propriety. He spread a rumor that a band of Louisiana vigilantes was coming to Anahuac to recapture the runaways. Bradburn summoned the garrison to repel the assault, and held the troops in readiness for several days, only to discover—to his chagrin and anger—that there were no vigilantes and no threat. Apparently Travis laughed too hard and gave himself away; Bradburn ordered him arrested.

By the mere fact of his arrest, Travis became a celebrity among the many Americans who deemed Bradburn a despot. A man who shared Travis's cell, Patrick Jack, had been arrested for raising an unauthorized militia, ostensibly against Indians but actually against Bradburn. Bradburn feared that the militia would attempt to free the prisoners, so he moved them from the ordinary guardhouse to an empty brick kiln. Word of their plight spread through Anahuac and north toward San Felipe and Nacogdoches. Bradburn tried to intimidate sympathizers by making additional arrests, but these merely caused the popular anger to spread even faster. A company of thirty armed colonists from Brazoria rode toward Anahuac to free the prisoners; by the time they reached the garrison town they numbered more than a hundred.

Bradburn reinforced the kiln-prison with cannons and threatened to shoot Travis and Jack in the event of attack. Travis for the first time felt the thrill of mortal danger, and discovered in himself a willingness to risk death for principle and glory. A witness recalled him shouting from captivity that the attackers should blaze away with no care for him.

But the crisis took a different turn. A band of soldiers sent out by Bradburn was captured by the insurgents, who used these hostages to bargain for the release of Bradburn's prisoners. Bradburn agreed to the deal but reneged after getting his soldiers back, leaving Travis and Jack in chains (and shooting up the American part of Anahuac to underscore his disdain). Meanwhile some of the insurgents went to Brazoria for a pair of cannons dumped there by a ship that got stuck in the sand; while bringing them out, the insurgents traded fatal fire with Mexican troops.

This escalation alarmed the Mexican commander at Nacogdoches, who hurried south to prevent the rebellion from becoming a revolution. Appraising the strength of the insurgents, he acceded to their central demands. He persuaded Bradburn to release Travis and the others to the civil court system, and then got Bradburn to relinquish his command to a replacement who had yet to alienate the locals.

At the time of his arrest, Travis had been merely another lawyer and speculator, younger and greener than most; two months later he emerged from jail a hero among the Texas rebels. Exploiting his opportunity, he wrote up his ordeal for publication. "Mexicans have learned a lesson," he declared. "*Americans know their rights and will assert and protect them.*" Virtue and honor had triumphed, and would continue to do so. "The Americans have gained every thing which they claimed. There is every prospect that this happy state of things will have a long and prosperous duration."

James Bowie was never a lawyer, largely because his other occupations kept him busy, often breaking the law. Bowie was a fighter (who killed at least one man in close combat), a speculator (with a particular gift for land fraud), a slaver (who made a fortune buying and selling human flesh), a smuggler (of slaves, mostly), a consorter with pirates (including the Laffite brothers), and a spinner of tales (which often ended by separating listeners from their money). Not least on account of his skill at tale telling, Bowie won the heart and hand of one of Texas's fairest maidens.

Bowie was born in Kentucky, in the bend of the Cumberland River, in 1776, two years before Moses Austin moved his family from Virginia to Spanish Louisiana. Rezin Bowie, James's father, was a farmer rather than a miner, but before long he too discerned possibilities in expatriation, and he likewise transported his clan across the Mississippi. The Bowies spent a couple of years in what would become Missouri, downriver from the Austins, but Rezin then relocated them farther south, to the bayou country of Louisiana. Like the Austins, the Bowies were repatriated when Jefferson purchased Louisiana.

James Bowie was eighteen when the War of 1812 came to Louisiana, and with his elder brother Rezin he enlisted for service under Andrew Jackson. But their enlistment was too late to win them any glory, for they hadn't found their way to the front by the time the British were beaten and the war ended. All the same, the militia stint got the Bowie boys off the farm and into the wider world, and the experience awakened in James a desire to be a man of his own. With twenty dollars in muster-out money, he set off to seek his fortune.

The first place he looked was along Bayou Boeuf, midway between New Orleans and Natchitoches. Without bothering to purchase the land or inform the owner, he took up residence on a parcel of property and commenced cutting cypress timber, which he floated to market. Between the proceeds from the wood sales and his willingness to live on venison and other game, he saved enough money to acquire the property honestly. He also bought a handful of slaves.

With these he continued to work and buy, expanding his domain tract by tract.

But even as his industry was rewarded, Bowie felt the pull of something larger. "He was young, proud, poor, and ambitious," recalled his brother John, who went on to describe James's appearance and character.

> After reaching the age of maturity he was a stout, rather raw-boned man, of six feet height, weight 180 pounds, and about as well made as any man I ever saw. His hair was light-colored, not quite red; his eyes were gray, rather deep-set in his head, very keen and penetrating in their glance; his complexion was fair, and his cheekbones rather high. Taken altogether, he was a manly, fine-looking person, and by many of the fair ones he was called handsome. He was possessed of an open, frank disposition, with rather a good temper, unless aroused by some insult, when the displays of his anger were terrible, and frequently terminated in some tragical scene. . . . He loved his friends with all the ardor of youth, and hated his enemies and their friends with all the rancor of the Indian.

He also exhibited a wild streak. "He was fond of fishing and hunting," John said, "and often afforded rare sport to his neighbors by his daring exploits in roping and capturing wild deer in the woods, or catching and riding wild unmanageable horses. He has been even known to rope and ride alligators."

In the bayou country Bowie met Jean Laffite. The pirate and smuggler was working from bases along the Louisiana and Texas coast, and had developed a large trade in slaves. Although slavery remained perfectly legal in the southern United States, and with it the domestic slave trade, the import of slaves from outside the country had been banned since 1808. In the East this presented no serious problem, as American slaves reproduced fast enough to meet demand. But in the Gulf states, where planters were rapidly expanding their cotton fields, the demand for slaves outstripped the local supply. Many slaves came legally (but unhappily, given the hard life that awaited them) down the Mississippi (hence the melancholy phrase "sold down the river"); others came illegally up from the Gulf. Jean and Pierre Laffite were procurers. Acquiring slaves from the flush markets of the Caribbean, they sold them to brokers who transported the unfortunate Africans to the Mississippi and unloaded them to planters there.

As with all contraband commerce, there were profits to be made by those willing to take risks. Both the profits and the risks appealed to Bowie, who entered the business with brothers Rezin and John. The partners devised an ingenious scheme for evading the laws designed to prevent slave smuggling. Those laws allowed that anyone who tipped the authorities regarding smuggled slaves would earn half the proceeds at auction of the slaves so seized. The Bowies simply turned informers against themselves—or, rather, they claimed to have found the slaves they actually purchased from the Laffites, and delivered them to the authorities. As the price they (illegally) paid the Laffites on the coast for the slaves was typically far less than the price the slaves commanded (legally) at sheriff's auction in the interior, even at a half share they came out well ahead. In some cases they bid on the slaves themselves; since half their bid price went to themselves, they had an advantage over other buyers. Either way the trade was very lucrative. "We continued to follow this business until we made $65,000, when we quit and soon spent all our earnings," John recalled.

James Bowie thereupon turned to land speculation. Like most westerners at one time or another, Bowie reckoned that there was a fortune to be made in land: that the same kind of folks Moses Austin had encountered in Tennessee in 1796 would pay for choice parcels. Louisiana in the early 1820s provided a particular opportunity for land speculation, especially if the speculator didn't mind forging a signature here and perjuring a witness there. Because Louisiana had changed hands three times in recent memory, land titles were tangled in three languages, three legal systems, three conceptions of ownership, and heaven knew how many bureaus, offices, and agents. Hoping to untangle the mess—or at least to cut the knot that bound up titles in the state—Congress decreed that land claimants under the previous regimes had until December 31, 1820, to register their claims. The General Land Office in Washington would then rule on the validity of the claims and determine ownership.

It occurred to Bowie that during the last weeks before the deadline the land office would be swamped with claims and would, therefore, be unable to check each individual claim. With an audacity that became his trademark, he forged Spanish claims to more than sixty thousand acres of Louisiana land. He made up names of sellers, fabricated sales prices, and purchased affidavits from "witnesses" to the transactions.

Meanwhile he divided his time between New Orleans and the bayou parishes Avoyelles and Rapides. In the bayou country, feuding was as common as the Spanish moss on the live oaks; where young men lived on the labor of others (slaves) or on the gamble of speculation (including fraud), they had plenty of leisure to take offense at real and imagined slights. Rivals in business and politics drew partners and allies into their disputes; towns split into feuding factions. Norris Wright, the sheriff of Rapides, took particular offense at Bowie's speculations and at his support of one of Wright's enemies, and cast public aspersions on Bowie's character. Bowie confronted Wright and demanded an apology; instead he got a bullet from point-blank range, which amazingly missed his heart. Bleeding profusely, Bowie set upon Wright bare-handed. "Had Wright not been rescued by his friends, James would have killed him with his fists," brother John asserted.

Wright's rescue merely delayed the reckoning. A disputatious sort, Wright got into a duel with another man, whom Bowie agreed to second. The duel took place on a sandbar by the Mississippi and drew spectators from the whole district. The formal gunplay was disappointing: the shooters both missed, twice. But the aftermath was everything the gawkers had hoped for. One of the seconds, believing honor yet to be satisfied, pulled a pistol, causing several other guns to appear as if by magic. Someone fired at Bowie, who fired back, missing the shooter but rearranging his cravat. More bullets flew, including one from Bowie's other pistol, which did even less damage than the ball from his first.

Yet Bowie's temper was up, and the depletion of his firepower didn't diminish it. His earlier run-in with Wright had prompted him to carry a large knife borrowed from his brother Rezin, sharpened near the tip on both sides for hand-to-hand combat and fitted into a scabbard laced to his belt. Now he drew the knife and began chasing his assailant. Wright entered the fray, firing at Bowie and putting a bullet through one of his lungs. Bowie took at least two more bullets, one to the chest, the other to a thigh, before going down. Wright then attacked Bowie with a sword-cane, inflicting several slashing wounds.

But as Wright closed in for the kill, Bowie grabbed his collar. Wright tried to pull away; Bowie, hanging on for life, was hoisted to his feet. With the better leverage thus afforded, Bowie thrust his fearsome blade into Wright's chest and "twisted it to cut his heart strings," as he explained later. Wright slumped to the ground, dead. The shock of this sudden reversal, and the sight of Bowie brandishing his bloody knife, brought the shooting and stabbing to an end. The spectators returned to their homes, marveling at Bowie's strength and will, and wondering where they could get a knife like his.

Bowie required several months to recuperate from the wounds he received in the Sandbar Fight (which became a proper noun almost before the Mississippi washed the blood from the fatal beach). For all his fighting prowess, Bowie recognized that he had been lucky to survive the scrape, and, while mending, he contemplated moving to a more placid neighborhood. Some of his Louisiana land claims had been disallowed, but a surprising number came through, demonstrating the value-for-money of purchased perjury. Encouraged, Bowie looked for new fields for speculation. He had heard good things about Austin's Texas colony, and he decided to explore the opportunities there.

He journeyed west via Natchitoches and Nacogdoches, then southwest to San Felipe. Austin was traveling, and rather than await his return, Bowie proceeded to San Antonio de Béxar. There he met Juan Martín de Veramendi, a former alcalde of San Antonio and the father of a charming daughter named Ursula. Bowie struck up a friendship with Veramendi, who was pleased to encourage the immigration of Bowie's money to Texas, if not necessarily of Bowie himself. For her part, Ursula found the rugged American intriguing.

Bowie returned to Louisiana to tend to certain business affairs.

He converted some of his land claims to cash while dodging investigators who were questioning some of his others. He was back in Béxar in the spring of 1829, to pay court to Ursula and learn more about Texas. On this visit he met José Antonio Menchaca, a friend of Veramendi and a man who told fascinating tales of silver mines in the Comanchería northwest of San Antonio. Many decades earlier, Spanish traders had carried silver to Louisiana, prompting questions about where the precious metal came from. Menchaca thought he knew the answer: a lost mine near the San Sabá River. Bowie couldn't resist the combination of danger (from the Comanches) and potential wealth, and he devoted weeks that summer to seeking the abandoned shaft. He was discouraged at discovering nothing, but not so discouraged as to preclude future visits to the area.

Returning again to Louisiana, Bowie learned that the federal investigators were getting closer. Not only did rejection of most of his remaining claims seem likely, but so, increasingly, did jail. To make matters worse, various Bowie creditors, sensing weakness, sued for nonpayment. If he somehow evaded the marshals on the fraud charges, he might still wind up in jail for debt. Under the circumstances, permanent relocation to Texas appeared more attractive than ever, and in the spring of 1830 he made the move.

He reached Texas amid the uproar surrounding the April 6 law—a state of affairs that pleased him, as he had always fished well in troubled waters. He presented himself as a rich man, one whom Mexican leaders would want for an immigrant, despite the ban on Americans generally, and one whom Juan Veramendi would wish for a son-in-law. That Veramendi was one of the leading figures in San Antonio, and thus that Bowie could pursue both goals at once, testified either to Bowie's luck in love or to his shrewdness.

Bowie explained to Veramendi that he hoped to build a cotton mill in Texas, which would significantly enhance the local economy. Veramendi, thinking of Texas, enthusiastically endorsed the plan. Bowie's mill would also make a nice profit; Veramendi, thinking of Ursula, found it doubly attractive. Veramendi recommended the Bowie plan to Erasmo Seguín, currently the alcalde of Béxar. Seguín soon began speaking favorably of Bowie to all who would listen.

Veramendi and Seguín encouraged Bowie to take his case to Saltillo, the capital of Coahuila y Texas, to receive the blessing of the state government there. Saltillo appealed to Bowie for a second reason: he wanted to resume his speculations in land. Although the April 6 law foreclosed the creation by Americans of new colonies in Texas, it didn't forbid the purchase of land from Mexican landholders. Bowie devised a scheme by which Mexican citizens would receive land from the government and then sell it to him.

He traveled to Saltillo in the summer of 1830 and remained there till fall. Through persistence and persuasiveness—aided by the timely arrival of Veramendi, who had just been named lieutenant governor of Coahuila y Texas—he won over the appropriate state officials, who in turn convinced the Mexican congress to award him a charter for his cotton mill (and grant him Mexican citizenship, effective upon completion of the mill). He also arranged for the purchase and transfer of more than a dozen eleven-league parcels of land. Assuming all the deals went through, Bowie would control three-quarters of a million acres. To complete his successful summer, Bowie persuaded Veramendi to betroth his daughter to him. Ursula was delighted, and the three returned to San Antonio together, discussing the wedding, the couple's prospects, and the future of Texas.

After a last trip to Louisiana—which confirmed the prudence of placing an international boundary between himself and American law—Bowie provided an accounting of his net worth to Veramendi, as stipulated in their prenuptial agreement. His balance sheet was impressive, showing $162,800 in his favor. What Bowie didn't tell Veramendi—or Ursula—was that most of his assets were either grossly inflated or simply spun of air, starting with land he didn't own and concluding with notes he could never collect. Veramendi probably didn't believe everything Bowie told him, but even allowing for exaggeration, Bowie still cut an imposing financial figure. In any case, Veramendi had grown to like this engaging American. Ursula had, too, and the father didn't want to disappoint his daughter.

The wedding took place in April 1831 in a small church near the plaza of San Antonio. For several months Bowie and Ursula lived genteelly among her family and friends. He dabbled in trade, doing just enough business to alert the Mexican tax collectors that he wasn't paying certain required duties. Veramendi, who had been Mexico's collector of foreign revenues at Béxar, was embarrassed, but not so much as to disown his son-in-law. Bowie talked about the cotton mill but made no visible progress toward building it.

Instead he dreamed about the silver mines he hadn't been able to locate earlier. And the more he dreamed about them, the more convinced he became that someone of his brass and cleverness ought to be able to find them. His confidence was infectious, and by the autumn of 1831 he had enlisted several partners, including Rezin, in the treasure hunt. Veramendi underwrote the expedition, which set out for the San Sabá in November.

Before Bowie and the others had a fair chance to find the lost mine, they learned why so few others had preceded them. Most of the Comanches at this time were at peace with the Mexicans, but certain of the Comanches' allies were not. During the expedition's third week out from San Antonio, it encountered a couple of Comanches who warned of a large party of Wacos, Caddos, and Tawakonis in the neighborhood. Some of Bowie's group wanted to seek shelter against a possible attack, but Bowie was determined to press on. For several days they examined the ground for traces of a mine—for wagon tracks that veered off into the brush, for telltale streaks of detritus—while scanning the horizon for hostile Indians. At night they chose campsites that afforded protection from ambush, and took turns keeping watch and listening for footfalls in the dark.

They had nearly reached the abandoned mission at San Sabá when they detected a Tawakoni scout on their trail. Behind the scout they spied the main body of Indians, numbering more than a hundred. Bowie and the silver-hunters dismounted from their horses, unloaded their pack animals, and arrayed the packs so as to provide protection against Indian arrows and bullets.

The Indians, apparently hoping to strip the interlopers of their possessions and animals without a fight, sent forward one of their own to parley. Rezin Bowie went out to meet him. The negotiation failed when Rezin made clear that there would be no surrender of property, despite the large disparity of numbers between the attackers and the besieged. Even before the parley ended, the Indians opened fire, hitting one of the whites and shattering his leg bone.

The attack began in earnest. The Indians stormed the spot where Bowie and the others were making their defense, but the defenders managed to kill the chief directing the attack, and his death flummoxed the rest, who fell back. Regrouping, they adopted a different approach, sniping at the intruders from various angles. Two more of Bowie's band were wounded. As the shooting continued, the Indians broadened their front until they encircled the treasure hunters, whose predicament now became most grave. But the Texans were better armed than the Indians, and they held their own for the next two hours.

At this point—near midday—the Indians decided to force the interlopers from their position by setting the brush afire. Checking the breeze, they kindled the sage and grass upwind of the redoubt and prepared to pick off the Texans as they fled the smoke and flames. But luck was with Bowie and friends, and the gusty wind turned the fire aside at the last moment.

The standoff continued through the afternoon. Not long before sundown, the Indians lit another fire. Burning hotter and higher than the first, this one bore straight toward the defenders' position. They beat at the flames with buffalo robes and blankets and frantically cleared the ground closest to them of everything flammable. They couldn't save the animals, which panicked at the fire and, breaking their leads, tore away. But they did manage to hold their ground—except that it was now exposed, having lost the cover of vegetation that had spoiled the Indians' aim. They also managed to stack stones for a low wall to lie behind.

Darkness and exhaustion ended the day's fighting. Expecting another—and probably final—attack in the morning, James and Rezin Bowie discussed a counterattack to be launched under the cover of night. Presumably surprise would be in their favor, and in the dark the Indians wouldn't be able to tell how few the able-bodied Texans had become. But on second thought they agreed that those few—there were only six who could still shoot—were too few, and that even if they could break through the Indian lines, they could never carry out the wounded, who would be left to the Indians' vengeance. This grim prospect compelled them to abandon the plan.

The only thing that gave hope was the wailing of the Indians during the night, as they mourned their dead. By the tone and constancy of the laments, Bowie and company guessed they had done serious damage to the attackers. In the typical confrontation with whites, Indians applied a rough cost-benefit analysis, calculating whether the prizes at issue were worth the cost in deaths and injuries.

Bowie and the others would surely die if the Indians insisted, but if the Texans displayed a determination to sell their lives dearly, the Indians might account the cost too high and abandon the effort. So the silver-hunters dug in and prepared for the next day's battle.

It never came. The Indians, tallying their casualties—and having rounded up the horses that escaped the flames—decided they had paid more than the Texans' remaining provisions were worth. In the hours after midnight they slipped away, leaving Bowie and the others alone in the San Sabá hills.

★

Bowie's defeat of the Indians added to the stories about the Sandbar Fight and burnished his reputation for bravery and skill in battle. Mexicans and Americans alike in Texas viewed the Louisianian with respect, if only because both parties felt a threat from the Indians. Moreover, in contrast to William Travis, who had flung himself into the political controversy that was swirling about the province, Bowie held back. He wasn't as attached to the status quo as Stephen Austin, but with a Mexican wife and father-in-law (a father-in-law who became, on the 1832 death of the governor of Coahuila y Texas, governor of the state), and with large landholdings under Mexican law, he had no incentive to agitate for an overthrow of the regime.

Yet those who did have an incentive agitated enough for everyone else, and during the summer of 1832 the troubles that made Travis a celebrity at Anahuac spread north to Nacogdoches. The Mexican commander there, José de las Piedras, ordered the settlers in the area to surrender their arms. Besides its obvious political overtones, the order threatened the security of the settlers against Indians and even—for those many who still hunted for food—against hunger. The settlers rejected the order and organized a militia to prevent Piedras from enforcing it. From Nacogdoches they sent word in all directions that despotism had arrived in the form of the Mexican colonel and must be resisted. The continuing struggle in Mexico between the centralists and the federalists, the latter led by Santa Anna, allowed the Texas militiamen to wrap their resistance in the philosophy of federalism; as federalists they demanded that Piedras withdraw his order. When he refused, fighting broke out. The militiamen attacked Nacogdoches in the early afternoon of August 2 and struggled street to street against uninspired Mexican defenders. That night Piedras decided to evacuate the town and head for San Antonio.

Bowie entered the fight at the behest of Stephen Austin. Austin had monitored the Anahuac disturbances with alarm, and he grew more alarmed at the spread of the troubles to Nacogdoches. Austin knew Bowie largely by reputation, but that reputation caused him to believe that Bowie was a man who could act decisively in a crisis. He urged Bowie to gallop to Nacogdoches to prevent the fighting there from triggering a revolution, but he left it to Bowie to determine how this might be accomplished.

Bowie accepted the assignment yet arrived too late to avert the street battle between Piedras and the militia. He wasn't too late, however, to pursue Piedras down the Camino Real, which he did with a company of some twenty men. Meeting the Mexicans at the Angelina River, Bowie's company harried them upstream till one of the junior Mexican officers decided he'd had enough and staged a mutiny. Most of the Mexican troops joined him, converting en masse to federalism. Bowie laconically reported the result to Austin: "I write to inform you that the 12th Regiment of Infantry, formerly of Nacogdoches and in command of Col. Jose de las Piedras, has been induced by certain American arguments to declare in favor of the Constitution of Santa

Anna, that Col. Piedras is a prisoner in town soon to be dispatched for Anahuac, and that the regiment has put itself under my command."

The capture of Piedras and the Mexican regiment by the greatly outnumbered American force further added to Bowie's reputation—at the same time that it identified him, almost against his will, with the insurgents in Texas. This wasn't what Austin had hoped for in sending Bowie to Nacogdoches, and it wasn't what Bowie had expected. Bowie accepted the plaudits; Austin tried to figure out what they portended.

Bowie's capture of a Mexican regiment in the name of Santa Anna would appear ironic before long, but in the summer of 1832 irony had yet to become the theme of Mexican politics, and Santa Anna remained the hero of the revolution—and the hope of the Texans. After his defeat of the Spanish at Tampico, the general could have made himself president, but he begged off, pleading poor health. "I find myself the victim of renewed attacks of illness, and must retire to the midst of my family to recuperate," he told his disappointed followers.

In truth, he simply wanted to let his support mature before he asserted himself. Elections were approaching, and Santa Anna declared, "Should I obtain a majority of suffrages, I am ready to accept the honor and to sacrifice, for the benefit of the nation, my repose and the charms of private life. My fixed system is to be called, resembling in this a modest maid, who rather expects to be desired than to show herself to be desiring."

Yet the maid knew better than to rely on the ballot. The government, currently controlled by the centralists, would count the votes and might well get whatever result it desired; as a hedge against such fraud, Santa Anna sounded out supporters in the military, determining who would back him in a coup. A clique of officers in Veracruz province said they would, and as a measure of their loyalty they helped him seize the customs house at the port of Veracruz. Its receipts being the single largest source of Mexico's public revenue, this action threatened to strangle the government financially and make Santa Anna's position impregnable.

The general's insurgent example reverberated across Mexico. The southern states of Chiapas and Oaxaca shouted for Santa Anna and federalism, as—at the other end of the country—did Texas. Stephen Austin wrote encouragement to the rebel leader. "I would not be a lover of the fundamental principles of the constitutional liberty of my adopted country," he told Santa Anna, "if I failed to respect the Chief whose arms have always been used to protect and sustain them." As Austin traveled about his colony, he urged the settlers to demonstrate their support of Santa Anna. They didn't require his urging. "On my arrival at Brazoria," he explained, "I met the whole people unanimous and enthusiastic in favor of the plan of Santa Anna." Austin added his endorsement, declaring that "the party of Santa Anna is truly the liberal republican and constitutional party" and that a victory by Santa Anna would be "the only means to bring civil war to an end and to secure peace and the constitutional liberty of the nation." So convinced was Austin of Santa Anna's rectitude and importance to Mexico that he was prepared to take up arms on the general's behalf. "The colony and all Texas have but one course left, which is to unite in the cause of the Santana party, and if necessary fight it out with the ministerialists."

By late summer of 1832, support of Santa Anna was becoming a solid majority opinion throughout Mexico. The government—the regime of the "ministerialists"—was being rapidly discredited, partly on account of the ministers' conservative and centralist views, partly from their failure to defeat this latest insurgency, and partly because, as incumbents, they were blamed for twenty years of unrest in Mexican society and politics. Many Mexicans simply wanted the turmoil to end and were willing to throw their support to anyone who promised peace.

In October 1832 Puebla fell to the Santanistas. A series of small battles around the Valley of Mexico followed, with Santa Anna's forces gaining additional ground. Finally, the discouraged government forces simply melted away.

Santa Anna accepted his victory from the people of Mexico City in January 1833. A grand parade was held in his honor; floats represented the Battle of Tampico (with Santa Anna explicitly portrayed), the Homeland (featuring the Constitution of 1824, of which Santa Anna was the most recent and successful defender), Valor (Santa Anna again) accompanied by Fame and Abundance, and the Mexican Nation surrounded by the twenty states of the Mexican federation (which Santa Anna was securing).

The hero basked in his glory and magnanimously called for grievances to be forgotten—for "indulgence with mistakes of opinion, an end to hatreds, and the erasure from memory of the word 'vengeance.' " "Thus," he said, "you will attain the object of your desires and sacrifices, long and happy days for the republic, durable happiness for all." And then, with a flourish of humility that frustrated his followers and bewildered his foes, he retired again to his hacienda. "My whole ambition is restricted to beating my sword into a plowshare," he said. Yet he assured his supporters he would not be far away, nor heedless of the popular will. "If any hand should again disturb the public peace and constitutional order, do not forget me.

I shall return at your call, and we shall again show the world that the Mexican Republic will not tolerate tyrants and oppressors of the people."

★

Manuel de Mier y Terán couldn't decide which was more discouraging: the revolt of the Texans or the revolt of Santa Anna. Not that he had to choose, for during that unsettled season they appeared to be woven of a single red thread of insurgency. But for a soldier who had devoted two decades of his life to establishing Mexican independence and defending its integrity, the trend of events was deeply disturbing.

In a world that was changing by the day, Terán often felt he was the only one keeping the faith. "I am not engaged in this fight on behalf of the ministers," he wrote at a critical moment for the centralists, "but on behalf of constitutional government. Neither did I enter it to be able to name government officials when it is over, but rather to put down rebellion in the territory under my command. I have worked and will work to that end." And what did he get for holding fast? The enmity of almost everyone. "I have come to be, as you will see, the target of the revolution," he told his brother.

From the village of Padilla, Terán wrote to Lucas Alamán, the government official to whom he was closest, lamenting the sad condition to which their country had fallen. "A great and respectable Mexican nation, a nation of which we have dreamed and for which we have labored so long, can never emerge from the many disasters which have overtaken it. We have allowed ourselves to be deceived by the ambitions of selfish groups; and now we are about to lose the northern provinces."

Terán saw no way back from the precipice. "What is to become of Texas?" he asked—once, and again, and again in this letter. And each answer only varied the theme of loss and blame. "How could we expect to hold Texas when we do not even agree among ourselves? It is a gloomy state of affairs. If we could work together, we would advance. As it is, we are lost."

Terán sought solace in an early love, his study of nature. "This morning dawned diaphanous, radiant, beautiful," he wrote on July 2. "The sky was blue; the trees green; the birds were bursting with joy; the river crystalline; the flowers yellow, making drops of dew shine in their calyces. Everything pulsed with life; everything gave evident signs that the breath of God had reached nature. In contrast to these, the village of Padilla is alone and apathetic, with its houses in ruin and its thick ashen adobe walls." Terán felt himself condemned to the ashes of this earth, though his spirit longed for that higher, better realm. "My soul is burdened with weariness. I am an unhappy man, and unhappy people should not live on earth. I have studied this situation for five years"—since receiving responsibility for Texas—"and today I know nothing, nothing, for man is very despicable and small, and—let us put an end to these reflections, for they almost drive me mad. The revolution is about to break forth, and Texas is lost."

It was more than a man could bear. "Immortality! God! The soul! What does all this mean? Well, then, I believe in it all, but why does man not have the right to put aside his misery and his pains? Why should he be eternally chained to an existence which is unpleasant to him? And this spirit which inspires, which fills my mind with ideas—where will it go? Let us see, now: the spirit is uncomfortable, it commands me to set it free, and it is necessary to obey. Here is the end of human glory and the termination of ambition." Again Terán asked, "What is to become of Texas?" And now he knew the answer: "What God wills."

The next morning—in another diaphanous dawn, with blue sky and green trees and singing birds and dew on the yellow flowers—Terán stood beside the ashen walls of the church of San Antonio de Padilla. Placing the handle of his sword against one of the adobe bricks and the tip against his heart, he fell forward and took his life.

Chapter 9

A Conspiracy of Volunteers

About the time the triumphant Santa Anna was entering Mexico City in early 1833, Andrew Jackson faced a revolt in his own country that, if currently less violent than the one Santa Anna headed, threatened gross bloodshed before long. The revolt centered in South Carolina, where opponents of a federal tariff approved in 1828 had been trying to prevent its collection. Citing such precedents as the American resistance to the Stamp Act of 1765, which started the chain of events leading to the American Revolution, and the opposition to the Alien and Sedition Acts of 1798, which helped drive John Adams and the Federalists from power, the South Carolinians developed a doctrine of "nullification," by which states might prevent enforcement of federal laws they found to be unconstitutional. Jackson had no personal investment in the "tariff of abominations," as its opponents called the measure passed during John Quincy Adams's last year in office, and as a westerner and a political heir of Thomas Jefferson, he was thought to be a states' rights man. But he was also president of the United States, and he took most seriously the threat that nullification posed to the Union. The logic of nullification pointed to secession, a prospect some of the nullifiers openly brandished.

The nullification struggle prompted an outpouring of rhetoric in the Senate, where Robert Hayne of South Carolina embraced nullification and secession as prerogatives of the states. Daniel Webster of Massachusetts answered Hayne in a speech that entered the annals of American oratory and ended with a ringing defense of the Union: "Liberty and Union, now and forever, one and inseparable!"

The debate continued at a Jefferson's Birthday dinner, an annual event for the party that included both the president and nearly all the nullifiers. The regular highlight of the evening was the series of toasts, the dozens of short speeches on topics of current interest. Robert Hayne cited the glorious resistance of Jefferson and the state of Virginia to the Alien and Sedition Acts, and concluded, "The Union of the States, and the Sovereignty of the States!"

All eyes and ears turned to Jackson, and strained to catch the president's response. Jackson was no orator, and his voice lacked the full-throated power of the Haynes and Websters of the day, but when he spoke the force of his will came through unmistakably. "Our Union," he declared: *"It must be preserved!"*

The president's statement produced an uproar at the dinner and shudders around the country. A showdown with the nullifiers loomed. Several days later, a congressman from South Carolina visited the White House. The president was polite, as always, but utterly determined. When the visitor asked if Jackson had any message for the citizens of South Carolina—who by now knew all about Jackson's toast—the president replied, "Yes, I have. Please give my compliments to my friends in your state, and say to them that if a single drop of blood shall be shed there in opposition to the laws of the United States, I will hang the first man I can lay my hand on engaged in such treasonable conduct, upon the first tree I can reach."

The nullification controversy had already divided the Jackson administration, alienating the president from Vice President John Calhoun, the South Carolinian who was the chief theoretician of the nullifiers; now it split the president's Democratic Republican party, driving a wedge between the West and the South that anti-Jacksonians like Henry Clay of Kentucky aimed to exploit. And it threatened to rend the country, as southern slaveholders exploited the tariff controversy to test the limits of states' rights against the authority of the national government.

Jackson understood the implications of the nullification contest, which was why he adopted his uncompromising stand against South Carolina's attempt to prevent the enforcement of federal laws. "Those who told you that you might peaceably prevent their execution deceived you," he warned the citizens of that state. "They could not have been deceived themselves. They know that a forcible opposition could alone prevent the execution of the laws, and they know that such opposition must be repelled. Their object is disunion. But be not deceived by names. Disunion by armed force is *treason*." And treason could never be ignored or forgiven. "On your unhappy State will inevitably fall all the evils of the conflict you force upon the Government of your country. It can not accede to the mad project of disunion, of which you would be the first victims."

To lend emphasis to his words, and to demonstrate that a passion for the Union was not simply an executive conceit, the president urged Congress to approve a Force Bill explicitly empowering him to ensure the enforcement of federal laws in South Carolina. The Force Bill provoked another angry debate in the Senate, with Calhoun—having been dropped from the Jackson reelection ticket in favor of Martin Van Buren of New York, and once more a senator—denouncing it as a declaration of war against his native state. But the bill passed overwhelmingly, giving Jackson a crucial victory.

Yet Jackson was artful as well as forceful, and even as he stood firm on the principle of an indissoluble Union, he gave ground on the tariff. A new measure reduced the 1828 schedule, leaving the South Carolinians room for a face-saving retreat. Though some in the Palmetto State still spluttered, most accepted this way out, and the crisis passed. Jackson accepted the victory, even as he recognized that it wasn't permanent. States' rights would remain the rallying cry for losers in the legislature until the question of national-versus-state sovereignty was finally settled. "The next pretext will be the negro, or slavery, question," he predicted.

Amid the fight for the Force Bill, Jackson received a letter from a supporter at Natchitoches. "I have with much pride and inexpressible satisfaction seen your messages and proclamations touching the Nullifiers of the South and their 'peaceable remedies,' " the writer declared. "God grant that you may save the Union! It does seem to me that it is reserved for you, and you alone, to render millions so great a blessing."

Jackson was naturally gratified at this support, especially coming at such a critical moment. But he received dozens of such letters every day (and many taking the opposite view). What made this letter stand out were its comments on another subject, and the signature at the bottom.

Having been as far as Bexar in the Province of Texas, where I had an interview with the Comanche Indians, I am in possession of some information that will doubtless be interesting to you, and may be calculated to forward your views, if you should entertain any, touching the acquisition of Texas by the Government of the United States. That such a measure is desirable by nineteen twentieths of the population of the Province, I can not doubt. They are now without laws to govern or protect them. Mexico is involved in civil war. The Federal Constitution has never been in operation. The Government is essentially despotic and must be so for years to come. The rulers have not honesty, and the people have not intelligence. The people of Texas are determined to separate from Coahuila, and unless Mexico is soon restored to order and the Constitution revived and reenacted, the Province of Texas will remain separate from the confederacy of Mexico. She has already beaten and expelled all the troops of Mexico from her soil, nor will she permit them to return. She can defend herself against the whole power of Mexico, for really Mexico is powerless and penniless to all intents and purposes. Her want of money taken in connexion with the course which Texas *must and will adopt*, will render a transfer of Texas inevitable to some power, and if the United States does not press for it, England will most assuredly obtain it by some means. . . .

I have traveled near five hundred miles across Texas, and am now enabled to judge pretty correctly of the soil and the resources of the country, and I have no hesitancy in pronouncing it the finest country to its extent upon the globe. . . . There can be no doubt that the country east of the River Grand of the North [the Rio Grande] would sustain a population of ten millions of souls. My opinion is that Texas will by her members in convention by the 1st

April declare all that country as Texas proper, and form a state constitution. I expect to be present at the convention, and will apprise you of the course adopted, so soon as its members have taken a final action. . . .

I hear all voices commend your course [regarding nullification] even in Texas, where is felt the liveliest interest for the preservation of the Republic.

Permit me to tender you my sincere felicitations and most earnest solicitude for your health and happiness, and your future glory, connected with the prosperity of the Union.

Sam Houston

Jackson wasn't exactly surprised to receive this letter, having been in touch with Houston on the subject of Texas for some time. But so erratic had Houston's behavior been during the previous few years that hardly anything he could have done would have surprised the old general.

With every other Tennesseean and many outside the state, Jackson had been shocked at Houston's ignominious flight from Nashville in 1829. As president, Jackson had no lack of informants to apprise him of Houston's progress—or regress—into the wilds of Arkansas and the haze of alcoholic oblivion. Houston initially drank to drown his hurt and shame, but at some point the drinking took on a life of its own. In one instance he and a fellow traveler encountered a third man, whom they engaged in a drinking contest that involved sacrificing their worldly cares to the god Bacchus—that is, throwing their clothing, item by item, on a campfire—with toasts following each burnt offering. The ceremony ended with the three in a naked stupor.

In the late spring of 1829 Jackson received a letter from Houston filled with self-pity, wounded pride, and boozy loquacity. Declaring himself "the most unhappy man now living," Houston told Jackson: "I can not brook the idea of your supposing me capable of an act that would not adorn, rather than blot, the escutcheon of human nature!" Houston had heard that his enemies were spreading falsehoods about him and his treatment of Eliza. "I do not directly understand the extent of the information, or its character, but I suppose it was intended to complete my ruin, in irremediable devastation of character!" Without more precise knowledge, Houston couldn't rebut the charges directly, but he appealed to his mentor and commander to recall the bravery and honor of better days. "You, sir, have witnessed my conduct from boyhood through life. You saw me draw my first sword from its scabbard. You saw me breast the forefront of battle, and you saw me encounter successive dangers, with cheeks unblanched, and with nerves which had no ague in them. You have seen my private and my official acts; to these I refer you." The fugitive required all the help he could get, for the world was against him. "I am to be *hunted down!* . . . an exile from my home and my country, a houseless unsheltered wanderer among the Indians." But he would not yield to enemy or misfortune. "I am myself, and will remain the proud and honest man! I will love my country and my friends. You, General, will ever possess my warmest love and most profound veneration! In return I ask nothing—I would have nothing, within your power to give me! I am satisfied with nature's gifts. They will supply nature's wants!!"

Houston closed this letter by explaining that he was heading off to live with the Cherokees, and that if the president wished to write he could reach him in care of the Cherokee Agency in Arkansas. After two months of hunting buffalo and smaller game, traveling among the Cherokees and other tribes of the territory, and drinking whatever alcohol he could lay hands on, Houston fell ill with the fever and shakes of malaria (perhaps combined with delirium tremens). "I am very feeble from a long spell of fever, which lasted me some 38 days and had well nigh closed the scene of all my mortal cares," he wrote Jackson as the illness was easing. By then he had decided to settle down in a wigwam—Wigwam Neosho, he called it—not far from the Arkansas River. The wigwam doubled as a trading post, which Houston operated with a woman who comforted him in his affliction and became his common-law wife. Diana Rogers—also known as Tiana—was the daughter of John Rogers, a Cherokee headman who was part Scot, and his Cherokee wife; Houston had known her as a girl during his days with Oolooteka—John Jolly—in Tennessee. Like Houston, Diana had been married, but in her case her spouse was actually, and not just figuratively, dead. Said to be tall and attractive, she saw something in Houston his bingeing and self-pity hid from others, and she took upon herself the responsibility of running the trading post in his absences and hauling him home after his drunks. That he was technically still married to Eliza apparently bothered neither her nor the neighbors.

For many months Houston drifted in and out of his fog. The Cherokees, who to their dismay knew quite a bit about alcoholism, were put off by Houston's heavy drinking; many of them derisively dropped his name Raven in favor of Big Drunk. Houston ran afoul of the local U.S. military commander for illegally importing liquor for resale; the charge was set aside when Houston explained, convincingly, that the nine barrels of whiskey, gin, rum, cognac, and wine were for his personal consumption.

On his good days he could still make himself useful. Living with the Cherokees and traveling among the various tribes inhabiting the trans-Mississippi region, he became an apostle of peace between rival tribes and between the Indians and whites. To Secretary of War

John Eaton he wrote regarding a conflict between the Osages and the Pawnees, in which each side had taken many prisoners, who thereby became an obstacle to ending the struggle. Houston urged Eaton to act as broker in a prisoner exchange. "Peace would cost a mere trifle to our Government," Houston said, "when compared to the advantages which must result from it!" After a band of Cherokees, angry at their tribe's treatment by the government and by nearby whites, threatened to go to war over the protests of John Jolly and other Cherokee leaders, Houston implored them not to, warning that they would simply bring down the greater wrath of the government and open the tribe to further depredations. When the U.S. Army, in a fit of cost cutting, considered closing a military post in the middle of the Indian territory, Houston assailed the measure as shortsighted and foolish. "I will predict, in the event of a removal of the U.S. troops from this post," he wrote the local commandant, "that in less than twelve months from the date thereof there will be waged a war the most sanguinary and savage that has raged within my recollection. Embers are covered, but whenever they are exposed, you will see the flame spread through five nations."

For his efforts on their behalf, the Cherokees made Houston a citizen of their nation, and sent him east as their envoy to the U.S. government. In Washington, Jackson received him graciously but dubiously. Houston reported how the Cherokees were being cheated by the agents supplying them beef under the terms of a treaty with the federal government; in persuading the War Department to fire the agents, he made himself the target of the agents' friends in the administration and in Congress.

Houston's visit to the East rekindled his interest in the larger world, reminding him, among other things, of how much more capable he was than many who held positions of public preferment. Traveling through Tennessee en route back west, he surveyed the political landscape and sized up Billy Carroll, the man who had succeeded him at the top of the state's politics. "My honest belief is that if I would again return to Tennessee I would beat him for governor," Houston confided to a friend. But the memories of Nashville and Eliza were too painful, especially when Carroll's allies revived them around the state as a way of warning Houston off. He halfheartedly defended himself against the renewed attacks, but, discovering that this merely afforded the slanders longer life, he finally threw up his hands in exasperation and posted a notice in Nashville's leading newspaper: "Know all men by these presents that I, Sam Houston, 'late Governor of the State of Tennessee,' do hereby declare to all *scoundrels whomsoever*, that they are authorized to accuse, defame, calumniate, slander, vilify, and libel me to any extent."

Convinced that he couldn't return to Tennessee, Houston sought a new arena for his abilities. Texas had been on his mind since the 1820s, when he had invested in the colonizing efforts of Robert Leftwich. Upon fleeing Nashville amid the ruin of his marriage and his former life, he was reported to have boasted, drunkenly no doubt, that he would "conquer Mexico or Texas, and be worth two millions in two years." Subsequently he was said to have sought support for an expedition against Texas, perhaps manned by his Cherokee friends.

Yet for three years Houston's Texas vision was nothing more than talk. To be sure, the talk alone was enough to cause Jackson to warn Houston against filibustering. Jackson was trying to negotiate the purchase of Texas from Mexico; discussions weren't going well, but Jackson understood that anything that smacked of extra-diplomatic pressure would make them go worse. "It has been communicated to me that you had the illegal enterprise in view of conquering Texas, that you had declared that you would, in less than two years, be emperor of that country by conquest," the president wrote Houston. "I must really have thought you deranged to have believed you had so wild a scheme in contemplation, and particularly when it was communicated that the physical force to be employed was the Cherokee Indians. Indeed, my dear sir, I cannot believe you have any such chimerical visionary scheme in view. Your pledge of honor to the contrary is a sufficient guarantee that you will never engage in any enterprise injurious to your country that would tarnish your fame."

Houston, suitably chastened, gave the required pledge and put Texas temporarily out of his mind. But despite two years of trying, Jackson made no progress toward the purchase of Texas. The president gradually discovered what every president through James Polk would learn: that no Mexican government could even consider selling Texas without jeopardizing its own existence. From the American perspective this appeared irrational: Mexico had made nothing of Texas so far and showed little promise of doing better in the future. The United States was offering gold for what was causing Mexico only grief. But Mexicans—following the lead of Manuel de Mier y Terán—wrapped Texas in the context of their revolution; to relinquish Texas would be to admit that the revolution had failed. No Mexican government was willing to make that admission.

In any event, during the latter part of his first term, Jackson began to consider alternative means of acquiring Texas. Houston's ambitions had clearly revived, and he was champing for action in a larger field than Indian affairs. Indeed, his champing had grown embarrassingly public. On a return visit by Houston to Washington, William Stanberry, an anti-Jackson congressman from Ohio, had mischievously impugned Houston's honor as a way of attacking the president. Houston sent Stanberry a note preparatory to issuing a formal challenge; after Stanberry refused to receive the note, Houston assaulted him with a cane (appropriately fashioned of hickory) on Pennsylvania Avenue. Stanberry responded to the blows by producing a pistol, which he aimed at Houston's chest and tried to fire. But the flint spark failed to ignite the powder, and the misfire additionally enraged Houston, who delivered several more blows about Stanberry's head and shoulders before finishing with one aimed below the belt that—in the decorous testimony of an eyewitness—"struck him elsewhere."

Now it was Stanberry's turn to feel aggrieved. The congressman brought charges against Houston in the House of Representatives, which voted to arrest the former member from Tennessee for breach-ing the rule that held members of Congress free from liability for words spoken on the legislative floor. The trial became a sensation, with Houston, although represented by Francis Scott Key (author of "The Star-Spangled Banner"), carrying the burden of his own defense. By Houston's later recollection, Jackson called him to the White House and declared angrily, "It's not you they are after, Sam; those thieves, those infernal bank thieves, they wish to injure your old commander." Giving him some money to buy a new suit of clothes for the trial, Jack-son continued, "When you make your defense, tell those infernal bank thieves, who talk about privileges, that when an American citizen is in-sulted by one of them, he also has some privileges." (Jackson had "bank thieves" on the brain at this time, for he was engaged in a bitter struggle to disincorporate the Bank of the United States, which he con-sidered an illegitimate bastion of moneyed privilege.)

Preparing his case till far into the night before the trial opened, Houston drank even more than he was recently used to. He sum-moned a bellboy and told the lad to wake a barber and send him in. "When he came I told him to bring me a cup of coffee at sunrise and his shaving traps," Houston later recalled. "Opening a drawer, I said, do you see this purse of gold and this pistol? If the coffee does not

stick when I drink it"—that is, if it failed to wake and sober him—
"take the pistol and shoot me, and the gold is yours." The coffee
stuck, however, and Houston made an impassioned defense of his
conduct. He couldn't well deny that he had attacked Stanberry, so he
pled extenuating circumstances, starting with the egregious insult to
his honor and including Stanberry's refusal to meet him in a manly
duel. Houston cited precedents, legal and political; he quoted poetry
("I seek no sympathies nor need/The thorns which I have reaped are
of the tree/I planted; they have torn me, and I bleed"); he drew upon
the wisdom of the ancients; he reminded his auditors of his honorable service under the flag of his country. "So long as that flag shall
bear aloft its glittering stars," he concluded (in imagery perhaps influenced by Key), "bearing them amidst the din of battle and waving
them triumphantly above the storms of the ocean, so long, I trust,
shall the rights of American citizens be preserved safe and unim-
paired, and transmitted as a sacred legacy from one generation to another, till discord shall wreck the spheres—the grand march of time
shall cease—and not one fragment of all creation be left to chafe on
the bosom of eternity's waves."

Houston's performance won over the gallery. Junius Brutus
Booth, a leading actor of the day (and the father of John Wilkes
Booth), rushed up to Houston at the close of his speech, pumped his
hand, and declaimed: "Houston, take my laurels!" Yet for all its
power, the speech had no effect on the outcome of the trial. The
House judged the accused guilty of a breach of its privileges and sentenced him to a reprimand by the speaker, which was duly delivered.

Despite this victory, Stanberry remained dissatisfied, and he
brought criminal charges against Houston. Another trial took place;
again Houston was convicted, this time of assault. He was fined five
hundred dollars.

Twice the loser, Houston nonetheless felt vindicated in the

court of honor. "I was dying out, and had they taken me before a justice of the peace and fined me ten dollars, it would have killed me," he said afterward. "But they gave me a national tribunal for a theatre, and that set me up again."

In setting Houston up again, his enemies—and Jackson's—prepared him for Texas. While in the East, Houston made the acquaintance of James Prentiss, a speculator who controlled tens of thousands of acres in the Leftwich grant. More precisely, he controlled the acres on paper; he offered to bring Houston in as a partner in exchange for a money payment and Houston's commitment to travel to Texas to make the paper claim good. He would finance Houston's journey and pay other expenses. If Houston succeeded, both men would become rich.

The prospect fired Houston's imagination. "So soon as matters can be arranged, I will set out for the *land of promise*," he wrote Prentiss in May 1832. Houston's twin trials in Washington delayed things, as did problems Prentiss encountered in funding Houston's trip. Houston grew impatient at the delays. "It is important that I should be off to Texas!" he wrote in June.

The news from Texas compounded Houston's impatience, even as it revealed that there was more to his project than redeeming land scrip. After passage of the law of April 6, 1830, the chances of Prentiss, Houston, or anyone else winning legal control of land under the terms of the Leftwich grant were vanishingly slim. What was required was some extralegal maneuver—a filibuster, for example. Presumably, an independent or American-affiliated Texas would be more likely to honor the Leftwich claims, but even if it didn't, the leaders of a successful filibuster would doubtless have other ways of compensating themselves.

The existence of ulterior motives was clear in Houston's correspondence with Prentiss. "The land which I bought, to be candid with
you, has claimed not much solicitude of me," he wrote. Yet the land
wasn't insignificant. Houston intended to sell some of it en route to
Texas in order to raise money for expenses, but he wouldn't liquidate
it all. "It might be well to have enough with me to form a pretext,
when I get there, for moving about." Prentiss responded by noting
that the reports from Texas—of the uprising against the Mexican government—boded well for Houston's mission. "The more conflict, the
more I am convinced of the expediency and practicability of our
plans," he said. Some weeks later, Prentiss urged Houston to make
haste west. "The field is now open for a great work in Texas—and you
must go and help reap the harvest."

Houston left Washington about the end of July and traveled west
via Tennessee. The closer he got to Texas, the more excited he became. "I have seen several friends here lately from Texas," he wrote
Prentiss from Nashville, "and all represent it as the most prosperous
state, and say it is a lovely region! Thousands would flock there from
this country, if the government were settled, but will not venture
without it!" Apparently Houston had made contact with people in
Texas, or at least they had caught wind of his coming. "Several persons have said to me that I was looked for, and earnestly wished for,
by the citizens of Texas," he told Prentiss.

Houston might have avoided Tennessee on his way to Texas; the
state still held painful memories for him. But Andrew Jackson was
summering at the Hermitage, and he wanted to speak to Houston
before the younger man left the country. What the two said is unknown, as it wasn't written down and there were no witnesses—
which was the point of the personal, private interview. But
apparently Jackson gave Houston five hundred dollars to finance the
journey—an essential sum, as Prentiss had run into cash-flow prob-

lems and hadn't fulfilled his front end of the deal. More important, the president gave Houston his blessing for a project that was ambitious and almost certainly illegal—under Mexican and perhaps American law.

Jackson's imprimatur helped provide Houston with a cover story more persuasive than land speculation. Continuing west through Arkansas, he obtained a passport from U.S. Army officers there requesting "all the Tribes of Indians, whether in amity with the United States, or as yet not allied to them by Treaties, to permit safely and freely to pass through their respective territories, General Sam Houston, a Citizen of the United States, Thirty-eight years of age, Six feet two inches in stature, brown hair and light complexion; and in case of need to give him all lawful aid and protection." Houston traveled as an agent investigating troubles among the Indians; to lend credibility to this guise he filed an advance report with the federal Indian commissioner at Fort Gibson, Arkansas. "It has been my first and most important object to obtain all the information possible relative to the Pawnee and Comanche Indians," Houston wrote. Such information, especially regarding the Comanches, could be gathered only by visiting Texas. "To reach the wild Indians at this season will be difficult, and only practicable by way of St. Antone. . . . It is probable at this time, or by the time I can reach there, that the Comanches may be within a few hundred miles of that place."

Having established his cover, Houston made a last visit to Wigwam Neosho. Perhaps Diana had guessed that one day he would leave her; probably he promised to return. But in the event he didn't, he left her the wigwam, the surrounding property, and the inventory of the trading post.

Riding south and west, he reached the Red River at Fort Towson, and at the beginning of December 1832 crossed into Texas. He traveled south to Nacogdoches and then southwest to San Felipe. He missed meeting Austin, who was traveling about the colony. But he did meet James Bowie, visiting from San Antonio. Each knew the other by reputation, and as they sized each other up, they doubtless shared intelligence: Bowie about the Indians he had fought on the San Sabá, the Mexicans he had captured on the Angelina, and perhaps the silver mines he still hoped to discover; Houston regarding the attitude of the Jackson administration toward Texas and Mexico. How far Houston tipped his hand in this regard is impossible to say. Bowie would have known that Houston and Jackson had once been close; whether he guessed—or was told—that they were again close, especially regarding Texas, cannot be determined.

But Bowie and Houston must have shared substantial information, for they shared the long road to San Antonio. The Comanches were a constant threat, and Bowie insisted that he and Houston travel with others and post a guard each night. Apparently the guards weren't always sober—or at least Houston wasn't. He came in after a predawn picket and recounted an unnerving experience he had just had. "He said he had been fired at more than a hundred times that morning—in imagination," remembered one of the other travelers. "He moved his head, and was sure an Indian arrow passed by him." He moved again. " 'Whiz' came an arrow." He moved yet again. "Another hissed by his head." Finally realizing that something was out of order, Houston looked for the arrows and discovered that the noise was nothing more than his hat brim brushing against the collar of his overcoat. (Either Bowie put Houston very much at his ease or Houston was still drunk, for him to tell this story against himself.)

At Béxar, Bowie introduced Houston to the Veramendis and other prominent residents of the town. As it happened, some Comanche chiefs—of currently friendly bands—were visiting San Antonio at the same time. Houston conveyed Jackson's regards and presented them with a medal bearing a likeness of the president. "I found them well disposed to make a treaty with the United States," he reported to the Indian commissioners in Arkansas, "and, I doubt not, to regard it truly and preserve it faithfully if made." If Houston's Indian mission had been serious, rather than an excuse for him to travel through Texas, he should have followed up this interview by going north from Béxar into the region where the Comanches and their allies were not friendly. But he didn't.

Instead he returned to Nacogdoches, where he learned more about the hostility that really interested him: the hostility among the Americans toward Mexico. In the wake of the uprising of the previous summer, the settlers had called a convention to discuss their grievances and petition the Mexican government for redress. The mere calling of the convention reflected the cultural rift between the Americans and the Mexicans, for where the right of assembly and petition was part of the Americans' English inheritance, it had no counterpart in the Spanish tradition. As a result, the convening itself—regardless of what might be said or done at the convention—connoted sedition to the Mexican authorities and put them on alert.

Their alert turned to alarm when the convention gathered at San Felipe in April 1833. The delegates numbered somewhat more than fifty (any records kept were subsequently lost) and included Stephen Austin, representing San Felipe, and Sam Houston, representing Nacogdoches, where the settlers had been sufficiently impressed by Houston's resumé and connections to select him after only a few weeks' acquaintance. Houston and the other delegates quickly concurred that they should petition the Mexican congress to repeal the anti-immigration clause of the April 6 law, as well as to restore the exemption from tariffs. Only a little more time was required for the convention to conclude that Texas must be allowed to separate from Coahuila and form its own state. The debate on this last point veered at times in a decidedly secessionist direction—with Houston at the helm. "Can Mexico ever make laws for Texas?" he asked the delegates. "*No*. . . . Mexico is acting in bad faith and trifling with the rights of the people. Plans formed without the assent of Texas are not binding upon Texas."

If Houston had any pangs of conscience in speaking this way, just two months after encouraging Jackson to crush the nullifiers of South Carolina, he gave no hint of it. On the contrary, he went further in the direction of separation by chairing a committee that drafted a constitution for a state of Texas. By chance—or very deep design—one of the delegates happened to possess a copy of the constitution of the state of Massachusetts; this provided a model for the convention's work. That the Massachusetts charter was scarcely adjusted to take account of the radically different setting and circumstances of Texas suggests the delegates wished to make a political statement rather than craft an actual government.

The statement was clear enough: Texas was determined to govern itself. Many of the delegates would have been happy with self-government within the Mexican federation; others apparently saw separation from Coahuila as a first step toward separation from Mexico, even if they deemed it impolitic at this point to say so. Stephen Austin was the leader of the first, minimalist camp; Sam Houston headed the second, radical group.

When critics of democracy in the age of Jackson lamented its deficiencies, they typically cited the ignorance of ordinary people regarding matters of state, and the likelihood that the yahoos would send their own to Congress. David Crockett was a case in point. "Colonel Crockett is perhaps the most illiterate man that you have ever met in Congress," declared an experienced Washington hand on meeting the Tennessee representative. "He is not only illiterate but he is rough and uncouth, talks much and loudly, and is by far more in his proper place when hunting a bear in a cane brake than he will be in the capital."

In the late 1820s Crockett was probably the third most famous Tennesseean, after Jackson and Houston. His fame rested on his prowess at hunting; bears were his preferred quarry, and the knife his favorite weapon. The knife, he explained, was silent—an especial advantage "if some skulking red-skin or vagabond should be upon your tracks for mischief"—besides "being a mighty saver of lead and powder." In the frontier districts of the West, where hunting was both a source of livelihood and a sport, a reputation as a hunter conferred the same kind of aura later enjoyed by successful entrepreneurs and athletes; and, as the aura would later, it often opened doors unrelated to the original success. Crockett, who had served under Jackson during the War of 1812, in turn became a justice of the peace, a town commissioner, a colonel of the Tennessee militia, and an assemblyman in the Tennessee legislature. Siding with the humble against the powerful, he began a career-long quest to make public lands more readily available to settlers. His quest was serious but his manner folksy. One legislator wanted to move the state capital from Murfreesboro to Nashville, complaining, by way of justification, of the miserable food and lodging in the former town. Crockett answered that he had never eaten nor slept so well as at his boarding-house during the legislative session; the state would save a great deal of money if, rather than moving the capital to Nashville, it moved the complaining legislator to Crockett's quarters. The same legislator asserted that the inhabitants of Murfreesboro were rude; Crockett replied that, speaking for himself, he hadn't found this to be so. Even black men in Murfreesboro tipped their hats to him, which was more than he could say for many white people in other parts of the state.

In 1825 Crockett was drafted by the Jackson machine to run for Congress. He lost, but respectably enough to run again two years later, this time victoriously. "I was, without disguise, the friend and supporter of General Jackson, upon his principles as he laid them down," he explained after the fact. Two years before Jackson brought the West to the White House, Crockett carried it to Congress, with an accent and an attitude that sometimes made even Old Hickory wince. Crockett talked of hunting "bar" and "coon," of "taking a horn" (having a drink), of being able to whip his "weight in wild cats." When a campaign opponent accused him of lying, he confessed to the charge. "Fellow citizens, I did lie," he said. "They told stories on me, and I wanted to show them, if it came to that, that I could tell a bigger lie than they could. Yes, fellow citizens, I can run faster, walk longer, leap higher, speak better, and tell more and bigger lies than my competitor, and all his friends, any day of his life."

His reputation spread. "His friends admit that he is somewhat eccentric, and that from a deficit in education, his stump speeches are not famous for polish or refinement," one editor explained. "Yet they are plain, forcible, and generally respectful." Another remarked, "To return from the capitol without having seen Colonel Crockett betrayed a total destitution of curiosity and a perfect insensibility to the Lions of the West." Alexis de Tocqueville, the French aristocrat who was slumming in America to learn about the novel phenomenon of democracy, knew about Crockett, or thought he did. "Two years ago the inhabitants of the district of which Memphis is the capital sent to the House of Representatives in Congress an individ-

ual named David Crockett, who has no education, can read with difficulty, has no property, no fixed residence, but passes his life hunting, selling his game to live, and dwelling continuously in the woods."
Now and then Crockett felt obliged to correct the most egregious
misconceptions about himself—he could read well enough, and lived
most of the year under a roof—but he hardly went out of his way to diminish the myth he was already becoming.

Crockett's growing fame didn't endear him to some in the Jackson
camp. James Knox Polk was younger than Crockett (by nine years),
better educated than Crockett (who wasn't?), more refined than
Crockett (ditto), and more ambitious than Crockett. This last trait
seems to have been what set him against Crockett, for though they
both entered Tennessee politics as Jacksonians, Polk evinced a desire
to make himself the heir of Old Hickory (now that Houston was out of
the way). Polk was also craftier than Crockett, and on some controversial issues—school funding, the tariff—he isolated Crockett from
the mainstream of Jacksonian sentiment. "Rely upon it," Polk told a
fellow Jackson loyalist, by way of attacking Crockett, "he can be and
has been operated upon by our enemies. We can't trust him an inch."

Crockett won reelection to Congress in 1829 (this was before
the states regularized their electoral calendars and settled on even-
year elections), but he felt the ground being cut from beneath his
feet. "To General Jackson I am a firm and undeviating friend," he
protested. "I have fought under his command, and am proud to own
that he has been my commander. I have loved him, and in the sincerity of my heart I say that I still love *him*. But to be compelled to love
every one who for purposes of self-aggrandizement pretends to rally

around the 'Jackson standard' is what I can never submit to. The people of this country, like the humble boatsmen on the Mississippi, ought to look out for breakers!" (Crockett knew about the Mississippi breakers, having nearly drowned when high water ran a flatboat of his into an anchored log raft, sweeping him and the boat under the raft. He barely escaped, losing every stitch of clothing and large patches of skin in the process.)

But it was Crockett who got slapped by the political waves. The more distance that developed between him and the president's advisers, the more attractive he became to Jackson's avowed enemies, who were busy forming the Whig party. Crockett innocently accepted their support and in doing so made himself even more of a target of the Jacksonians. Nearly every measure he supported—on land sales, Indian policy, highways—met resistance from the administration. Eventually Crockett had to admit that the problem wasn't merely Polk but Jackson himself. When the president endorsed a rival in Crockett's 1831 reelection campaign, the rift between the two old comrades in arms burst into the open. Crockett accused Jackson of abandoning his own beliefs, saying, "I have not left the principles which led me to support General Jackson; he has left them and *me*; and I will not surrender my independence to follow his *new opinions*, taught by interested and selfish advisers, and which may again be remolded under the influence of passion and cunning." On another occasion Crockett indignantly declared, "I have not got a collar round my neck marked 'My dog,' with the name of Andrew Jackson on it. Because I would not take the collar round my neck, I was hurled from the party." When defeat became all but certain, Crockett asserted, "I would rather be beaten and be a man than to be elected and be a little puppy dog. . . . I would rather be politically buried than to be hypocritically immortalized." (The pleasure of the Polk faction at Crockett's downfall was captured in a remark by one of them on the eve of the balloting: "I think Crockett is going to be beat at this election. . . . I hope the name of David, the mighty man in the River Country, will no longer disgrace the Western District in the National Legislature.")

Crockett employed his freedom from politics to hunt bears (successfully, as always) and try to work down his debts (unsuccessfully, as usual). He cleared a tract of land along the Obion River in western Tennessee and built a cabin and outbuildings and planted corn and fruit trees. He also cultivated friends among the Whigs, who encouraged him to attempt to take back his congressional seat in 1833. He made the race and, running as an explicit anti-Jacksonian at a time when Jackson's hard line against states' rights had dented his popularity in Tennessee, emerged triumphant.

The Whigs knew an opportunity when they saw it. Having lost the 1832 presidential election to Jackson with the elegant Henry Clay at the top of the ticket, they sought a candidate for 1836 who could tap the popular desire for democratic authenticity. The vogue of the West had given rise to numerous books and plays, starting with the works of Washington Irving and James Fenimore Cooper and extending to *The Lion of the West,* a stage production that toured the country and featured a character unmistakably based on Crockett. Biographies of Crockett, unauthorized and romanticized, appeared in bookshops and were immediately snatched up. Observing the large sales and the royalties they produced for their authors, Crockett decided to write his own biography.

The memoir struck a balance between the homespun and the serious—as befit a frontiersman being bruited for president. Crockett apologized for presuming on readers' patience by writing the book at all, but he explained that "obscure as I am, my name is making considerable deal of fuss in the world." He didn't apologize for his lack of proper grammar, but simply said, "I hadn't time to learn it, and make no pretensions to it." On this point he linked himself to the early Jackson even as he distanced himself from the current version. "While the critics were learning grammar, and learning to spell, I, and 'Doctor Jackson, L.L.D.' [Jackson had just received an honorary degree from Harvard] were fighting in the wars. . . . Big men have more important matters to attend to than crossing their *t*'s and dotting their *i*'s, and such like small things." Crockett recounted his bear hunts ("At the crack of my gun, here he came tumbling down; and at the moment he touched the ground, I heard one of my best dogs cry out. I took my tomahawk in one hand, and my big butcher-knife in the other, and run up within four or five paces of him, at which he let my dog go and fixed his eyes on me. I got back in all sorts of a hurry, for I know'd if he got hold of me, he would hug me altogether too close for comfort. I went to my gun and hastily loaded her again, and shot him the third time, which killed him good"). He applied frontier aphorisms and figures of speech to political life, thereby making them part of the larger lexicon ("Root, hog, or die"; "My heart would begin to flutter like a duck in a puddle"; and, most famously, "Be sure you're always right—*then go ahead!*"). He described a stint as justice of the peace and his preference for natural law over statute ("I gave my decisions on the principles of common justice and honesty between man and man, and relied on natural born sense, and not law-learning to guide me, for I had never read a page in a law book in all my life"). He confessed his ignorance of the workings of government at the time of his first campaign for office ("I had never read even a newspaper in my life, or any thing else on the subject"). He defended his split from Jackson ("I was willing to go with General Jackson in every thing that I believed was honest and right; but further than this I wouldn't go for him, or any other man in the whole creation. . . . I would sooner be honestly and politically damned than hypocritically immortalized").

The book was an instant success, running through several printings in its first year and inspiring numerous pirated editions (which prevented Crockett from realizing his royalty hopes). Crockett became even more of a celebrity, and even more of a threat to the Jacksonians.

Chapter 10

The General Is Friendly

Mary Holley hadn't seen her cousin Stephen Austin for twenty-five years, and she might not have seen him for twenty-five more had her husband not suddenly died, leaving her to puzzle out how to support herself and her young son. She knew that Stephen was in Texas, as was her brother Henry. She also knew that many Americans were going to Texas and many more were thinking about going, despite the Mexican efforts to curb the immigration. Being a writer by inclination, and as enterprising in her own way as any of the empresarios, she determined to make some money out of Texas, too. She would travel there and keep an account of her journey, and then publish a book that would serve simultaneously as a travelogue for stay-at-homes whose interest in Texas was merely vicarious and as an immigrants' guide for persons preparing to undertake the journey themselves. Hers wouldn't be the only such account; reports from Texas were already appearing in modest numbers. But in her pitch to publishers she noted two distinctions working in her favor: her tie to Austin and her feminine perspective. The former gave her—and would give her readers—special access to the most famous of the empresarios; the latter would appeal to women who, as Texas became more populated and civilized, formed an ever-growing part of the immigrant stream. Her pitch succeeded, and she found a publisher. In the autumn of 1831 she set off for Texas with a boatload of passengers from New Orleans.

"They were all bound, like myself, to *the land of promise*," she wrote. "A better assortment of professions and character, for an infant colony, could not have been selected: an editor of a gazette from Michigan, a civil engineer from Kentucky, a trader from Missouri with his bride along and an outfit of dry goods, a genteel good-looking widow on a visit to her son, with a suitable proportion of the working class." Seasickness struck the group, sending editor, engineer, working class, and author running for the rail. For two days she couldn't keep anything in her stomach except fruit juice. "I would advise all who take this voyage to carry a liberal supply of oranges with them," she wrote upon reaching land.

At the mouth of the Brazos the ship encountered one of the military posts established under the law of April 6, 1830, to control immigration. "The officer of the garrison boarded us to examine our passports, a ceremony the Mexicans are very tenacious of from their known jealousy of foreigners. He was a young man, dark and rather handsome, in a neat Mexican uniform. . . . He very politely addressed our captain in a few words of English, probably his whole vocabulary; while the latter displayed to best advantage, in reply, his whole stock of Spanish." The documents of most of the passengers were produced, inspected, and approved. Mary Holley's visa, however, was in her luggage. The officer let it go. "With courtly complaisance and gallant reliance upon a lady's word, he waived the ceremony of examination and saved us the trouble of searching our trunks."

The voyage continued up the Brazos to the town of Brazoria, some thirty river miles from the mouth, at the head of tidewater. The town was only three years old and showed the callowness of youth.

"One street stretches along the bank of the Brazos, and one parallel with it farther back, while other streets, with the trees still standing, are laid out to intersect these at right angles, to be cleared at some future day as the wants of the citizens may require. Its arrangements, as well as its wealth and greatness, are all prospective."

Fifty families made the town their home, after the frontier fashion. "Some families, recently arrived, are obliged to camp out, from the impracticability of getting other accommodation. The place, therefore, has a busy and prosperous air, which it is always agreeable to notice, but has not yet advanced beyond the wants of first necessity. There is neither cabinet-maker, tailor, hatter, shoe-maker, nor any other mechanic, except carpenters." There were no hotels, either, but there was one boardinghouse. "The proprietors of it are from New York and know how things should be, and have intelligence and good sense enough to make the best of circumstances they cannot control."

There was much about Texas beyond the control of immigrants, which was why they should concentrate on those things they *could* control. Weather worried many who had heard of the Texas heat. Mary Holley counseled: "The best month to arrive in is October. The first impression at that time is delightful, as well as just, and there is less inconvenience and trouble at that time than at any other season. It is also the most favourable season on account of health. The change to the hot months of the succeeding year is then gradual. Those persons who come from the northern states or from Europe, in the spring and summer, experience too sudden a change and are always more or less affected by it."

Immigrants must come prepared with provisions, knowledge, and proper attitude. This applied particularly to women.

> House-keepers should bring with them all indispensable
> articles for household use, together with as much common

clothing (other clothing is not wanted) for themselves and their children, as they conveniently can. Ladies in particular should remember that in a new country they cannot get things made at any moment, as in an old one, and that they will be sufficiently busy the first two years, in arranging such things as they have, without occupying themselves in obtaining more. It should also be done as a matter of economy. . . .

Those who *must* have a feather-bed had better bring it, for it would take too long to make one; and though the air swarms with live geese, a feather-bed could not be got for love or money. Every body should bring pillows and bed linen. Mattresses, such as are used universally in Louisiana—and they are very comfortable—are made of the moss which hangs on almost every tree. They cost nothing but the case and the trouble of preparing the moss. The case should be brought. Domestic checks are best, being cheap and light, and sufficiently strong. The moss is prepared by burying it in the earth until it is partially rotted. It is then washed very clean, dried and picked, when it is fit for use. These mattresses should be made very thick, and those who like a warmer bed in winter can put some layers of wool, well carded, upon the moss, taking care to *keep this side up.*

Every emigrant should bring mosquito bars. . . . They are indispensable in the summer season, and are made of a thin species of muslin, manufactured for the purpose. Furniture, such as chairs and bureaus, can be brought in separate pieces and put together, cheaper and better, after arrival, than they can be purchased here, if purchased at all. But it must be recollected that very few

articles of this sort are required, where houses are small
and building expensive. . . . Tables are made by the house
carpenter, which answer the purpose very well, where no-
body has better and the chief concern is to get something
to put upon them. The maxim here is, nothing for show
but all for use.

Immigrants would discover a society appealing in its simplicity
and egalitarianism. "The people are universally kind and hos-
pitable. . . . Every body's house is open, and table spread, to accommodate the traveler. There are no poor people here, and none
rich—that is, none who have much money." Immigrants received
equal amounts of land on arrival, regardless of circumstances back
home. "And if they do not continue equal, it is for want of good management on the one part, or superior industry and sagacity on the
other. All are happy, because busy; and none meddle with the affairs
of their neighbors, because they have enough to do to take care of
their own." Even some persons who might least have expected to
thrive in Texas did so. "Delicate ladies find they can be useful, and
need not be vain. . . . Privations become pleasures; people grow ingenious in overcoming difficulties. They discover in themselves
powers they did not suspect themselves of possessing."

Texas wasn't for everyone. "Those persons . . . who are established in comfort and competency, with an ordinary portion of domestic happiness; who have never been far from home, and are
excessively attached to personal ease; who shrink from hardship and
danger, and those who, being accustomed to a regular routine of pre-
scribed employment in a city, know not how to act on emergencies or
adapt themselves to all sorts of circumstances, had better stay where
they are."

For many others, though, Texas afforded opportunities they

wouldn't find elsewhere. "He whose hopes of rising to independence in life by honourable exertion have been blasted by disappointment; whose ambition has been thwarted by untoward circumstances; whose spirit, though depressed, is not discouraged; who longs only for some ample field on which to lay out his strength; who does not hanker after society nor sigh for the vanished illusions of life; who has a fund of resources within himself, and a heart to trust in God and his own exertions; who is not peculiarly sensitive to petty inconveniences but can bear privations and make sacrifices of personal comfort—such a person will do well to settle accounts at home and begin life anew in Texas."

Stephen Austin appreciated Mary Holley's spreading the word about Texas, but she meant more to him than good publicity. He hoped that with her husband dead and her brother in Texas, he could persuade her to move to his colony. He had had a crush on her as a youth, and the fond memories of that time returned when he heard she was coming for a visit. To Austin, Mary Holley represented grace and beauty and refinement—qualities often absent on the frontier. Austin was no elitist, and he never spoke ill of the plain folks who formed the majority in his colony, but he was a college man who knew something of literature and the arts, and he hoped to attract at least a few kindred spirits to his corner of the wilderness.

Their first meeting in Texas increased his estimation of Mary Holley. "She is a very superior woman, and the most agreeable company I have met with for many years," he wrote his sister, Emily. Austin spent ten days with Mary, at her brother Henry's house above Brazoria. She inquired about the origins of the colony; Austin recounted the trials of the early days. She asked about Mexican politics; he explained the tortuous course of the revolution. She wanted to learn about the Indians; he told her of the Comanches and Karankawas and Wacos and Tonkawas. All this she included in the draft of the book she was writing; she read sections for his comment and correction. She taught Austin and others in Henry's household a song she had composed, called the "Brazos Boat Song," which became a family anthem.

Austin was enchanted. "Mrs. H. is a *divine* woman," he told James Perry. As she departed east to finish her book and consider whether to relocate permanently, Austin bade her the warmest farewell. "There is a pleasure in meeting with congenial feelings and tastes and sympathies, that few—very few—in this cold and selfish world can appreciate and enjoy," he said. "It is therefore like the diamond to the miser: invaluable." Austin allowed himself to dream of life in Texas when she returned, and others like her followed. "We will then arrange our cottages—rural, comfortable, and splendid—the splendor of nature's simplicity. Gardens and rosy bowers, and ever-verdant groves, and music, books, and intellectual amusements can all be ours; and that confidence and community of feeling and tastes which none but congenial minds can ever know; all these, without excessive wealth, we can have."

Between the dream and the reality lay a long journey—literally for Austin. In the spring of 1833 he departed for Mexico City, to deliver to the national government the petition of the San Felipe convention calling for statehood for Texas separate from Coahuila. The season was a bad one for cholera, which Austin encountered at the Rio Grande. Unsettling symptoms laid him low there, and though they passed, they prompted him to choose a sea voyage south, via Veracruz, rather than an overland trek, to avoid further exposure. The passage reminded him why he hated boats. "I had a wretched trip," he wrote. "*One month* from Matamoros to Vera Cruz in a little schooner— ten days on short allowance of water—none but salt provisions—and sea sick all the time."

Mexico City was no better. Cholera was rampant in the capital. "There were 43,000 sick here at one time," Austin wrote. "The deaths, I believe, have been about 18,000. I have never witnessed such a horrible scene of distress and death." The epidemic carried off many government officials and frightened the rest, many of whom fled the capital till cooler weather should stem the disease.

Despite the difficulties (including another unnerving round of symptoms in himself), Austin devoted all his energies to lobbying for Texas statehood. "I explained at large and with some detail the situation of Texas and the necessity of erecting it into a state," he reported to a standing committee of the San Felipe convention, after at length he obtained a meeting with Vice President Valentín Gómez Farías and several cabinet ministers. Austin said he had anchored his argument for statehood to several points: the desire of the people of Texas to govern themselves, their separate identity from that of Mexicans, an 1824 law that anticipated a separate government for Texas, the stronger ties that would develop between Texas and Mexico without Coahuila in the way, and "the right and duty of every people to save themselves from anarchy and ruin!" Austin explained to San Felipe: "On this last point I enlarged very much. I distinctly stated as my opinion that self-preservation would compel the people of Texas to organize a local government, with or without the approbation of the General Government—that this measure would not proceed from any hostile views to the permanent union of Texas with Mexico, but from absolute necessity, to save themselves from anarchy and total ruin.

How such a measure would affect the union of Texas with Mexico, or where it would end, were matters worthy of serious reflection."

This was strong stuff, amounting to an ultimatum. Austin shouldn't have been surprised if Gómez Farías had thrown him out of his office. In fact, on another occasion the vice president did respond angrily. "I told the vice president the other day that Texas must be made a state by the Government or she would make herself one," Austin wrote to James Perry. "This he took as a threat and became very much enraged." Austin tried to mollify Gómez Farías by explaining that he intended no threat but was merely describing the mood in Texas. "When he understood that my object was only to state a positive fact which it was my duty to state, he was reconciled." (This wasn't quite true, as Austin would discover.)

Even while pressing the Mexican government on Texas statehood, Austin attempted—from a distance—to restrain the radicals in Texas, knowing that another outbreak of anti-government violence would make his difficult task impossible. He wrote home putting the best face on his discussions with Gómez Farías and the other officials. Following one interview, which he characterized as "long and frank," he declared, "I believe that Texas will be a state of this Confederation with the approbation of this Government before long." Austin urged the Texans to show resolve but avoid provocation. Under no circumstances should they speak of anything other than statehood within the Mexican union. "Should our application be refused, Texas ought to organize a local government with as little delay as possible—but always on the basis that it is a part of the Mexican Confederation, a younger sister who adopts this mode of entering upon her rights, now that she is of age, because unnecessary embarrassments are interposed which are unconstitutional, unjust, inexpedient and ruinous."

Austin himself, however, in moments of exasperation, some-times spoke of an alternative to a Mexican connection. Not long after reaching Mexico City, he wrote to settler and friend John Austin (perhaps a distant relative) that he supposed that the Mexican con-gress, when it reconvened, would vote in favor of statehood for Texas, but that the legislature would then ask the other states for their ap-proval. This would cause additional delay and cast the whole state-hood issue into doubt. Austin wasn't sure he could stand it. "I have had a hard trip so far and more difficulties to work through here than you can well form an idea of. But I hope to get along and that Texas will be a State of *this*, or the *U.S.*, republic before another year, for I am so weary that life is hardly worth having, situated as we are now."

Had Mexican officials read this letter, they would have doubted Austin's integrity even more than they did. As it happened, they read other letters he wrote, with precisely that result. In October he sent a letter to the *ayuntamiento* (town council) of San Antonio de Béxar, urging the members to coordinate with the other town councils of Texas in preparing to move unilaterally toward Texas statehood. Be-tween the cholera and the ongoing political struggles of the capital, he explained, nothing had been done on Texas. "And in my opinion, nothing is going to be done." He said he would play out his hand in Mexico City, but in the likely event he failed to get what he came for, the inhabitants of Texas must act together. "And so I hope that you will not lose a single moment in directing a communication to all the Ayuntamientos of Texas, urging them to unite in a measure to organ-ize a local government independent of Coahuila, even though the general government should withhold its consent." To underline his resolve, Austin replaced the standard closing in the correspondence of revolutionary Mexico—"God and Liberty"—with a new coinage: "God and Texas."

Had Austin been writing to friends or allies, this encouragement to sedition might never have reached the eyes of the Mexican authorities. But many of the (mostly Mexican) inhabitants of San Antonio feared that a separate state of Texas, even one attached to Mexico, would be dominated by Americans, and the town's ayuntamiento included persons who were as skeptical of Austin as any ministers in Mexico City. They passed his letter on to the government of Coahuila y Texas, which, delighted at receiving such damning information on the insurgent empresario, forwarded the letter to the federal government.

This took time, which the unsuspecting Austin put to use. Though (sanctioned) statehood appeared a lost cause for the present, other progress seemed possible. Austin hammered against the ban on American immigration and finally succeeded in winning its repeal. This was no small feat, and Austin thought it augured well—at least well enough to warrant continued patience. "Texas matters are all right. Nothing is wanted there but *quiet*," he wrote. It also warranted his return to Texas, to ensure the quiet. "I shall be at home soon," he predicted on November 26.

Austin's trip north went smoothly until he reached Saltillo in January 1834. He had ridden hard to catch the newly appointed commandant general for the northern district, Pedro Lemus, so that the two might travel together. To his amazement, when he presented himself to Lemus, the general arrested him. Lemus explained that he had received an order from the war ministry to capture Austin and return him to the capital to answer charges raised by the state government of Coahuila y Texas.

Austin was hurt and dismayed. "All I can be accused of is that I have labored arduously, faithfully, and perhaps, at particular moments, passionately and with more impatience and irritation than I ought to have shewn, to have Texas made a State of the Mexican Confederation separate from Coahuila," he wrote to Sam Williams. "This is all, and this is no crime." If he had erred in writing frankly to the people of San Antonio—Austin guessed the source of the complaint against him—he had done so from honorable motives. "I considered that very great respect and deference was justly due to them as native Mexicans, as the capital of Texas, and as the oldest and most populous town in the country. And I knew the importance of getting them to take the lead in all the politics of Texas. Besides this, I was personally attached to those people as a sincere friend and wished to act in concert with them." But they had betrayed his confidence—which was all the more hurtful given that events were tearing Texas apart and no one else was trying to mend it. "My object was to smother the party spirit and violent and ruinous divisions which I saw brewing in the colony."

General Lemus appreciated Austin's plight and transported him south in his own carriage. But the kindness ended when Austin reached Mexico City. On February 13, 1834, he was placed in a prison that once had held victims of the Inquisition. He spoke briefly with a prosecutor a few days later, but beyond this he received no information regarding the charges against him or his prospects of coming to trial. He had no cellmate and no visitors except Padre Miguel Muldoon, an Irish cleric he had met earlier. "Time drags on heavily," Austin wrote in a diary he kept during his detention. "What a horrible punishment is solitary confinement, shut up in a dungeon with scarcely enough light to distinguish anything."

The lonely days facilitated reflection. He asked himself what the "true interest of Texas" was, and answered, "It is to have a local government to cement and strengthen its union with Mexico instead of weakening or breaking it. What Texas wants is an organization of a local government, and it is of little consequence whether it be part of Coahuila or as a separate state or territory, provided the organization be a suitable one." As this conclusion was more moderate than the line he took with Gómez Farías, one suspects that either Austin had learned the lesson his imprisonment presumably was supposed to teach him—that Texas must forever remain a part of Mexico—or he thought someone would be reading his journal. His musings often sound like the defense he would make at trial, should he ever get one. "My intentions were pure and correct. I desired to cement the union of Texas with Mexico, and to promote the welfare and advancement of my adopted country, by populating the northern and eastern frontier. I have been impatient, and have allowed myself to be compromised and ensnared by the political events of last year, and by the excitement caused by them in Texas." But he had committed no crime. "My conscience acquits me of anything wrong, except impatience and imprudence."

Yet if Austin was defending himself to a potential prosecutor, he was also defending himself to himself. In prison the Mexican republic assumed a solidity it had often seemed to lack on the outside, where the roils of revolution left everyone—Austin included—wondering whether the government could hold itself together, let alone hold the country together. If Mexico was falling to pieces, simple self-preservation dictated that the Texans look to their own security. In prison, however, the view changed. The stone walls of his cell had stood longer than the republic of the North, and they gave every indication of standing for a long time to come. Under the circumstances, it was easy for Austin to revert to his earlier thinking about Texas and Mexico, and to conclude—again—that the future of his adopted province lay within the embrace of his adopted country.

But there were things about Mexico that had to change, starting with a legal code that could lock a prisoner away with no means to defend himself. "What a system of jurisprudence is this of confining those accused or suspected without permitting them to take any steps to make manifest their innocence or to procure proofs for their trial? They can neither consult with counsel, lawyer, friend or anybody. I do not know of what I am accused; how can I prepare my defense? . . . This system may be in conformity with law, but I am ignorant of which law. . . . It is very certain that such a system is in no wise in conformity with justice, reason or common sense."

After three months in prison, Austin spied a glimmer of hope, in the person of Santa Anna. The hero of Tampico had been elected president the previous March, despite continuing illness, which, he said, prevented his attending his own inauguration. "I am in such a condition that I cannot even put on my shoes," he told Gómez Farías, who became acting president.

Gómez Farías happened to be a physician, but he didn't require a medical degree to know that Santa Anna's illness was political, an allergic reaction to responsibility for the liberal reforms the progressive vice president and a similarly inclined congress began to put in place. Santa Anna was allowing the liberals their moment, yet he was hedging his bets by distancing himself from the reforms. The losers in the latest round of the revolution—a group that included some of the wealthiest and most influential persons in the country—had yet to formulate a response to the government's program, and Santa Anna didn't want to commit himself before they did. If the reforms proved popular, Santa Anna would claim credit; if they failed, he'd let Gómez Farías take the blame.

Santa Anna's health recovered sufficiently for him to visit the capital at the end of May; while there he reaffirmed his devotion to the revolution and the constitution of 1824. A conservative alliance of bishops and generals had called for Santa Anna to assume emergency powers against the liberals; the president condemned the very thought. "I swear to you," he told the Mexican people, "that I oppose all efforts aimed at the destruction of the constitution and that I would die before accepting any other power than that designated by it. . . . My firmest determination is to defend without the slightest hesitation the constitution as our representatives gave it to us in 1824."

Yet during the subsequent several months Santa Anna reconsidered his attachment to the 1824 charter. The bishops and generals, joined by the landed gentry, descended upon Santa Anna's hacienda and implored him to move against the liberals. They argued that the revolution had gone awry, that the Mexican masses weren't ready for republicanism, that progress for Mexico required stronger leadership than the current system could deliver.

Santa Anna allowed himself to be persuaded. Having observed the congress flail haplessly at the numerous problems facing Mexico, and having watched one set of politicians fall out murderously with the next, the general decided that he alone—ruling alone—held the key to Mexico's salvation. To many observers, this turnabout was nothing less than a betrayal of the republic and the revolution. A former American minister to Mexico, Joel Poinsett, charged the president with abandoning his liberal convictions. Santa Anna replied in measured tones. "Say to Mr. Poinsett that it is very true that I threw up my cap for liberty with great ardor, and perfect sincerity, but very soon found the folly of it. A hundred years to come my people will not be fit for liberty. They do not know what it is, unenlightened as they are, and under the influence of a Catholic clergy, a despotism is the proper government for them."

Despotism was what Santa Anna began to provide the Mexican

people in the spring of 1834. "When I returned to the capital," he explained, by way of justifying what happened next, "I encountered stormy sessions of the Congress. One faction was endeavoring to confiscate the property of the church and to deny to the clergy its rights and ancient privileges. The public was dismayed by these actions and opposed violently any usurpation of the clergy's rights. Obeying the dictates of my conscience and hoping to quell a revolution, I declined to approve the necessary decree to put these edicts into law."

He did more than that. He sent the congress home, expressing confidence that he could govern quite well without the legislature. He chased off Gómez Farías (who fled to New Orleans) and unilaterally repealed most of the liberal reforms. The wealthy sighed in relief; the generals rallied to their old commander; the bishops offered benedictions. "We were perishing," one of the churchmen explained, "but God mercifully turned over a blessed leaf for us and had mercy on our sufferings. At the end of last April there appeared unexpectedly a brilliant star, whose beauty, clarity and splendor announced to us, as in other times to the three Wise Men, that justice and peace were drawing near and were already in our land." The star, of course, was "the Most Excellent Señor President Don Antonio López de Santa Anna . . . whose religious and patriotic sentiments qualify him eternally as a hero of the love and recognition of the nation."

Stephen Austin wasn't quite so enthusiastic, but from the pinched perspective of his cell he accounted Santa Anna's assumption of sweeping power a good thing. For one thing, Santa Anna eased the conditions of Austin's imprisonment. Not long after the general reached Mexico City, Austin was allowed the run of the Inquisition prison. "Our doors are now open from sun rise to 9 o'clock at night," Austin wrote James Perry. "We have the free use of the *patio* and can visit another extensive range of dungeons in the 2nd story of the main building. . . . From this range there is a passage onto the *asotea* or roof of our range of dungeons, which is so flat that we can walk over our dungeons and all around our patio and have sufficient room for exercise." The loosening of his bonds, which shortly followed the dismissal of Gómez Farías, suggested to Austin that the acting president had been responsible for his incarceration, and he hoped that Santa Anna's return would set things right.

In any event, the weeks dragged on with Austin still in custody. He was transferred to a less austere prison in the suburbs, where visitors could come and go freely. One visitor, an American businessman who admired Austin's determination, offered to help him escape. But Austin declined, putting his faith in Santa Anna. "I have no doubt that the political intentions of the President General Santa Anna are sound and patriotic," he wrote in August. As for his own prospects and those of Texas, Austin had every confidence in Mexico's supreme leader. "President Santa Anna is friendly to Texas and to me," he said. "Of this I have no doubt."

PART THREE

Blood on
the Sand
(1835–1836)

Chapter 11

The Sword Is Drawn

When Sam Houston read the letter Austin wrote from Mexico City in August 1834, he thought the prisoner had gone mad. For Austin to place his trust in Santa Anna, and to ask others to do the same, seemed to Houston to raise serious doubt about Austin's sanity—or his integrity. "It awakened no other emotion in my breast than pity mingled with contempt," Houston told a contemporary. "He showed the disposition of the viper without its fangs. The first was very imprudent, the second pusillanimous."

Beyond what he perceived to be Austin's woeful misunderstanding of Santa Anna, Houston took personal offense at aspersions Austin cast on his good faith and that of others in Texas who were less sanguine than he—Austin—regarding the prospects of continued attachment to Mexico. In his August letter, Austin hinted darkly at machinations by his enemies in Texas to keep him imprisoned. "I have even been told," Austin wrote, "that if I am not imprisoned for life and totally ruined in property and reputation, it will not be for the want of exertions or industry on the part of some of my countrymen who live in Texas." Austin had gone on to say, "Whether all this be true or not, I do not know. I am unwilling to believe it." But then he proceeded—twice—to repeat the charge, only to reiterate—twice—that he couldn't believe it. And he asserted that Santa Anna was a better friend of Texas than were those insisting on greater rights for Texans. The rambling recitation was enough to drive Houston to distraction, and to conclude that prison had addled Austin's brain.

Or perhaps interest had corrupted his soul. It was well known, even to Texas newcomers, that Austin owed his position in Texas to the government of Mexico. Mexico had made him an empresario, had conferred on him the authority to assign lands in Texas to colonists and to establish and enforce laws in the colony. If Texas remained part of Mexico, Austin would remain a great man in Texas. But if Texas became independent of Mexico, Austin would be . . . what?

Houston wouldn't have come to Texas if he hadn't believed that independence—from Mexico, if not necessarily from the United States—was the proper and likely future of Texas. He had no desire to spend his days as a Mexican citizen, and if he nodded in that direction—by nominal conversion to Catholicism, for instance—it was only to further his larger aim. Whether Austin would contribute to that larger aim was up to Austin. On current evidence—on the evidence of his enthusiasm for Santa Anna and his suspicion of those willing to press for the rights of Texans—he would hinder rather than help.

While Austin languished in prison, Houston traveled around Texas and back to the United States. He didn't publicize his whereabouts, and for months he dropped from sight. He was in Washington in April 1834, where he encountered David Crockett. Crockett's alienation from Jackson must have made the conversation uncomfortable—but only momentarily, as Houston and Crockett "took a horn" and shared memories of old times in Tennessee. Crockett doubtless plied Houston for news about Texas, and as the purpose of Houston's visit was to prime American interest in Texas, he surely told Crockett as much as the congressman wanted to hear. In Washington, Houston must also have met with Jackson, although the meeting was so discreet as to leave no record. Houston talked Texas with enough other political figures to discover that acquisition of Texas by the United States was improbable, given the bitterness of the minority opposition to Jackson, and given the clause of the Constitution that allowed a third of the Senate to veto any treaty. This meant that the Texans would have to look to themselves—which wasn't a bad thing, in Houston's view. "As to Texas, I will give you my candid impressions," Houston wrote James Prentiss. "I do not think that it will be acquired by the United States. I do think within one year it will be a sovereign state and acting in all things as such. Within three years I think it will be separated from the Mexican confederacy, and remain so forever." As for Santa Anna, in whom Austin placed such faith: "I assure you that Santa Anna aspires to the *purple*, and should he assume it, you know Texas is off from them and so to remain."

Sightings of Houston were rare and sketchy during the next several months. He was reported to be traveling with a band of Indians in the Arkansas district. A British traveler, G. W. Featherstonhaugh, told of stopping over at Washington, Arkansas, in late 1834:

> General Houston was here, leading a mysterious sort of life, shut up in a small tavern, seeing nobody by day and sitting up all night. The world gave him credit for passing his waking hours in the study of *trente et quarante* and *sept à lever*; but I had been in communication with too many persons of late, and had seen too much passing before my eyes, to be ignorant that this little place was the rendezvous where a much deeper game than faro or rouge-et-noir was playing. There were many persons at this time in the village from the states lying adjacent to the Mississippi, under the pretence of purchasing government

lands, but whose real object was to encourage the settlers in Texas to throw off their allegiance to the Mexican government.

Featherstonhaugh wanted to learn more, but, perceiving that curiosity might be mistaken by the conspirators ("The longer I staid the more they would find reason to suppose I was a spy"), he declined to ask.

By early 1835 Houston was back in Texas. He settled in Nacogdoches, where he resumed the practice of law. (It was his desire to join the bar that prompted his Catholic baptism, which entailed his assumption of the saint's name—Paul, or Pablo—that he now included in signing documents intended for the courts.) He observed the growing tension between the Texans and the Mexican government, and awaited his opportunity.

While Houston watched and waited, Santa Anna tightened his grip on the Mexican government. One by one he dismantled the institutions of federalism, dissolving the state legislatures, disbanding the state militias, and finally doing away with the states altogether, demoting them to mere departments of the national government. Meanwhile he made the national government an instrument of his own authority. He repealed the liberal reforms of Gómez Farías and engineered elections that transformed the congress into his rubber stamp.

The changes provoked resistance in various parts of the country. Federalists in Zacatecas, northwest of Mexico City, refused to comply with the order to disband the militia, insisting on retaining this last defense of states' rights. Santa Anna thereupon determined to teach the Zacatecans a lesson—the lesson he had learned from

General Arredondo years earlier in Texas. He personally led an army against Zacatecas, crushing the militia before turning his men loose on the populace at large to make a brutal example of what insurgents could expect from him. The slaughter exceeded that of the Medina, and it included hundreds of women and children. The message was unmistakable: all who opposed the will of the president-general should expect no mercy if their opposition failed.

As part of his plan to restore order to the northern frontier, Santa Anna dispatched his brother-in-law, General Martín Perfecto de Cos, to Texas with several hundred men. Cos's orders were to accomplish in Texas what had been accomplished in Zacatecas—the disarming of the citizenry and the preemption of future resistance. Cos was not an evil man; he doubtless preferred that the disarming take place peacefully. But he had his orders, and he had the example of Zacatecas. If peaceful methods didn't suffice, the Texans should expect the sword, wielded as harshly as necessary. Nor would Cos be lulled by Texan protests of adherence to the Mexican constitution. "The plans of the revolutionists of Texas are well known to this commandancy," Cos announced. "And it is quite useless and vain to cover them with a hypocritical adherence to the federal constitution. The constitution by which all Mexicans may be governed is the constitution which the colonists of Texas must obey, no matter on what principles it may be formed."

William Travis, as a lawyer, might have argued this point with Cos on constitutional grounds, but circumstance and temperament took him in a different direction. After the 1832 fight at Anahuac, Travis had moved to San Felipe, where he got to know Stephen Austin and the early settlers, enrolled some of them as law clients, and gained a greater appreciation of their concern lest rash action jeopardize all they had accomplished since coming to Texas. Meanwhile Travis himself acquired a stake in the status quo when he earned appointment as secretary to the San Felipe ayuntamiento.

Something else toned down the rebelliousness that marked Travis's early manhood: he fell in love. For many months after reaching Texas, Travis sowed wild oats with reckless abandon. A diary he kept during this period recorded his conquests. "Chingaba una mujer que es cincuenta y seis en mi vida," he wrote on September 26, 1833, in the Spanish he reserved for matters romantic. "I fucked a woman that is the fifty-sixth in my life." His exhausting pace occasionally caught up with him. "No pudiera," he wrote regarding the night of February 21, 1834. "I could not." Another night, with a prostitute ("Pagaba un peso," he wrote: "I paid one peso") proved "malo." Worse than impotence was infection. "Venereo mala," he lamented on March 28.

But a case of the clap—which he medicated with mercury—didn't prevent the frontier Lothario from maintaining the chase. What *did* slow him down was love, as opposed to mere sex. Travis met Rebecca Cummings during the winter of 1833–34. She was the sister of an innkeeper whose Mill Creek premises Travis frequented, and after catching the young lawyer's eye she captured his heart. By mid-February he had told her how he felt, and she reciprocated. "Proposals &c agreeably received," he wrote triumphantly on February 16. During the following weeks he devoted every spare moment to Rebecca. "Spent day pleasantly in la sociedad de mi inamorata," he wrote on March 21. When work or bad weather derailed a rendezvous, he cursed his bad luck. "Started to Mill Creek; waters all swimming & prairie so boggy," he wrote one rainy night. "Could not go. *The first time I ever turned back in my life.*"

The couple agreed to wed, assuming certain difficulties could be

resolved. The first was Travis's reluctance to leave off with the prosti-
tutes, whom he continued to visit while courting Rebecca. The second
was his previous—and persisting—marriage to Rosanna. Precisely
how Travis explained Rosanna to Rebecca is unclear; doubtless his
version of their separation favored his current case. Rebecca wasn't
easily persuaded, but his passion wore down her resistance. "Reception cold, but conclusion very hot," he recorded on April 1. The next
day they reached "a simple understanding"—apparently that they
would be married as soon as Travis could divorce Rosanna. This would
take time, as Rosanna had to petition the Alabama legislature for a
special bill dissolving the marriage, and because the likeliest ground
for the action was abandonment, which legally required three years of
absence and nonsupport. As things happened, Rosanna herself found
someone else, and in her new suitor discovered cause to hasten her
release from Travis. But the Alabama legislature could not be hurried,
and though the process moved forward in late 1834 and early 1835, it
did so with southern deliberation.

If Travis wasn't the reflexive rebel he had been at twenty-two (he
turned twenty-six in 1835), he remained touchy on the issue of Texan
rights. In the spring of 1835 trouble again developed at Anahuac, and
again over import taxes. Since 1832 the collection of the duties had
been intermittent and haphazard; those importers who seriously objected to paying resorted to smuggling, with little worry about legal
sanction. But as part of Santa Anna's campaign for law and order in
Texas, a new contingent of troops was sent to Anahuac to ensure collection of the customs duties. This irked the merchants there, one of
whom, Andrew Briscoe, sputtered his exasperation:

I landed at this place near 4 weeks. Since, I have had some damned rough usage, having my goods landed against my will by military force. The people would calmly stand by and see me lose all. God damn them. I went to Miloska to get justice but failed. The roughest affair and most dangerous exertions implied. My business has been delayed. My provisions and groceries have been [confiscated] as contraband, and the whole duties claimed on balance and the goods withheld till the duties shall be paid. And all this by deputy collector and 40 soldiers!!!

The merchants' annoyance prompted acts of sabotage and evasion, which provoked a further crackdown. When a cargo of lumber consigned to the government and landed at Anahuac mysteriously caught fire, the authorities stepped up patrols and confiscations. When passengers aboard a schooner belonging to one of Travis's clients were discovered without passports, the schooner was seized and its cargo impounded. The boat, with the offending passengers as prisoners, was taken to Veracruz.

Nearly every American in Texas knew—and the few who didn't were quickly informed—that precisely such actions had triggered the American Revolution, which started with disputes over import taxes and escalated when offenders were hauled off to Britain for trial. Travis appreciated the parallel, and the fact that his friends and clients were among the victims of the new crackdown gave him additional reason to get involved. In June, Andrew Briscoe and another man tussled with some Mexican soldiers enforcing the customs rules; the two men were arrested. Although the second man was soon released, Briscoe remained in custody. The news of the arrest reached San Felipe roughly coincident with word of the approach of General Cos, and with the publication of an intercepted letter written by

Colonel Domingo Ugartechea, the Mexican commander in Texas, predicting, "In a very short time the affairs of Texas will be definitely settled. . . . These revolutionaries will be ground down."

This was more than Travis could bear. He organized a band of volunteer soldiers, who elected him captain. They rode to Anahuac, where, supported by a boat bearing a small cannon, Travis ordered the Mexican commander to surrender his post. When the commander demurred, Travis threatened to kill every member of the garrison. Unsure how large the rebel force was, and how committed his own men were to holding the fort, the commander put the question to his officers, who voted for discretion over unthinking valor. Upon receiving assurances that they wouldn't be harmed if they complied with Travis's ultimatum, the Mexicans evacuated Anahuac and rode off toward the Rio Grande.

Travis was understandably proud of himself for facing down those he deemed the minions of the tyrant Santa Anna, but not everyone in Texas shared his pleasure. Most of the established property owners continued to hope the current troubles would blow over, and they feared anything that might bring Santa Anna's wrath upon them. They muttered against Travis and considered how to rein him in.

Travis grew more popular when Cos ordered his arrest. "As it is impossible that the attack made upon the garrison of Anahuac should pass with impunity," Cos wrote to Colonel Ugartechea, "I require and stimulate the patriotism of your honor to proceed immediately and without excuse to the apprehension of the ungrateful and bad citizen, Juliano Barret Travis, who headed the revolutionary party. . . . He ought to have been punished long since."

The old settlers worried more than ever at this escalation of events, but among the newcomers Travis again became a hero. The local authorities refused to carry out the arrest orders, and by their refusal joined the resistance to Santa Anna. When the Mexican gov-

ernment placed a thousand-dollar bounty on Travis's head, his reputation was ensured.

Travis was delighted. "I discharged what I conceived to be my
duty to my country to the best of my ability," he said, as modestly as
he could. Lowering his reserve, he added, "Thank God! Principle has
triumphed over prejudice, passion, cowardice, and slavery. Texas is
herself again. . . . I feel the victory we have gained, and I glory in it."

Arrest did even more for James Bowie than for William Travis. The
two years till 1835 were the most difficult in Bowie's life: hard on his
reputation and hard on him personally. His personal troubles began
with the cholera outbreak that had coincided with Austin's departure
for Mexico City. Bowie was traveling in the United States at the time,
and Juan Veramendi evacuated himself and his family, including
Bowie's bride, Ursula, to Coahuila to escape the infection. But the
epidemic outpaced them, and first Veramendi's wife, then the governor himself, then Ursula succumbed to the disease. As it happened,
Bowie, at Natchez, Mississippi, fell gravely ill with malaria at about
the same time, and though he managed to beat back the parasites that
infested his bloodstream, the news of Ursula's death provoked a re-
lapse. Bowie's marriage had begun in part as a match of (his) conve-
nience, but it had grown into much more, and with Ursula's passing
he wondered whether his own life was worth living. For months he
could think of little besides his loss. "Strong man that he was," said
Noah Smithwick, who had known Bowie before and reencountered
him in the wake of Ursula's death, "I have seen the tears course down
his cheeks while lamenting her untimely death."

But Bowie had survived bullets and arrows and infectious disease, and he survived his broken heart. He returned to Texas to settle

the Veramendi estate (thereby letting himself off the hook he had fashioned by his exaggerated claims of prenuptial wealth). And notwithstanding his mourning, his old feistiness reemerged. After a brawl in San Antonio, he complained that a friend had witnessed the fight without coming to his aid. "Why, Jim," the friend said (according to the recollection of a third party), "you were in the wrong." Bowie replied, "Don't you suppose I know that as well as you do? That's just why I needed a friend. If I had been in the right, I would have had plenty of them."

The speculative instinct also resurfaced. For several years the residents, merchants, and politicians of Monclova, the historic capital of Coahuila, had been trying to recapture the state government of Coahuila y Texas from Saltillo, the seat of government of the dual state since 1824. In 1833 the Monclovans succeeded. But the Saltillans contested the transfer, and the turmoil surrounding the fight produced unusual opportunities for turning state power to private purposes. Among the opportunists were speculators who persuaded the Monclova government to sell them public land in Texas for a small fraction of its market value. Samuel Williams, Austin's partner, was one of this clique, as was Bowie, who wound up with title to more than a half million acres near Nacogdoches. When word of the deal surfaced, Williams's reputation for probity was ruined among the Texans (as was his relationship with Austin, who furiously distanced himself from Williams and the sweetheart deal). Bowie's reputation suffered less damage, on account of having less far to fall. But to those who had hoped his connection to the Veramendis might make an honest man of him, the reeking scandal suggested a dismaying reversion to form.

Luckily for Bowie, he was arrested by General Cos's soldiers while heading from Monclova toward the Rio Grande. Cos wasn't after land jobbers but rather the Monclova officials with whom Bowie was traveling. And in fact the general lowered his guard long enough for Bowie to escape after two weeks in captivity. Yet in fleeing to the American settlements with word that Cos was right behind, Bowie became something of a Texan Paul Revere, and his speculative excesses were largely forgotten.

Bowie's reputation rose further in the weeks that followed. The alarm at the approach of the Mexican army spurred the spontaneous gathering of militia units, one of which, at Nacogdoches, elected Bowie its colonel. Seizing the moment, Bowie led his men to the local Mexican armory, where they helped themselves to its contents while the overwhelmed Mexican commander stood by speechless. With his men now armed, Bowie directed a flying squadron to intercept some dispatches addressed to the Mexican consul at New Orleans. When these were read in the town square at Nacogdoches, they confirmed the growing feeling that the Mexican government was engaged in a nefarious plot to subvert the rights and freedoms of the people of Texas.

While Bowie, Travis, and Houston were doing their best to start a war, Stephen Austin was trying just as hard to stop it. Part of Austin's pacifism was, as Houston and the others surmised, a reflection of the empresario's self-interest in maintaining his ties to the Mexican government. Another part of Austin's hesitancy reflected his stubborn belief that Santa Anna had the best interests of Texas at heart. And a final part reflected the simple weariness of a man imprisoned for many months very far from home. "You must look upon me as dead, for a long time to come," Austin wrote James Perry in October 1834. "My innocence will avail me nothing. There seems to be a net wove around me which I cannot understand, and of course cannot resist. . . . A foreigner and a *North American* by birth, shut up in prison, almost destitute of friends and money, far removed from all resources, and in the midst of enemies . . . what have I reasonably to expect except a long imprisonment and perhaps total ruin?" Prison wore a man down, and for one whose health had never been robust—and who had been ill before entering prison—a lengthy sentence might be a death sentence. Had Austin been wealthier, he might have hoped for early release. "It has been hinted to me more than once that a sum of money, say $50,000, would stop my enemies and set me at liberty," he remarked. As it was, his prison time cost him dearly. Inmates were expected to pay for their upkeep; Austin reckoned his out-of-pocket expenses at $10,000, beyond his pain, suffering, and lost time.

The irony of his situation, as he saw it, was that he was being punished for being too loyal to his adopted country. "I have been much more faithful to the Government of my adopted country . . . than this Government deserved. What a recompense am I now receiving for all my fidelity to Mexico, all my labors to advance its prosperity, to settle its wilderness, to keep peace and tranquility in Texas? Do I deserve such treatment? No. In place of imprisonment I deserve rewards from the Government."

Austin's one hope, he believed, remained Santa Anna. From prison Austin observed and applauded the developments that were delivering more and more power to Santa Anna, and he hoped that an expected reorganization of the government would make Santa Anna even less answerable to others. "If that change gives Santa Anna absolute power, or extra facultades [powers], I shall be set at liberty. He is my friend, and he is an honest man as well as an able one."

More-wishful words were rarely written. Santa Anna indeed acquired more power, but Austin remained at the mercy of the Mexican system of justice. Although he was released from prison after posting bail and promising not to leave the capital, his case moved no faster during the first months of 1835 than it had during the previous year. Austin inferred that with Zacatecas and other states in revolt against the central government, Santa Anna was reluctant to intervene on behalf of one accused of separatism. But Austin didn't lose faith in the president-general. "Santa Anna leaves in three days for the interior (Zacatecas)," he wrote in April. "He informed me yesterday that he should visit Texas and take me with him, after these other matters are settled. He is very friendly to Texas and it would be an advantage to that country if he would pay it a visit."

Awaiting Santa Anna's mercy, Austin continued to monitor Mexican politics. He learned of a mutiny in Veracruz and wondered what it meant. "All the rest of the country is quiet," he observed. "To say how long it will remain so would be the same as to say when Vesuvius will or will not explode." The affairs of his adopted country were more puzzling than ever. "I do not understand those of the day—who does?" Rumors about Texas were rife in the capital. "I believe that the most of them originate with persons who wish the Government to send the most of the army there so as to leave an open field for revolution here."

Finally, in August 1835, Austin was allowed to leave Mexico City, no wiser regarding the charges against him than he had been at the start of his detention. Preferring the perils of the deep to the risk of rearrest, he traveled by boat from Veracruz to New Orleans, where he could catch another boat to Texas.

At New Orleans, Austin began to realize that the Texas he was returning to in 1835 wasn't the Texas he had left in 1833. The Crescent City was the jumping-off point for most of the thousand or so immigrants who were pouring into Texas each month, in most cases asking leave of neither empresarios nor the Mexican government. Although no one knew just how many Americans there were in Texas at this time, the total was probably about thirty thousand (compared to perhaps

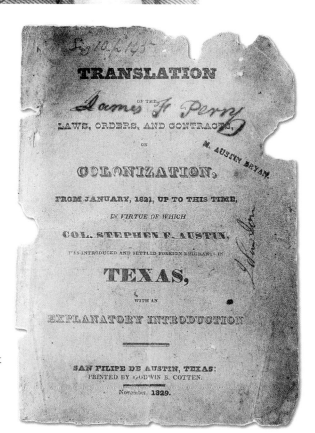

TRANSLATION

OF THE

LAWS, ORDERS, AND CONTRACTS,

ON

COLONIZATION,

FROM JANUARY, 1821, UP TO THIS TIME,

IN VIRTUE OF WHICH

COL. STEPHEN F. AUSTIN,

HAS INTRODUCED AND SETTLED FOREIGN EMIGRANTS IN

TEXAS,

WITH AN

EXPLANATORY INTRODUCTION

SAN FILIPE DE AUSTIN, TEXAS:
PRINTED BY GODWIN B. COTTEN.

November, 1829.

The legal framework
for Austin's colony

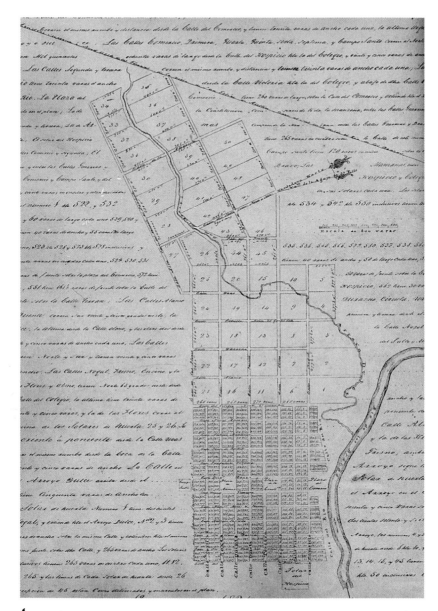

Austin's plan for San Felipe

William Barret Travis
(perhaps; it might be a fake)

James Bowie

David Crockett

Martín Perfecto de Cos

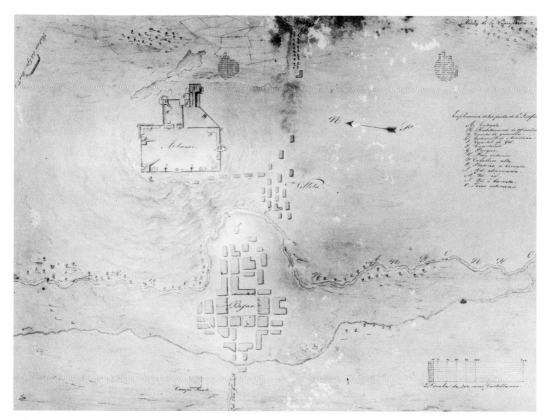

Santa Anna's map of the Alamo battlefield

The Alamo chapel after the battle

The Texas declaration of independence

UNANIMOUS
DECLARATION OF INDEPENDENCE,
BY THE
DELEGATES OF THE PEOPLE OF TEXAS,
IN GENERAL CONVENTION,
AT THE TOWN OF WASHINGTON,
ON THE SECOND DAY OF MARCH, 1836.

TEXAS
FOREVER!!

The usurper of the South has failed in his efforts to enslave the freemen of Texas.

The wives and daughters of Texas will be saved from the brutality of Mexican soldiers.

Now is the time to emigrate to the Garden of America.

A free passage, and all found, is offered at New Orleans to all applicants. Every settler receives a location of

EIGHT HUNDRED ACRES OF LAND.

On the 23d of February, a force of 1000 Mexicans came in sight of San Antonio, and on the 25th Gen. St. Anna arrived at that place with 2500 more men, and demanded a surrender of the fort held by 150 Texians, and on the refusal, he attempted to storm the fort, twice, with his whole force, but was repelled with the loss of 500 men, and the Americans lost none. Many of his troops, the liberals of Zacatecas, are brought on to Texas in irons and are urged forward with the promise of the women and plunder of Texas.

The Texian forces were marching to relieve St. Antonio, March the 2d. The Government of Texas is supplied with plenty of arms, ammunition, provisions, &c. &c.

A poster appealing for help

Sam Houston

Antonio López de Santa Anna

John Quincy Adams

Andrew Jackson

three thousand Mexicans and a smaller, and even more approximate, number of Indians). The Mexican government had utterly lost control of the border of Texas. But so had Austin and the empresarios.

It was a sobering hour for Austin, for the uncontrolled immigration threatened everything he had worked for in Texas. Austin's Texas was designed to be part of Mexico; his Texas colony was to be filled with law-abiding citizens of Mexico. Many of the newcomers weren't law-abiding, and almost none had any desire to become Mexican citizens. Against Austin's expectation and desire, Texas was being Americanized. In 1822 Austin had faced a choice between the United States and Mexico, and had chosen Mexico. Now he faced another choice, between Mexico and Texas. He had sworn allegiance to the former and had served it loyally for most of his adult life. But he had fathered the latter and guided it from infancy to its current raging adolescence.

There was never really any question as to which he would choose. Texas came before all else. Yet that didn't mean the choice would be painless. Sam Houston and many of the other newcomers were already a headache; more to the point—and far more serious— Santa Anna and Mexico could hardly be expected to let Texas go without a fight.

Considering the momentous nature of Austin's decision, he accepted its consequences with surprising equanimity. "It is well known that my object has always been to fill up Texas with a North American population," he told Mary Holley. This object was being realized, in spades. The Mexican government might try again to stem the tide, but it was too late; the Americans in Texas would refuse to let that happen. "It may become a question of *to be*, or *not to be*. And in that event, the great law of nature—self-preservation—operates and supersedes all other laws." Austin wouldn't have said so just weeks before, but he now asserted that the large immigration was a good thing. "The cause of philanthropy, and liberty also, will be promoted by *Americanizing* Texas." Indeed, against everything he had affirmed since arriving in Texas, he now endorsed the logical conclusion of the large American immigration: "The fact is, we must and ought to become a part of the United States." Austin judged that this would be good for the United States, which would then have Texas as a western outpost. It would be good for the western world as a whole, in that it would expand the area of liberty and democracy. "The political importance of Texas to the great Western world . . . is so great that it can not fail to have due weight on all reflecting men." And it would be good for Texas, which would benefit from the protection and stability afforded by American arms and institutions.

Austin wasn't ready to call for a break from Mexico. But the break would come, whether he called for it or not. "A gentle breeze shakes off a ripe peach. Can it be supposed that the violent political convulsions of Mexico will not shake off Texas so soon as it is ripe enough to fall?"

Regarding Santa Anna, who had beguiled him so long, Austin felt the scales falling from his eyes. At New Orleans he learned of the latest Anahuac troubles and of the approach of General Cos. Austin wasn't willing to write Santa Anna off entirely, if only because he had staked so much on the president-general. But he no longer placed any confidence in Santa Anna's promises. "General Santa Anna told me he should visit Texas next month—*as a friend*," Austin wrote. "His visit is uncertain, his friendship much more so." This left the fate of Texas in the hands of the Texans. "We must rely on ourselves, and prepare for the worst."

From New Orleans, Austin sailed for Texas, arriving on September 1 at the mouth of the Brazos, where he observed firsthand the tension between the colonists and the Mexican government. His boat entered the Brazos estuary amid a naval battle between a Mexican warship and two merchant vessels, one American and one Texan. The American ship was smuggling a cargo of trade goods when the Mexican gunboat tried to seize it; shortly after the shooting started, the Texan craft—a steamboat—came chugging to the Americans' aid. As it happened, Austin's nephew William Joel Bryan was aboard the Texas steamboat, and when he and a shipmate recognized Austin on the arriving boat, they broke off their engagement with the Mexicans to greet the returning empresario. Austin was pleased at their consideration but alarmed at the degree to which violent resistance to Mexican authority had apparently become an everyday affair.

His homecoming elicited a tremendous celebration. "A grand dinner and ball were got up for the occasion on two days' notice," Henry Austin reported to Mary Holley. No expense was spared—though Henry thought it could have been. "The only thing I did not like was seven dollars a head for ball and supper, and thirty more for a decent suit of clothes, which I had not and could have done without." Yet Henry handed over the money, as did many others. "There were sixty covers, and despite the short notice the table was three times filled by men alone. In the evening the long room was filled to a jam. At least sixty or eighty ladies . . . danced the sun up. And the Oyster Creek girls would not have quit then had not the room been wanted for breakfast. You never saw such enthusiasm."

The dinner had a purpose beyond welcoming the exile home. Though the recent events had heightened popular concern about the intentions of Santa Anna toward Texas, opinion remained deeply divided on the appropriate response. On one side were the newcomers, with little to lose, who advocated immediate independence from Mexico, accomplished by war if necessary. On the other were the old settlers, with much to lose, who hoped for a peaceful resolution of the

current difficulties, perhaps by a restoration of the Mexican constitution of 1824, perhaps by legal transfer of Texas to the United States.
The war party wanted to ratchet up tension with Mexico, to bring the
issue to a head; the peace party prayed for calm, to let matters sub-
side. And now that Austin was back, each party looked to him to furnish the leadership and guidance that no one else, to date, had been
able to deliver. "His arrival unites all parties," Henry Austin told
Mary Holley, adding, "United we have nothing to fear."

Austin understood what was expected of him, and after the
toasts in his honor, he rose to speak. He mentioned only briefly his
ordeal in prison: "My efforts to serve Texas involved me in the
labyrinth of Mexican politics. I was arrested, and have suffered a long
persecution and imprisonment." He concentrated instead on the
challenges facing Texas upon his release and return.

> I fully hoped to have found Texas at peace and in tranquil-
> ity, but regret to find it in commotion, all disorganized, all
> in anarchy, and threatened with immediate hostilities.
> This state of things is deeply to be lamented; it is a great
> misfortune, but it is one which has not been produced by
> any acts of the people of this country. On the contrary it is
> the natural and inevitable consequence of the revolution
> that has spread all over Mexico, and of the imprudent and
> impolitic measures of both the general and state govern-
> ments, with respect to Texas.

The people of Texas were not to blame, Austin said. "They are farmers, cultivators of the soil, and are pacific from interest, from occupation, and from inclination. They have uniformly endeavored to
sustain the constitution and the public peace by pacific means, and
have never deviated from their duty as Mexican citizens." Perhaps a

few individuals had acted rashly, but such actions resulted from the anarchic conditions of Mexican politics and the lack of local government in Texas.

The Mexican revolution had entered a new and alarming phase, Austin said. "The federal constitution of 1824 is about to be destroyed, the system of government changed, and a central or consolidated one established." The omens were dire. Reports from the south indicated that General Cos was moving toward Texas with thousands of troops; he was said to be planning to burn the houses of leading Texans and incite the slaves to rebellion. How should Texans respond?

On this public occasion, just days after his return, Austin wasn't ready to go beyond recommending another convention—a "consultation"—of the people of Texas. This was the crucial prerequisite to anything that might follow, for it would allow Texans to speak with a single voice and to act with a common will. "Let all personalities, or divisions, or excitements, or passion, or violence, be banished from among us. Let a general consultation of people of Texas be convened as speedily as possible, to be composed of the best, and most calm, and intelligent, and firm men in the country, and let them decide what representations ought to be made to the general government, and what ought to be done in the future."

Caution came naturally to Austin; no one who knew him was surprised to hear him try to banish passion from the affairs of Texas. The peace party went home from the dinner happy, the war party with indigestion.

But events soon took a turn that made caution appear dangerous and passion patriotic. Eschewing the long march overland, General

Cos loaded his five hundred men (not the rumored thousands) on ships and sailed for Texas. Within two weeks of Austin's homecoming the Mexican troops were upon the Texas coast. The fate of Zacatecas was notorious throughout Texas; Cos, as Santa Anna's brother-in-law, was assumed to share the dictator's view of the appropriate treatment of rebels.

Austin was stunned. "Things have come on us much sooner than I expected," he wrote. Committees of safety were hastily organized; Austin headed San Felipe's. He circulated a letter to other towns, sharing the latest information regarding the current crisis. "The substance of this information is that General Cos was expected at Béxar on the 16th of this month with more troops, that he intended to make an immediate attack on the colonies, that there was a plan to try and foment divisions and discord among the people, so as to use one part against the other, and prevent preparation—and that the real object is to destroy and break up the foreign settlements in Texas." Urging every community to mobilize and drill, Austin extinguished the hopes of the peace party that he would continue to counsel restraint. "All kind of conciliatory measures with General Cos and the military at Béxar are hopeless. . . . Nothing but *ruin* to Texas can be expected from any such measures. They have already and very properly been resorted to, without effect."

Doubtless cursing his folly for having trusted Santa Anna so long, Austin now determined to meet the president-general on the ground he had chosen. "War is upon us," he declared. "There is no remedy." Cos, speaking for Santa Anna, was demanding abject surrender. "The people must unconditionally submit to whatever the government chooses to do for them; he lays down the principle that General Government have the right to force us to submit to any reform or amendments or alterations that congress may make in the consitution, &c." Texans would do better to abandon the country than to accept such demands, "for we shall be, under Cos' doctrine, without any rights or guarantees of any kind." But Texans would not abandon the country, and they would not submit to dictation. "War is inevitable."

The duty of Texans was inescapable. "There must now be no half way measures—war in full. The sword is drawn and the scabbard must be put on one side until the military are all driven out of Texas."

Lexington on the Guadalupe

Noah Smithwick was the kind of immigrant Austin had always sought to exclude from Texas. He was irreverent, impatient of authority, and openly disdainful of Mexico and Mexicans. A North Carolinian by birth, a Tennesseean by youth, and a gunsmith by vocation, Smithwick was living in Kentucky in 1826 when Sterling Robertson, an empresario with a grant north of Austin's colony, came to the bluegrass to recruit colonists. "The glowing terms in which he descanted on the advantages to be gained by emigration were well-calculated to further his scheme," Smithwick recalled. Like Austin, Robertson offered a league of grazing land and a *labor* for crops; beyond that he extolled the exemption from tariffs and other taxes, the abundance of game, the fertility of the soil, the healthfulness of the climate in Texas. "In short, there the primitive curse was set at defiance." Smithwick was eighteen; with his brothers he talked of emigrating to this new Eden. One thing and another distracted his siblings. "But it had taken complete possession of me, so early in the following year, 1827, I started out from Hopkinsville, Kentucky, with all my worldly possessions, consisting of a few dollars in money, a change of clothes, and a gun, of course, to seek my fortune in this lazy man's paradise."

Smithwick arrived in Texas to discover that though it resembled paradise in some respects, it was no place for a lazy man. Land was plentiful, all right, but that simply meant that it was worth very little, at least to one like himself with no desire to become a farmer. "I had a strong aversion to tearing up God's earth," he said, adding, "A league of land those days was of less consequence than a horse." He bounced about for a few years, servicing the guns of the settlers and learning about life in this curious land. As a southerner, Smithwick was no stranger to slavery, but the anomalous status of the institution in Texas made it especially peculiar. A slave-holding settler named Thompson, a generally good-hearted man, was on the verge of returning to the United States, where his property interest in his servants would be legally secure; one of those servants decided to flee for Mexico proper rather than go back. "But he soon wearied of 'husks' [tamales], and, returning voluntarily, surrendered himself to his old master, preferring slavery under Thompson's lenient rule to freedom in Mexico." Smithwick believed that by the end of the 1820s most slaves in Texas were aware that slavery was illegal on Mexican soil; it was the strangeness of Mexican culture that kept them from insisting on their freedom. Sometimes, though, violence was involved, as the case of a slaveholder with the ironic name of "Pleasant" McNeal demonstrated. "Jim, one of McNeal's slaves, openly announced his determination to leave, and, acting on the impulse, threw down his hoe and started away. Pleasant McNeal, to whom he communicated his intention, ordered him to return to work, but Jim went on, whereupon Pleasant raised his rifle. 'Jim,' said he, 'if you don't come back, I'll shoot you!' Jim, however, kept on, and, true to his threat, McNeal shot him dead."

Smithwick discovered that the Mexican insistence on Catholic conversion had an odd effect on certain social practices. For weddings to be legal, they had to be solemnized by a priest. But priests were rare, and young lovers often couldn't wait. So they had the local alcalde officiate at a ceremony in which they exchanged promises and put their signatures to a bond saying they would find a priest to finish the job at first opportunity. Yet such were the vagaries of love that the newlyweds might fall out before the priest appeared, in which case they would simply reclaim their bond from the alcalde, tear it up, and resume their single lives.

The priests who *were* present were often no recommendation for their faith. Miguel Muldoon, the cleric who visited Austin in the Mexico City prison, was a regular at San Felipe (where he reverted to Michael). "Padre Muldoon was a bigoted old Irishman, with an unlimited capacity for drink," Smithwick declared. One day Muldoon and a fellow convivialist were making the rounds of San Felipe's watering holes when the pair wandered into the grocery store of Frank Adams, where a group of townsfolk were already at work on a bottle. "Frank politely invited the newcomers to join them. Old Muldoon elevated his nose. 'No, I never drink with any but gentlemen,' said he. Adams promptly drew back and dealt the Padre a blow between the eyes which had the effect of considerably modifying his ideas of gentility." Stephen Austin, knowing the respect in which priests were held by most Mexicans, and fearing repercussions from the government, attempted to persuade Adams to make amends. "But the sympathy of the populace was with Adams, regardless of consequences. Muldoon, who was no fool, seeing that he had few friends, apologized for his offensive language and accepted the proffered drink to assist him in swallowing his medicine."

Another regular at San Felipe prompted Smithwick to reflect on what brought people to Texas. This person, a man named Clay, was highly intelligent and of good family and means. Although he drank heavily, his brilliance shone more clearly the drunker he got. "I have seen him sit and talk politics when he could not rise from his seat, and not a man among us could begin to hold his own against him." His evident gifts made Smithwick wonder why he had come to Texas. "There was nothing whatever to indicate that Clay's emigration had been compulsory, but with a family educated and refined, and ample means, it was difficult to account for his presence in the colony on any other hypothesis."

Smithwick's emigration to Texas hadn't been compulsory, but his emigration *from* Texas was. Weary of smithing, he ventured into smuggling: of tobacco southwest across the Rio Grande. He managed to avoid arrest, but the overhead of the operation consumed nearly all the profits. He briefly hunted for silver in the Mexican mountains, but that yielded even less return. He traveled to Nacogdoches, which he found to be a "gamblers' heaven" with "a regular organization for roping in the greenhorn and relieving him of his cash." (Smithwick added, in hindsight: "Several of its members afterward took an active part in the revolution, one at least being a signer of the Declaration of Independence.") Smithwick ultimately returned to San Felipe, where he nearly killed a man he had hired to cut wood for his forge, but who had drunk away his advance wages without delivering any wood. "I told him I would give him no more till he cut wood enough to pay for what he had already. Upon that he grasped his ax in both hands and, raising it above his head, came at me. I was working at the anvil with a heavy hammer, and, being quicker than my assailant, planted it between his eyes, felling him senseless to the ground." Blood burst from the man's nose and mouth, and he lay as one dead. But he eventually came to, and the authorities accepted Smithwick's argument that he was merely defending himself.

They were less accepting of his part in another act of violence.

An acquaintance of Smithwick murdered the alcalde of Gonzales, and despite a common feeling in Gonzales that the alcalde ("an overbearing man," Smithwick said) deserved killing, the murderer fled to San Felipe, where he thought he'd have a better chance at trial. The authorities in San Felipe, however, said he'd have to be sent to Saltillo for a crime such as this, and they asked Smithwick to fashion shackles for the prisoner. Along with many other Americans in Texas, Smithwick questioned Mexican justice and was reluctant to see the man sent so far away for trial. "The prisoner was a friend of mine, and, becoming incensed at the treatment to which he was subjected, I gave him a file to cut his irons off, also providing him with a gun and other essentials with which to leave the country." Smithwick's good deed backfired when the escaped prisoner, instead of departing, loitered about the town. In time he was shot and killed—with Smithwick's gun in his possession. For his complicity in the escape, Smithwick was banished from San Felipe and Texas. As he was being taken from the town, a friend approached him with a bottle and a glass and asked if he wanted to deliver a final toast to the community. Raising his glass, Smithwick said, "If there is an honest man in the place, may he be conducted to a place of safety, and then may fire and brimstone be rained down upon this iniquitous town."

Smithwick's exile from Texas lasted four years, which he spent in western Louisiana, where he got to know James Bowie and others who wandered back and forth between Mexican territory and American. He returned to Texas in 1835, "just at the time the growing dissension between Mexico and the colonists began to assume warlike proportions," as he put it—and at a time when Austin and the respectable element in Texas might be willing to overlook his past indiscretions.

With war approaching, Austin recognized the virtue in the kind of unruliness he had previously tried to bar from the province. Smithwick's contempt for authority, troublesome when Austin sided with authority, became useful when Austin opposed it.

Smithwick discovered that though the Texans were increasingly willing to fight against Santa Anna, they couldn't agree on what they were fighting *for*. "Some were for independence; some for the constitution of 1824; and some for anything, just so it was a row," he remembered. "But we were all ready to fight."

Smithwick also discovered how ignorant the Texans were of what a war against Mexico would entail, and how unprepared they were for it.

> Our whole available force could not have amounted to more than 250 men, while Mexico had an organized army of several thousand, and there were thousands of Indians eagerly watching for an opportunity to swoop down on us and wipe us from the face of the earth and thus regain their lost hunting grounds, which they had always been able to maintain against the Mexicans. . . . Our only arms were Bowie knives and long, single-barreled, muzzle-loading flintlock rifles, the same that our fathers won their independence with, and that the famous Kentucky brigade used with such telling effect in the battle of New Orleans.

What the Texans did know of the Mexicans inclined them to anticipate success.

> The Mexican soldiers had not shown themselves brave, the army, indeed, being largely composed of peons and convicts—men who had no incentive to patriotism or

bravery, and over whom it was necessary to keep a strong guard to prevent them from deserting. Then, too, the seat of war was a long way from the Mexican base of supplies, a weary waste of desert infested by hostile Indians intervening, and no means of communication except by courier. Perhaps, too, we unconsciously relied on the active sympathy of the United States, whose offspring we were; still, as a rule, I do not think we apprehended the remotest possibility of such assistance being necessary.

The self-confidence of the Texans rose on the first battle of the war. Actually, the clash at Gonzales in early October 1835 was hardly more than a skirmish. A few years earlier, Green DeWitt, the empresario whose Guadalupe River colony included Gonzales, had requested a cannon from the Mexican authorities at San Antonio to defend the town against Indians. The government complied, sending a small bronze cannon, which was installed in a blockhouse at Gonzales. In September 1835, as part of the campaign by General Cos to disarm the Texans, Colonel Ugartechea of San Antonio requested the cannon's return, and sent several soldiers to retrieve it. As Ugartechea's bad luck would have it, a Mexican soldier had recently got in a fight with a Gonzales townsman, leaving the townsman injured and community feelings bruised. With Santa Anna obviously determined to suppress Texas liberties, many in the formerly loyal DeWitt colony experienced a change of heart, becoming suspicious of Mexican motives. Their suspicion prompted the alcalde and other town leaders to refuse Ugartechea's request that they return the cannon. To underline their point, they seized the soldiers sent to retrieve it.

Ugartechea responded by dispatching a much larger force—some hundred dragoons—to Gonzales to insist on the cannon's return. But by now the word had spread that trouble was brewing, and volunteers began arriving by the score. Late-summer rains had swollen the Guadalupe River, and the defenders of Gonzales had removed the ferry to the east bank of the river, beyond the reach of the arriving Mexican troops. When the Mexicans got to the west bank, their commander, Lieutenant Francisco de Castañeda, was forced to shout across the stream that he had a message for the alcalde. The defenders of Gonzales replied, similarly shouting over the rush of the river, that the alcalde was absent. Castañeda, whose orders from Ugartechea were to avoid violence if possible, said he'd wait for the alcalde to return. He had his men pitch camp on the west bank of the river, opposite the town.

While Castañeda waited, more volunteers arrived at Gonzales, until they substantially outnumbered the Mexicans. Following the frontier tradition, they elected officers, including John Moore as colonel. During the night of October 1, the Texans crossed the river, carrying with them the controversial cannon, mounted on a makeshift carriage. Their plan was to attack and disperse the Mexican force at first light. But a heavy fog developed before dawn, obscuring the vision of both sides and casting confusion over the whole scene. Nonetheless, on the morning of October 2, the Texans, approaching the Mexicans in the mist, opened fire.

Castañeda wanted neither to start a war nor to see his troops decimated, and so, after retreating to a more defensible position, he offered to parley with the Texans. A participant on the Texas side left an account of the discussion:

> The Mexican commander, Castañeda, demanded of Colonel Moore the cause of our troops attacking him, to which Colonel Moore replied that he had made a demand of our cannon, and threatened, in case of refusal to give it up, that he would take it by force; that this cannon had been

presented to the citizens of Gonzales for the defense of themselves and of the Constitution and laws of the country; that he, Castañeda, was acting under the orders of the tyrant Santa Anna, who had broken down and trampled underfoot all the state and federal constitutions in Mexico, excepting that of Texas, and that we were determined to fight for our rights under the Constitution of 1824 until the last gasp.

Castañeda replied that he himself was a republican . . . that he did not wish to fight the Anglo-Americans of Texas; that his orders from his commander were simply to demand the cannon, and if refused, to take up a position near Gonzales until further orders.

Colonel Moore then demanded him to surrender with the troops under his command, or join our side, stating to him that he would be received with open arms, and that he might retain his rank, pay, and emoluments; or that he must fight instantly.

Castañeda answered that he would obey orders.

Castañeda was obviously surprised at the aggressiveness of the Texans, although perhaps he shouldn't have been. Their attitude reflected both the alarm they felt at the recent political developments and the entirely practical consideration that they weren't regular soldiers and had farms and ranches to tend to. Castañeda might enjoy the luxury of patience, of awaiting further orders, but they did not—and anyway, acknowledging no higher authority than themselves, they had no one to await orders from. In coming to Gonzales, the Texans had left their homes unguarded; for all they knew, Indians even at that moment might be taking advantage of their absence and wreaking havoc on their families and homesteads. Under the circumstances, prudence dictated a forward defense of their rights against Santa Anna.

By this time some of the Texans had raised a banner beside the disputed cannon, with black letters on a white field issuing a challenge: "COME AND TAKE IT." As soon as Moore returned to the Texan lines, the cannon roared a challenge of its own, firing a charge of metal scraps toward the Mexicans. The Kentucky rifles of the Texans threatened more actual damage as the Texans advanced. But neither the cannon nor the rifles in fact inflicted much harm, for Castañeda quickly abandoned the field and headed for San Antonio. "Your Lordship's orders were for me to retire without compromising the honor of Mexican arms," he reminded Ugartechea, by way of explanation.

The casualties from this first clash were light: a handful on the Mexican side, and even fewer among the Texans. Yet the Texans accounted it a stirring victory and a fateful step, as Noah Smithwick explained (in simultaneously tallying its cost): "It was our Lexington, though a bloodless one, save that a member of the 'awkward squad' took a header from his horse, thereby bringing his nasal appendage into such intimate association with Mother Earth as to draw forth a copious stream of the sanguinary fluid. But the fight was on. Not a man of us thought of receding from the position in which this bold act had placed us."

Like Lexington in April 1775, Gonzales in October 1835 signaled a transformation in the troubles between the insurgents and the government they opposed. In each case the insurgents had previously engaged in violence against the government (the Stamp Act riots and

the Boston Tea Party in the first instance, the Anahuac and Nacogdoches disturbances in the second), but in each case the violence had
been sporadic, more or less spontaneous, and inspired by particular,
remediable grievances. At Lexington, and again at Gonzales, the insurgency became more deliberate, better organized, and more pur-
poseful. In short, insurgency became rebellion—which would
become revolution.

Before long the rhetoric of the American Revolution would trip
off the tongues of the Texas rebels. Indeed, the parallels were already
being drawn: the defenders of Gonzales rode into battle after hearing
a sermon by a local Methodist preacher that perorated: "The same
blood that animated the hearts of our ancestors in '76 still flows in
our veins." But just as the American rebels of the 1770s required time
to determine the ultimate objectives of their struggle against King
George, so the Texas rebels of the 1830s had to argue about what their
fight against Santa Anna should yield. As of the battle of Gonzales,
there was no body that could speak for all the Texans—or even for the
American majority. In other words, Texas lacked its Continental
Congress. Stephen Austin and others were trying to remedy this deficiency, by means of the consultation Austin had endorsed at his
welcome-home dinner. But as late as September, even this comparatively innocuous undertaking continued to meet resistance from
those who hoped to avoid provoking Santa Anna. By backing the consultation, Austin increased the likelihood that it would take place,
and the landing of General Cos made the consultation more likely
still. With the outbreak of fighting at Gonzales, the question was no
longer whether it would meet, but whether it could meet soon
enough. Ironically, though, the fighting delayed the gathering by
drawing many of the potential delegates to the front. Given a choice
between fighting and talking about fighting, most Texans preferred

the real thing. An October call to the delegates failed to achieve a quorum, which wasn't attained till early November.

Yet the campaign against Cos and the Mexicans required some kind of organization, and the Texas rebels supplied it in their typical ad hoc mode. The various communities raised companies of volunteers, which elected their own commanders (with Gonzales choosing John Moore, San Felipe Stephen Austin, and Nacogdoches Sam Houston). As the companies coalesced after Gonzales, their officers recognized the need for a commander in chief. Several budding George Washingtons thought they fit the bill; unable to choose among them, the group offered the post to Austin, who accepted.

From the standpoint of politics, the choice was logical enough. Austin remained the most unifying figure in Texas. Although committed by now to independence, he appreciated the need to bring the diffident along slowly. "No more doubts, no submission," he wrote privately. "*I hope to see Texas forever free from Mexican domination of any kind.*" He added, however, "It is yet too soon to say this publicly. . . . That is the point we shall aim at, and it is the one I am aiming at. But we must arrive at it by *steps*, and not all at one jump."

Austin discerned a tactical advantage in appealing to Mexican federalists, who resented Santa Anna's usurpation and might cooperate in his overthrow. One group of federalists was known to be in New Orleans, organizing an expedition against central Mexico. Austin and Texas were in no position to offer anything other than moral support to this venture, but to the extent it even began to succeed, it would distract Santa Anna and perhaps require him to pull Cos and his troops south. And this—the expulsion of Mexican forces from Texas—was the primary goal at present.

Austin, moreover, hoped to bring aboard as many Mexican Texans as possible. At this point, with the Americans in Texas outnumbering the Tejanos by about ten to one, many of the Americans were speaking of the struggle against Santa Anna as a contest of cultures or races. Noah Smithwick put this view quite baldly. "It is not in the nature of things for the superior race to long remain under the domination of the inferior," he said. The Mexicans had had their chance to conquer Texas and subdue the Indians there, and had failed. "And it was mainly because of Mexico's inability to hold the territory against them that it was thrown open to the Anglo-American. It was he who beat back the savage and converted the wilderness into civilized homes. Why then should he not control its destiny?"

Austin wasn't immune to such reasoning; almost no American, in an age that thought in racial terms, was. (Most upper-class Mexicans, including the late Mier y Terán, held comparably hierarchical attitudes, distinguishing between themselves and the lower castes and classes of Mexico.) But Austin realized that it would be counterproductive to treat Texas's struggle as a contest of civilizations so long as there were Tejanos willing to join the fight against Santa Anna. Juan Seguín, the son of Erasmo Seguín, was a devoted federalist; Austin had hardly taken over as commander in chief before the younger Seguín arrived at San Felipe leading a company of Tejanos from the district below San Antonio de Béxar who were as eager to defend the rights of Texas as any of the Americans. How ardent they would be for independence was another matter, given that the Americans so greatly outnumbered them; consequently Austin did what he could to keep the independence issue quiet.

Even more believable as a Mexican federalist was a man who shared living quarters with Austin during this period. Lorenzo de Zavala, formerly a Mexican senator from Yucatán, governor of the state of Mexico, and federal Treasury secretary, was high on Santa Anna's enemies list; having fled central Mexico, he took refuge in Texas among the rebels there. Zavala's presence gave credibility to the argument that the Texans were simply insisting on their constitutional rights vis-à-vis the government of Mexico. Whether he would endorse independence, and whether, in doing so, he would maintain his credibility, were open questions.

★

Amid the excitement at Gonzales, General Cos marched from the coast toward San Antonio. A company of Texans in the vicinity of Matagorda, inspired by the revolutionary spirit, determined to give chase. The Texans were also inspired by rumors that Cos was carrying tens of thousands of dollars in silver to pay the troops and otherwise fund the suppression of Texan liberties. The rebels guessed that they could find much better uses for the silver. Some hoped, in addition, to capture Cos himself; as kin (if only by marriage) to Santa Anna, he ought to be a valuable hostage.

But Cos moved quickly, and by the time the company, headed by George Collinsworth (lately of Mississippi), hit the road, the Mexican general was out of reach. Rather than retire empty-handed, the company—numbering more than a hundred, including some thirty Tejanos—marched to La Bahía, or Goliad, as it had come to be called. The town's garrison consisted of a handful of officers and perhaps fifty men, none of whom were eager to risk their lives in defense of the post. Collinsworth sent a message to the largely Tejano civil authorities of the town, demanding that they surrender and encouraging them to join the rebellion. The civil leaders weren't any more eager than the soldiers to tangle with the rebels, but neither were they sufficiently convinced of the rebels' staying power to risk taking their part, despite the Texans' assurance that they were fighting not for independence but for the constitution of 1824.

As a result, Collinsworth and the Texans decided to storm the town. The attack took place on the morning of October 10, and was over in less than half an hour. The Mexican resistance was mostly perfunctory, so that the commander could say he had surrendered to superior force. The Texans captured an arsenal of small arms, including, in the words of a post-action inventory that partly explained the Mexicans' reluctance to fight: "200 stands of muskets and carbines, some of which might be made serviceable by small repairs but the greater part are broken and entirely useless."

More important than the Goliad arsenal was the location of the town, astride the main route from San Antonio to the sea. Cos might have traveled up the San Antonio River without a fight, but he wouldn't travel back down without one. Even more to the point, he wouldn't be reinforced except overland, across the hundreds of empty miles that had always made travel between Saltillo and San Antonio such a challenge. Cos held San Antonio, but San Antonio simultaneously held Cos.

Sam Houston was egotistical enough to believe he would make a better commander in chief of Texan forces than Stephen Austin, and tactful enough not to say so. Houston had more military experience than Austin, more political experience, and greater ambition to be the liberator of Texas. His military experience made him respect the capacity of Mexican forces to inflict damage on the Texans. The Texans might be brave, but they were unorganized and undisciplined; the rank and file of the Mexicans might feel little stake in the future of Texas, but they had been trained to obey orders, a habit that could count for everything in pitched battles, as opposed to the skirmishes that had constituted the fighting thus far. Houston's political experience caused him to see the necessity of grounding the Texas rebellion in a democratic consensus. Austin, the patriarch, could lead the rebellion only so far. His command of the army—such as it was—rested on nothing more substantial than the whim of the officers and men. What they had given easily they might as easily take away. A war against Santa Anna—and Houston had no doubt that it would be a war, not a mere battle or two—required solid leadership based on genuine authority.

As to Houston's ambition, the man who had been the rising son of Tennessee, the heir apparent of Andrew Jackson, sought redemption in Texas. He had tried to drown his love-broken ambition in drink and bury it in the wilderness, but it refused to die. He had been a great man; he must be a great man. Destiny had called him before, and he had bungled his opportunity. It called again. It wouldn't call a third time.

While Austin's obvious constituency was Texas, Houston's was the world beyond the Sabine. In a summons sent to newspapers in the United States, Houston implored liberty-minded men to join the Texans in their struggle. *"War in defense of our rights, our oaths, and our constitutions is inevitable in Texas!"* he declared.

> If *volunteers* from the United States will join their brethren in this section, they will receive liberal bounties of land. We have millions of acres of our best lands unchosen and unappropriated.
>
> Let each man come with a good rifle, and one hundred rounds of ammunition, and come soon.
>
> Our war-cry is "Liberty or death."
>
> Our principles are to support the constitution, and *down with the Usurper*!!!

On the day he wrote this—October 5—Houston spoke with scant authority beyond his own. He certainly had no right to offer land to volunteers from the United States. Besides, any prospective American volunteer must have hesitated to enlist on behalf of the Mexican constitution. Wasn't that the weak reed that had led to all this trouble in the first place?

Houston recognized the contradictions within his appeal, but until the consultation met—whenever that might be—he couldn't avow what had been his design all along: to detach Texas from Mexico and make it part of the United States. Till then he spoke ambiguously, hoping his listeners and readers in America would understand.

On the day after he issued his summons for volunteers, Houston gained a bit more authority. The Nacogdoches militia elected him commander in chief for their district, "with full powers to raise troops, organize the forces . . . and to do all things in his power to sustain the principles of the constitution of 1824." This last clause afforded some leeway, in that the *principles* of the constitution might differ from the constitution itself. Houston, in his first proclamation as Nacogdoches commander, still cited the constitution but placed more emphasis on rights and liberty:

> The time has arrived when the revolutions in the interior of Mexico have resulted in the creation of a dictator, and Texas is compelled to assume an attitude defensive of her rights. . . . War is our only alternative! *War, in defense of our rights,* must be our motto! . . . The morning of glory is dawning upon us. The work of liberty has begun. Our actions are to become a part of the history of mankind. Patriotic millions will sympathize in our struggles, while nations will admire our achievements. . . . Our only ambition is the attainment of rational liberty—the freedom of religious opinion, and just laws. To acquire these bless-

ings, we solemnly pledge our persons, our property, and our lives.

Such was Houston's public policy. Meanwhile he pursued a second agenda, one aimed at tying the interests of the United States to the future of Texas. Several weeks earlier Houston (and several other members of a Nacogdoches "committee of vigilance and safety") had written to Andrew Jackson regarding "a subject of grave and serious importance" to the people of Texas. An army of five thousand Creek Indians, Houston's committee said, was being raised in the western territories of the United States for an invasion of Texas. Houston and the others implored Jackson to prevent the invasion and thereby preserve "a sparse and comparatively defenseless population . . . from the evils which were so tragically manifested on the frontiers of Georgia and Alabama, evils which can only be remedied by the skill and generalship of a Jackson."

On its face, this request to Jackson was odd. Why should the chief executive of the United States assume responsibility for the defense of the residents of a foreign country, especially when most of those residents were Americans who had turned their backs on their homeland? And even supposing Jackson did feel for the safety of his former compatriots, Houston offered no evidence to support his claim that the Creeks were massing on the American side of the Sabine to swoop down on Nacogdoches and the Texas settlements. There was a good reason for Houston's failure to do so: he had no such evidence, because there was no such threat.

Yet if Houston's request for troops lacked evidence, it didn't lack purpose. In his private talks with Jackson at Washington and Nashville, the president and his protégé must have discussed pretexts by which the United States could intervene in the Texas troubles. Jackson himself had employed the Indian threat—perhaps significantly, from the Creeks—to detach Florida from Spain; he and Houston doubtless reasoned that the same rationale might be used to sever Texas from Mexico. The purpose of Houston's request was to give Jackson an excuse to gather U.S. forces in western Louisiana; once there they could find cause to cross over into Texas, where their presence might be very useful to the Texas rebels.

While Austin and Houston worried about the strategy of the war with Mexico, James Bowie focused on tactics—to wit, on fighting Mexicans. Bowie was in Nacogdoches when news of the Gonzales battle arrived, and he might have enlisted under the command of Houston. But enlistment wasn't Bowie's style; a free lance by spirit and now by choice, he headed straight for the front. Austin, as commander in chief, had ordered an advance against San Antonio de Béxar, to corner and capture Cos. Bowie caught up with Austin's army, which was growing by scores of volunteers a day, on Cibolo Creek, a half day's ride east of San Antonio.

Anyone other than a frontier veteran might have been alarmed at the ragged appearance of the army of Texas. "It certainly bore little resemblance to the army of my childhood dreams," Noah Smithwick recalled.

> Buckskin breeches were the nearest approach to uniform, and there was wide diversity even there, some being new and soft and yellow, while others, from long familiarity with rain and grease and dirt, had become hard and black and shiny. Some, having passed through the process of wetting and drying on the wearer while he sat on the

ground or a chunk before the camp fire, with his knees elevated at an angle of eighty-five degrees, had assumed an advanced position at the knee, followed by a corresponding shortening of the lower front leg, exposing shins. . . . Boots being an unknown quantity, some wore shoes and some moccasins. Here a broad-brimmed sombrero overshadowed the military cap at its side; there a tall "beegum" rode familiarly beside a coonskin cap, with the tail hanging down behind, as all well regulated tails should do. Here a big American horse loomed up above the nimble Spanish pony ranged beside him; there a half-broke mustang pranced beside a sober, methodical mule. Here a bulky roll of bed quilts jostled a pair of "store" blankets; there the shaggy brown buffalo robe contrasted with a gaily checkered counterpane on which the manufacturer had lavished all the skill of dye and weave known to the art—mayhap it was part of the dowry a wife brought her husband on her wedding day, and surely the day-dreams she wove into its ample folds held in them no shadow of a presentiment that it might be his winding sheet.

Bowie fit right in, as did some Louisiana friends who accompanied him to the Cibolo—"all spoiling for a fight," as Smithwick observed. Smithwick added, "Bowie's prowess as a fighter made him doubly welcome, and Austin at once placed him on his staff." Austin's reliance on Bowie indicated the degree to which the rowdies were coming to the fore; the hero of the Sandbar and the San Sabá might not have made a good settler, but he could fight like the devil, and fighters were what Texas needed now. Austin handed Bowie and James Fannin—a West Point dropout from Georgia who had arrived in Texas a year earlier—responsibility for reconnoitering around San

Antonio: for determining how the town could be sealed off from the outside, how it was being fortified, how it might be taken.

As one of the few former residents of San Antonio among the Americans, Bowie retained contacts in the town, including Antonio Menchaca, a Béxar native and father of four. Bowie smuggled a letter to Menchaca, who sympathized with the rebels and relayed Bowie's letter to like-thinking townsmen. Within days dozens of *bexareños* slipped out of the town and joined the rebels, bringing intelligence about the Mexican defenses and adding to the ranks of the Tejanos in the rebellion. On October 22, Bowie and Fannin reported to Austin from the Espada mission, nine miles below San Antonio:

> A large number of the citizens of Bexar and of this place are now laying out, to prevent being forced to perform the most servile duties. . . . Great consternation was manifested there when our approach to this point was made known. . . . They have 8 pieces (4 lb.) [i.e., cannon] mounted, and one of larger size preparing for us. They have none on the Church, but have removed all their ammunition to it, and enclosed it by a wall, made of wood, six feet apart and six feet high, filled in with dirt, extending from the corners to the ditch, say sixty yards in length.

Bowie and Fannin went on to explain that provisions in the town were running low. "The men with whom we have conversed are decidedly of the opinion that in *five days* they can be *starved* out."

Bowie and Fannin recommended raising the pressure on Cos by approaching the town from two directions at once; when Austin ignored their recommendation, they repeated it. "Permit us to again suggest—nay *urge*—the propriety, the necessity of some movement which will bring us *nearer together and shut in the enemy*, and either starve them out, whip them out, or dishearten and beat them in small parties, in all of which our *two parties may agree on an hour* and cooperate with each other, and never fail of success."

Austin reluctantly consented to move forward, but too slowly to suit Bowie and Fannin. On October 27 they led some ninety men through the trees along the San Antonio River to the Concepción mission, scarcely a mile from the town. There, in a bend of the river, they established a position—in defiance of Austin's orders to reconnoiter and return. With reason, Austin feared that sentries or spies from the town would learn that the rebel force had been divided, and that Cos would exploit the opportunity and attack. Moreover, although the position Bowie and Fannin established had the advantage of putting the river around and behind them, so they needn't fear assault from the sides or rear, it had the same disadvantage, making retreat difficult or impossible.

When Austin learned what the headstrong officers had done, he ordered the rest of the army forward to reinforce them. But before the additional troops arrived, the battle began. Cos had indeed learned of the rebels' exposure, and dispatched a force to exploit it. A heavy fog fell on the river during the night of October 27; in the mist the next morning the Mexicans and Texans stumbled onto one another. Initial shots were exchanged, but aiming was useless in the fog, and Bowie ordered his men to hold their fire. Gradually the mist parted, revealing that Cos had outmaneuvered the rebels, crossing the river below their position and threatening to tie the noose of the river loop, with them inside.

"When the fog lifted, we found ourselves pretty well surrounded," Noah Smithwick wrote, "though the bluff and heavy timber on the west side of the river secured us against attack in the rear. In front was a field piece flanked by several companies of infantry; and across the river, to cut off retreat, were two companies of cavalry." The Mexicans opened fire with cannon loaded with grapeshot. "But we lay low and their grape and canister crashed through the pecan trees overhead, raining a shower of ripe nuts down on us, and I saw men picking them up and eating them with as little apparent concern as if they were being shaken down by a norther."

Bowie's famous coolness under fire paid dividends. "Bowie was a born leader, never needlessly spending a bullet or imperilling a life," Smithwick said. "He repeatedly admonished us, 'Keep under cover, boys, and reserve your fire; we haven't a man to spare.' " Between the cannon volleys, the Mexican infantry charged, only to be decimated by the rifle rounds of the Texans, who similarly harassed the cannon crews. "Our long rifles—and I thought I never heard rifles crack so keen, after the dull roar of the cannon—mowed down the Mexicans at a rate that might well have made braver hearts than those encased in their shriveled little bodies recoil," Smithwick said, not bothering to disguise his scorn for the foe.

> Three times they charged, but there was a platoon ready to receive them. Three times we picked off their gunners; the last one with a lighted match in his hand; then a panic seized them and they broke. They jumped on the mules attached to the caisson, two or three on a mule, without even taking time to cut them loose, and struck out for the fort, leaving the loaded gun on the field. With a ringing cheer we mounted the bank and gave chase. We turned their cannon on them, giving wings to their flight. They dropped their muskets, and, splashing through the shallow water of the river, fled helter skelter as if pursued by all the furies.

It was a stunning victory for the Texans. Less than a hundred rebels, in a precarious position, had repulsed four times as many

Mexicans. The latter lost some sixty dead or wounded, the former but one, killed by a Mexican musket ball. Austin, arriving with the main column of the rebel army shortly after the battle ended, was amazed at what Bowie and the others had accomplished. "The overwhelming superiority of force, and the brilliancy of the victory gained over them, speak for themselves in terms too expressive to require from me any further eulogy," the commander in chief recorded.

Chapter 13

Behind Ben Milam

In the heady aftermath of the battle of Concepción, the long-awaited consultation took place. Considering the mood of the rebels, its proceedings were remarkably cautious and its results surprisingly restrained. Fifty-five delegates from thirteen municipalities convened at San Felipe; the principal question before the body was whether the fight currently under way was for independence or something less. The independence advocates had the benefit of the blood that had flowed between the Texans and the Mexican forces; to assert that the dead and wounded had suffered simply to restore the status quo ante—Santa Anna was both anticlimatic and at least mildly implausible. Such a halfhearted claim would also complicate the call for aid from the East. Noah Smithwick remembered Sam Houston advocating independence to the volunteers. "He made a speech to us, urging the necessity of concerted action among the colonists, arguing that it should be for independence; otherwise we could expect no assistance from other powers." (Smithwick also remembered that Houston initially cut an unprepossessing figure among the officers. "He rode into our camp alone, mounted on a little yellow Spanish stallion so diminutive that old Sam's long legs, incased in the conventional buckskin, almost touched the ground"). Whatever Houston's continuing connections in Washington, he knew—from his own futile experience promoting aid to Greek freedom fighters, if from nothing else—that diplomatic recognition would have to precede any official American support for the Texas rebels, and that diplomatic recognition required a declaration of independence.

Against the advocates of independence were the conservative defenders of the status quo. These included, as always, those early settlers who had grown comfortable under Mexican rule and who now became alarmed at the ascendancy of such late arrivals as Houston and Travis and Bowie. Mexico—before Santa Anna—had been good to them, granting them more land and opportunity than they had ever possessed and experienced in the United States. Independence was a stormy ocean and Texas a small bark; better the safe harbor they had known. As for attachment to the United States: what had the United States ever done for Texas? Some slaveholders in Texas contended that the peculiar institution would be secure only under the protection of the American Union; skeptics—including many from Texas's majority of nonslaveholders—pointed out that with the recent rise of abolitionism in America, slavery might be no more secure under Old Glory than under the eagle of Mexico.

Tactical matters shaped the arguments over independence. The independence advocates were at a disadvantage from the fact many of those most ardent for freedom from Mexico were closest to the front—that is, not at San Felipe for the consultation. In addition, the independence men had to answer the objection that independence was a leap that didn't have to be made all at once. The consultation could continue the war under the banner of the constitution of 1824 and thereby continue to appeal to Mexican federalists. If the federalists failed to respond, or if conditions in Mexico deteriorated further and the constitution of 1824 became an undeniably dead letter, Texas could then take the next step, to independence.

This was the argument that ultimately carried the consultation. The independence party offered a motion for an immediate break with Mexico; it lost by a vote of fifteen to thirty-three.

Yet if the consultation failed to take the most decisive action, it did accomplish two important feats. First, it created a provisional government for Texas. In form this was a state government, with a governor (Henry Smith of Kentucky, an early Texas settler and political activist) rather than a president, but little imagination was required to envision the state government evolving into the government of an independent Texas. In any event, under the Texans' states'-rights interpretation of the 1824 constitution, their state government would have nearly all the prerogatives and privileges of an independent government, save on matters of foreign policy.

The consultation's second accomplishment was the replacement of Stephen Austin as commander of the army by Sam Houston. What might have been a difficult decision was made easier by Austin's ill health, and by his belated recognition that he wasn't cut out to be a general. Austin had never recovered from his ordeal in Mexico City, and his condition worsened during the autumn campaign against Cos. "My health has been very bad since I left the Cibolo more than a month ago," he wrote to James Perry in November, "and I have been unable to attend personally to the duties of my station with that activity which the service required." Looking ahead, he added, "My constitution is much too worn out and too feeble for the exposure and hardships and activity of a winter's campaign, destitute of everything like comforts. . . . I have had a hard and difficult task to perform, and am *really so worn out, that I begin to require rest.*"

Had Austin been more gifted at command, he might have borne the trials of the field better. His initial appointment had served its purpose: to hold the various militia companies together at a crucial moment. But with the war now truly begun, the command of the army ought to go to someone with greater experience. Austin didn't dispute this judgment, and in fact seconded it. "It is an office I never sought, and tried to avoid, and wish to be relieved from if another who is more competent can be appointed," he told the consultation. "I believe that my worn out constitution is not adapted to a military command; neither have I ever pretended to be a military man."

Conveniently, but not by accident, the consultation had an able replacement for Austin in its midst. While many of the other independence men remained at the front, disdaining the politics of the consultation, Houston went to some effort to get himself elected a delegate and to attend. He campaigned for the command, but not so blatantly as to put off sensitive souls. "He made the best speech yesterday I have ever heard," wrote delegate Gail Borden (who would gain fame as the inventor of a process to condense milk). "The whole tenor of it went to harmonize the feelings of the people and to produce unanimity of sentiment." Houston's tact and diplomacy counted for more in the minds of the delegates than reports that he was drinking again, and the consultation unanimously elected him general in chief of the Texas army.

Meanwhile the consultation assigned Austin work better suited to his native skills: as envoy to the United States. Austin's abilities had always been in the diplomatic realm; for more than a decade he had shown unmatched adroitness in coaxing, cajoling, appeasing, and misleading the Mexican government, to the benefit of Texas. Now he would turn his gifts upon the American government, seeking aid that might prove crucial in keeping the Texan army in the field.

And if his health improved in the American East, all the better for Texas and for him.

★

Houston's appointment as commanding general was a large first step toward achieving his ambition of liberating Texas. But the appointment came with a catch: the army he would command didn't exist. The fighting thus far had been the work of irregulars, men who fought when the spirit struck them. They reported for battle when they chose and took leave when they felt like it, and acknowledged as commanders none besides officers they elected themselves. Austin's role as commander in chief had been largely symbolic and exhortatory. Following the victory at Concepción, he called for an immediate attack on San Antonio. Some of the men were ready to follow orders; Andrew Briscoe reported, regarding his company of three dozen from Liberty: "Of these I think there are six or eight who will refuse to follow me into San Antonio. The rest will go, intending to conquer or die." But a majority of the officers—including Bowie and Fannin, the heroes of the hour—took a different view and effectively overruled Austin. He might have tried to demand compliance, but between his appreciation of his own military inexperience and his recognition that he couldn't court-martial anyone or shoot deserters, he was compelled to accede to what amounted to insubordination. "We are all captains and have our views," wrote Robert Coleman, a volunteer from Columbia whose fellows had been unable to choose a single captain and so elected a committee. Coleman's statement might have been the motto of the Texas army.

As long as the army consisted of barely organized militia, the problem of indiscipline persisted. The Texan soldiers made fierce fighters, but for the other aspects of soldiering they had no patience.

Any protracted operation—a siege, for example—drove them away. And who could blame them? Their defense of Texas against Santa Anna left no one to defend their homes against Indians. William Dewees, who fought at Gonzales before joining Austin's larger force before San Antonio, wrote, "While we were busy in Gonzales preparing for more active exertions in the tented field, the Comanche Indians came down with a considerable force near the town and committed some depredations." As it happened, the Texans took time from their anti–Santa Anna efforts to inflict reprisals on the Comanches, but the mere fact of the Indians' appearance so far into the settled regions of Texas suggested how vulnerable the settlers—meaning, in particular, the wives and children of the soldiers—were. Under the circumstances, one didn't have to be a sunshine patriot to be a summer soldier.

Beyond this, camp duty could be hazardous to a man's health—even a man less delicate than Austin. With no organized supply chain, the soldiers foraged in the countryside or went hungry. Foraging alienated the locals, which did nothing good for the rebel cause; going hungry alienated the soldiers, whose homes and hearths looked better with each meal skimped. Moreover, these soldiers knew nothing about digging latrines and employing other sanitation measures; they were a medical disaster waiting to happen. Upon appointment as general in chief, Houston wrote to James Fannin urging a withdrawal from San Antonio. "The army at present without tents and the necessary comforts for the men, I fear may produce an epidemic and destroy more than would have fallen in storming the place," Houston explained. The current strategy, such as it was, entailed starving the Mexicans into surrender. Houston thought the hunger weapon cut both ways. "So long as there is subsistence in the neighborhood, the enemy will command it as well as you! So that by the time they are starved out, you will have nothing to subsist the troops or the people."

To ease their hunger and boredom, the men turned to alcohol, which had predictable effects on discipline. Austin, before relinquishing his command, wrote an urgent letter ("By express—very important, to be sent without delay") to the president of the provisional government pleading with him to do something about the liquor problem. "In the name of Almighty God," Austin told Henry Smith, "send no more ardent spirits to this camp. If any is on the road, turn it back or have the head knocked out."

Houston never succeeded in shaping his men into a regular army. From the beginning of the Texas revolution to the end, the rebel troops were irredeemably democratic. This was hardly surprising in an age that made a mantra of democracy, and on a frontier where the democratic ethos was especially pervasive. But it drove Houston to distraction and almost despair. And it nearly cost Texas its revolution. In real armies, authority flows from the top down; in the Texas army it bubbled from the bottom up. Gravity being more reliable than effervescence, authority among the Texans often failed, sometimes at critical moments.

But Houston never stopped trying to make soldiers of his men. From the start he harangued the provisional government to put its resources where its proclamations were. "An immediate organization of the army should take place," he wrote in early December. The government said it wanted an army, yet it was withholding the means to create one. "The field officers proper to command and superintend the several recruiting rendezvous have not been appointed. The regiment of artillery so necessary for the defense of our seacoast, as well as for field service, has no basis on which it can be raised. No officers are appointed, and it will be impossible for me ever to enlist the rank and file of the army until the officers are appointed." The president and council, Houston said, were acting on the principle that officers would somehow spring from the ranks of the enlisted men. Militias might operate this way, but real armies worked differently. "An army has never been raised for regular service until the officers had all been appointed." The council acted as though time was on the side of Texas. So it might seem at the moment, but that moment would pass. Recent intercepts of letters from Santa Anna revealed plans for a major offensive against Texas. "An army of the enemy amounting to 10,000 men, with suitable munitions of war, must be met and vanquished or Texas will be overwhelmed for years to come." Texas might have three months to prepare, which meant that the preparations had to begin at once. "Unless the officers are appointed at an early day, it will be impossible to have an army at the opening of the campaign, which can not, in my opinion, be delayed with safety to the country longer than the 20th of February or the first day of March, at farthest." Half measures would yield half results, when a wholehearted effort was absolutely essential. "We must have an army or abandon all hope of defending the country!"

While pressing the provisional government as hard as he could, Houston appealed, in even more impassioned terms, to Texans at large.

Citizens of Texas, your rights must be defended. The oppressors must be driven from our soil. . . . Union among ourselves will render us invincible; subordination and discipline in our army will guarantee us victory and renown. Our invader has sworn to extinguish us, or sweep us from the soil. He is vigilant in his work of oppression, and has ordered to Texas ten thousand men to enforce the unhallowed purposes of his ambition. . . . The hopes of the usurper were inspired by a belief that the citizens of Texas were disunited and divided in opinion. . . . That alone has been the cause of the present invasion of our rights. He shall realize the fallacy of his hopes, in the union of her citizens, and their ETERNAL RESISTANCE to his plans against constitutional liberty. We will enjoy our birth-right, or perish in its defense.

The irregulars before San Antonio seemed bent on confirming every bad thing Houston said about militias. They defied Stephen Austin until the moment he gave up the command. Austin repeatedly tried to organize an assault on the town, but neither orders nor pleas availed. "I have at various times submitted the question of storming the fortifications to a council of officers," Austin wrote James Perry, "and they have uniformly decided against it. Yesterday I was in hopes the Army was prepared to do it, and I issued a positive order to storm at daylight this morning; but on trial I found it impossible to get half the men willing for the measure, and it was abandoned from necessity." Austin's frustration, as much as his poor health, made him happy to turn the problem of the army over to Houston. "I have done the best I could. This army has always been composed of discordant elements, and is without proper organization. The volunteer system will not do for such a service."

Although Houston agreed with Austin that the volunteer system would never do, he agreed with the militia that an assault on San Antonio was unwise. In fact, he went further, arguing that if an assault didn't make sense, neither did a siege. In the Creek campaign with Jackson in Tennessee, Houston had seen militia melt away when there was no active fighting to be done, and he now concluded that it would be better to withdraw in good order from San Antonio than to have the army disintegrate.

Yet having reached this conclusion, he appreciated that such influence as he could exert on the volunteers at Béxar would be by persuasion only. No more than Austin could he enforce obedience. Consequently he wrote to James Fannin, asking the captain to reconsider the siege, especially as it was less than complete. "Would it not be best to raise a *nominal* siege—fall back to La Bahía and Gonzales, leaving a sufficient force for the protection of the frontier (which, by the bye, will not be invaded), furlough the balance of the army to comfortable homes, and when the artillery is in readiness, march to the combat with sufficient force and at once reduce San Antonio?" Artillery, Houston judged, was the key to driving the Mexicans from their fortified position at the Alamo and in the town. He had sent an agent to New Orleans to acquire cannon, but they wouldn't arrive for weeks or months. Till then, the army should husband its resources. "Remember one maxim: it is better to do well late, than *never!* The army without means ought never to have passed the Guadalupe without the proper munitions of war to reduce San Antonio. Therefore the error cannot be in falling back to an eligible position."

Talk of retreat, however reasonable, inevitably struck some of the Texans as defeatist. The conspiracy-minded had previously sensed a plot by Houston to take over the army. Two settlers from the DeWitt colony warned the provisional council against "the insidious attempts of designing and ambitious men who have an eye to their own ambitious projects rather than to the good of the country." Foremost among these "traitors in the ranks," they said, was Houston: "a vain, ambitious, envious, disappointed, discontented man who desires the defeat of our army, that he may be appointed to the command of the next." When Houston did indeed gain command of the regular army—notional though it was as yet—the plot appeared to have succeeded.

There was something to the arguments of the conspiracy theorists. Houston was almost everything they said of him: vain, ambitious, envious, disappointed, and discontented. And he certainly believed he'd make a better general than Austin—which was true enough, as Austin himself essentially admitted. But to say that Houston desired the defeat of the army was absurd. The army was Houston's protection as much as anyone else's; if the rebellion failed, he'd be lucky to reach the Sabine alive. And with his last chance of rehabilitation shattered, he wouldn't have much to live for.

More to the point, Houston was right in arguing that San Antonio wasn't essential to the Texan cause. It was too far from the American settlements, too close to the rest of Mexico, too hard to defend. The war would never be won at San Antonio, but it might be lost there. The proper line of defense was the Guadalupe.

Had anyone actually commanded the troops at San Antonio, Houston's argument might have taken hold. But the army had a mind of its own—many minds, in fact, and they kept changing. After weeks of refusing to attack the town, the volunteers suddenly decided that an attack was precisely what was called for. The catalyst for the decision was a report that a Mexican relief column was approaching from the Rio Grande. Somehow a rumor arose that the column was carrying a large quantity of silver. Many of the rebels were bored with the siege and intrigued by the thought of booty, and they determined to capture the column and claim its prize. To lend a semblance of order to the expedition, Edward Burleson, who had been elected by the volunteers at the front to replace Austin (by which election the volunteers spat in Houston's face), ordered James Bowie to lead the group.

Bowie and about forty men intercepted the Mexican column a

mile from Béxar but still within sight of the town, across the open plains that surrounded it. Although outnumbered three or four to one, the Texans hardly hesitated before galloping against the Mexican train. The surprised Mexicans fought their way to an arroyo, where they dug in. Meanwhile General Cos, hearing the shooting and seeing the predicament of the relief column, dispatched a contingent from the town. At this, the Texans took cover in an arroyo close by the one that held the Mexicans.

The two sides traded fire. The Mexicans, hoping to capitalize on their greater numbers, charged the Texan line, only to be forced back by the rebels' rifles. The battle raged for some time, till Texan reinforcements—additional volunteers, who refused to stay in camp while Bowie's group seized all the silver—reached the scene. Their arrival prompted the Mexicans to make a dash for the safety of the town, covered by artillery Cos had ordered out for that purpose. With the cannons holding the Texans off, the Mexicans escaped, although they left their baggage behind.

The Texans approached their prize with plunder foremost in mind. To their dismay and chagrin, all they found was fodder: grass the Mexican soldiers had cut in the meadows outside San Antonio and were taking to feed the horses and mules there. This was no relief column but a foraging party; its booty was nothing the Texans couldn't have gathered peacefully on their own.

The ludicrous affair acquired the derisive label "Grass Fight," and it increased the restiveness of the Texas troops. Many had already gone home; others threatened to do so imminently. A rambunctious few, with perhaps no homes to go to, decided to carry the fight to Mexico, via an attack on Matamoros. Though they claimed patriotism as their motive, many apparently hoped to find more worth seizing there than they had discovered in Texas.

Edward Burleson, unable to keep the men in camp by orders or threats, resorted to promises—of an attack on San Antonio. As luck would have it, Cos released three Americans lately held prisoner in the town; arriving in the Texan camp, they reported that the garrison was more vulnerable than Burleson and the rebels had believed. Burleson announced that an assault would begin the next morning, December 2.

But again the broken—or nonexistent—chain of command fouled the operation. Polling their men, the company captains told Burleson they wouldn't attack. Burleson, like Austin earlier, had no choice but to acquiesce in what in any normal army would have been mutiny.

The double reversal profoundly discouraged the troops—many of whom, it turned out, were quite ready to fight. Hundreds more abandoned the camp, on grounds that if they weren't going to fight Mexicans, there was no reason to remain. "All day we get more and more dejected," wrote Samuel Maverick, one of the dwindling faithful. "The general [Burleson] mustered the remaining men and begged them to not all go, but some stay and retreat with the cannon to La Bahía. A retreat seems our only recourse. The spectacle becomes appalling."

Herman Ehrenberg was the son of a Prussian official of the court of Frederick William III, which made the lad's liberal leanings a problem for both himself and his father, not to mention the court. In his student years at Jena in the early 1830s, young Herman practiced the kind of demonstrative politics that spilled from the campus onto the streets of the city and landed many of the student leaders in jail. But Ehrenberg seems to have been comparatively unimportant or particularly clever, for he eluded the Prussian police until he decided, sometime around his seventeenth birthday, to flee the country for America.

New York, the first stop for most immigrants from Europe then and later, didn't suit him, for reasons unclear. After assorted adventures he found himself in New Orleans in October 1835, as news of the incipient revolution in Texas crossed the Sabine and floated down the Red and Mississippi Rivers. "Reports of the events in Texas filled the newspapers of the city, and the whole press, indifferent for once to party politics, supported the colonists in their rising," Ehrenberg remembered. "Democratic as well as Whig and Independent papers vied with each other in their efforts to arouse public interest in the cause of the rebellious settlers. The success of this propaganda was complete, for all the citizens of New Orleans, native-born Americans as well as immigrants from Europe, Protestants as well as Catholics, were ready to help the brave men who were fighting against Mexican oppression."

A group calling itself the Committee for Texas, organized by Adolphus Sterne—who happened to be the landlord of Sam Houston in Nacogdoches—announced a rally to be held at eight o'clock in the evening of October 11. On every corner of New Orleans placards two feet high called lovers of liberty to the cause of their Texas neighbors. Ehrenberg, inclined to be indignant toward any trespass on personal freedom, and not gainfully employed at the moment, couldn't resist the invitation.

> While the cathedral clock slowly tolled its eight strokes, crowds of men poured into the coffee-house of the Arcade. This place was soon packed, and a deafening din prevailed until the appearance of the first speaker on the

platform. Uproarious cheers greeted his arrival, then a deep silence fell upon the assembly; for everyone was eager to hear the message of the colonists, whose delegates and friends now came forward to explain the cause of the rebellion and to ask for support and sympathy. But these official representatives were not the only speakers who addressed the public; several citizens, carried away by the excitement of the moment, stood up and in a fervid if informal manner expressed their wishes and hopes in behalf of Texas. These short, spontaneous speeches roused the enthusiasm of their hearers to the highest pitch.

As the orations wound down, a subscription was taken up. Within minutes the committee collected ten thousand dollars for the Texas fighters. A second list circulated, for those who would join the rebel ranks. "A Kentuckian, six feet tall, mounted the now empty platform and wrote his name at the head of the list, while the spectators boisterously clapped their hands," Ehrenberg recorded. "Old Kentucky was as ready as ever to fight for a just cause!"

Ehrenberg resisted the impulse, but only till the next morning, when he enlisted in the first of two companies of volunteers that came to be called the New Orleans Greys. (The color referred to their uniforms, which distinguished them from the Tampico Blues, another anti–Santa Anna company mustered at New Orleans, bound for the east coast of Mexico.) Besides their uniforms, the Greys were outfitted with rifles, pistols, Bowie knives, and several pieces of artillery. One company of the Greys would approach Texas by river and land, via Natchitoches. The other would travel by sea, through the Gulf.

Ehrenberg, who was one of six Germans among the Greys, was

assigned to the company that traveled upriver to Natchitoches. At each stop of the steamboat, Louisianians turned out to cheer the brave soldiers. The Alexandria militia mustered to salute the Greys; the citizens of Natchitoches sent hams, pies, and other treats to their camp and invited the men into their homes for a real meal. Ehrenberg and his comrades savored the hospitality and passed the transit time marveling at the moss-draped oaks and shooting at the sluggish alligators (which seemed more annoyed than injured by the bullets). But they itched to shoot Mexicans and wanted to get to Texas. "News had come that the colonists intended to make an early attack on San Antonio. This report troubled us, for we feared that the great distance which still separated us from our friends would prevent us from reaching San Antonio in time to assist them."

As they approached the international border, the Greys moved carefully. The Mexican government had protested the use of American soil for staging attacks on Texas, and the Jackson administration publicly adopted a policy of strict compliance with American neutrality laws. American officers at frontier posts had orders to forbid the passage of the Greys into Texas. These orders, however, didn't compel the American soldiers to patrol the woods in search of the volunteers. "We therefore advanced very cautiously, and spent the night at the home of a gentleman named Thomas, a few miles from the border and entirely beyond the reach of any observation post at the fort," Ehrenberg explained. "On the next day we left the plantation and came without hindrance to the Sabine."

They were greeted in Texas even more warmly than in Louisiana. Settlers lined the bank of the river where they crossed. "A pretty Texas girl held out to us a beautiful banner of blue silk, bearing the following inscription: 'To the first company of volunteers sent by New Orleans to Texas.' " At San Augustine, members of the local militia who had stayed home to protect the community from Indians turned out to cheer the newcomers. Their drummer evidently knew but a single tune, a funeral dirge. "The mournful thoughts which this kind of music suggested were not at all in unison with the mood of the enthusiastic Greys. Our drummer, therefore, began to roll out the lively march of 'Beer in the Mug.' " The Greys got the better of this percussive battle, and the somber mood lifted. Two small cannons in the town square fired salvos to honor the guests; barbecued steaks eased their hunger.

At Nacogdoches the Greys obtained mounts, horses acquired from friendly Cherokees by Adolphus Sterne. This saved the soldiers' legs and mitigated their impatience, as they made better time toward the front. They crossed the Brazos at Washington, which, though raw, appeared to Ehrenberg to have a future. "There were several coffee houses, an inn, and a few shops where every kind of article was on sale, from brass tacks to groceries and ready-made garments." From Washington the road led toward Bastrop, as the Colorado River community of Mina had been renamed, for the man who had rescued Moses Austin and aided his son. They reached Bastrop at midnight, but despite the late hour the inhabitants threw them a party. Large bonfires illuminated each intersection of the town's few streets, and everyone made merry till morn.

West of Bastrop the Greys entered Comanche country. The newcomers had heard of the fearsome horsemen of the plains, and all scanned the horizon for the first sign of the Indians. But though the Comanches made no appearance, the Greys felt their presence. A Comanche band, either on a hunt or simply managing the range—to keep trees from encroaching on the buffalo grass—had set a prairie fire, which now threatened to engulf the Greys. "In apprehensive wonder," Ehrenberg wrote, "we saw that boundless sea of fire sweep over the prairie. The flames leapt closer and closer; dark clouds rose up and rolled slowly over the burning grass." The fire died out before singeing the travelers, but it left them in a fix, as their horses, already haggard from the four-hundred-mile march from Nacogdoches, now had nothing to eat. "Leaves, shrubs, grass—everything had gone; nothing remained but an appalling blackness."

Yet the rebel reinforcements made it to San Antonio almost intact. An English member of the Greys got lost and then encountered a Mexican patrol, which shot his horse dead and wounded him. Another man, the drummer who knew the drinking songs, likewise became separated from the main body of Greys. Surrounded by a party of Mexicans, this Louisiana Creole feared for his life. But thinking quickly, he declared that he bore a flag of truce. His captors were skeptical, yet when he said that four thousand American volunteers were right behind him, the Mexicans decided they'd let their superiors sort out the truth in his story, and they took him back to Béxar.

The Greys reached the rebel camp at a critical time for the Texas revolution. With many of the colonists among the insurgents returning to their homes, the new arrivals kept the rebel column from disintegrating entirely. And having traveled so far to engage the Mexicans in battle, they had no desire to return home with their carbines unfired and their Bowie knives unbloodied. Consequently, when in early December Edward Burleson decided to follow Houston's advice and withdraw the rebel force to the east side of the Guadalupe, they joined the few resident stalwarts in objecting.

The man who spoke loudest against retreat was Ben Milam, an old settler of cussedly democratic instincts and a habit of resisting authority. "Colonel Milam is a native of Kentucky," explained a Texan who was a member of a patrol that had encountered Milam most unexpectedly some weeks earlier. "At the commencement of the Mexican war of independence he engaged in the cause, and assisted in establishing the independence of the country. When Iturbide assumed the purple, Milam's republican principles placed him in fetters—dragged him to the city of Mexico, and confined him in prison until the usurper was dethroned. When Santa Anna assumed the dictatorship, the republican Milam was again thrust into the prison at Monte Rey." But Milam's patriotism appealed to his jailers, who discreetly allowed him to escape and provided a horse. "The noble horse did his duty, and bore the colonel clear of all pursuit to the place where our party surprised him. At first he supposed himself in the power of his enemy. But the English language soon convinced him that he was in the midst of his countrymen." Between his imprisonment and his stealthy escape, Milam hadn't heard that the Texans were in arms against Santa Anna. "When he learned the object of our party, his heart was full. He could not speak—for joy." Milam took part in the capture of Goliad, and his joy increased. "I assisted Mexico to gain her independence," he said in the hour of victory. "I have endured heat and cold, hunger and thirst; I have borne losses and suffered persecutions; I have been a tenant of every prison between this and Mexico. But the events of this night have compensated me for all my losses and all my sufferings."

And now Milam wasn't inclined to surrender what had cost him so much. When Burleson spoke of dropping the siege of San Antonio, Milam declared he'd attack the place on his own. Frank Johnson, another old settler, seconded the sentiment. Volunteer Creed Taylor described the crucial moment in the rebel camp:

Ben Milam and Frank Johnson were heard in animated conversation, and presently they were observed walking rapidly in the direction of the commander's quarters. Minutes now passed as hours. Suddenly the flap of General Burleson's tent was thrown back and a man stepped boldly out and forward. He drew a line on the ground with the stock of his rifle. Then waving his old slouch hat above his head, he cried in stentorian voice, "Boys! Who will go with Ben Milam into Bexar?"

The quick, commingled responses, "I will," were almost deafening.

"Well, if you are going with me, get on this side," shouted Milam. And with a rush, animated cheers, and loud hurrahs, the men formed in a line to the number of about three hundred—every one eager to follow the old hero in any venture and at all hazards.

In fact, not quite everyone joined the hazardous venture, which still seemed to some as reckless as it had before Ben Milam spoke up. But Burleson, canceling plans for the retreat, shamed most of those who wanted to go home into staying in the camp as a reserve force. "Remain like men," Creed Taylor recalled him saying, "and, win or lose, you will share the glory with your brave comrades. Abandon us, and you will merit the contempt of posterity!"

The attack began before dawn on December 5. Milam led one column of volunteers; Frank Johnson led the other. An artillery company under James C. Neill diverted Mexican attention with several salvos against the Alamo, across the meandering San Antonio River, about a third of a mile from the town proper. "The hollow roar of our cannon was followed by the brisk rattling of drums and the shrill blasts of bugles," wrote Herman Ehrenberg, whose New Orleans Greys enthusiastically joined the assault. "Summons, cries, the sudden trampling of feet, the metallic click of weapons mingled in the distance with the noisy blare of the alarm and the heavy rumblings of the artillery. Our friends had done the trick. Their cannonading had put the Mexicans on the alert, and many of them would probably rush to the defense of the fortress. The success of this first part of our scheme encouraged us, for we thought that in the midst of the din and confusion we should have a better chance of slipping into the city unnoticed."

A Béxar native, Jesús Cuellar (called "Comanche," for having been an Indian captive in his youth), who had taken a dislike to Cos and recently come over to the rebels, led the attackers into the town. "Not a word passed his lips, and his eyes were constantly turned toward the Alamo, as if the dense shadows about the fortress held the secret fate of our adventure," Ehrenberg wrote. Suddenly several rockets shot up from the fortress. Cuellar, relieved, explained that this was the distress signal, calling the defenders of the town to the defense of the Alamo. "It meant, he said, that the road was free and that we were safe."

Ehrenberg, Cuellar, and the others ran through the dark for the nearest buildings of the town. They saw several Mexican soldiers standing guard around a fire. Cuellar told his fellows not to shoot, lest the noise betray the attack. The key to success was to penetrate as far as possible before the defenders discovered the nature and angle of the assault. "The farther into the city we ran, the more stone houses we should be able to occupy."

They reached the edge of town without opposition and worked toward the central square. Ehrenberg's company of Greys took a route that ran near the river. "Sometimes our way led across small Mexican gardens, which afforded us a good deal of shelter; sometimes over bare, exposed patches of ground close to the edge of the stream."

They were almost to the square when the defenders spotted them and opened up with grapeshot. The rounds were especially lethal in the narrow streets, which funneled the shrapnel toward the attackers, forcing them to dive into doorways and behind whatever projected from the walls or ground.

"It was quite early yet," recorded Ehrenberg, who took shelter in a stone building that had served as a guardhouse. "Most of the objects around us were still wrapped in the receding shadows of departing night, but in spite of this semi-darkness, we easily detected the enemy's position. The lurid glow of the explosions lit up the central quadrangle of the city, from which the Mexican artillery poured forth continuous volleys of shot. A dozen or more six-pounders seemed to have chosen our small fortress as a special objective, and one of them, which stood within eighty feet of us, gave us a good deal of anxiety. . . . Cannon-balls and bullets whizzed and crashed above our heads, leaving us frightened and bewildered."

What had started as a coordinated assault degenerated into a confusion of individual combats, with the rebels by twos and threes fighting their way from house to house, and from room to room within the houses. At times it was hard to tell enemies from friends. "On our right and somewhat farther back than we were, little clouds of smoke were rising at intervals from several stone buildings," Ehrenberg said. "Judging from the intermittent shooting that these were held by a small number of our adversaries, we promptly made up our minds to seize the houses and use them as part of our quarters. Just as our plans were completed, several discharges from these same houses informed us that they were in the hands of our friends, who likewise had mistaken us for enemies. While they were firing upon us, one of their bullets had hit a tall Mississippian named Moore, but fortunately it had glanced off a two-dollar piece which he had in his coat pocket. The second bullet struck another very tall fellow, also from Mississippi, tore off a part of his forehead, and dashed its fragments on the flagstone and on those of us who stood around him." Before the friendly shooters could be apprised of their mistake, they claimed another casualty, a German who was badly wounded in the shoulder.

By signals and shouts, Ehrenberg's company finally got their fellow rebels to stop shooting at them. Thereupon both parties began reckoning how to link forces. Crossing the street between the two houses could cost one's life. "Scores of lead and copper bullets greeted the appearance of volunteers bold enough to run the gauntlet of this well-sustained fusillade," Ehrenberg recalled. They set to work digging a trench from one house to the other, a task made doubly difficult by the lack of proper tools and the compacted character of the soil that constituted the thoroughfare.

Meanwhile the Texans sought to silence the artillery that continued to batter the walls of their refuge. The Greys had a six-pounder of their own, which they brought to bear on the Mexican position. But they lacked much ammunition and had to ration their fire. Their supply of rifle bullets was more ample, and they employed these to good effect against the Mexican cannon closest to them. "Several of our best sharpshooters stationed themselves close to the loop-holes in our walls and mercilessly struck down every bluecoat who came near the artillery piece, which was very soon reduced to silence because the Mexican soldiers were unable to reach it."

Despite the lateness of the season and a chill that had frosted the neighborhood in recent days, the fighters grew hot and consequently thirsty in the close quarters of combat. Initially the invaders ran to the river with pails to quench their thirst, but once the defenders realized the rebels' predicament, they lay in wait for the buck-

eteers and sniped at them en route. A few hours into the fight, Ehrenberg and some of his fellows found themselves in a house with a Mexican woman, whom they persuaded to make breakfast for them.
Realizing they were without water, she offered to go to the river and
fetch some herself. Ehrenberg and the others wouldn't hear of it; a
snipers' alley was no place for a woman, they declared. "But she
laughed at our objections, saying that we did not begin to realize the
fondness of the Mexicans for the fair sex. She added that since there
was no danger it would be foolish to stop her, and was off before we
had time to hold her back." The woman made it to the river without
incident, as Ehrenberg and the others watched anxiously. "She had
filled the buckets and was preparing to go back when the enemy
opened fire on her. Four bullets went through her body and she fell
lifeless on the green grass. Our men, horror-stricken, gazed over the
walls, and after a few moments several of them rushed outside and
dragged in the well-meaning but unfortunate woman." Perhaps the
Mexican troops were similarly horrified upon realizing what they had
done, or perhaps they just needed time to reload, but in the pause in
their fire that followed the woman's death, some of the Greys got to
the river and back with water.

All day the fighting raged. The Mexican fire was active enough to
make the rebels' advance harrowing but inaccurate enough to make it
possible. "The enemy's fire increased as we drew nearer the plaza,
where the buildings were stronger and more compact, all of them being of stone or adobe, with flat roofs, and a wall projecting around
and about four feet above the surface of the roofs," Creed Taylor remembered. "These walls were manned by Mexican troops who kept
up a brisk fire upon us during the day, and if they had been trained
marksmen, armed with any other gun than the 'escopeta,' few of us
would have escaped death. I saw volley after volley fired from an

'aratea' in our front and not a man's head to be seen. Crouching behind the roof-walls, those Mexican soldiers would load, thrust their
guns over the crest of the low wall, and send a constant shower of balls
in our direction, with harmless effect." Yet the Mexicans' inaccuracy
wasn't entirely a matter of poor training and inferior arms. "It was a
matter of self-preservation, since no sooner did a head appear above
the walls than it served as a target for a dozen hunting rifles, and there
was always another dead Mexican."

The fall of darkness brought a respite and an accounting. The
rebels had gained a foothold in the town, at the cost of one dead and
several wounded. The Mexicans had lost at least several killed and
others wounded, but still controlled the central plaza and the Alamo.
The Texan side maintained communications with Burleson's camp,
from which it received food under the cover of darkness. Burleson
himself arrived to take stock with Milam and Johnson; though all
three were surprised at the strength of the Mexican resistance, they
agreed to resume the assault the next morning.

The fighting on the second day proceeded much as on the day before.
"At daylight of the 6th," explained Frank Johnson, in his after-action
report to Burleson, "the enemy were observed to have occupied the
tops of houses in our front, where, under the cover of breastworks,
they opened through loop-holes a very brisk fire of small arms on our
whole line, followed by a steady cannonading from the town, in front,
and the Alamo on the left flank, with few interruptions during the
day." The rebels extended their flank to the right, dug trenches to
connect their previously separated columns, moved up cannon to return the Mexican bombardment, and continued to pick off whatever
careless defenders showed their heads above walls and in windows.

Late the second day, the row of mesquite trees that lined the river caught fire—probably set by some of the Texans, as the Mexicans had used the cover the trees provided to improve their shooting angle against the rebels. The fire, and the continued construction of trenches by the rebels to connect the buildings they controlled, allowed the attackers to consolidate their position and narrow the options of the Mexicans. Even so, the latter kept fighting long after dark, pounding the Texans with artillery. "Yet our labors on the preceding day had been so strenuous," Herman Ehrenberg recalled, "that in spite of the noise and danger we slept as soundly as if we were residing in one of the large, peaceful communities of the Eastern states."

On the third day, to the surprise of the Texans and probably of the Mexicans, the outcome of the battle still hung in the balance. The Texans had the advantage in arms, the Mexicans in position. At one point Creed Taylor's company was trapped in an adobe house that came under Mexican cannon fire. With each round, another large chunk of the wall blew out. It appeared a matter of little time before the rebels would be blasted themselves. A stone house across the street promised greater protection, but its roof was held by Mexican infantrymen who added their fire to the cannons'. One of Taylor's comrades, named Henry Karnes, determined not to wait on death. Taking up a crowbar and pointing at the door of the stone house, he yelled (in Taylor's recounting), "Boys, load your guns and be ready. I am going to break open that door. . . . I want you to pour a steady hot fire into those fellows on the roof and hold their attention till I reach the door, and when I break it in I want you boys to make a clean dash for that house." Taylor and the others objected that the building was full of Mexicans; couldn't he see their *escopetas* in the windows? "Damn the Mexicans and their escopetas," Karnes answered. "It's that house or retreat. You men do as I tell you." Taylor added, in his own voice, "And with rifle in one hand and crowbar in the other, he flew across the street, and after a few well-directed blows, the door gave way, by which time our whole company was at his heels."

As the rebels entered by the street door, the defenders attempted to escape out a back way. Some were killed, others taken prisoner. But because the Texans couldn't spare guards to watch them, the prisoners were paroled—released on their promise not to resume the fight—almost as fast as they were taken.

By noon the third day, the battle was shifting in the attackers' direction, but still slowly and sometimes lethally. After the rebels captured the Veramendi house, Ben Milam employed its courtyard to scan the Mexican position with a telescope. He failed to spot a Mexican sniper in a cypress tree near the river—one of a small number of Mexican soldiers armed with top-flight British-made Baker rifles. Frank Johnson was later told by a Mexican officer that the sniper, Felix de la Garza, was the best shot in the Mexican army. At this moment he lived up to his reputation, for with a single shot he hit Milam in the head. The man who had forced the decision to storm the town slumped down, lifeless. De la Garza almost instantly joined him in death, for the telltale puff of white smoke from his rifle gave him away, and several angry Texans, seeing their leader die, blasted the sniper's aerie.

A cold rain began falling on the night of December 7, chilling the combatants on both sides, wetting their powder, and suppressing most of their fire. The rebels filled and placed sandbags to reinforce their position; the defenders consolidated within their diminishing perimeter. General Cos sought to regain the initiative by a sally against Burleson's camp, and at first made a good show. "It appeared we were to be swept off by a general charge by the cavalry, infantry, and lancers, playing more music than I ever heard," one of Burleson's men declared. But Burleson held steady. As the Mexicans approached, his artillery opened fire with grapeshot. On the uncovered plain the effect was murderous, and the Mexicans fell back.

Mexican morale surged on news that a relief column was nearing the town. Cos sent two hundred troops to cover its advance. But the news was premature, and the troops deserted. The psychological damage was even greater than the actual blow. "The reaction of those who yet remained was that the deserters had changed sides in the war," recalled Mexican general Vicente Filisola. "There was a feeling that General Cos was dead." Filisola added, "The fact that many of the women and children of the town had sought refuge in the Alamo depressed the troops which yet remained. They became obsessed with the idea that their cause was already lost, and increasing rumors of more desertions persisted."

Mexican morale revived somewhat when, on the afternoon of the fourth day, reinforcements really did arrive. Five hundred troops from the Rio Grande, led by Colonel Ugartechea, eluded rebel patrols and marched into the part of the town the defenders still held. "We entered the town by the trail to cadet Flores' house and from there to the plaza, where we were greeted with rifle fire, acclamations and ringing of bells by 300 valiant souls who for 55 days had been preparing breastworks day and night without regard for distinction of rank," wrote José Juan Sánchez-Navarro, a lieutenant colonel of engineers, who was one of the newcomers.

But Sánchez was forced to add: "What poor support we offered!" The new troops were tired and hungry from their forced march north. Sánchez had been forty-eight hours in the saddle, and after wolfing a small meal of beans, rice, and tortillas, he fell dead asleep. "I slept so soundly that nearby cannon and rifle fire did not wake me." He regained consciousness only at being shaken violently by another officer, a captain, who declared, "We are lost!" The arriving soldiers had

brought almost nothing in the way of provisions; as a result, they became a drain on the dwindling supplies of the town. Making his way
to the Alamo, Sánchez discovered how dire the situation was. "I saw
about 50 horses that were eating the capes of the troops and even the
trails of the artillery. . . . I found out there were no supplies at all, not
even water." Sánchez heard that Cos had been killed, and again the
cry, "We are lost!"

Soon they were. Cos in fact was alive, as Sánchez learned when
he received an order to report to the general. "Sánchez," Cos said,
"by reason of cowardice and perfidy of many of our companions, all
is lost." An intrepid band of Mexican troops, of the Morelos battalion, still held the plaza. "Go save those brave men," Cos said. "I authorize you to approach the enemy and obtain the best terms
possible." Pausing a moment, he went on, "Save the dignity of our
Government, the honor of its arms, and honor, life, and property of
chiefs, officials, and troops that still remain with me, even though I
myself perish."

Sánchez attempted to follow orders, but the Morelos men
weren't ready to quit. When they discovered Sánchez's mission, they
refused to let him pass. "You will not go, for the Morelos Battalion has
never surrendered," their colonel declared. Several soldiers surrounded Sánchez, shouting at him and threatening bodily harm. One
pulled a gun. But Sánchez explained that he was acting under Cos's
orders, and the diehards finally gave in.

Approaching the rebel lines, Sánchez discovered his own reasons for disliking to parley. "We were surrounded with crude bump-
kins, proud and overbearing," he said. "Whoever knows the
character of North Americans may appreciate the position in which
we found ourselves."

But he got what he came for, and more than he or Cos had any
right to expect. According to the cease-fire document, the Mexicans

would "retire with their arms and private property into the interior of the republic under parole of honor" and would "not in any way oppose the reestablishment of the federal constitution of 1824." Moreover, the rebels would supply the Mexicans with provisions for their journey, albeit "at the ordinary price of the country."

Chapter 14

The Army of Operations

By the time of the Texas rebellion, Santa Anna had begun casting himself as the Napoleon of the West. "Some journalists had tried to compare my campaigns to those of Napoleon," he wrote, neglecting to mention that he was the one who suggested the comparison. Yet, egotistical as it was, it wasn't entirely unwarranted. Like Bonaparte, Santa Anna had lived through a revolution that tore his country to pieces; like Bonaparte, he had rescued his country from foreign foes; like Bonaparte, he came to believe that a single guiding genius might divine the general will better than the untutored masses. Bonaparte had concluded that he *was* France, with a mission to save the French from themselves; Santa Anna concluded the same thing with regard to Mexico and the Mexicans.

His assumption of dictatorial power in the autumn of 1835 simply formalized this conclusion. Dissolving the state legislatures placed entire lawmaking authority in the hands of the central government, which was to say in the hands of Santa Anna. For one who had never shown much interest in governing, as opposed to acquiring power, this might have been a burden. But then the Texans rose in revolt, giving the hero another chance to demonstrate his indispensability to Mexico and to the Mexican revolution, and a reason to leave the chores of governing to someone else. He appointed an acting president and headed north.

Santa Anna had no doubt of his ability to dispose of the rebels, for whom he had only contempt. They were opportunists and mercenaries aiming to rape and plunder Mexico. "Our country found itself invaded not by an established nation that came to vindicate its rights, whether true or imaginary; nor by Mexicans who, in a paroxysm of political passion, came to defend or combat the public administration of the country," he wrote. "The invaders were all men who, moved by the desire of conquest, with rights less apparent and plausible than those of Cortés and Pizarro, wished to take possession of that vast territory extending from Béxar to the Sabine, belonging to Mexico. What can we call them? How shall they be treated? All the existing laws, whose strict observance the government had just recommended, marked them as pirates and outlaws."

The appropriate punishment for pirates was death, and death they would receive. Santa Anna informed General Joaquín Ramírez y Sesma, the commander of his advance brigade, of the policy to be adopted toward the rebels: "The foreigners who are making war against the Mexican nation, violating all laws, are not deserving of any consideration, and for that reason no quarter will be given them."

The most difficult part of the campaign, Santa Anna judged, would be the journey north. He established temporary headquarters at San Luis Potosí, where he gathered troops and arranged financing for the expedition. As he had before, he cajoled various wealthy persons into extending emergency loans to the government; as before, this provoked protest and charges that some of the money was being diverted to private accounts. But Santa Anna ignored the protests; as before, he reasoned that all would be forgiven in the flush of his victory.

The grumbling grew louder once the march began. The Chihuahuan desert was never an easy passage, as Stephen Austin and everyone else who had crossed that stretch of northern Mexico discovered. But winter presented special challenges, especially for an army, with its large retinue of draft animals. Their forage—or what would have been their forage—had withered the previous summer and hadn't yet grown back (which was why travelers tried to cross in the spring). Water was marginally more available than it would be later, but in this arid zone that margin couldn't quench the thirst of an army. The weather, though often mild, could turn bitterly cold within hours, freezing the sweat of the men and animals on their skin and chilling their bones. And the distance was daunting, some eight hundred miles from San Luis Potosí to San Antonio de Béxar.

Napoleon knew that an army travels on its stomach; if the Napoleon of the West knew that, he apparently forgot. Midway through the march, he ordered the five thousand men of the army placed on half rations. "I have been unable to find out the reason for this unjust and mysterious order," wrote Ramón Martínez Caro, Santa Anna's secretary for the campaign. Martínez Caro called the order unjust "because it marks the beginning of the privations of the soldiers, just as they set out on their long journey over deserts, in the middle of the winters, which is very severe in those regions, without sufficient clothes, particularly among the wretched recruits who in the main were conscripts and were practically naked." The order was mysterious in that sufficient provisions and supplies to feed the men had been made available to the commissary general of the army, a

man who happened to be Santa Anna's brother-in-law. "What became of these provisions and supplies?" Martínez Caro wondered.

José Enrique de la Peña, a lieutenant colonel of engineers,
thought the expedition poorly conceived. "In an immense, open, and
uninhabited country, it was necessary to take everything along, and to
proceed in a manner heretofore unknown," de la Peña said. "The
Texas expedition should have been considered as a fleet taking to the
high seas or, more strictly speaking, as a colonial enterprise. It was
necessary to select the season, to assemble foodstuff beforehand, and
to provide adequate means of transportation of all descriptions. The
presence of good surgeons and well-equipped ambulatory hospitals
was indispensable, not only for the wounded but also for the many
illnesses caused by prolonged and difficult marches." The troops
needed tents lest they fall ill; their weapons and powder needed protection lest they become damp and useless. The expedition required
intelligence and special expertise. "It was necessary to know the
depth of the rivers, their width, and the steepness of their slopes, as
well as the force of their currents and the advantages and disadvan-
tages of the woods surrounding them."

De la Peña was only twenty-eight, but he had been in the Mexican military long enough to see the damage the interminable revolution had done to the institution of arms in his country. "The army had
been infiltrated by a demoralizing force, which unfortunately was
present in all classes. . . . It had been destroyed during the civil war,
particularly during the years of 1832, 1833, and 1834. The flower of
our veterans had perished without glory, killing each other, at times
to uphold freedom, at others abuses. . . . Its losses were filled by recruits snatched away from the crafts and from agriculture, by heads of
families, who usually do not make good soldiers, by men in cells
awaiting the punishment of their crimes, at times by men con-

demned by one corps yet finding themselves as part of another." With so many reluctant soldiers, Santa Anna felt obliged to order deserters shot, yet the very reluctance of the soldiers made them resent such harsh treatment the more.

De la Peña, originally a navy man, thought Santa Anna could have avoided many problems by transporting his army north by ship, as Cos had done. The troops would have arrived in Texas sooner, fresher, and at less expense. Ships could have carried their provisions far more easily than did the pack mules and oxcarts they drove overland; traveling by sea, the expedition would have been able to leave at home the retinue of wives, mistresses, and children that invariably followed Mexican armies in the field.

Santa Anna wasn't ignorant of the difficulties he faced, yet, like Bonaparte, he believed they simply promised larger glory. "The great problem I had to solve," he said, "was to reconquer Texas and to accomplish this in the shortest time possible, at whatever cost." Mexico remained vulnerable to other insurgencies, and for the army to spend many months subduing Texas would lay the rest of the country open to intolerable danger. "A long campaign would have undoubtedly consumed our resources and we would have been unable to renew them." Time was of the essence. "If the only four favorable months of the year were not taken advantage of, the army, in the midst of the hardships of a campaign, would perish of hunger and of the effects of the climate. . . . In order that the soldier, by means of repeated marches and frequent battles, should forget the immense distance which separated him from his family and home comforts; in order that his courage might not fail; and, in short, to maintain the morale which an army obtains from its activity and operations, it was of the utmost importance to prevent the enemy from strengthening its position or receiving the reinforcements that the papers from the North asserted were very numerous." Critics might carp at this or that aspect of the campaign, but they weren't the ones responsible. Mexico had chosen Santa Anna. "It left everything to my genius."

★

Sam Houston longed for such freedom of action. The bane of Houston's existence during the final weeks of 1835 was his lack of authority commensurate with the responsibility he bore. As general in chief he was supposed to defend Texas from Santa Anna, but in fact he commanded few of the instruments required for the defense. Almost alone among the Texans, Houston had a sound grasp of military strategy. Others were as good on tactics—on the details of attacking this town or holding that fort—but no one else so appreciated how the pieces of the puzzle of Texan defense ought to fit together. "I propose placing a field officer in command of San Antonio de Bexar with a sufficient number of troops for the defence of the station," he explained a week after the capture of the town. "I also design the employment of an engineer, and to have the fortifications and defences of the place improved. La Bahia must be occupied by a force amounting to from 50 to 100 men, and commanded by a competent officer. The main force will be placed where it can command the port of Copano. Refugio Mission will probably be the best situation for a force to be stationed. San Patricio will also be within the range of the cordon of posts to be established for the purpose of the reception of troops until the campaign of the spring will open."

It was one thing to devise strategy, however, and another to effect it. The provisional government was no help. Indeed, the meddling of the politicians made Houston's task doubly difficult. The government ordered that the headquarters of the army be established at Washington, the new town on the Brazos River whose chief recommendation was that its promoters wanted the business and had pull with the general council. "It will give me great pleasure to obey the order at the earliest possible moment," Houston told Henry Smith sarcastically. The meddling only grew worse. "It is extremely painful to me to feel what I am compelled to experience, and believe to exist," Houston wrote Smith. "I have never failed to render any information when called on by the chairman of the military committee"—Wyatt Hanks of the Bevil District of eastern Texas—"and to furnish such books as he wished for his instruction. Yet I am constrained to believe that he has interposed every obstacle to the organization of the army and, so far as I am identified with it, to delay the placing of Texas in a proper state of defence."

Houston's most consistent complaint was lack of funds. He was supposed to raise an army but wasn't given the money to do so. He couldn't hire recruiting officers, nor even provision those men who came to his camp on their own. And when monies *were* appropriated, they found their way into the pockets of jobbers and speculators. "The brave men who have been wounded in the battles of Texas, and the sick from exposure in her cause, without blankets or supplies, are left neglected in her hospitals," Houston told Smith during the first week of 1836, "while the needful stores and supplies are diverted from them, without authority and by self-created officers, who do not acknowledge the only government known to Texas and the world." Houston implored Smith to rectify the situation. "No language can express my anguish of soul. Oh, save our poor country! Send supplies to the wounded, the sick, the naked, and the hungry, for God's sake!"

Lack of money wasn't Houston's sole problem. Although he was the commanding general, most of those fighting in Texas had taken no oath of allegiance to his army, to the Texas government, or to anything else. They acted as free agents, sometimes subject to the authority of their elected officers, often not even to that. They decided when they would fight and when they wouldn't, as Stephen Austin and then Edward Burleson discovered at San Antonio. Many of the recently arrived Americans had been motivated to come by a love of liberty and a feeling of solidarity with the Texans, but even these expected to get something tangible for their pains.

James Grant was a native of Scotland who emigrated to Texas in 1823. Although a physician by training, he became interested in the politics of his new home, and was elected to the legislature of Coahuila y Texas. In the spring of 1835 he was secretary of the Monclova assembly that delivered the hundreds of leagues of Texas land to James Bowie and the other speculators, among whom Grant contrived to include himself. Shortly thereafter he fled Monclova with the rest of the government Santa Anna dispersed. Grant might well have opposed Santa Anna on constitutional grounds alone; that the dictator was trying to deprive him of a prospective fortune in land gave him a second reason to join the Texas rebels, which he did. He participated in the siege of San Antonio in the autumn of 1835 and spoke loudly for Texan rights. Yet Grant's Coahuila connection distanced him from such as Stephen Austin and Sam Houston, and where they were moving—more slowly in the first case than in the second—toward independence, Grant opposed the break. Most Texans considered the Monclova deal a blatantly corrupt speculation; there seemed little chance that an independent Texas would honor the backroom bargain. For this reason, perhaps among others, Grant embraced the 1824 constitution, rather than independence. And he argued that the Texans ought to try to get other states and districts of Mexico, starting with Coahuila, to join the revolt. As a first step, he proposed an attack on Matamoros, at the mouth of the Rio Grande. By taking the fight south, he contended, the Texas rebels would give heart to opponents of Santa Anna in Coahuila and force the dictator to defend that district. If nothing else, control of the customs house at Matamoros would yield revenue the rebels could devote to the defense of Texas.

His personal stake aside, there was logic to Grant's argument, but there was sounder logic against it. The shady dealings of the late Monclova legislature were no secret; their existence, and the fact that the beneficiaries included, besides Grant and Bowie, such other rebel leaders as Ben Milam and Frank Johnson lent credence to Santa Anna's claim that the rebels were merely pirates bent on looting Mexico's patrimony. As for their goal of seizing the Matamoros customs, this was the sort of thing brigands had been doing for centuries. Finally, the idea that an attack on Matamoros might ignite a rebellion elsewhere in Mexico was problematic, to say the least. The opposite result—that Mexicans would rally around the flag—was equally likely. Several weeks earlier, a band of anti-Santanistas recruited in New Orleans by José Antonio Mexía (and including the Tampico Blues of Herman Ehrenberg's acquaintance) had landed at Tampico, hoping to ignite local opposition to the dictator. The expedition turned out to be a fiasco: the schooner carrying the rebels ran aground, and Santa Anna's loyalists were waiting for them when they struggled ashore. Mexía managed to escape, but thirty-one of his men were left behind. Three died of wounds incurred in the operation; the others were executed for piracy.

Houston opposed the Matamoros expedition, but he lacked the authority to stop it. He had tried to persuade the San Felipe consultation to nullify the Monclova grants in order to demonstrate the bona fides of the rebels. He had failed then, for the same reason he failed now to forestall the Matamoros expedition: influential members of the consultation, and now of the provisional government, had interests in the speculation. Henry Smith joined Houston in opposition, but he couldn't control the general council, which proceeded to over-rule him and Houston. When Houston discovered that the expedition was going to go forward, he bowed to the inevitable yet still tried to shape it. He ordered James Bowie to take charge. "In the event you can obtain the services of a sufficient number of men for the pur-pose," Houston wrote Bowie, "you will forthwith proceed on the route to Matamoros, and, if possible reduce the place and retain possession until further orders." Better Bowie, Houston reasoned, than Grant or Johnson or someone he didn't know. "Should you not find it within your power to attain an object so desirable as the reduction of Mata-moros, you will, by all possible means, conformably to the rules of civilized warfare, annoy the troops of the central army, and reduce and keep possession of the most eligible position on the frontier, us-ing the precaution which characterizes your mode of warfare. You will conduct the campaign. Much is referred to your discretion." Houston directed Bowie to apprise the provisional government of his actions by reporting "through the commander-in-chief of the army." And he added, in a non sequitur that was significant precisely for not follow-ing from what came before, "Under any circumstances, the port of Copano is important."

Bowie was pleased at the prospect of action, even a prospect as clouded as the Matamoros expedition. After the rousing tussle at Concepción, things had turned in a decidedly unsatisfactory direc-tion for him. The "Grass Fight" won no one any glory, and by bad luck Bowie missed the battle for San Antonio. Impatient at the (pre-Milam) refusal of his comrades to attack the town, he accepted an as-signment to ride to Goliad and assess the state of that town's defenses. What he discovered was not encouraging, and he headed back to San Antonio to report the bleak news. By the time he got there the rebels had taken the town, and things were as dull as ever, if less frustrating.

The dullness disposed many of the victors, including Herman Ehrenberg and the New Orleans Greys, to join James Grant and Frank Johnson in the expedition to Matamoros. Bowie was inclined to go, too—which was why Sam Houston appointed him to head the affair.

Houston's rivals, however, had other ideas. His reasoning in naming Bowie to head the Matamoros expedition was translucent, if not quite transparent; the council accordingly denied Houston's authority to appoint Bowie, and appointed Johnson in his place. Johnson initially accepted the appointment but changed his mind when the council overruled some of his choices for junior officers, whereupon the council put James Fannin, Bowie's comrade from Concepción, in charge. The situation grew more confusing when the political skirmishing between Governor Smith and the council erupted into open warfare. Smith tried to dissolve the council and send the members home; the council, likening Smith to Santa Anna, called for the governor's impeachment. Meanwhile Johnson changed his mind again and joined Grant in assuming—with the approval of neither council nor governor—command of the Matamoros expedition, for which they began recruiting volunteers.

Bowie was in no mood to sort out the mess, and when Houston, acknowledging defeat in this part of the affair, offered him another assignment, he gladly accepted. What Houston disgustedly called the "Matamoros rage" had stripped the garrison left to guard San Antonio, till it was a shadow of the force that had conquered it. Houston had never considered the town strategically important, and its weakness—and the distraction provided by the Matamoros fever—supplied him an excuse to arrange its evacuation. Bowie, he decided, was just the man for the job. "Colonel Bowie will leave here in a few hours for Bexar with a detachment of from thirty to forty men," Houston wrote Smith on January 17. "I have ordered the fortifications in the town of Bexar to be demolished, and if you should think well of it, I will remove all the cannon and other munitions of war to Gonzales and Copano, blow up the Alamo and abandon the place."

While remedying—he thought—the weakness on his western flank, Houston turned his attention south. The Matamoros expeditionaries were gathered at Goliad, eager for another try at the Mexicans and a first chance at some real booty. "Our party now mustered six hundred men," Herman Ehrenberg explained, "and only the lack of food and ammunition kept us idle." The troops initially accepted the delay as an inevitable aspect of campaigning. "But as time went by without bringing the stores we needed, our inactivity grew more irksome. . . . It enraged us to think that if we had been provided at once with powder and lead, we should by now have already stormed and captured Matamoros. As it was, the procrastination of the Government helped the enemy and diminished our chances, for the Mexicans, aware of our plans, were strengthening the defenses of their city and every day making it more nearly impregnable." The delay discouraged the most impatient members, who abandoned the project and headed for their homes back in the States. Before long the ranks had dwindled to 450. To keep the remainder from following, Grant and Johnson decided to start south, hoping the promised supplies would overtake them on the road.

At Refugio the expedition rested several days, albeit more for the purpose of delay than recuperation. They were ready to resume the march for Matamoros, 150 miles farther on, when Houston rode into their camp. "Tenseness and excitement prevailed in our ranks," Ehrenberg recalled, "for Sam Houston was the most famous and popular leader of the Texans. The vigor of his patriotism, the sincerity of his democratic faith, the liberal tenor of his conduct had won him the love and confidence of all his fellow-citizens." In this latter sentence, Ehrenberg spoke more for the rank and file than for the politically ambitious, but even Houston's rivals had to acknowledge the man's gifts of leadership, which were put here to the test. "The eminent commander had now a delicate mission to perform," Ehrenberg said, "for he came to allay the suspicions, calm the impatience, and restore the satisfaction of the restless, discontented troops. Nor was this all. The army was at present broken up, and the concentration of its forces at some point was as urgently needed as it would be difficult to achieve."

Houston entreated the volunteers to reconsider their campaign. Even as they were heading south, Santa Anna was driving north; why did they wish to leave Texas to fight when the enemy was coming to them? Houston had to admire the daring and zeal of the troops. But such qualities "must not be wasted in profitless labors," he said (according to Ehrenberg's reconstruction of the speech). "In order to win, we must act together. United we stand, divided we fall. I am told that you intend to take Matamoros. I praise your courage, but I will frankly confess to you, my friends, that I do not approve of your plans. The capture of a city that lies outside the boundaries of our territory is useless, and the shedding of Texas blood in such unprofitable warfare is a mistake." The volunteers wanted to fight the enemy. "Will you not do so more effectively by falling upon its armies after long marches and other hardships have exhausted and demoralized them?" The Texas forces weren't large enough or strong enough to be divided. "Since our military power is weak, let our strength be in our unity."

Many of the soldiers were openly skeptical of Houston's argument. One of their officers, a Captain Pearson, stepped forward to rebut the commander. "However great my esteem for General Houston," Pearson said, "I cannot accept his proposal. We have already tarried here too long. What has been the result? Most of our men have left because they grew tired of our inaction. . . . There is no sense in our staying here idle. Why should we bear all the hardships of the campaign and receive so little in return? . . . Let us march on, and I ask all those who agree with me to be on the road to Matamoros by noon."

Ehrenberg was torn, as were many of his comrades. "These two speeches, following close upon each other, excited mingled feelings in our hearts," he said. "The army was overwhelmingly in favor of storming Matamoros, yet the eloquence and popularity of General Houston induced most of the volunteers to postpone their departure for this city until the arrival of Fannin's regiment." But others wouldn't wait, no matter how eloquent Houston was. "There were still quite a few who wanted to follow the immediate promptings of their impatience. Forty of our comrades decided to go at once to San Patricio, forty miles farther south, and they marched away that very day."

In early December 1835, Stephen Austin and his fellow "agents of the people of Texas," William Wharton and Branch Archer, received their diplomatic charge from the provisional government. They were to travel without delay to "the United States of the North," entering that country at New Orleans, where they were to procure and outfit naval vessels for the defense of Texas's coast and commerce, obtain arms and other provisions for the Texas army, negotiate a loan of up to

$100,000 "on the best terms that you can," and solicit donations from supporters of the Texas cause. After that:

> You will proceed to the City of Washington with all con-
> venient speed, endeavoring at all points to enlist the sym-
> pathies of the free and enlightened people of the United
> States in our favor by explaining to them our true political
> situation and the causes which impelled us to take up
> arms, and the critical situation in which we now stand.
> You will approach the authorities of our Mother Country,
> either by yourselves or confidential friends, and ascertain
> the feelings of the Government toward Texas, in her pres-
> ent attitude. Whether any interposition on the part of that
> Government in our favor can be expected, or whether, in
> their opinion, any ulterior move on our part would, to
> them, be more commendable and be calculated to render
> us more worthy of their favor, or whether by any fair and
> honorable means, Texas can become a member of that
> Republic. If not, if we declare independence, whether
> that Government would immediately recognize and re-
> spect us as an independent people, receive us as allies,
> and form with us a treaty of amity both offensive and de-
> fensive.

The tentative, conditional nature of this last part of the charge—
"if we declare independence"—reflected the ambivalence that officially characterized the policy of the provisional government, and
which was mirrored in the views of the commissioners. William
Wharton thought timidity ill became Texas and would doom the mission, and he initially declined to participate. "From the papers of the

United States and my correspondence," Wharton wrote Archer, "I believe that under any declaration short of absolute independence, we will receive no efficient or permanent aid or pecuniary assistance from the United States, they believing it an internal domestic quarrel about which they can feel but little interest. So that situated as we are, we encounter all the evils of a declaration of independence without realizing one 50th of the advantages."

Austin, however, judged that ambiguity still served a purpose. He left San Felipe in mid-December; between there and the coast he encountered José Mexía, who despite his recent reverse at Tampico hoped to continue the fight against Santa Anna. Austin thought Texas could benefit from the support of Mexía and other Mexican federalists; for this reason he believed that the declaration of November 7, calling for the reinstatement of the constitution of 1824, ought to remain the banner under which Texas fought. "A change of the basis now, to that of independence, would give us no more than is secured by the declaration . . . ," Austin wrote the provisional government, "but it would injure us abroad by giving an idea that we are unstable in our opinions, and it would paralyze the efforts of the federal party which are now in our favor, and no doubt turn them against us."

By the time he got to New Orleans, however, he had changed his mind. The question of what the Texans were fighting for could no longer be hedged. Finally Austin found himself agreeing with Sam Houston, to whom he wrote at length explaining the change in his thinking:

When I left Texas I was of opinion that it was premature to stir this question, and that we ought to be very cautious of taking any steps that would make the Texas war purely a national war, which would unite all parties against us, instead of it being a party war, which would secure to us the aid of the federal party. In this I acted contrary to my own impulses, for I wish to see Texas free from the trammels of religious intolerance and other anti-republican restrictions, and independent at once; and as an individual have always been ready to risk my all to obtain it; but I could not feel justifiable in precipitating and involving others until I was fully satisfied that they would be sustained.

Since my arrival here, I have received information which has satisfied me on this subject. I have no doubt we can obtain all and even much more aid than we need. I now think the time has come for Texas to assert her natural rights; and were I in the convention I would urge an immediate declaration of independence.

I form this opinion from the information now before me. I have not heard of any movement in the interior by the federal party, in favor of Texas; on the contrary, the information from Mexico is that all parties are against us, owing to what has already been said and done in Texas in favor of independence; and that we have nothing to expect from that quarter but hostility. . . . Our present position in favor of the republican principles of the constitution of 1824 can do us no good, and it is doing us harm by deterring those kind of men from joining us that are most useful.

At New Orleans, Austin proselytized on behalf of Texas to audiences large and small. The response was gratifying. "There is a Louisiana Battalion, a Georgia Battalion, a Mississippi Battalion, an Alabama Battalion, and a Tennessee Battalion," he reported. Money also signed on. "We have effected a loan for *two hundred thousand* dollars and expect to procure another for 40 or 50,000." The terms were generous to the lenders, to be sure: eight percent, repayable in Texas land, which made the lenders as much speculators as vindicators of liberty. And not surprisingly, the lenders insisted that Texas declare independence as soon as possible. "The universal wish and expectation in this quarter is that Texas ought to declare herself *independent at once,*" Austin said.

From New Orleans, he steamed upriver. Natchez was strong for Texas independence, a meeting there having just "Resolved: That the proud dictator, Santa Anna, like the fort Alamo, must fall. And the purple current of valiant gore that has moistened the plain in the cause of liberty and glory must be avenged." Donations were accepted and volunteers enlisted. Nashville was even warmer. "I have never been in a place where I have met with more genuine hospitality and enthusiastic patriotism," Austin wrote.

Austin found the experience gratifying both politically and personally. "I had no idea before I left home of the deep and general interest that is felt for the cause of Texas, or of the influence which my opinions seem to have in this country." It made him reconsider his past actions—but not to renounce them. "Had I known it sooner, I should have been less cautious than I have been about precipitating the people of Texas into a declaration of independence. The responsibility, however, would have been very great on me had I contributed to involve the settlers whom I had been instrumental in drawing to that country, before I was certain they would be sustained." Yet all was turning out well. "I am now confident they *will* be fully and promptly sustained in their independence."

At Louisville, Austin gave the speech of his life, on behalf of the cause of his life. He spoke of the sins of Santa Anna: of promises broken, laws ignored, innocents brutalized for defending their rights.

Beyond the specific grievances and incidents that had provoked the current conflict, Austin addressed a deeper issue: the *meaning* of Texas. Americans had traveled to Texas to find a better life for themselves and their children. They had entered a Mexico that boasted a republican constitution promising fundamental rights of self-government. Yet the usurper Santa Anna had destroyed that constitution and suspended those rights. Like the American patriots of 1776, the Texans had been forced to fight for what was theirs. Indeed, Austin said, the cause of the Texans was better than that of the American revolutionaries, for the danger to Texas was more immediate. The patriots of 1776 had resisted "a *principle*, the theory of oppression." "But in our case it was the *reality*. It was a denial of justice and our guaranteed rights; it was oppression itself." The Texans were accused of ingratitude in accepting Mexican land and then throwing off Mexican rule. Again Austin cited American precedent. "I will ask, if it was not ingratitude for the people of the United States to resist the throng of oppression and separate from England, can it be ingratitude in the people of Texas to resist oppression and usurpation by separating from Mexico?" The Texans were charged with land theft, with taking what didn't belong to them. But to whom did the land of Texas—"a country which we have redeemed from the wilderness, and conquered without any aid or protection whatever from the Mexican government"—really belong? Just as the American colonies had belonged to those who settled them, and not to the English king, so Texas belonged to the Texans. "We have explored and pioneered it, developed its resources, made it known to the world, and given to it a high and rapidly increasing value. . . . The true and legal owners of Texas, the only legitimate sovereigns of that country, are the people of Texas."

The cause of the Texans was just, and a victory for Texas would be

a victory for everything America cherished and humanity desired.
"The emancipation of Texas will extend the principles of self-
government over a rich and neighboring country, and open a vast
field there for enterprise, wealth, and happiness. . . . It will promote
and accelerate the march of the present age, for it will open a door
through which a bright and constant stream of light and intelligence
will flow." The cause of Texas was one to which virtuous people everywhere could rally, and it was one upon which the Texans could fairly
hope for heavenly blessing. "With these claims to the approbation
and moral support of the free of all nations, the people of Texas have
taken up arms in self-defence, and they submit their cause to the
judgment of an impartial world, and to the protection of a just and
omnipotent God."

Had Austin reached Tennessee a bit earlier on his journey east, he
might have encountered David Crockett heading west. In the mid-
1830s Crockett was more famous than ever, but he was discovering
that fame had its price. The publication of his autobiography was followed by a tour of the sort that would become mandatory for celebrity
authors a century and a half hence. Crockett covered the East Coast,
traveling for his first time via train; enthusiastic audiences greeted
him at Baltimore, Philadelphia, New York, Newport, Providence, and
Boston. They clamored to hear his stories of "grinning" bears to
death and outwitting and outshooting wild Indians. The Whigs and
anti-Jackson Democrats among his listeners—and the farther east he
went, the more unpopular Jackson grew—delighted to hear him lash
"King Andrew." Jackson's administration had no principles, Crockett asserted, and accordingly it had led the country astray. "This re-

minds me of an anecdote of an old man in the barrens of Illinois," he said.

> He took his boy out to plow, and there was no trees in the barrens. Says he, Boy, do you see yon red heifer? Yes, says the boy. Well, do you plow straight to her. The old man left the boy. The boy he plowed toward the heifer, and she moved and the boy followed, and so kept plowing on all day. The old man in the evening came, and was astonished. Says he, You rascal, what sort of plowing is this you have done? Why, says the boy, you told me to plow to the red heifer, and I have been plowing after her all day.

As with the book itself, the tour was as much about Crockett's eastern future as about his western past. This was his first exposure to the Northeast and vice versa. The Whigs were happy to host some of Crockett's events; whether or not he became their presidential nominee in 1836, as an anti-Jackson westerner (and a Tennesseean, at that) he demonstrated that the president didn't speak for everyone in the West. Crockett understood that the Whigs loved him less than they hated Jackson, but he also understood that shared antipathies were the lifeblood of many alliances. The Whigs were using him; he would use them. Both might benefit.

After his popular triumph, Crockett found life in Congress a bore. "You look tired, as if you had just got through a long speech in the House," said a visitor to the Capitol, encountering Crockett on the steps and thinking he was winded from addressing his colleagues. "Long speech to thunder!" Crockett replied. "There's plenty of them up there for that sort of nonsense, without my making a fool of myself at public expense. I can stand *good nonsense*—rather like it—but *such nonsense* as they are digging at up yonder, it's no use trying to." When

Crockett did address the House, it was primarily to savage Jackson; when Jackson's lieutenants called him to task or order, he turned his fire their way. "I am not certain that the people will object to being transferred by Jackson over to that political Judas, little Van," he said of Martin Van Buren, Jackson's heir apparent. "I have sworn for the last four years that if Van Buren is our next president I will leave the United States. I will not live under his kingdom. . . . I would vote for the devil against Van and any man under the sun against Jackson." Speaking, at this point, more for dramatic effect than from careful reflection, he said, "I will go to the wilds of Texas. I will consider that government a paradise to what this will be."

Crockett intended to provoke the Jacksonians, and he succeeded. Jackson himself raged against Crockett as a ringleader of a "wicked plan to divide and conquer the Democracy of the union." "How is it," the president thundered, "that there is no man in the Republican ranks to take the stump and relieve Tennessee from her degraded attitude of abandoning principle to sustain men who have apostatized from the Republican fold for sake of office?" James Polk duly discovered such a man. Crockett initially underestimated Adam Huntsman—or, rather, he underestimated the ability of the Jackson machine to get out the vote for Huntsman. The two tramped across western Tennessee, with Crockett lambasting Jackson and Huntsman defending him. As always, Crockett campaigned as the man of the people. "If his vocabulary was scanty, he was master of the slang of his vernacular, and was happy in his coarse figures," observed a reporter sent from New York to cover Crockett. "He spurned the idle rules of the grammarians and had a rhetoric of his own." When Huntsman tried to embarrass him by producing a coonskin and asking him to assess it, as if that were the sum of his expertise, Crockett rejoined, "Sir, 'tis not good fur. My dogs wouldn't run such a coon, nor bark at a man that was fool enough to carry such a skin." As the election approached, Crockett was confident. "I have him bad plagued," he said of Huntsman.

Yet Crockett's cleverness and confidence couldn't overcome Jackson's organization, and the incumbent lost a close race. "The great *Hunter*, one Davy, has been beaten by a *Huntsman*," a happy Jacksonian gloated to Polk. Another boasted: "We have killed blackguard Crockett at last."

It wasn't the first time Crockett had lost, and he didn't think it signaled an end to his political career. Jackson had won this round, and his protégé Van Buren might win the next round, in 1836. But then again, Van Buren might not win, in which case an office for Crockett under a Whig administration wasn't out of the question. Even if Van Buren did win, he was no Jackson and would be vulnerable in 1840.

The question for Crockett was how to fill his time till then. A return to farming didn't appeal, especially after his taste of fame. A journey to the West made more sense. He could hunt, and if he went to Texas he could chase buffalo, a prize to pique the interest of any hunter. Besides, with all the news coming out of Texas lately, including reports about his old friend Sam Houston, a man would have to be dead to curiosity not to want to find out more about that country.

A more personal consideration as well made Crockett look west. Like Sam Houston, William Travis, and countless others who found their way to Texas, Crockett left behind a broken marriage. His first wife had died young, leaving him three children. Desperate for help tending them, he remarried quickly and, as soon appeared, unwisely. His new spouse, Betsy, showed scant tolerance for her husband's long absences, his aversion to regular work, and his growing enchantment with politics and fame. She spent more and more time with her relatives, till finally she didn't come home. Crockett couldn't fault her,

and he concluded that perhaps wedlock simply wasn't for him. Whatever its cause, the breakup left him with few domestic ties to Tennessee.

In the early autumn of 1835 he made up his mind to go to Texas,
and by the end of October he was ready to set off. "I am on the eve of
starting to Texas," he wrote a friend on October 31. Crockett said he
wasn't leaving America permanently, at least not yet. This was a reconnaissance trip. But it would be a thorough one. "I want to explore
Texas well before I return."

At the time he embarked for Texas, Crockett had taken no position on the quarrel between the Texans and Santa Anna. And at first
he didn't intend to get involved. But during the journey west, his
thinking took shape and his intentions changed. Everyone in Tennessee knew Crockett, and everyone in Tennessee knew about the
Texas troubles. With scores of Tennesseeans heading west to join the
fight against Santa Anna, it was easy for observers to assume that
Crockett was going for the same purpose. Crockett was too much the
politician to disabuse those who congratulated him on joining the
noble cause. Yet he was honest—and irreverent—enough to put a
characteristically modest interpretation on his journey. His explanation improved with practice; by the time he reached Nacogdoches in
early January 1836, he had it in good shape. "I am told, gentlemen,"
he explained to his hosts at a welcoming dinner, "that when a
stranger like myself arrives among you, the first inquiry is, what
brought him here. To satisfy your curiosity at once as to myself, I will
tell you all about it. I was, for some years, a member of Congress. In
my last canvass, I told the people of my district that if they saw fit to
reelect me, I would serve them as faithfully as I had done before. But,
if not, *they might go to hell, and I would go to Texas.*"

The audience roared appreciatively, making Crockett feel he

had found kindred spirits. And his introduction to Texas made him consider staying longer than he had anticipated. "It is the garden spot of the world," he wrote to his children from San Augustine. "The best land and the best prospects for health I ever saw, and I do believe it is a fortune to any man to come here. There is a world of country here to settle." The people of Texas evidently loved him. "I have got through safe and have been received by everyone with open ceremony of friendship. I am hailed with hearty welcome to this country. A dinner and a party of ladies have honored me with an invitation to participate both at Nacogdoches and at this place. The cannon was fired here on my arrival." Crockett had entered Texas from the north, and below the Red River he saw land "that I have no doubt is the richest country in the world—good land and plenty of timber and the best springs and wild mill streams, good range, clear water and every appearance of good health and game aplenty."

It was a land worth fighting for, and Crockett decided to do just that. "I have taken the oath of government and have enrolled my name as a volunteer and will set out for the Rio Grand in a few days with the volunteers from the United States," he explained. Yet already he was looking beyond the battlefield. He couldn't have known before arriving how readily his fame would transfer to Texas; now that he did know, he conceived of making a new start in politics in Texas. "All volunteers is entitled to vote for a member of the convention or to be voted for, and I have but little doubt of being elected a member to form a constitution for this province." What had seemed a reversal the previous summer now appeared a stroke of fortune. "I am rejoiced at my fate. I had rather be in my present situation than to be elected to a seat in Congress for life." Obviously, he would be in Texas longer than he had supposed. He wanted his children to know that everything was working out well. "Do not be uneasy about me. I am among friends."

Victory or . . .

While Crockett and his new friends rode west and south from Nacogdoches with the other volunteers, José Enrique de la Peña marched north and east from Monclova with comrades of his own. "We had set out with a fierce norther and had suffered all day long, facing its cutting winds and rain," de la Peña wrote, "and by seven that night the rain had turned to snow." De la Peña had only just received his assignment in Santa Anna's army, and he was hurrying to catch the cavalry brigade, which had left earlier and, as it happened, got lost on the road. The brigade was backtracking when he overtook it. "The countermarch had been executed in the dark, in a wooded area," he explained, "and, on a narrow road, all was confusion and chaos. Some muledrivers took advantage of the disorder to escape, and those who did not, neglected their mules because the agonizing cold kept increasing, and dire necessity forced the men to neglect their duties, to think only of taking care of themselves." With difficulty the brigade pitched camp. "A few fires were started, which served as a converging point to the wandering multitude. Officers, soldiers, women, and boys, all shivering, gathered around the fires; circumstances had made equals of us all, and the soldier could crowd against his officer without fear of being reprimanded." But there wasn't enough space by the fires to warm everyone, and those who did get close didn't want to give up their places to fetch more wood. The fires dwindled as the weather worsened. "The snowfall increased and kept falling in great abundance, so continuous that at dawn it was knee-deep; it seemed as though it wished to subdue us beneath its weight." Men who made the mistake of lying down to sleep were soon buried under the drifts; even those who dozed sitting had to shake themselves periodically lest they be buried, too. Most of the soldiers were from warmer regions; many had never seen snow or felt such cold. They prayed for dawn, only to be astonished and dismayed at what it brought.

This night of agony, which our soldiers spent around the fires, adding to the clamor the curses desperation evoked from many; this night, which the torment of cold and hunger made longer, was followed by the day, which, so longed for and looked for, presented to our eyes an indescribable spectacle, the most enchanting that can be imagined. What a bewitching scene! As far as one could see, all was snow. The trees, totally covered, formed an amazing variety of cones and pyramids, which seemed to be made of alabaster. The Tampico Regiment had left its cavalry unsaddled, and the mounts, covered to the haunches, could not be distinguished by their color. Many mules remained standing with their loads; others, as well as some horses, died, for those that fell and tried to get up inevitably slipped from being so numb, and the weight of their loads would make them crack their heads. The snow was covered with the blood of these beasts, contrasting with its whiteness.

De la Peña, with every other officer in Santa Anna's army, knew the commander in chief fancied himself another Napoleon; the blood on the snow made de la Peña think of Bonaparte's disastrous retreat from Moscow.

The snow fell for twenty-four hours; as it melted it mired the men and animals in slush and mud. Now it was the turn of the oxen to suffer. "The oxen pulling the carts, by nature cumbrous animals and used to working only certain hours of the day, were being needlessly worked to death, harnessed even before sunrise until some hours after sunset, with no care taken to pasture them during the night." Because many of the drivers had deserted, the oxen were left to soldiers who knew nothing about such beasts. "The soldiers, not satisfied with striking the oxen, would torment them with the points of their bayonets or their sabers." The animals stumbled, clogging the road still further; many died in harness, bringing the column to a halt.

A second storm hit the army two days later. "A cloud charged with hail and lightning descended on us with all its fury. A wild wind kept us from advancing, holding men and horses back by its force, but the rain, which was more copious, hit even harder." In a painful irony, amid the rain the men and horses could find little to drink, as the water ran off the desert landscape quickly or made undrinkable mud. "Between five and six in the afternoon we encamped on the prominence of Armadillo, spending the night in the mud and tormented by thirst."

Another few days brought the column to the Río Bravo del Norte—what the Americans called the Rio Grande—"a stream quite wide at this point, beautiful without being picturesque, somewhat shallow and slow of current," de la Peña wrote. The river relieved the thirst of the men and animals, and most had little difficulty wading across. But a few oxen, worn by the march, beset by their inexperienced drivers, and pulling carts overloaded on account of the loss of other animals, tripped and drowned in the yard-deep stream, over-loading the survivors still more.

The army ought to have rested before making the crossing of the desert between the Rio Grande and the Nueces. But Santa Anna, who already had gone ahead with his First Division, wanted his troops massed at San Antonio before the Texans were ready to defend the town. De la Peña's group pushed north to San Ambrosio, "a place without water but with such an abundance of rabbits that the soldiers could catch them by hand as easily as chickens from a hen." Perhaps distracted by the prospect of rabbit stew, the soldiers of one battalion allowed their stores of gunpowder to catch fire, with frightening but not fatal results. The army struggled forward as fast as it could, only to receive orders to move faster. "Suddenly a message arrived from the commander-in-chief. He communicated that on the 23rd he had entered Béjar and that the enemy had retreated and had barricaded themselves in the fortress of the Alamo. He ordered the sapper bat-talions from Aldama and Toluca to start forced marches."

De la Peña pressed ahead with the sappers. The stretch from the Rio Grande to the Nueces was daunting not only from the lack of wa-ter but also from the threat of attack by Comanches, who had helped make this region a desert to Mexicans (and Americans). Yet no Indi-ans appeared, to the relief of the soldiers. Across the Nueces, de la Peña—like so many others, most of whom had fewer distractions—was struck by the beauty of the land. "On the 29th, the last day of Feb-ruary, the troops took the ranch on Leona Creek, which dominates the scene as it courses over a beautiful plain, an inviting scene that begs to be inhabited. . . . The whole belt between this creek and the Nueces River is pleasant and rather beautiful and varied, and as one explores it, the soul expands and fills with joy; the sight of nature in its brilliant splendor brings an indescribable sense of wonder; the most delightful feelings follow one another to converge all at once and leave the recipient in a state of sublime ecstasy." Doubtless the strain of the journey and apprehension over what lay ahead made de la Peña more emotional than he might otherwise have been, but he could hardly contain his feelings as he surveyed the landscape. "Those who may have enjoyed the pleasure of love during the flower of youth and the heat of a passion irritated by obstacles and stirred up by desires might be the only ones who could feel what my soul felt on this day in the midst of nature so full of beauty and life."

After a day's march of forty miles, de la Peña's company reached the Rio Frio—"which did not betray its name, for a bitter cold was brought on by a blustery norther." After twenty-five miles the next day, they camped in an arroyo that shielded them from the wind but not from another snowstorm, which prevented all but the weariest from sleeping. One man died of exposure that night and was hastily interred the next morning. The weather disrupted communications, as the ink froze in its bottles. Late the following afternoon the party crossed the Medina River, which bore special significance to those, including de la Peña, who knew their history. "This was the place where General Arredondo had fought against the colonists who had rebelled during the Spanish regime." Another man died that night, apparently of exhaustion.

The next day they achieved their goal. "On the 3rd of March, between eight and nine in the morning, after the troops had put on their dress uniforms, we marched toward Béjar, entering between four and five in the afternoon within sight of the enemy, who observed us from inside their fortifications."

By March 3 the defenders of the Alamo—the fortifications to which de la Peña referred—had been observing the Mexican forces for ten days. James Bowie had arrived in San Antonio at the end of the third week of January, bearing Houston's order to demolish the Alamo and abandon the town. But Bowie was the wrong person to carry such an order, for as a recent resident of Béxar he had a greater attachment to the place than most of the Texas rebels. Moreover, his memories of Ursula—which were all he had left of her—were closely tied to the Veramendi house on Soledad Street; he couldn't lightly consign those memories to Santa Anna.

And after he examined the defenses of the Alamo, he decided that perhaps he didn't have to. James Neill had been left in charge of San Antonio's defense after Frank Johnson and James Grant lured most of the garrison toward Matamoros. Fortunately for Neill, the Matamoros battalion was too eager for its booty, and therefore in too much of a hurry, to be bothered hauling artillery; so, although he was left with only seventy men, he retained nearly all the cannons the Texans had captured from Cos on taking the town. He and his faithful few made themselves useful building emplacements for the guns and fortifying the walls of the Alamo compound; by the time Bowie arrived, the place appeared almost formidable and was becoming more so. Green Jameson, the engineer in charge of the work, was quite proud of what he called "Fortress Alamo." In a letter to Houston, Jameson wrote, "I send you herewith enclosed a neat plot exhibiting its true condition at this time." The map, helpfully indexed, showed "batteries and platforms where cannon are now mounted . . . strong stone walls . . . a large stone quartel for horses . . . the magazine in the Church San Antonio: two very efficient and appropriate rooms 10 feet square each, walls all around and above 4 feet thick . . . the aqueduct around the fortress by which we are supplied with water . . . a lake of water where we contemplate supplying the fortress by ditching from one of the aqueducts laid down . . . a pass from the present fortress to a contemplated drawbridge across a contemplated ditch inside a contemplated half-moon battery . . . the half-moon battery at each end of the fortress as contemplated . . . a twelve-feet ditch around the half-moon battery as contemplated." Jameson acknowledged that the garrison needed more men but, in light of recent intelligence regarding Santa Anna's movements, not so many more as to be out of the question. "We heard of 1000 to 1500 men of the enemy being on their march to this place. . . . In case of an attack we will move all into the Alamo and whip 10 to 1 with our artillery." Jameson concluded, "I can give you full assurance that so far as I am concerned there shall be nothing wanting on my part, neither as an officer or a soldier to promote and sustain the great cause at which we are all aiming."

Such confidence was infectious, and Bowie didn't take long to succumb. "All I can say of the soldiers stationed here is complimentary to both their courage and their patience," Bowie wrote Henry Smith. "I cannot eulogize the conduct and character of Col. Neill too highly." Houston's evacuation order had been conditional, anyway, on approval by the political authorities, and because Bowie hadn't heard of that approval he assumed it hadn't been given. And he did his best to forestall it. "The salvation of Texas depends in great measure in keeping Béjar out of the hands of the enemy," he asserted. "It serves as the frontier picket guard, and if it were in the possession of Santa Anna, there is no stronghold from which to repel him in his march toward the Sabine." Perhaps Bowie had never taken Houston's order as more than a recommendation—which was how he took most orders, as Stephen Austin had discovered—but now he disregarded it entirely. "Col. Neill and myself have come to the solemn resolution that we will rather die in these ditches than give it up to the enemy. These citizens deserve our protection, and the public safety demands our lives rather than to evacuate this post to the enemy."

Even if Houston had exercised iron control over the army, he would have had difficulty denying Bowie and the others at San Antonio the right to take a stand for Texas. Houston's situation wasn't helped by the bickering that continued to afflict the provisional government. Smith and the council couldn't agree on anything, let alone where the defense of Texas ought to begin; and without the backing of one or the other, Houston couldn't make any decisions that anyone felt obliged to obey. As a result, the decision to defend the Alamo—like every other decision so far in the war—was made by those who would have to carry it out.

But they needed help. Every few days Bowie, Jameson, or Neill (sometimes all three) wrote to Houston, Smith, or the council pleading for reinforcements. "*Relief* at this post, in men, money, and provisions is of *vital* importance and is wanted instantly," Bowie told Smith in the letter in which he announced his decision to fight to the end at the Alamo. "Our force is very small; the returns this day to the commandant is only one hundred and twenty officers and men." The latest intelligence from the Rio Grande was that Santa Anna had more than five thousand men. "It would be a waste of men to put our brave little band against thousands."

In answer to the pleas, Smith ordered William Travis to join Bowie and the others at the Alamo. Travis was reluctant at first, sensing that neither Smith nor Houston nor anyone else except Bowie and those already at Béxar was serious about defending the place. Travis asked for five hundred men to accompany him; Smith said he could have one hundred and would have to raise them himself. In the event, Travis was able to raise fewer than three dozen, outfitted from his own pocket. "I must beg that your Excellency will recall the order for me to go to Bexar in command of so few men," he wrote Smith. "I am willing, nay anxious, to go to the defense of Bexar, but, sir, I am unwilling to risk my reputation (which is ever dear to a soldier) by going off into the enemy's country with such little means, so few men, and with them so badly equipped."

Smith, however, who was more intent on fighting his enemies in the provisional government than on fighting the Mexicans, neither recalled the order nor increased the resources to carry it out. Travis, perhaps deciding that his reputation as a soldier would suffer more from refusing to accept this assignment than from complying, reluctantly headed off to San Antonio with his small company. "I shall march today with only about thirty men," he told Smith. "I shall, however, go on and do my duty." He was not hopeful. "Our affairs are gloomy indeed. The people are cold and indifferent. They are worn down and exhausted with the war, and, in consequence of dissensions between contending and rival chieftains, they have lost all confidence in their own government and officers. . . . The patriotism of a few has done much; but that is becoming worn down. I have strained every nerve; I have used my personal credit, and have neither slept day nor night since I received orders to march, and, with all this, I have barely been able to get horses and equipments for the few men I have."

Travis's gloom persisted after his arrival at San Antonio on February 3. His commission as lieutenant colonel placed him in rank below James Neill, who nominally commanded the entire garrison but in reality controlled only those men who had enlisted in the regular army and the organized volunteers. About half the garrison still consisted of individuals who had never enlisted for anything and who—as before—insisted on choosing their own officers. These men elected Bowie, who shared their independent spirit and their scorn for such niceties as chains of authority. Yet Bowie habitually deferred to Neill, which made for an orderly, if tenuous, command of the post.

Ten days after Travis arrived, however, Neill received word of serious illness in his family, and he took a leave of absence. He conferred his command on Travis—to whom Bowie, with the advantage of thirteen years and considerably more fighting experience, saw no reason to defer. A divided command resulted, with the regulars following Travis and the volunteers Bowie.

"My situation is truly awkward and delicate," Travis complained to Smith. What made it even more awkward was that Bowie was behaving with utter irresponsibility. "Since his election he has been roaring drunk all the time, has assumed all command, and is proceeding in a most disorderly and irregular manner—interfering with private property, releasing prisoners sentenced by court martial and by the civil court, and turning everything topsy turvy." Only Travis's sense of honor kept him at his post. "If I did not feel my honor and that of my country compromitted I would leave here instantly for some other point with the troops under my immediate command, as I am unwilling to be responsible for the drunken irregularities of any man."

Travis would stay, but for the sake of Texas he must have reinforcements. "I hope you will immediately order some regular troops to this place, as it is more important to occupy this post than I imagined when I last saw you," he told Smith. "It is the key of Texas. Without a footing here, the enemy can do nothing against us in the colonies."

Eventually Bowie sobered up, and when he did he agreed to share the command with Travis. Although this was hardly less awkward than the situation Travis complained of to Smith, it improved morale. Meanwhile, the approach of Santa Anna encouraged cooperation between the Texas commanders. Travis couldn't claim the loyalty of the volunteers, but Bowie could; and if Travis hoped to keep the volunteers in the fort, he had to heed Bowie's advice and opinions. Bickering continued but less egregiously than before.

★

Santa Anna knew of the hardships suffered by de la Peña's brigade and the rest of the Army of Operations. But he deemed swiftness essential in crushing the Texas rebellion before it advanced any further. Among the Mexicans of Texas were many who willingly provided intelligence to Santa Anna against the Americans. He probably knew that Houston and the others weren't expecting to have to fight till spring ("By the 15th of March, I think, Texas will be invaded," Travis wrote on February 13), and he knew that more Americans were arriving in Texas by the week. Indeed, Santa Anna's foreign minister made regular complaints to the Jackson administration in Washington about the raising of Texas-bound volunteers in the United States. Jackson's secretary of state, John Forsyth, replied that President Jackson had taken "all the measures in his power . . . to prevent any interference that could possibly involve the United States in the dispute, or give just occasion for suspicions of an unfriendly design on the part of this Government to intermeddle in a domestic quarrel of a neighboring state." Santa Anna could not have been reassured by this bland statement, which left a great deal of room for persons not associated with the American government to intermeddle as they chose—as Forsyth himself acknowledged in saying, "For the conduct of individuals which the Government of the United States cannot control, it is not in any way responsible."

By all evidence, the Texas revolt united the Mexican people more effectively than anything Santa Anna had been able to do on his own. "This country is in a perfect tempest of passion in consequence of the revolt in Texas, and all breathe vengeance," Jackson's minister in Mexico, Anthony Butler, informed the American president. Santa Anna was capitalizing on this support in waging his war against Texas, which he was portraying as a war against the United States. Butler was hardly an unbiased observer on the subject of Santa Anna, but he probably got the outlines of the president-general's reaction right when he said, "Santa Anna is perfectly furious, mad, and has behaved himself in the most undignified manner, boasting of what he would do not only with the insurgents of Texas but also with the United States, who he has identified with the revolt, charging our Government and people with promoting and supporting that revolt with sinister views, with the view of acquiring the territory. He has sworn that not an inch of the territory shall be separated from Mexico, that the United States shall never occupy one foot of land west of the Sabine." Butler related a story he heard from an eyewitness regarding a reception given by Santa Anna for the British and French ministers. "Santa Anna as usual very soon began to speak of the affairs of Texas, and as a consequence introduced the United States. He spoke of our desire to possess that country, declared *his full knowledge* that we had instigated and were supporting the revolt, and that in due season he would *chastise us* for it." Butler thought this threat so extraordinary that it required repeating. "Yes, Sir," he told Jackson, "he said *chastise us*. He continued: I understand that Gen. Jackson sets up a claim to pass the Sabine, and that in running the division line hopes to acquire the country as far as the Neches. 'Sir,' said he (turning to a gentleman present), 'I mean to run that line at the mouth of my cannon, and after the line is established, if the nation will only give me the means, only afford me the necessary supply of money, I will march to the capital. I will lay Washington City in ashes, as it has already been done once' (turning and bowing to the British minister)."

Some of Santa Anna's expression of outrage was probably for effect, but he doubtless was sincere in believing that Mexico was under assault from the United States. It was this belief that led him to treat the Texas rebels as pirates and adventurers rather than disaffected citizens of Mexico. Politically, the rebellion in Texas served Santa Anna's purposes by letting him reprise his role as defender of Mexico against its enemies, and by this means rally the Mexican people around his banner. The farther north he got and the closer his army approached to the Americans defending San Antonio and the rest of Texas, the more plausible his patriotic role became. As his troops rested briefly on the banks of the Nueces before making the last march to San Antonio, the commander in chief appealed to their love of country:

> Comrades in arms! Our most sacred duties have conducted us to these plains, and urged us forward to combat with the mob of ungrateful adventurers, on whom our authorities have incautiously lavished favors. . . . They have appropriated to themselves our territories, and have raised the standard of rebellion in order that this fertile and expanded department may be detached from our republic, persuading themselves that our unfortunate dissensions have incapacitated us for defense of our native land. Wretches!—they will soon see their folly.
>
> Soldiers! Your comrades have been treacherously sacrificed at Anahuac, Goliad and Béjar; and you are the men chosen to chastise the assassins.
>
> My friends! We will march to the spot whither we are called by the interest of the nation in whose service we are engaged. The candidates for acres of land in Texas will soon learn to their sorrow that their auxiliaries from New Orleans, Mobile, Boston, New York and other northern ports, from which no aid ought to proceed, are insignificant, and that Mexicans, though naturally generous, will not suffer outrages with impunity, injurious and dishon-

orable to their country, let the perpetrators be whom they may.

Until Santa Anna was almost within sight of San Antonio, the Texans knew nothing specific of his approach. The undermanned garrison couldn't maintain regular reconnaissance but had to rely on rumors filtered through the populace in the path of Santa Anna's army. The reliability of that populace, and hence of those rumors, was subject to the usual vicissitudes of war; like most ordinary people in most armed conflicts, the Tejanos wished primarily to be left alone. Some had sided with the Americans; even now Juan Seguín walked step for step with Travis and Bowie along the walls of the Alamo. Others cast their lot with Santa Anna. There weren't many convinced *centralistas* among the Tejanos (local control made as much sense to northern Mexicans as to western Americans), but many of the Tejanos took umbrage at the flood of illegal immigrants from the United States and agreed with Santa Anna that they were pirates and filibusters. Moreover, the example of Zacatecas wasn't lost on the Tejanos. Perhaps—just perhaps—the Americans in the Alamo could preserve themselves from Santa Anna's wrath. But who would save those outside the walls? A man might wish to oppose the dictator, and many had till now; but who would defend that man's family? Even Travis, at a moment when each man in the Béxar garrison might make the difference between survival and disaster, acknowledged the higher claim of family upon his troops, and after Seguín relayed an eleventh-hour request from several of the Tejano volunteers for furloughs, he let them go.

Between the lack of reliable intelligence and the speed of Santa Anna's approach, the Mexican army was almost upon the rebels before they realized the imminence of their peril. Travis had given his men the night of February 22 off from their labors about the Alamo;

some were still carousing in the small hours of the next morning when they observed townsfolk loading wagons and carts as if for a journey. Inquiry elicited unhelpful answers: that they were going to visit relatives in the country, that with the approach of spring they needed to tend distant fields. Travis, alarmed, questioned them further, even threatening to lock them up till they told what they knew. At this point someone revealed what had started the exodus: Santa Anna's army was at the Medina River, less than ten miles away, and approaching fast.

Travis naturally sought to confirm the report. He ordered two good horsemen to ride toward the Medina till they made contact with the enemy or proved the rumor wrong. If they saw the Mexicans, they should gallop back at once.

Travis and several others climbed to the roof of the San Fernando Church, the highest point in town, to watch the riders depart. For more than a mile the horsemen remained in view, growing smaller but still visible on the prairie. After several hundred yards more they topped a modest elevation and were about to slip from sight when they reined in their horses, apparently spotting something beyond the view of those on the roof of the church. Then, after but a moment, they turned and tore back toward the town, racing as if Satan himself were on their heels.

Travis didn't wait for their report; their haste told him all he needed to know. He ordered the entire garrison to withdraw to the Alamo, to the positions they had been preparing these last weeks. At almost the same time, he dispatched another appeal for help, this time to Gonzales, the garrison closest to Béxar and the one from which reinforcements might arrive soonest. "The enemy in large force is in sight," Travis wrote. "We want men and provisions. Send them to us. We have 150 men and are determined to defend the Alamo to the last."

Had the Texans been even slightly less attached to their individualism, the sudden appearance of Santa Anna must have solved the problem of the divided command between Travis and Bowie. Badly outnumbered, the Texans should have realized that their sole hope for survival lay in unity. But the democratic spirit died hard, and Bowie and the volunteers continued to refuse to subordinate themselves to Travis and the regulars.

The split became freshly apparent on the day of Santa Anna's arrival. As the Mexican troops streamed into the undefended town, across the river and several hundred yards from the Alamo, Santa Anna ordered a red flag raised above the San Fernando Church. The Texans interpreted this as a signal that no quarter would be given. Travis responded defiantly, ordering a cannon shot fired in the direction of the church. But Bowie wanted to talk. Pleading confusion, he addressed a letter to Santa Anna (as "Commander of the invading forces below Bejar"). "Because a shot was fired from a cannon of this fort at the time that a red flag was raised over the tower," Bowie said, "and a little afterward they [some of Bowie's comrades, presumably] told me that a part of your army had sounded a parley, which, however, was not heard before the firing of the said shot, I wish, sir, to ascertain if it be true that a parley was called for." The letter closed, "God and Texas!" and was signed by Bowie alone, as "Commander of the volunteers of Bexar." A Bowie aide carried it across the plain and the river to Santa Anna's headquarters.

Santa Anna answered indirectly. "As the Aide-de-camp of his Excellency, the President of the Republic," José Batres wrote, "I reply to you, according to the order of his Excellency, that the Mexican army cannot come to terms under any conditions with rebellious foreigners to whom there is no other recourse left, if they wish to save their lives, than to place themselves immediately at the disposal of the Supreme Government from whom alone they may expect clemency after some considerations are taken up." Batres closed: "God and Liberty!"

Actually there was another recourse left to the rebels, although they might not have been fully aware of it. During the first forty-eight hours after the arrival of the Mexican army, Santa Anna made little effort to seal all the exits from the Alamo. José de la Peña believed that the Texans could easily have withdrawn—indeed, de la Peña spoke of "the certainty that Travis could have managed to escape during the first nights"—had the rebels chosen to leave.

Instead they remained. Their decision to do so reflected their confidence in their skill at arms, their ignorance of the opposition they faced, and their trust in their fellow rebels. Before Santa Anna's arrival, Travis and Bowie hardly doubted that they could defend the Alamo against any force the Mexicans might send against them. Bowie, especially, had made a habit of outnumbered victory—over his Louisiana foes at the Sandbar, over the Indians at San Sabá, over the Mexicans at Concepción—and with the walls and cannons of the Alamo on his side, he didn't flinch at a numerical disadvantage of even ten to one. Anyway, he and Travis expected reinforcements: from Goliad, from Gonzales, or from the contingent that had marched off to Matamoros. Santa Anna's arrival evoked a reassessment of what they faced; the sight of the columns pouring into Bexár would have sobered anyone. But from the ramparts of the Alamo, Travis and Bowie couldn't count the Mexican troops, and they had no good idea of what they were up against. They still expected reinforcements, and even if the odds were worse than before, the rebels were sufficiently belligerent to hold their ground.

The decision to stay came more easily on account of a recent addition to the garrison. David Crockett took his time riding across Texas from Nacogdoches; his journey had the air of a political campaign as much as a military march. Young John Swisher encountered the Tennesseean at the Swisher farm above San Felipe and was most impressed. "At the time I saw Colonel Crockett," Swisher recalled, "I judged him to be about forty years old [Crockett was forty-nine]. He was stout and muscular, about six feet in height, and weighing 180 to 200 pounds. He was of a florid complexion, with intelligent gray eyes. He had small side whiskers, inclining to sandy. His countenance, although firm and determined, wore a pleasant and genial expression. Although his early education had been neglected, he had acquired such a polish from his contact with good society that few men could eclipse him in conversation. He was fond of talking and had an ease and grace about him which, added to his strong natural sense and the fund of anecdotes that he had gathered, rendered him irresistible." Stopping a few days at the Swisher place, Crockett engaged John in a series of shooting contests, good-naturedly handicapping himself to level the field. "My recollection is that we had a drawn match of it," Swisher said. At night, Crockett and the elders, with Swisher listening, talked late. "During his stay at my father's, it was a rare occurrence for any of us to go to bed before 12 or 1 o'clock. . . . He told us a great many anecdotes, many of which were common place and amounted to nothing in themselves, but his inimitable way of telling them would convulse one with laughter."

Crockett learned that action was expected at San Antonio, and he made his way there, arriving during the second week of February. His coming heartened the officers and troops of the garrison, who reasoned that their cause must be just if it could attract such a figure as Crockett. His coming also steeled the resolve of the garrison to stay and fight, for if Crockett, who had no land in Texas, no family in Texas, and no prior connection to Texas, had chosen the moment of maximum danger to enter the Alamo, it must be a mean and cowardly soul who would choose that moment to flee. In addition, Crockett's appearance eased the tension between Travis's regulars and Bowie's volunteers. By virtue of age, military experience, and national prominence, Crockett outranked everyone at the Alamo. Yet he refused to accept a commission, declaring that he would be honored to serve as a private. His goal was not glory but vindication of liberty and the right of common folks to shape their future.

Crockett's presence buoyed the entire garrison. Antonio Menchaca remembered Travis calling a halt to the labors on the fortress specifically to celebrate the arrival of the famous man. "Let us dance tonight, and tomorrow we will make provisions for our defense," Travis said. Crockett's personality leavened the atmosphere of a company surrounded and outnumbered. He regaled the men with stories, doubtless of his exploits against Indians, against the bear population of Kentucky, and against the ruling classes of Washington City. He challenged his new comrades to contests with the rifle and the fiddle. Travis and Bowie inevitably included him in their strategy sessions; his sense of humor took the edge off the competition between the two younger men.

As the days passed, Crockett's experience assumed added importance. Bowie became ill, mildly at first but then debilitatingly. The source of the illness was some infectious agent, perhaps from the water supply, although this was the wrong season for cholera or typhoid. Other men fell ill, but there was no epidemic, as would have been expected with a water-borne pathogen. The surviving accounts are unclear as to Bowie's symptoms; certain versions suggest pneumonia or tuberculosis. Whatever the nature of his illness, the consequence was that within days after Santa Anna's arrival, he was unable to function in any command capacity. Travis had effective control of the entire garrison, with Crockett assuming the role Bowie had played among the volunteers but clearly and willingly subordinate to Travis.

★

In one of their last joint statements, written February 23, Travis and Bowie appealed to James Fannin at Goliad for help. "We have removed all our men into the Alamo, where we will make such resistance as is due to our honor, and that of the country, until we can get assistance from you, which we expect you to forward immediately," they said. "In this extremity, we hope you will send all the men you can spare promptly." If either Travis or Bowie, upon seeing the size of Santa Anna's force, had had second thoughts about remaining at the Alamo, these were now banished. "We have one hundred and forty-six men, who are determined *never to retreat*. We have but little provisions, but enough to serve us till you and your men arrive. We deem it unnecessary to repeat to a brave officer, who knows his duty, that we call on him for assistance."

As the burden of command fell on Travis, he grew into his authority in a way that must have surprised those who had known him chiefly as a bellicose young buck. He had been glib; now he became eloquent. He had been headstrong; now he was heroic. A letter written on February 24, just a day after the joint appeal to Fannin, revealed the change that was coming over the beleaguered commandant. Addressed not to his fellow soldiers but to a far broader audience—and, one suspects, to posterity—the frontier lawyer and failed journalist scribbled a message that stirred the heart of everyone who read it.

To the People of Texas and all Americans in the world:
Fellow Citizens and Compatriots—I am besieged by a thousand or more of the Mexicans under Santa Anna. I

have sustained a continual bombardment and cannonade for 24 hours and have not lost a man. The enemy has demanded a surrender at discretion; otherwise, the garrison are to be put to the sword, if the fort is taken. I have answered the demand with a cannon shot, and our flag still waves proudly from the walls. *I shall never surrender or retreat.*

Then, I call on you in the name of Liberty, of patriotism and every thing dear to the American character, to come to our aid with all dispatch. The enemy is receiving reinforcements daily and will no doubt increase to three or four thousand in four or five days. If this call is neglected, I am determined to sustain myself as long as possible and die like a soldier who never forgets what is due his own honor and that of his country. VICTORY or DEATH.

> *William Barret Travis*
> *Lt. Col. Comdt.*

P.S.

The Lord is on our side. When the enemy appeared in sight we had not three bushels of corn. We have since found in deserted houses 80 to 90 bushels and got into the walls 20 or 30 head of beeves.

Travis entrusted this letter to Albert Martin, a volunteer from Gonzales who had taken part in the first battle of the revolution, the fight over the disputed cannon. Martin slipped between the Mexican forces under cover of darkness and galloped the seventy miles to Gonzales, where he relayed Travis's message to the world. While Martin was still on the road, and long before Travis could expect to know whether his plea had any effect, the rebel colonel penned another message, more informative and only slightly less exhortatory, to Sam Houston. Travis explained how he had rejected Santa Anna's surrender demand and how Mexican cannons had begun bombarding the Alamo shortly after that initial parley and continued till the present. He described the latest developments: "Today at 10 o'clock A.M., some two or three hundred Mexicans crossed the river below and came up under cover of the houses until they reached point blank range, when we opened a heavy discharge of grape and canister on them, together with a well directed fire from small arms which forced them to halt and take shelter in the houses about 90 or 100 yards from our batteries. The action continued to rage about two hours, when the enemy retreated in confusion, dragging off many of their dead and wounded."

Travis commended the performance of the garrison. "I take great pleasure in stating that both officers and men have conducted themselves with firmness and bravely." He mentioned several by name, ending with one Houston knew well: "The Hon. David Crockett was seen at all points, animating the men to do their duty." Travis added, "The whole of the men who were brought into action conducted themselves with such undaunted heroism that it would be injustice to discriminate."

As before, he pleaded for help. "Our numbers are few, and the enemy still continues to approximate his works to ours. I have every reason to apprehend an attack from his whole force very soon. But I shall hold out to the last extremity, hoping to secure reinforcements in a day or two. Do hasten on aid to me as rapidly as possible, as from the superior number of the enemy, it will be impossible for us to keep them out much longer." Yet, relieved or not, the garrison would do its duty. "If they overpower us, we fall a sacrifice at the shrine of our country, and we hope posterity and our country will do our memory justice." He prayed, however, that things wouldn't come to that. "Give me help, oh my Country!" He closed, defiant as ever: "Victory or Death!"

★

If Travis had known what little effect his messages were having on his fellow rebels, he might have saved his ink (and quite possibly reconsidered his decision to defend the Alamo). Houston spent the six weeks after mid-January doing nothing very constructive. Having failed to talk the expedition to Matamoros out of continuing, he attempted to sabotage the project politically. "Who is Dr. Grant?" he asked Henry Smith derisively. "Is he not a Scotchman, who has resided in Mexico for the last ten years? Does he not own large possessions in the interior? Has he ever taken the oath to support the organic law? Is he not deeply interested in the hundred-league claims of land which hang like a murky cloud over the people of Texas?" Was he not the man who, to further his chimerical project, had usurped authority to strip the defenses of San Antonio, "leaving the sick and wounded destitute of needful comforts?" Was he not, in short, a person with interests other than those of Texas at heart? "Yet this is the man whose outrages and oppressions upon the rights of the people of Texas are sustained and justified by the acts and conduct of the general council!"

Houston judged Grant's co-conspirators in the Matamoros campaign to be hardly better. James Fannin was a colonel in the regular army, having switched over from the volunteers. "By his oath he was subject to the orders of the commander-in-chief, and, as a subaltern, could not, without an act of mutiny, interfere with the general command of the forces of Texas," Houston said. Yet Fannin had taken it upon himself, against the clear wishes of his commander, to raise a regiment to ride south. Morever, Fannin had utterly discredited the expedition to Matamoros—or, rather, showed its true nature—by promising that the soldiers would be paid from the spoils of war. This statement revealed the mercenary motives of the expedition and divested it "of any character save that of a piratical or predatory war." It also guaranteed the campaign's failure, as the people of Matamoros, far from rising in support of the Texans' resistance to Santa Anna, would unite in opposition. "They will look upon them as they would look upon Mexican mercenaries, and resist them as such."

Houston's complaints availed little. To many among the rebels he was a sodden old soldier who had lost the will to fight. Every victory thus far had come through the efforts of such go-ahead types as Travis and Bowie and Ben Milam (rest his brave soul) and Frank Johnson and James Grant. If the prospect of booty was required to motivate the men, so be it. Wasn't Texas itself a great prize?

Muttering (and probably drinking), Houston wandered off toward Nacogdoches. His own officers and soldiers wouldn't listen to him, but perhaps his old friends the Cherokees would. During most of February, while Travis and Bowie and Crockett were preparing the Alamo for its final defense and Travis was daily pleading for help, Houston was hundreds of miles away, sharing a pipe with Chief Tewulle. His efforts produced a treaty of friendship with the Cherokees and their forest-Indian allies, an agreement that had scant connection to the current crisis in the war against Santa Anna.

★

Fannin came closer than Houston to answering Travis's pleas. John Brooks was Fannin's aide-de-camp at Goliad; on February 25 he scribbled a letter to his sister: "From the hurry of a preparation to march, I have stolen a moment to write you. An express from San Antonio de Bexar received here, a few moments since, with intelligence that the Mexican Army under Santa Anna were in sight of that place and preparing to attack it. He heard the firing of cannon after he had gained some distance toward us. He estimated their strength at from three to five thousand. Bexar has a garrison of 156. They have retired to the Alamo, determined to hold out to the last, and have solicited reinforcements from us." Brooks explained that the Texan army as a whole was woefully undermanned—and that nearly all those who were in the army weren't even Texans. "The only troops in the field at this time are volunteers from the United States, and they probably do not exceed 800." The garrison at Goliad comprised 420 men, who were busy strengthening what they had called Fort Defiance. Fannin, in response to Travis's request for reinforcements, decided to leave 100 at Goliad and take the rest to Béxar. "With a forlorn hope of 320 men," Brooks related, "we will start tonight or tomorrow morning at the dawn of day in order to relieve the gallant little garrison, who have so nobly resolved to sustain themselves until our arrival."

In this letter to his sister, Brooks suggested that the rescue mission might—just might—succeed. "Our force is small compared with that of the enemy," he acknowledged. "It is a desperate resort." But it was worth the try. "If by forced marches we can reach Bexar, a distance of more than a hundred miles, and cut our way through the enemy's lines to our friends in the fort, our united force thus advantageously posted may perhaps be sufficient to hold out until the militia can be collected to reinforce us." Heaven had blessed the brave before, and it might do so again. "We hope the God of Battles will be with us—that victory will again perch on the bright little banner of Texian liberty."

Yet in a second letter, written to his father that night, Brooks conceded that the relief party was probably riding to its death. "We have less than 350 men; the force of the enemy is possibly 3000—a vast disparity. We are almost naked and without provisions, and very little ammunition. We are undisciplined in a great measure; they are regulars, the elite of Santa Anna's army: well fed, well clothed, and well appointed and accompanied by a formidable battery of heavy field and battering pieces. We have a few pieces but not experienced artillerists and but a few rounds of fixed ammunition, and perhaps less of loose powder and balls." Only a miracle would prevent annihilation. "My dear Father, I frankly confess that without the interposition of Providence, we can not rationally anticipate any other result to our Quixotic expedition than total defeat." Nonetheless, Brooks was willing to go. "If we perish, Texas and our friends will remember that we have done our duty."

Fannin was willing to go, too—at first. The relief column set out from Goliad hauling four small artillery pieces in ox-drawn wagons. But only two hundred yards beyond the gates one of the wagons broke down. Then the crossing of the San Antonio River proved difficult and slow, disabusing the rescuers of any idea that they might reach Béxar quickly. If they got there at all, it would be by painful march. Indeed, the odds were against even reaching the town. "Not a particle of bread stuff, with the exception of half a tierce of rice, with us," Fannin informed the provisional council. "No beef, with the exception of a small portion which had been dried, and not a head of cattle, except those used to draw the artillery, the ammunition, etc., and it was impossible to obtain any until we should arrive at Seguín's rancho, seventy miles from this place."

These remarks were Fannin's preface to a message saying that the relief mission had been aborted. He explained that after the unpromising start the officers had requested a council, which he duly convened. "The Council of War consisted of all the commissioned officers of the command," Fannin said, "and it was by them unanimously determined that, inasmuch as a proper supply of provisions and means of transportation could not be had; and, as it was impossible, with our present means, to carry the artillery with us; and as, by leaving Fort Defiance without a proper garrison, it might fall into the hands of the enemy . . . it was deemed expedient to return to this post and complete the fortifications."

There was reason, if not much courage, in Fannin's decision. If the Alamo was doomed, and if the relief column couldn't alter that fate, there was no point sacrificing three hundred men who might yet save Goliad—which, Fannin belatedly came to believe, was more important than San Antonio.

Whatever the logic of Fannin's decision, it was no comfort to Travis and the defenders of the Alamo, who in fact never learned that Fannin wasn't coming. Day after day they scanned the prairie to the southeast of the Alamo; night after night they strained to hear the shots that would signal that reinforcements were fighting their way through Santa Anna's siege lines.

Their hopes were rewarded but almost simultaneously disappointed in the hours after midnight of February 29. A mounted volunteer unit from Gonzales had looped to the northeast to evade the dragoons of General Joaquín Ramírez y Sesma, who guarded the road from Goliad. The first opposition the Gonzales volunteers encountered came from the Alamo itself, as guards there heard movement in the dark under the walls and fired on the presumed attackers. They hit one rebel volunteer before the others hissed out, in English, to stop shooting, for God's sake: these were friends. The defenders rushed to help them in, their delight diminishing only—and sharply—when they counted the newcomers and discovered a mere thirty-two.

The day of their arrival—March 1—was the day the long-awaited convention on independence was scheduled to begin at Washington-on-the-Brazos. Travis couldn't know that a quorum in fact had been achieved, but, assuming that it had, he wrote to the president of the convention, whoever that might be. An unmistakable bitterness informed his opening sentence: "In the present confusion of the political authorities, and in the absence of the commander-in-chief, I beg leave to communicate to you the situation of this garrison." For six days the enemy had maintained a steady bombardment with howitzers and long guns, the latter from across the river, beyond the answering reach of anything within the Alamo. Meanwhile, enemy infantry and sappers had been encircling the fort with trenches; these were nearly complete, although they hadn't prevented the arrival of the volunteers from Gonzales. Travis explained that his own men had been active, too. "I have fortified this place, so that the walls are generally proof against cannon balls; and I shall continue to entrench on the inside, and strengthen the walls by throwing up dirt." He was pleased to report that his men had inflicted more damage than they had incurred. "At least two hundred shells have fallen inside of our works without having injured a single man; indeed, we have been so fortunate as not to lose a man from any cause, and we have killed many of the enemy." The spirits of the men remained high, "although they have had much to depress them." Travis estimated the Mexican forces at between fifteen hundred and six thousand, with more arriving daily. "The reinforcements will probably amount to two or three thousand."

Travis reminded the convention how often he had requested aid, and he wondered why, with the exception of the company from Gonzales, none had appeared. "Col. Fannin is said to be on the march to this place with reinforcements, but I fear it is not true, as I have *repeatedly* sent to him for aid without receiving any." Travis detailed what was needed: five hundred pounds of cannon powder, two hundred rounds

of cannonballs of various sizes, ten kegs of rifle powder and a commensurate quantity of bullet lead, and as many men as could be spared.
"If these things are promptly sent and large reinforcements are has-
tened to this frontier, this neighborhood will be the great and decisive
ground. The power of Santa Anna is to be met here or in the colonies;
we had better meet them here than to suffer a war of devastation to rage
in our settlements." If relief didn't arrive soon, Travis would have no
choice. "I shall have to fight the enemy on his own terms."

It was war to the death. "A blood red banner waves from the
church of Bejar, and in the camp above us, in token that the war is one
of vengeance against rebels. They have declared us as such, demanded
that we should surrender at discretion, or that this garrison should be
put to the sword." Travis and his fellows didn't mind the danger.
"Their threats have no influence on me or my men"—except "to make
all fight with desperation and that high-souled courage that characterizes the patriot, who is willing to die in defense of his country's liberty
and his own honor." Travis renewed his vow to battle till the end, and
he promised similar resolve from his subordinates. "I feel confident
that the determined valor and desperate courage heretofore exhibited
by my men will not fail them in the last struggle; and although they may
be sacrificed to the vengeance of a Gothic enemy, the victory will cost
the enemy so dear that it will be worse for him than defeat." Travis's
closing was as defiant as ever: "God and Texas—Victory or Death."

Travis wrote two more letters that day. To the convention he
urged a declaration that would confer real meaning on the fight
against Santa Anna and on the sacrifices it entailed. "Let the Convention go on and make a declaration of independence, and we will then
understand, and the world will understand, what we are fighting for.
If independence is not declared, I shall lay down my arms, and so will
the men under my command. But under the flag of independence, we

are ready to peril our lives a hundred times a day, and to drive away the monster who is fighting us under a blood-red flag, threatening to murder all prisoners and make Texas a waste desert."

To a trusted friend he sent a personal message: "Take care of my little boy. If the country should be saved, I may make him a splendid fortune; but if the country should be lost and I should perish, he will have nothing but the proud recollection that he is the son of a man who died for his country."

★

Although the siege was going well for Santa Anna, it wasn't everything the Mexican commander had hoped. His original plan entailed attacking directly from the march, to crush the rebels before they had a chance to retreat to the Alamo. "With the speed in which this meritorious division executed its marches in eighty leagues of road," he wrote to the Mexican minister of war, "it was believed that the rebel settlers would not have known of our proximity until we should have been within rifle-shot of them." But heavy rains had raised the Medina River, slowing the army's crossing and allowing word of the Mexican approach to reach the rebels, who withdrew into the Alamo.

Yet he couldn't complain. "The national troops, with the utmost order, took possession of this city, which the traitors shall never again occupy." And over the next several days the Mexican lines advanced toward the Alamo, pinning the rebels down. "They are not even allowed to raise their heads over the walls." The defiance of the rebels wouldn't last. "Up to now they still act stubborn, counting on the strong position which they hold, and hoping for much aid from their colonies and from the United States of the North, but they shall soon find out their mistake." The assault on the Alamo—"which will take place when at least the first brigade arrives"—would be the initial step toward eradicating the rebellion. "After taking Fort Alamo, I shall continue my operations against Goliad and the other fortified places, so that before the rains set in, the campaign shall be absolutely terminated up to the Sabine River."

The following days brought word that the rebel-eradication campaign was proceeding nicely. Despite Houston's opposition, Johnson and Grant had pressed ahead with the Matamoros expedition. They mustered men and scoured the country around San Patricio for horses to carry them south. But their actions, besides advertising their presence and aims, alienated many of the local Tejanos, who informed the Mexican army of the rebels' whereabouts. General José Urrea, in charge of the security of Matamoros, put the intelligence to good use. At ten o'clock on the night of February 25, Urrea's informants reported that the rebels had occupied San Patricio. The weather was miserable, with rain falling and snow threatening. A less resolute commander might have waited for it to clear, but Urrea seized the opportunity for surprise. Setting out at once, he pushed his men through the night and the following day. The weather got worse. "The night was very raw and excessively cold," Urrea recorded in his journal. "The rain continued, and the dragoons, who were barely able to dismount, were so numbed by the cold that they could hardly speak." Six infantrymen of the Yucatán battalion died from exposure.

The Mexican forces reached San Patricio before dawn on February 27. Urrea quietly ordered forty dragoons to dismount. "Dividing them into three groups under good officers, I gave instructions for them to charge the position of the enemy, protected by the rest of our mounted troops." The surprise was devastating. "The enemy was attacked at half past three in the morning in the midst of the rain, and although forty men within the fort defended themselves resolutely, the door was forced at dawn, sixteen being killed and twenty-four being taken prisoners."

Johnson managed to flee north toward Refugio, but Grant, still raiding along the Rio Grande, was unaware of what had happened. Urrea exploited his ignorance. "I decided to wait for the enemy ten leagues from San Patricio, at the port of Los Cuates de Agua Dulce, where he would have to pass. I divided my force into six groups and hid them in the woods." The rebels approached early on March 2, and again the surprise was overwhelming. "Between ten and eleven in the morning, Dr. Grant arrived. He was attacked and vanquished by the parties under my command and that of Colonel Francisco Garay. Dr. Grant and forty of the riflemen were left dead on the field, and we took six prisoners besides their arms, munitions, and horses."

Santa Anna heard of Urrea's victory a short while later. He congratulated the general on his victory but judged he had to steel Urrea's spine on an issue the triumph raised. Urrea asked what he should do with the prisoners his men had captured; these included the two dozen Americans and five Tejanos. Santa Anna responded that the law of Mexico was clear: "Foreigners invading the republic, and taken with arms in their hands, shall be judged and treated as pirates." The president-general added, "An example is necessary, in order that those adventurers may be duly warned and the nation be delivered from the ills she is daily doomed to suffer." Regarding the Tejanos: "As, in my opinion, every Mexican guilty of the crime of joining these adventurers loses the rights of a citizen by his unnatural conduct, the five Mexican prisoners whom you have taken ought also to suffer as traitors." In other words, the prisoners were to be executed, every one.

The prisoner question came up the next day in a different context. Urrea's success at San Patricio spurred Santa Anna to move against the Alamo. "Twelve days had passed since Ramírez y Sesma's division had drawn up before the Alamo, and three since our own arrival at Béjar," José de la Peña wrote. "Our commander became more furious when he saw that the enemy resisted the idea of surrender. He believed, as others did, that the fame and honor of the army were compromised the longer the enemy lived. General Urrea had anticipated him and had dealt the first blow, but we had not advanced in the least. . . . It was therefore necessary to attack him in order to make him feel the vigor of our souls and the strength of our arms."

Santa Anna called a council of war on the evening of March 4. Some of the officers apparently believed that the rebel garrison could be reduced with minor loss of Mexican life, if Santa Anna were willing to wait for more artillery to arrive. "They could not have resisted for many hours the destruction and imposing fire from twenty cannon," de la Peña wrote. But the commander refused to continue the siege. The rebels, he declared, must be destroyed at once. No one at the council openly opposed this decision, evidently considering opposition futile. The discussion then turned to tactics: what columns would approach from which directions, how many units should attack at once and how many he held in reserve. The question of prisoners arose. "The example of Arredondo was cited," de la Peña recorded. "During the Spanish rule he had hanged eight hundred or more colonists after having triumphed in a military action, and this conduct was taken as a model." A few of the officers present voiced concern at such a harsh policy. "But their arguments were fruitless."

The order to ready the final assault was circulated on the afternoon of March 5. "The time has come to strike a decisive blow upon the enemy occupying the fortress of the Alamo," Santa Anna declared. "Tomorrow at 4 o'clock a.m., the columns of attack shall be stationed at musket-shot distance from the first entrenchments, ready for the charge, which shall commence at a signal to be given with the bugle from the northern battery." The general specified the preparations: "The first column will carry ten ladders, two crowbars, and two axes; the second, ten ladders, the third, six ladders; and the fourth, two ladders. . . . The companies of grenadiers will be supplied with six packages of cartridges to every man, and the center companies with two packages and two spare flints." No concession would be made to the foul weather. "The men will wear neither overcoats nor blankets, nor anything that may impede the rapidity of their motions." They would retire early the night before the attack. "The troops composing the columns of attack will turn in to sleep at dark, to be in readiness to move at 12 o'clock at night."

Santa Anna entreated his men to consider the opportunity fortune had placed in their way. "His Excellency expects that every man will do his duty, and exert himself to give a day of glory to the country, and of gratification to the Supreme Government, who will know how to reward the distinguished deeds of the brave soldiers of the Army of Operations."

Inside the Alamo, Travis weighed his options. By now Bowie was confined to bed, too weak to get up, too delirious to argue with Travis even if he had been so inclined. Crockett was helpful, encouraging the men and lifting spirits wherever he went; but he didn't trespass on Travis's authority. The twenty-six year-old colonel made decisions on his own.

Not that the men didn't voice their opinions. More than a few were less adamant than Travis about fighting to the death. According to witnesses who reached Mexican lines before and after the battle, a groundswell for surrender emerged in the ranks during the last days of the siege. De la Peña cited "a lady from Bejar" who fled the Alamo on March 5, "a Negro who was the only male who escaped" (this was Travis's personal slave, Joe), and "several women who were found inside" after the battle, as authority for his statement that "Travis's resistance was on the verge of being overcome." De la Peña elaborated: "For several days his followers had been urging him to surrender, giving the lack of food and the scarcity of munitions as reasons; but he had quieted their restlessness with the hope of quick relief, something not difficult for them to believe since they had seen some reinforcements arrive. Nevertheless, they pressed him so hard that on the 5th he promised them that if no help arrived on that day they would surrender the next day or would try to escape under the cover of darkness."

This hearsay may or may not have accurately reflected what Travis told the garrison. It would be unnatural to think that none of the defenders—most of whom were recent arrivals to Texas—were having second thoughts about their predicament. That Travis actually contemplated surrender seems unlikely given all that he had written during the past two weeks. But he may have *told* the men he was contemplating surrender, in order to keep them at their posts another day. According to one version of the story, the "lady from Béjar" carried an offer from Travis to surrender on condition that the defenders' lives would be spared. According to this version, Santa Anna rejected the offer, as he had rejected Bowie's offer to parley earlier. Travis must have known that Santa Anna would reject the offer, but in making it—if he did—he gave his men a warrant of his willingness to consider their views.

Quite conceivably, Travis *was* considering a fighting retreat. After all, by now the chances of surviving a Mexican attack appeared negligible; the Alamo simply could not be held. The men could either die where they were or die trying to get out—and in the latter case some might survive. There would be no dishonor in trying to save his force now that it had become clear—as a result of the refusal of the provisional government, of the rest of the army, and of the citizens of Texas to relieve the garrison—that the Alamo could not be saved. In any event, Travis knew that once the shooting started, he would have little control over what the men did. Would they fight harder in the Alamo, with no hope of surviving, or on the road to Gonzales, with some hope? It wasn't an easy question.

According to de la Peña, conventional wisdom in the Mexican camp held that Travis was contemplating surrender or escape. This was what the "lady from Béjar" said (whether or not she brought a surrender offer), and it was simply common sense. Who wouldn't want to abandon a patently lost cause?

Ironically, the prospect of surrender was what prompted Santa Anna to attack. "He wanted to cause a sensation, and would have regretted taking the Alamo without clamor and without bloodshed," de la Peña said.

So the attack went forward. The Mexican troops retired early on the night of March 5; if Travis and the men inside the Alamo noticed the unusual calm across the river, they gave no sign. By midnight both camps were quiet.

But soon the Mexican camp stirred, as silently as fifteen hundred men could. They spoke in whispers; every effort was made to keep metal from clanging on metal. By one o'clock four columns were moving toward the river, which the men crossed, two by two, on plank bridges built during the twelve days of the siege. "The moon was up," de la Peña recalled, "but the density of the clouds that covered it allowed only an opaque light in our direction, seeming thus to contribute to our designs. This half-light, the silence we kept, hardly interrupted by soft murmurs, the coolness of the morning air, the great quietude that seemed to prolong the hours, and the dangers we would soon have to face: all of this rendered our situation grave. We were still breathing and able to communicate; within a few moments many of us would be unable to answer questions addressed to us, having already returned to the nothingness whence we had come." The fear of death sobered them all; even more sobering was the prospect of agony short of death. Yet another sentiment, a common determination, spurred them forward. "An insult to our arms had to be avenged, as well as the blood of our friends spilled three months before within these same walls we were about to attack."

Within those walls, the defenders of the Alamo slept. Travis had retired about midnight, according to the recollection of his slave Joe. He had made a final round of the fort and posted sentries outside the walls to warn of enemy approach. His brain doubtless swirled with questions—Would relief come tomorrow? Would an attack? Would the men stand or run? How would he meet death?—until exhaustion overcame him.

He was still asleep when the attack began. The four Mexican columns crept toward the walls of the Alamo. The first, under General Cos, who had disregarded his parole and returned to Texas, filed toward the west wall, the one closest to the town. The second column was assigned the shorter north wall, which held the strongest battery. The third circled around to the east, to the rear of the fort. The fourth was to assault the main gate, on the south side of the fort. A fifth, including de la Peña's sappers, was held in reserve, to be thrown into battle at the critical moment wherever their weight would be decisive.

The approach went smoothly. The rebel pickets must have fallen asleep, for none called out or fired a shot before being surrounded and silently killed. The attackers were in place before dawn, awaiting the bugle that would announce the attack. Nervous anticipation kept most of the men alert; a few, including de la Peña, dozed.

The signal—"that terrible bugle call of death," de la Peña said—came with the first light of dawn. Their secret revealed, the attackers rushed forward, crying, "Viva Santa Anna! Viva Mexico!"

In that moment the fortress came to life. The sentries on the walls shouted and fired; the noise awoke Travis, who leaped from his cot, seized a rifle in each hand, and raced for the north battery, yelling as he crossed the yard for all to man their posts.

Travis's strategy, such as it was against such numbers, depended on keeping the Mexicans from reaching the walls in force. The Texan rifles could do lethal damage against individual enemy soldiers, but they were slow to reload, and even though each defender had three or four weapons, these simply couldn't kill Mexicans fast enough. For such wholesale slaughter Travis relied on the cannons. Loaded with shrapnel—lacking grapeshot, Travis substituted nails, links of chain, pieces of horseshoes, and anything else that might survive the blast of powder—the cannons could mow down Mexicans by the score. Loaded with balls—many recovered from the incoming Mexican fire during the previous twelve days—they cut narrower but still fearsome swaths.

The Mexican tactics played into the Texan hands. Always thinking himself another Napoleon, Santa Anna employed the European method of massed attack, which allowed a few seasoned officers and veteran enlisted men, positioned at the edges of the advancing columns, to keep the hundreds of terrified conscripts from fleeing at the first enemy fire. This mode of warfare had the additional advantage of conveying implacability: try as the defenders might to resist the advancing columns, the columns kept coming. Yet the massed method was horribly wasteful of life (which was why the ranks had to

be continually replenished with those terrified conscripts), especially when the columns faced entrenched artillery, as Santa Anna's
did now.

During the opening phase of the battle, the defenders held their
own. Their cannons wreaked frightful havoc among the Mexicans. "A
single cannon volley did away with half the company of chasseurs
from Toluca," de la Peña said; and other rounds did like damage.
Limbs and bones flew everywhere; muskets and bayonets blown from
the infantrymen's hands became missiles of death. Those who escaped the cannon fire tripped over their comrades' fallen bodies and
slipped in the blood and gore. All wanted to run, to escape the carnage, but those who tried to do so found themselves facing Santa
Anna's lancers, whose gleaning weapons reiterated that safety lay
ahead in victory, not behind in defeat.

By sheer numbers—there were more of them than the Texan rifles and cannons could possibly kill—the Mexicans reached the walls.
Here they were relatively safe, for the makeshift fortress lacked the
forward projections that would have allowed the defenders to control
their walls with flanking fire. Yet the Mexicans still had to scale the
walls, and the first over the top could count on being hacked or shot
to death. The ladders Santa Anna had ordered were insufficient, having been poorly made, blasted by the cannon fire, or abandoned on
the field where their bearers fell. The bravest attackers began clam-
bering up the walls using their comrades as stepstools; in most cases
they came tumbling back down, bayoneted or shot by the Texans. But
there were enough of them, compared to the defenders, that eventually they gained a foothold on the ramparts. Once inside, several
fought their way to the gates, which they threw open to their fellows.

As the fighting shifted to the interior of the Alamo, the real
butchery began. The Texans swiveled their cannons and commenced

firing on the Mexicans inside the walls, who had nowhere to turn for shelter and no choice but to charge into the very mouths of the guns. Eventually the attackers' numbers told again, and they captured the cannons, which they employed against the defenders. The Texans beat a fighting retreat to the chapel and other rooms of the compound.

Amid the smoke, the dust, and the dimness of the dawn, the combatants locked in mortal confusion. "Our soldiers, some stimulated by courage and others by fury, burst into the quarters where the enemy had entrenched themselves, from which issued an infernal fire," de la Peña wrote. "Behind these came others who, nearing the doors and blind with fury and smoke, fired their shots against friends and enemies alike, and in this way our losses were most grievous. They turned the enemy's own cannon to bring down the doors to the rooms or the rooms themselves; a horrible carnage took place, and some were trampled to death. The tumult was great, the disorder frightful; it seemed as if the furies had descended upon us; different groups of soldiers were firing in all directions, on their comrades and on their officers, so that one was as likely to die by a friendly hand as by an enemy's."

Facing certain death where they fought, some of the defenders tried to surrender. They made white flags of kerchiefs or socks and waved them in doorways or poked them through holes in the walls. By de la Peña's account, some Mexican soldiers initially tried to honor their surrender. "Our trusting soldiers, seeing these demonstrations, would confidently enter their quarters; but those among the enemy who had not pleaded for mercy, who had no thought of surrendering, and who relied on no other recourse than selling their lives dearly, would meet them with pistol shots and bayonets." The Mexicans quickly learned to ignore the surrender pleas. Some of the

Texans went over the walls in an attempt to escape; these were ridden down by the Mexican cavalry and sabered to death.

The last redoubt of the defenders was the chapel. Its thick stone walls stood proof against the cannons the attackers now leveled against it, but eventually its oaken doors were splintered by the eighteen-pound balls of the fort's large gun. The attackers surged through the entrance and didn't stop shooting and hacking till all resistance had ceased.

Chapter 16

At Discretion

Of the Alamo's approximately two hundred defenders, all but a handful were killed in the battle. Travis was one of the first to fall, from the northern parapet where the fighting was heaviest, of a Mexican bullet that pierced his forehead and killed him instantly. James Bowie died in his bed, too feverish to fight, perhaps mistaken by the attackers for a malingerer or a coward.

Where and how David Crockett died has exercised the historical imagination for more than a century and a half. De la Peña said that seven men survived the battle and were presented as prisoners by General Manuel Fernández Castrillón to Santa Anna.

> Among them was one of great stature, well proportioned, with regular features, in whose face there was the imprint of adversity, but in whom one also noticed a degree of resignation and nobility that did him honor. He was the naturalist David Crockett, well known in North America for his unusual adventures, who had undertaken to explore the country and who, finding himself in Béjar at the very

moment of surprise, had taken refuge in the Alamo, fearing that his status as a foreigner might not be respected.

Santa Anna answered Castrillón's intervention in Crockett's behalf with a gesture of indignation and, addressing himself to the sappers, the troops closest to him, ordered his execution. The commanders and officers were outraged at this action and did not support the order, hoping that once the fury of the moment had blown over, these men would be spared.

But several officers who were around the president and who, perhaps, had not been present during the moment of danger, became noteworthy by an infamous deed, surpassing the soldiers in cruelty. They thrust themselves forward, in order to flatter their commander, and with swords in hand, fell upon these unfortunate, defenseless men just as a tiger leaps upon his prey. Though tortured before they were killed, these unfortunates died without complaining and without humiliating themselves before their torturers.

This version was corroborated, in substance if not in detail, by the account of Fernando Urizza, as told to Nicholas Labadie after the battle of San Jacinto. Urizza was an officer in Santa Anna's army; Labadie was a rebel medic who treated his wounds. Urizza told Labadie:

As I was surveying the dreadful scene before us, I observed Castrillón coming out of one of the quarters, leading a venerable-looking old man by the hand; he was tall, his face was red, and stooped forward as he walked. The President stopped abruptly, when Castrillón, leaving his prisoner, advanced some four or five paces toward us, and with his graceful bow, said: "My General, I have spared the life of this venerable old man, and taken him prisoner." Raising his head, Santa Anna replied, "What right have you to disobey my orders? I want no prisoners." And waving his hand to a file of soldiers, he said, "Soldiers, shoot that man." And almost instantly he fell, pierced with a volley of balls.

Labadie asked Urizza the name of the prisoner. "I believe," Urizza replied, "they called him *Coket*." In his retelling, Labadie commented, "At that time, we knew very little of David Crockett. . . . All I knew was that I had heard of David Crockett passing through Nacogdoches in the month of February to join the army, with some fifteen others. But I have never since had any doubt but that Urizza's account gave the fate of Crockett truly. This statement was made some four or five days after the battle of the 21st [of April], and Urizza could have had no motive to misrepresent the facts."

Perhaps not, but a third eyewitness told a different story. Francisco Antonio Ruiz, the alcalde of San Antonio, observed the storming of the Alamo from the Mexican lines, along with other officials of the town. As the firing ceased and the smoke drifted away, they received a summons.

Santa Anna sent one of his aide-de-camps with an order for us to come before him. He directed me to call on some of the neighbors to come up with carts to carry the dead to the cemetery, and also to accompany him, as he was desirous to have Col. Travis, Bowie, and Crockett shown to him.

On the north battery of the fortress lay the lifeless body of Col. Travis on the gun carriage, shot only in the forehead. Toward the west, and in the small fort opposite the city, we found the body of Col. Crockett. Col. Bowie was found dead in his bed, in one of the rooms of the south side.

It is hard to know what to make of these conflicting accounts. De la Peña's has the advantage of having been recorded close to the events, as a diary (subsequently transcribed). Yet de la Peña had never seen Crockett before the battle and would have required someone else to identify him. The same was true of Urizza, who apparently didn't hear or remember the name quite right. (Though Crockett wasn't exactly "old," as Urizza said, he might well have seemed so after the horrendous battle.) Ruiz, by contrast, must have met Crockett (and Travis and Bowie) before the siege began and almost certainly would have been able to identify their bodies, as Santa Anna expected. Yet Ruiz didn't record his version till years later (precisely when is unclear), by which time the heroic myth that the Alamo's defenders fought to the last might have influenced what he remembered or chose to record. Labadie, likewise, didn't record Urizza's story till years later, but if the myth was acting by then, Labadie didn't succumb. It may be significant that Ruiz said nothing about *any* prisoners, whereas a fourth eyewitness account, by Santa Anna's secretary, Ramón Martínez Caro, agreed with de la Peña that some rebels were captured alive and subsequently executed. Then again, Martínez Caro—who put the number at five, rather than de la Peña's seven—didn't identify any of the prisoners by name. This is curious if in fact one of the prisoners was Crockett, the most famous man at the Alamo and one whom Santa Anna wanted specifically identified (according to Ruiz).

The details of Crockett's death must remain a mystery, like so much else in the past. (Why they generate such debate is a mystery of a different sort. Many of Crockett's admirers doubt that he would have let himself be taken prisoner while he retained the breath of life, and they argue that he must have gone down fighting. Yet it casts no aspersions on Crockett's resolve to imagine that he was physically overwhelmed by the attackers—perhaps dazed or otherwise wounded—and was simply unable to resist capture. If courage is the question, de la Peña's testimony that he endured torture uncomplainingly is proof of that.)

Wherever Crockett—or any of the others—died, they proved their point. Texas wouldn't be taken easily. Santa Anna lost some six hundred men in achieving his victory, and though at this stage of the war he could afford the losses, he might not enjoy that luxury for long. On a different plane, the glorious demise of the Alamo garrison gave the Texans a rallying cry that lifted their political struggle against Santa Anna to the moral realm. In life, Travis and Bowie and Crockett were hardly the sort to inspire reverence, hardly the kind parents would name their sons after. But in death they transcended their flaws; absolved of their sins, they entered the pantheon of American heroes. The specifics of the Texans' dispute with Mexico were unknown to most of those outside Texas, yet in the wake of the Alamo the specifics shaded into inconsequence. Whatever motivated men to die such a death must be righteous. Santa Anna's great blunder at Béxar was not to lose so many of his own men but to kill so many of the enemy (and after the battle to burn their bodies, which added to the sacrificial significance). A military struggle he might win; a moral struggle, never.

★

Not everyone in the Alamo that March day died. Susanna Dickinson, the wife of Almaron Dickinson, the captain of rebel artillery, had taken refuge in the Alamo with her husband and their infant daughter, Angelina, upon the approach of Santa Anna's army. When the battle began, Almaron told her to save herself and the baby, and as he ran to his post and his death, she and Angelina found a hiding place (in either the church or the powder magazine; accounts differ). Discovered by Mexican soldiers afterward, mother and child were brought before Santa Anna, with several other women and children who similarly survived the carnage. An undetermined number of slaves, including Travis's Joe, also escaped death, although Joe and perhaps some of the others were wounded.

Santa Anna could be a hard man, as he had revealed in Zacatecas in loosing his convict-troops on the civilian populace and as he had shown just now at the Alamo in expending hundreds of his own men lest the rebels surrender without a fight. But even he had no stomach for killing women and children in cold blood. Besides, he needed envoys to carry the grim tidings of the Alamo east to the American settlements. His decision to spare Joe and the slaves perhaps reflected his judgment that slaves weren't responsible for their masters' misdeeds; it might also have evinced his desire to encourage defection by Joe's fellow slaves among the rebels' bondsmen. Many of the Texans' slaves seemed to think Santa Anna would be their liberator; one Texan reported slaveholders on the lower Brazos saying that "their negroes, God damn them, were on the tip-toe of expectation, and rejoicing that the Mexicans were coming to make them free!"

Santa Anna did set the Alamo slaves free, although Joe, for one, returned to the American settlements, where the executors of Travis's estate reenslaved him. (He subsequently escaped.) As for the women and children, Santa Anna gave each woman a blanket and two dollars in silver and let them and their little ones go.

Susanna and Angelina Dickinson received special treatment. Wishing to ensure their safe passage to Houston's camp, Santa Anna dispatched the servant of one of his officers to accompany them east.

En route they encountered Joe, and the three were eventually intercepted by Houston's scouts, who guided them to the rebel commander at Gonzales, where Susanna and Joe told of the final hours of the Béxar garrison.

★

At Gonzales the bloody news from the Alamo met a less sanguinary report from Washington-on-the-Brazos. The convention had gathered on March 1; on March 2 it unanimously approved a declaration of Texas independence. The obvious model was the declaration of American independence of 1776; the obvious spur was Santa Anna's impending destruction of the Alamo, which made the Texas declaration both imperative, lest the heroes there die in vain, and dangerous, in that nothing worth noting stood between Santa Anna and the convention. As the American declaration had indicted King George for a litany of sins, so the Texas declaration indicted Santa Anna: for revoking the Mexican constitution, for establishing a military despotism, for suppressing the liberty of the Texans, for endangering their lives and property, for rejecting their petitions and imprisoning their emissaries, for demanding that they give up their arms, for sending mercenaries to war against them, for inciting the Indians, for dictating religious practice, for denying trial by jury, and for failing to provide public education. The Texas declaration asserted that the people of Texas had borne these injuries patiently, until patience ceased to be a virtue. The Texans then had risen in defense of their rights and the Mexican constitution. They had appealed to their fellow Mexicans to join them, but their appeal had been ignored, and continued to be ignored.

> We, therefore, the delegates with plenary powers of the
> people of Texas, in solemn convention assembled, appeal-

ing to a candid world for the necessities of our condition, do hereby resolve and declare that our political connection with the Mexican nation has forever ended, and that the people of Texas do now constitute a FREE, SOVEREIGN, and INDEPENDENT REPUBLIC.

As with most such manifestoes—including the American Declaration of Independence—the Texas declaration mingled honest grievances with the exaggerated or imaginary in its charge against the Mexican government. Santa Anna had indeed revoked the constitution under which most of the American settlers came to Texas, and he was ruling as a military despot. But the lack of religious freedom, of trial by jury, and of public education in Mexico was no surprise except to the willfully ignorant. Santa Anna's attempt to disarm the Texans followed years of unrest in Texas, and his army was no more mercenary—indeed, considerably less mercenary—than that of the Texans, which, at this point, consisted largely of foreigners enticed to Texas by promises of land.

In multiplying their grievances, the Texans actually weakened their case, which rested most firmly on Santa Anna's usurpation and the failure of federalists in Mexico to resist him. Or, rather, the Texans would have weakened their case if their primary audience had been the generalized "candid world" of which their declaration spoke. In fact, the primary audience was more specific: American citizens and the American government. The Texas declaration was partly a statement of principles but equally an appeal for American help. The more Texas looked like the United States—starting with a declaration modeled on Jefferson's—the more appealing it would be to Americans.

This is not to say that the Texans who drafted the declaration (chiefly George Childress, who seems to have arrived at Washington with a draft in his pocket) or those who signed it (including Sam Houston, returned from his peace-piping with the Cherokees; Lorenzo de Zavala, having despaired of reforming Mexico from within; Sterling Robertson, the old empresario; Samuel Maverick, the refugee from Béxar; and José Antonio Navarro, a former federal congressman from San Antonio) were disingenuous. They were in the middle of a war, which they were currently losing. Their property and quite possibly their lives depended on receiving help from across the Sabine. They were in no position to split hairs on Mexican malfeasance.

The convention had business besides declaring independence; it had to create the instruments by which its declaration might be realized. All the rebels agreed, in the wisdom of hindsight regarding the cost of their past disagreements on the subject, that the army must answer to a single head. If a unified command had existed from the start of the revolution, the garrison at the Alamo might never have found itself in such a fix. At this point there was no credible alternative to Sam Houston, and on the second day after endorsing independence, the convention unanimously confirmed Houston as major general and "commander in chief of the land forces of the Texian Army, both Regulars, Volunteers, and Militia while in actual service." No less to the point, the convention made all able-bodied males between seventeen and fifty liable for military service, subject to punishment for failure to serve but also subject to reward (in land) for compliance.

The convention went on to write a constitution for the Republic of Texas. The new Texas government would have a legislature of two houses and an executive headed by a president and a vice president. Texas law would be based on the common law. Local government would be provided by counties, with boundaries to be determined in due course. As the constitution would not take effect until ratified by the people, the convention created an interim executive to manage the war. David Burnet was elected interim president, Lorenzo de Zavala vice president, Thomas Rusk secretary of war.

★

The leisurely pace of communications in the 1830s, an era before the telegraph and largely before railroads, was typically a hindrance to the conduct of public affairs. But it benefited the Texans in the aftermath of the Alamo, for as the news of the disaster was making its way east, many volunteers from the United States headed west under the mistaken belief the Texans were winning their war.

J. H. Barnard left Chicago in the flush of the Texans' first victories. "Goliad had been taken in a gallant manner, and the Texan forces were collecting to capture San Antonio," Barnard wrote. He read the recruiting appeals and felt an instant kinship to the Texans. "They were in arms for a cause that I had always been taught to consider sacred, viz.: republican principles and popular institutions. They had entered into the contest with spirit, and were carrying it out with vigor." Chicago in late 1835 was nothing like the metropolis it would become, and the village on the swampy shore of Lake Michigan, with winter winds that rattled the rafters of its houses and the bones of its residents, couldn't hold Barnard, a medical doctor with few patients, against the warm promise of Texas. "I was instantly possessed of a desire to render my personal services, however insignificant they might be, in their behalf. Accordingly, I hastily closed my business and left Chicago on December 14, 1835, in company with two young men bound for Texas."

The trio descended the Mississippi to New Orleans, where they bought weapons and provisions and, with a handful of emigrants and almost a score of volunteers, boarded a schooner for the Texas coast. The captain kept a sharp eye for Mexican cruisers, fearful of losing his craft and having all aboard imprisoned or worse as pirates. But the only vessel they raised was another charter, carrying a similar complement of volunteers, from Alabama. "We ran alongside and were saluted with three cheers, which were heartily returned," Barnard wrote.

The enthusiasm diminished on landing at Matagorda, near the mouth of the Colorado. Barnard had come to Texas to join the rebel army. "But now there seemed to be no army, at least no regular troops. There were, to be sure, some parties in the west. Colonel Fannin had a company at Goliad, and Colonel Travis one at San Antonio." But most of the Texans who had taken part in the assault on San Antonio had gone home, and most of the volunteers from the States were involved in the campaign against Matamoros—"which seemed to me wild and visionary, and I felt no inclination to join." Stephen Austin had told Barnard at New Orleans to report to General Houston. "This course I would have been glad to pursue, but no one could inform me where he was or where his headquarters were established." The only fighting Barnard could detect was "the disgraceful row between Governor Smith and the council."

Barnard decided to explore the area while waiting for things to sort out. With two other young men he embarked on a tour of the estuary of the Colorado. "We cruised around here several days, and amused ourselves by hunting and fishing and examining the bay." They reencountered the Alabama volunteers and became better acquainted. The "Red Rovers" were captained by Jack Shackelford, like Barnard a physician but farther along in life. "Of mature age, surrounded by an amiable family and possessing a lucrative practice, the

first call [from Texas] for sympathy and aid struck a responsive chord
in his breast. He immediately collected a company from his neighborhood, and left home and business to take part in the struggle for
freedom." Barnard happened to be with Shackelford when the Alabama captain received instructions from the provisional council to
take his company to Goliad and put them at the disposal of Colonel
Fannin. Shortly thereafter a letter from Fannin himself arrived, asking for volunteers. "I no longer felt any hesitancy as to what I should
do," Barnard wrote, "but immediately joined Captain Shackelford's
company and prepared to march with them to Goliad."

About seventy volunteers—sixty Rovers and ten others, including Barnard—began the march up the Lavaca River. All were in high
spirits, enjoying the adventure of travel and the excitement of
prospective danger. But some of the men got drunk and then quar-
relsome. "Knives were drawn, pistols presented, and I fully expected
to witness a scene of tumult and death," Barnard wrote. Shackelford
was compelled to intervene, and by force of character and threat of
blows he persuaded the belligerents to retreat.

On February 12 the column reached Goliad. Barnard was a
novice in military affairs, but he sized up the town with an eye toward
its defense.

> It is built upon a rocky elevation and is a good military po-
> sition. A square of about three and one-half acres is en-
> closed by a stone wall of eight or ten feet in height, the
> sides facing nearly to the cardinal points. The entrance or
> gate-way is about the middle of the south wall. . . . The
> walls are built of stone and are about three feet in thick-
> ness; they are carried up about twenty feet, when they are
> turned over in an arch for the roof, which has a parapet

around it about four feet in height. The whole structure impresses one strongly with the idea of solidity and durability.

At the time of Barnard's arrival, the Goliad garrison included around three hundred officers and men. The Shackelford group, with some others who arrived about the same time, increased the garrison's strength to more than four hundred. "We were abundantly supplied with provisions, and with arms and ammunition," Barnard wrote. "Almost every man had his rifle and brace of pistols, besides there were a good number of English muskets captured from the Mexicans, and we had five or six pieces of artillery." The men improved the fort's defenses, strengthening walls and building a covered passageway to the river to protect their water supply. This accomplished, the garrison confidently awaited the approach of the enemy. "Prepared as we were, we fully believed ourselves able to stand against many times our number, not doubting that on being attacked the citizens would at once come to our support."

The first slight breach in this wall of confidence occurred with the arrival of Frank Johnson and a few others who had narrowly escaped the debacle at San Patricio and now brought word that General Urrea was marching north with a large army. Not much later came the news that Santa Anna was at Béxar with another large force. The approach of the Mexicans had provoked an exodus by settlers from the vicinity of Refugio; many passed through Goliad in their flight, raising the level of concern among the garrison still more.

Barnard was one of the party Fannin organized to relieve Travis and the Alamo defenders at the end of February. With the others Barnard crossed the San Antonio; with the others he crossed back after Fannin and the officers decided to abandon the relief expedition. This reversal additionally eroded morale among the Goliad garrison, and the erosion started to feed on itself. "The signs of coming danger began to produce a feeling of anxiety, which was further increased by many vague and groundless rumors that circulated among the men. The confinement in the garrison became irksome; our provisions, of which we had at first an abundance, were becoming short; the restraints of discipline, now more necessary than ever in their enforcement, produced discontent and murmurs and a loss of confidence in their commander."

Had Fannin known either more or less than he did about military affairs, his command might not have met the fate it did. An utter novice might have pushed on to the Alamo and perhaps, by tripling the size of the garrison there, helped it hold out until relieved by Houston, who likely would have been compelled by the raised stakes to go to its assistance. A thorough veteran would have realized that with Santa Anna at Béxar and Urrea on the Nueces, Goliad had become both superfluous and untenable. Already outflanked, Goliad could neither hinder the Mexican advance nor defend itself from a pincer assault.

But Fannin stayed where he was, unable to decide what to do. At times he breathed defiance. "I have about 420 men here, and if I can get provisions in tomorrow or next day, can maintain myself against any force," he wrote on February 28. "I will never give up the ship, while there is a pea in the ditch. If I am whipped, it will be *well done*." But at other moments—sometimes in the same letter—he complained at being badly used by the people and leaders of Texas. He especially resented the failure of the colonists to come to their own defense, which they had left to the foreign volunteers. "I have but three citizens in the ranks," he said. "Though I have called on them for six weeks, not one yet arrived, and no assistance in bringing me provisions. . . . I feel too indignant to say more about them. If I was honorably out of their service, I would never re-enter it. . . . If I am lost, be the censure on the right head, and my wife and children and children's children curse the sluggards forever."

As the noose tightened around the Alamo, Fannin and the garrison at Goliad anticipated finding themselves similarly besieged. "We are in hourly expectation of an attack," John Brooks wrote on March 4. "But, from the want of horses, we are unable to obtain any accurate information on the strength or movements of the enemy." The waiting and the not knowing elicited reflection in the men. "My life has indeed been a wayward and useless one," Brooks told his sister, who apparently had chided him on the subject, "and you can not be more sensible of it, or more sincerely deplore it, than myself." Of late, however, he had discovered his calling, such as it was. "*I am a soldier of fortune*. . . . My profession, perhaps for life, be it short or long, will be that of *arms*. It is the only pursuit in which I could feel a throb of interest." Yet it wasn't an ignoble calling, at least not when devoted to a worthy cause, as it was now. "It is the cause of liberty, of the oppressed against the tyrant, of the free man against the bigoted slave, and, what recommends it more strongly to me, of the weak against the strong. If I fall, let me fall—it is one of the chances of the game I play—a casualty to which every soldier is liable. My prayer has been, since my earliest recollection, to die on the field of battle, with the shout of victory in my ears; and if it is the will of high Heaven that that fate should meet me now, I will not murmur."

While hoping for relief, Fannin tried to assist the refugees from Refugio. He sent Amon King and a company of men to aid in the evacuation. But King decided to punish some Tejanos in the area who sympathized with Santa Anna, and in the process he tangled with an advance guard of Urrea's army. The latter forced King's company to take refuge in the mission at Refugio, where they were surrounded.

King managed to get a message out to Fannin, who thereupon dispatched a company of Georgians under William Ward. The Georgians lifted the siege, but then Ward and King, rather than returning at once to Goliad, as prudence dictated, lingered in the area. King insisted on completing his punishment of the local Mexican loyalists, while Ward stayed at Refugio. In King's absence Ward was surrounded by the main force of Urrea's army. King and his men returned to attempt a rescue, only to be pinned down themselves by Urrea's rifles. The double battle was a standoff until the Texans ran out of bullets and powder. Under the cover of dark the two Texas companies tried to escape. But the numbers of the enemy and the antipathy of the locals, who reported to Urrea on the rebels' progress, doomed both Texan contingents. King and his men were captured the next day and sent back to Refugio. Ward's battalion got farther but eventually surrendered as well.

The Refugio affair gravely weakened Fannin's force at a time when it needed every man, if only to conduct a successful retreat. On March 11 Houston sent Fannin two letters. The first relayed the grim news of the Alamo's fall; the second instructed Fannin to abandon Goliad and retreat to Victoria, on the Guadalupe below Gonzales. "Previous to abandoning Goliad, you will take the necessary measures to blow up that fortress, and do so before leaving its vicinity," Houston said. Haste was essential. "The immediate advance of the enemy may be confidently expected, as well as a rise of water. Prompt movements are therefore highly important."

But if decisiveness wasn't in Fannin's character, neither was promptness. He delayed nearly a week before obeying Houston's order, hoping Ward and King would return. If they had, Fannin's procrastination might have been repaid, for the combined force could have retreated more strongly than Fannin's reduced force did alone. But the delay also allowed Urrea to close in. And even after Fannin discovered that Ward and King would not be returning, he dallied at Goliad. He held a council of war and then wasted a day allowing one of his companies to chase loyalist scouts around the neighborhood of the town—and letting the rest of the garrison watch rather than make ready for the retreat. "As the affair was nearly all visible from the fort," J. H. Barnard recalled, "it produced considerable excitement, and all left the work to see the 'sport.' " The effort yielded a minor victory and a momentary feeling of satisfaction. "The events of the day had animated all, and good humor and cheerfulness prevailed," Barnard said. But they also wasted dwindling time.

The garrison got away the next morning, after putting the town to the torch. The first leg of the march was ominously labored. "The country around us seemed entirely deserted," explained Herman Ehrenberg, whose New Orleans Greys had joined Fannin after heeding Houston's plea not to go to Matamoros. "Even the usual spies had stopped prowling around. . . . A large number of wagons laden with foodstuffs and ammunition encumbered and slowed up our march, for, unwilling at first to lose all our belongings, we had taken with us much heavy baggage." To speed the column, Fannin ordered some of the baggage abandoned. When this afforded only marginal improvement, he took more-drastic measures. "Several wagons were broken up or merely abandoned, and their teams hitched to the remaining carts," Ehrenberg said. "After crawling on a little farther, disgust at the creeping pace of our column induced us finally to abandon all our equipment."

But they didn't abandon it soon enough. Despite keeping a lookout all morning, Fannin's column saw not a single Mexican, encouraging the commander to call a noon halt. The men were nervous at this additional delay, but Fannin dismissed their worries. "His former experience in fighting Mexicans had led him to entertain a great

contempt for them as soldiers, and caused him to neglect such pre-
cautionary measures as were requisite from their great numerical
strength and superiority," Barnard wrote. The march resumed, and
the column advanced toward Coleto Creek, where timber along the
banks promised protection.

They were still a mile from the creek when a unit of Mexican
cavalry, Urrea's advance guard, rode into sight. Fannin's officers
urged that the column dash for the creek, where the cover would
make up for their lack of numbers. Fannin rejected the advice and
ordered the men to form a hollow square, with the four artillery
pieces they still possessed at the corners.

"Our army now waited for the approach of its adversaries,"
Ehrenberg recalled. The Mexicans fired, futilely, from several hundred yards, then from closer range, with no more effect. The Texans
continued to wait. "We did not return their fire because they were still
beyond the reach of our rifles. Our artillery officers, tall fine-looking
Poles, decided likewise to let the enemy's cavalry draw nearer before
opening fire. Finally, when the Mexican horsemen had come close
enough to us, our front line moved aside so as to leave free range to
our cannon, which poured heavy shot upon our hasty and over-
confident assailants." The Texans' patience was well rewarded. "The
effect of our artillery fire was immediate and horrible. Frightened by
the noise, the horses of the enemy plunged and kicked wildly. Many
of the Mexicans were thrown off their saddles, and their riderless
horses galloped aimlessly across the field, while wounded men and
beasts lying prostrate in the dust were trampled upon by the advancing or retreating cavalry squadrons."

The Texans held their own throughout the afternoon. The Mexicans charged, then charged again, but each time were repulsed by
the defenders' fire. Yet the bleakness of the Texans' predicament was

evident to all. By now the bulk of Urrea's army had arrived, and it encircled the Texans, who were running low on ammunition and lacked water to cool their cannons, which became inoperable from overheating, and to assuage their thirst, which became unbearable, especially for the hemorrhaging wounded. Darkness brought a respite from the shooting but not from the Texans' danger and discomfort. "We heaped, around our small camp, wagons, dead horses, and human corpses, so as to have some kind of shelter if the enemy made a night attack," Ehrenberg wrote. "The groans of the wounded increased the misery and horror of our situation. The cries of pain uttered by the stricken soldiers, the muffled thuds arising from the building of our barricades, and the challenges of the Mexican sentries broke the silence of the prairie, which lay dark and cheerless around us. There was not the smallest breath of air, and the moisture of the atmosphere added to the discomfort of our wounded companions. A few of them, consumed by burning fever . . . begged pitifully for water. Our canteens were empty, and although it wrung our hearts to see them suffer, we could not even moisten their parched lips with a drop of water." A light rain began to fall, easing the fever of the wounded and some of their thirst, but it also dampened the unprotected powder of the Texans, rendering much of it useless.

Another argument broke out among the officers. Several, including those leading Ehrenberg's Greys, wanted to risk everything in an attempt to fight through the Mexican lines to Victoria, ten miles away. Others, including Barnard's Captain Shackelford, refused to countenance any scheme that would leave the Texan wounded (about fifty, besides the nine or ten killed thus far) to the mercy of the Mexicans, who, on the evidence of the Alamo, had none for rebels. Fannin, himself wounded, albeit not seriously, sided with Shackelford.

With dawn the Texans' position appeared hopeless. Additional

Mexican artillery had been positioned in the night, trained from high ground down upon on the Texans' wall-less square. Fannin had been hoping that some scouts who hadn't been trapped the previous day might bring relief from Victoria. But when no help arrived, and when the Mexican cannons began pounding the Texas troops, he signaled to Urrea a desire to parley.

★

At this point the story becomes confused. "I immediately ordered my battery to cease firing and instructed Lieut. Col. Morales, Captain Juan José Holzinger, and my aide, José de la Luz González, to approach the enemy and ascertain their purpose," Urrea recalled. "The first of these returned soon after, stating that they wished to capitulate. My reply restricted itself to stating that I could not accept any terms except an unconditional surrender." This prompted some back-and-forth with the Texans. Then, Urrea continued, "desirous of putting an end to the negotiations, I went over to the enemy's camp and explained to their leader the impossibility in which I found myself of granting other terms than an unconditional surrender. . . . Addressing myself to Fannin and his companions in the presence of Messrs. Morales, Salas, Holzinger and others, I said conclusively, 'If you gentlemen wish to surrender at discretion, the matter is ended; otherwise I shall return to my camp and renew the attack.' " Urrea was acting under the duress of Santa Anna's no-quarter policy; he seems to have been speaking sincerely when he said, "In spite of my great desire of offering them guarantees as humanity dictated, this was beyond my authority. Had I been in a position to do so, I would have at least guaranteed them their lives." Urrea added: "Fannin was a gentleman, a man of courage, a quality which makes us soldiers esteem each other mutually. His manners captivated my affection, and if it had been in my hand to save him, together with his companions, I would have gladly done so. All I could do was to offer him to use my influence with the general-in-chief. . . . After my ultimatum, the leaders of the enemy had a conference among themselves, and the result of the conference was their surrender according to the terms I proposed."

The Texans remembered things differently. Ehrenberg found himself in the middle of negotiations when it was discovered that none of the Mexican officers spoke much English and none of the Texans much Spanish. But Mexican captain Holzinger, like Ehrenberg, spoke German, and so the parley was conducted largely in German, with Holzinger interpreting to the Mexicans and Ehrenberg to the Texans. As Ehrenberg recalled, "After a long debate, Fannin finally agreed to the surrender of all our arms, but we were to retain our private property and were to be sent by ship from Copano or Matamoros to New Orleans, where we would be set free on condition that we gave our word of honor not to fight any longer against the present government of Mexico." Ehrenberg added parenthetically: "This promise would not have been a serious obstacle to us, since in Mexico governments changed almost every year."

Barnard, who apparently learned the terms of the surrender along with the rest of the Texans, remembered the events much as Ehrenberg did. "After some parley," Barnard said, "a capitulation with General Urrea was agreed upon, the terms of which were that we should lay down our arms and surrender as prisoners of war; that we should be treated as such, according to the usages of civilized nations; that our wounded men should be taken back to Goliad and properly attended; and that all private property should be respected. These were the terms that Colonel Fannin distinctly told his men on his return had been agreed upon, and which was confirmed by Major Wallace and Captain Dusaugue." Barnard corroborated, for the most part, Ehrenberg's recollection regarding transport to New Orleans. "We were also told, although I cannot vouch for the authority, that as soon as possible we should be sent to New Orleans under parole not to serve any more against Mexico during the war with Texas. . . . It seemed to be confirmed by an observation of the Mexican Colonel Holzinger, who came to superintend the receiving of our arms. As we delivered them up, he exclaimed: 'Well, gentlemen, in ten days, liberty and home.'"

Barnard remembered that Fannin, upon returning to the Texan lines, sat down to record the terms of the surrender. What Fannin wrote confirmed—confusingly—both versions of the story.

Art. 1st. The Mexican troops having placed their artillery at a distance of one hundred and seventy paces from us, and having opened fire, we raised a white flag. . . . We proposed to them to surrender at discretion, and they agreed.

Art. 2nd. That the wounded and the commandant Fannin shall be treated with all possible consideration upon the surrender of all their arms.

Art. 3rd. The whole detachment shall be treated as prisoners of war and placed at the disposition of the supreme government.

Camp on the Coleto between the Guadalupe and La Bahia. March 20, 1836.

B. C. Wallace, commandant. I. M. Chadwick, adjutant to the commandant.

Approved: J. W. Fannin, Jr., commanding.

To this statement was appended a note:

Because, when the white flag was raised by the enemy, I
made it known to their officer that I could not grant any
other terms than a surrender at discretion, without any
other condition, and this was agreed to through the officers stated above; the other petitions which the sub-
scribers of this surrender make will not be granted. I told
them this, and it was agreed to. I must not, nor can I, grant
anything else.

José Urrea

Fannin, apparently, tried to have things both ways—as did Urrea. On their own, the two could have agreed on a capitulation that
would have guaranteed the rebels their lives and perhaps passage out
of Texas. Urrea made his feelings on this subject apparent to the Texans, as he admitted afterward. "They doubtless surrendered confident that Mexican generosity would not make their surrender
useless, for under any other circumstances they would have sold their
lives dearly, fighting to the last." But Urrea wouldn't countenance
anything on paper except an unconditional surrender. Fannin knew
his men couldn't continue the battle without inviting a massacre, and
he didn't want to be responsible for another Alamo. He wrote the
terms he wanted into the surrender document, including the contra-
diction—in light of announced Mexican policy—between surrender at
discretion and treatment as prisoners of war. And he almost certainly
stressed the latter in explaining the capitulation to the men. He was
in no position to prevent Urrea from adding his own interpretation at
the end of the document, and he was in no mood to share that interpretation with his men, lest some of them reject the agreement and
resume fighting on their own, jeopardizing the safety of everyone

else. In other words, Fannin was throwing his men on the mercy of
Urrea without telling them so.

Implicit in Fannin's action was a belief, or a hope, that Urrea could
persuade Santa Anna to soften his policy toward the rebels. Santa
Anna wasn't admitting at this point how many men he had lost at the
Alamo, but Urrea must have known that the Mexican army couldn't
stand many more such victories. A policy of no quarter might terrorize the Texans into abandoning their revolution, as Santa Anna obviously intended, but it might instead have the opposite effect, turning
every battle into an Alamo. The rebel army was small, yet the reser-
voir from which the Texans were drawing recruits—the United
States—was vast. A war of attrition hardly favored Mexico. Besides,
paroled prisoners returned to New Orleans could serve as harbingers
of defeat, discouraging other volunteers from taking up the Texas
cause.

Urrea knew better, however, than to argue policy with his commander. Instead he appealed to Santa Anna's soldierly sense. In his
report of the victory at Coleto Creek, Urrea praised the performance
of his men, citing "the bravery and daring of the gallant officers and
soldiers who, with so much honor and courage, added luster to the
characteristic valor of the Mexican army." He went on to explain that,
as formidable as they were in battle, they were equally magnanimous
in victory. "Immediately upon the surrender of the enemy, their fury
was changed to the most admirable indulgence. This show of generosity after a hotly contested engagement is worthy of the highest
commendation, and I can do no less than to commend it to Your Excellency." Urrea told how his men had taken three hundred prisoners, who were currently "all in my power." He wasn't so bold as to say

so directly, but his implication—that Santa Anna wouldn't want to stain this great victory by ordering the execution of the prisoners—was clear.

Santa Anna grew livid on receiving this message, probably less from Urrea's failure to follow orders than from his presumption in trying to push the commander into a corner. The whole point of the no-quarter policy was to kill the rebels on the battlefield, where such killings could be rationalized as occurring in the heat of the fight. By taking prisoners, Urrea had maneuvered Santa Anna into having to give a positive order for a mass execution, which Urrea apparently believed Santa Anna wouldn't do.

Perhaps Santa Anna hesitated. Perhaps he weighed magnanimity for its political and diplomatic effects, if not for its own merits. But if he did so, he never let on. He claimed to be bound by Mexican law and by a higher duty. "Law commands, and the magistrate has no power to mitigate its rigor; for him it is to put it into execution," he said afterward. "If, in the execution of law, no discretion is allowed a judge, how can a general in a campaign be expected to exercise greater freedom? The prisoners of Goliad were condemned by law, by a universal law, that of personal defense, enjoyed by all nations and individuals. . . . How could I divert the sword of justice from their heads without making it fall upon my own?" Santa Anna conceded that he thought the law just; but even if it wasn't, he was not to blame for carrying it out. "Can there be greater blindness than to impute the crime to the dagger and not to the hand that wields it?"

His orders to the field were less philosophical. Following the surrender, the Texan prisoners were marched back to Goliad and imprisoned in their old fort. Colonel Nicolás de la Portilla had charge of them; Urrea, doubtless fearing that his ploy regarding the prisoners wouldn't work, and not wishing to have their blood directly on his hands, proceeded to Victoria, which he occupied. Santa Anna wrote straight to Portilla, knowing that while a triumphant general might try to disobey orders, a mere colonel wouldn't dare.

> I am informed that there have been sent to you by General Urrea two hundred and thirty four prisoners. . . . As the supreme government has ordered that all foreigners taken with arms in their hands, making war upon the nation, shall be treated as pirates, I have been surprised that the circular of the said government has not been fully complied with in this particular. I therefore order that you should give immediate effect to the said ordinance in respect to all those foreigners who have yielded to the force of arms, having had the audacity to come and insult the republic, to devastate with fire and sword, as has been the case in Goliad, causing vast detriment to our citizens, in a word, shedding the precious blood of Mexican citizens, whose only crime has been their fidelity to their country. I trust that, in reply to this, you will inform me that public vengeance has been satisfied by the punishment of such detestable delinquents.

Santa Anna's order, which the commander in chief copied to Urrea as a reminder of who was in charge, caused Portilla real anguish. "At seven in the evening I received orders from General Santa Anna by special messenger, instructing me to execute at once all prisoners taken by force of arms agreeable to the general orders on the subject," he wrote in his diary for March 26. "I kept the matter secret, and no one knew of it except Colonel Garay. . . . At eight o'clock on the same night, I received a communication from General Urrea by special messenger in which, among other things, he says, 'Treat the prisoners well, especially Fannin. Keep them busy rebuilding the town and erecting a fort. Feed them with the cattle you will receive from Refugio.' What a cruel contrast in these opposite instructions! I spent a restless night."

The prisoners slept better than Portilla that night. Fannin's decision to surrender had outraged many of his men, with the Greys nearly mutinying at the prospect of handing themselves over to the authors of the Alamo. "Their indignation soon broke out in violent protests," Ehrenberg wrote. "After upbraiding Fannin for his weakness, they reminded him of the disastrous fate which had overtaken the other volunteers who had sought safety in a truce with the treacherous Mexicans." But the opponents found themselves in a minority. "Their words roused no response among their comrades. Many of the volunteers in Fannin's army were tired of soldiering. They resented the restraints of military life and were therefore not averse to a capitulation which held out to them the hope of an early return to the United States. . . . My companions and I saw very quickly that Fannin's move in favor of peace met with the approval of the majority of his troops, so that further opposition would have been futile." Yet they continued to display their dissatisfaction. One man named Johnson was especially upset. "Unable to control his anger, he gnashed his teeth, clenched his fists, and stamped furiously on the ground." A short while later, the Texans' powder wagon exploded in a brilliant burst of light and with a concussion that knocked down prisoners and guards on all sides. As luck would have it, the injuries were relatively slight, except to one man, Johnson, who died. Ehrenberg concluded that Johnson had touched off the powder deliberately, preferring instant death to the uncertainty of remaining a prisoner.

The march back to Goliad calmed the fears of some of the prisoners but not of all. Barnard heard Captain Dusaugue, the translator in the surrender negotiations, solemnly declare, "I am now prepared for any fate," after an encounter with one of the Mexican officers. "The words and his manner struck us with surprise," Barnard recalled, "and we asked if he had ascertained by anything the captain had said that treachery was meditated. He said no, but repeated his former remark." About that time, the Texans and their guards were wading across the San Antonio River. Darkness had fallen, and fatigue and inattention were overtaking the guards. "The idea struck me that here was a chance for escape, by silently dropping into the water while the guard and the captain were on the other side and from the darkness could not see me," Barnard said. "In two or three minutes I would have floated beyond their reach, and being a good swimmer could then easily escape." But before Barnard could make up his mind to move, the guard approached and the moment passed.

Barnard and the other American physicians were separated from the rest of the prisoners and made to tend the Mexican wounded, after which they were allowed to treat the Texans. For them, with something useful to occupy their time, the imprisonment was not especially unpleasant. Other prisoners were added to the Coleto group, including William Ward and the remainder of the Georgians, captured after their flight from Refugio. Fannin and his adjutant, Chadwick, were taken to the coast at Copano, evidently to arrange transport to New Orleans. They returned on Saturday, March 26. "They were in good spirits and endeavored to cheer us up," Barnard wrote. "They spoke of the kindness with which they had been treated by the Mexican Colonel Holzinger, who went with them, and their hopes of our speedy release. Fannin asked me to dress his wound, and then talked of his wife and children with much fondness until a late hour." Fannin's optimism was heartening. "I laid down to rest this evening," Barnard wrote, "with more pleasure and happier anticipations than I before had allowed myself to indulge in."

Captivity weighed more heavily on most of the other prisoners. Fatigue, crowding, and hunger were the principal complaints. "Several of my comrades were so exhausted that they slept standing, for the crowded state of the prison prevented us from lying down," Ehrenberg recalled. "A few of our smaller companions who could sit down enjoyed greater repose than the others. But even then they could not remain in their sitting position very long, for the atmosphere grew so close that squatting on the floor was bearable for a short time only."

During the first few days the men had almost nothing to eat. They grew restive in their hunger; some suggested that they would die better trying to escape than slowly starving. Ehrenberg thought he detected a design in the withholding of food. "The cannon in front of the door were loaded and the Mexicans who stood by held lighted wicks in their hands. It was evident that any rebellion on our part would end only in blood and death. I firmly believe that the enemy's plan was to starve us into rebellion and then to massacre us when we tried to secure our rights by force. Such conduct would have given a very plausible excuse to Santa Anna and his colleagues for our deaths."

If this indeed was the plan, not all the Mexican officers got the word. A herd of cattle was brought in, and the prisoners were allotted several ounces of beef per man. Some managed to cook their cuts over small fires fueled by wood stripped from the walls of the building that housed them; others ate their meat raw. The meal didn't cure the hunger of the men, but it eased the desperation that might have provoked an uprising. On subsequent days the prisoners were allowed to purchase tortillas from the Mexican soldiers in exchange for personal effects and items of clothing. By the time they reached the prisoners, the tortillas were "about as tough as leather," Ehrenberg said. "But we were all so hungry that we were glad to eat them."

At one point Mexican colonel Holzinger pulled his fellow Germans among the prisoners aside, with an offer that they abandon the Americans and join the Mexican army. They rejected the offer, Ehrenberg most indignantly. "It was mere nonsense to talk of belonging to different nations when feeling and misfortune made us one," Ehrenberg wrote. "Nothing stood between us now. We were no longer English, German, or American; we were Texans."

As Texans they were summoned from their quarters on Sunday morning, March 27. "Grey clouds hung over the horizon, and the air was hot and sultry," Ehrenberg recalled. The prisoners were told to make ready to march. Some asked where they were going but received no reply. The Mexicans wore parade uniforms, which seemed odd, and none carried knapsacks or other gear for a journey.

"Mexican soldiers met us on either side as we came out of the main entrance," Ehrenberg wrote. "They were drawn up in two lines, one man behind the other, so that we were closely guarded on both sides when we marched forward." The prisoners numbered about four hundred, the guards almost twice that many. The Texans expected to take the road to the coast, but they were directed toward Victoria instead. "The motive of this unforeseen change of plans gave us food for meditation." The mood grew more ominous with each step. "The Mexican soldiers, who were as a rule very talkative, were unbearably silent; our men were grave; the atmosphere hot and close."

The prisoners and guards had marched less than a mile from

the fort when the officer in charge ordered a detour off the road. "On our left there stood a row of mesquite trees, five or six feet high, stretching in a straight line as far as the bank of the San Antonio River, which lay some way off," Ehrenberg remembered. "The river flowed between banks thirty or forty feet high, which on our side rose almost perpendicularly from the water. We followed the hedge toward the river, wondering why we were being taken in this direction."

Ehrenberg and his fellows weren't the only ones with questions. At dawn that day, Barnard, Shackelford, and the others with medical training had been summoned by Colonel Garay, one of the few Mexican officers who spoke English. Garay ordered them to report to his quarters, which lay in an orchard a quarter mile from the fort. "He was very serious and grave in countenance," Barnard remembered, "but we took but little notice of it at the time." Barnard and the others assumed they were to treat more of the Mexican soldiers, yet when they reached Garay's quarters, they saw no wounded men. An enlisted man—a boy, really, named Martínez—who said he had lived in Kentucky engaged them in idle conversation. Barnard and the others grew impatient at this curious performance and said they would return to the fort. Martínez, however, explained that he had orders from Garay to keep them there. The colonel, he said, would appear shortly.

Puzzled and annoyed, the medics were surprised to hear a volley of muskets. They asked Martínez what the shooting was about. He responded vaguely that some of the soldiers must be discharging their weapons to clean them.

"My ears had, however, detected yells and shouts . . . ," Barnard wrote, "which, although at some distance from us, I recognized as the voices of my countrymen. We started, and turning my head in that direction, I saw through the partial openings in the trees several prisoners running with their utmost speed and directly after them Mexican soldiers in pursuit of them." Now Colonel Garay appeared. "Keep still, gentlemen, you are safe," he said. "This is not my orders, nor do I execute them." He explained that the previous night he had been commanded to shoot all the prisoners, but he had determined to save the surgeons and a few others and would plead that they had been captured without arms.

So Barnard and the others listened as the executions proceeded. "In the course of five or ten minutes, we heard as many as four distinct volleys fired in as many directions, and irregular firing that was kept up an hour or two before it ceased. Our situation and feelings at this time may be imagined, but it is not in the power of language to express them. The sound of every gun that rang on our ears told but too terribly the fate of our brave companions, while their cries that occasionally reached us heightened the horrors of the scene."

Shackelford, who sat beside Barnard through all this, was in agony. "His company of 'Red Rovers,' that he brought out and commanded were young men of the first families in his neighborhood—his particular and esteemed friends," Barnard recorded. "Besides, two of his nephews who had volunteered with him, and his eldest son, a talented youth, the pride of his father and beloved of his company, were there." Shackelford could hear them being killed but could do nothing to save them.

Barnard later learned that Fannin had been executed separately from the other prisoners. "When told he was to be shot, he heard it unmoved, but, giving his watch and money to the officer who was to superintend his execution, he requested that he might not be shot in the head and that he might be decently buried." His request was ignored. "He was shot in the head and his body stripped and tumbled into a pile with the others."

Barnard discovered that such mercy as the Mexicans displayed was largely the work of a Señora Álvarez—"whose name ought to be perpetuated to the end of time for her virtues," he declared. This woman, the wife of one of General Urrea's officers, upon hearing of the execution order, had pleaded with Colonel Garay to save whomever he could. Her entreaties, combined with Garay's own revulsion at the order, had caused him to pull aside the surgeons and the handful of others. "In consequence," Barnard wrote, "a few of us were left to tell of that bloody day."

★

But not those few alone. By a miracle, Herman Ehrenberg escaped the slaughter. In the line with the others on the bank above the San Antonio River, Ehrenberg became aware of what was in store for the prisoners at about the same time Barnard did. "A command to halt, given in Spanish, struck our ears like the voice of doom, for at that very moment we heard the distant rattle of a volley of musketry." The officer at hand spoke again, ordering the prisoners to kneel. The Mexican guards moved close and put the muzzles of their guns against the prisoners' chests.

Briefly Ehrenberg and the others thought the Mexicans were bluffing, that this was a device to get the prisoners to turn coat and join the Mexican army. But they soon realized the dead earnestness of the action. "A second volley of musketry came to our ears from another direction; this time a wail of distress followed it." Before Ehrenberg had time to absorb the meaning of what was happening, the soldiers with his group opened fire. "Thick clouds of smoke rolled slowly toward the river. The blood of my lieutenant spurted on my clothes, and around me the last convulsions of agony shook the bodies of my friends."

Somehow the point-blank volley spared Ehrenberg. Though stunned by the mass killing, he retained sufficient presence of mind to dive to the ground, then to scramble beneath the smoke toward the river. A Mexican soldier slashed at him with a sword, but he hurtled forward, plunging down the steep bank into the water. The Mexicans fired at him from the top of the bank, yet between the obscuring effects of the smoke and his repeated dives under the surface, the bullets missed. He reached the other side and pulled out to catch his breath. "I looked back at the place where my friends lay bleeding to death. The enemy was still shooting and yelling, and it was with a sorrowful heart that I listened to these shouts of triumph which in my fancy were mingled with the groans of pain of my dying friends."

Runaway

Ehrenberg's safety was hardly ensured when he reached the east bank of the San Antonio River. His miraculous escape from the Goliad slaughter bought him a reprieve from danger but no more than that, for on commencing his flight eastward, away from the Mexican lines, he discovered that he was one of thousands similarly running for their lives. Precisely as Santa Anna intended, word of the Mexican commander's unsparing treatment of rebels spread before his advancing forces, provoking dismay among the rebels and panic among the populace. "It is said that Santa Anna designs driving all the Americans beyond the Sabine," John Brooks reported to his father, in one of the last letters he wrote before his execution with the others at Goliad.

This wasn't Santa Anna's public position. For the record, the president-general assured all law-abiding Texans that they would be secure. He issued a statement blaming a rebel minority for the current troubles of Texas, and went on to declare, "The inhabitants of this country, let their origin be whatever it may, who should not appear to have been implicated in such iniquitous rebellion, shall be respected in their persons and property. . . . The good will have nothing to fear. Fulfill always your duty as Mexican citizens, and you may expect the protection and benefit of the laws."

Santa Anna's private position was quite different. In fact he did intend to drive the Americans out of Texas. Even as he acted to suppress the rebellion on Mexico's northern frontier, he pondered how to prevent such rebellions from recurring. "I am convinced that we ought not to risk either Anglo-American or European colonists to remain on the frontier," he told War Secretary Tornel. Even if some Anglo-Americans were not taking part in the rebellion—"a rare coincidence indeed," he said—their loyalty would always be suspect. For those American colonists of established residence in Texas, Santa Anna recommended removal to the interior of the country, "in order not to expose ourselves, as at present, to the sad experiences of our inadvertence, a lesson that is costing us so dearly." Yet he surely realized that many, probably most, of the Americans would return to the United States rather than be compelled to the interior. In either case, Texas would be cleansed of American presence and influence. And, of course, regarding the large number of immigrants who had come illegally: "They should be immediately expelled from Mexican territory."

By the end of March 1836 Santa Anna had made a promising start on his campaign of expulsion. Each Mexican victory and each advance by Santa Anna's army launched a new wave of refugees fleeing his wrath. Creed Taylor, the teenager who had helped take San Antonio the previous December, and his brother left the army to assist their mother in the evacuation of the family farm on the Guadalupe. "We reached home about sundown," Taylor recalled, "and found mother hastily preparing to begin her flight that very night. Some of the neighbor women were there, and all were making haste to get away." Mrs. Taylor was happy to see her boys, but their arrival didn't diminish her desire to escape before all were murdered or ravished. Taylor described an incident that illustrated the panic. "Mother had prepared supper, and while at the table just at dark, the discharge of guns not faraway was heard. 'The Mexicans are on us,' the younger women shouted, and their alarm for a while was extreme. Later in the night it was learned that some of the men who lived below us on the river, and who were coming home from the army to save their families, had fired their guns merely to announce their arrival."

The scattered nature of the settlements contributed to the fright and confusion. Rumor traveled on the wind (literally, in the case of the heard gunfire) and often got distorted in the transmission. Listeners imagined the worst and, in the absence of calming evidence, acted on their imagination. Because the colonists lived far apart, each family felt peculiarly exposed. In many cases the men had gone off to fight; those who went to the Alamo and Goliad wouldn't be coming back, and their families typically had no one to protect them. John Swisher was in Gonzales, the town that had sent the last thirty-two defenders to the Alamo, when the word of the fall of the fortress arrived. "There was not a soul left among the citizens of Gonzales who had not lost a father, husband, brother or son in that terrible massacre. I shall never forget the scene which followed the confirmation of the dreadful news. The mad agony of the widows and the shrieks of the childless and fatherless beggars all description."

When the interim government appointed Sam Houston commander in chief, it expected that he would shortly lead the Texas troops against Santa Anna. For weeks, however, Houston did everything he could to avoid battle. Upon appointment he headed for Gonzales, with the stated intent of relieving the Alamo. But he took his time getting to Gonzales, requiring five days for a trip that most travelers made in two. What he did on the way has remained a mystery, and it became a bone of contention after the Alamo fell, unrelieved by Houston or anyone else. Some supposed he fell off the wagon again, drinking his way from San Felipe to Gonzales, perhaps out of fear at the magnitude of the task before him. Others, still less charitable, concluded that he wanted the Alamo to fall in order that he could take uncontested control of the army. There is no positive evidence for either charge, nor for the simpler claim that he was a coward, afraid to risk his life for those of Travis and the Alamo garrison.

On the other hand, there is abundant evidence that Houston refused to go to the Alamo because he believed, as commander in chief, that his overriding objective was victory in the war, not victory in a single battle. To race to the Alamo might be emotionally satisfying, but with the small number of troops in his command it wouldn't prevent a Mexican victory there, and it might well end the war at once—in defeat for Texas. "We could have met the enemy, and avenged some of our wrongs," Houston asserted upon learning of the Alamo's fate, "but, detached as we were, without supplies for the men in camp, of either provisions, ammunition, or artillery, and remote from succor, it would have been madness to hazard a contest." Houston's army at this point numbered less than four hundred—"without two days' provisions, many without arms, and others without any ammunition." They were brave enough; most wanted only a chance to avenge the death of their comrades. But besides their lack of supplies, they knew nothing of organized maneuvers or combat. "They had not been taught the first principles of the drill." Against Santa Anna's army, which outnumbered the Texans ten to one, they wouldn't stand a chance. Nor, even supposing it was possible to retake the Alamo, would holding that fort serve any strategic purpose (which was why Houston had wanted to abandon it in the first place). "Troops pent up in forts are rendered useless." Santa Anna would simply station a modest number of his own men to maintain a siege and would send the rest to ravage the countryside.

The only hope for Texas lay in retreat. The army would buy time in falling back before Santa Anna's advance: time to recruit new troops, time to train those recruited. Moreover, in falling back, the Texans would lengthen Santa Anna's supply lines and render his position more precarious. "By falling back," Houston explained, "Texas can rally, and defeat any force that can come against her."

This pragmatic attitude hardly made Houston popular. Creed Taylor still held it against Houston years later. "Sam Houston had at Gonzales 500 men," Taylor declared, exaggerating in his anger. "Of these at least one half of them had been at Concepción and San Antonio, and he didn't have a man in his army who didn't have a blood grievance against the Mexicans and that did not *know* that he could do as we had done before—whip ten to one of the carrion-eating convicts under Santa Anna." Taylor asserted that if any of several other men had commanded the army at Gonzales, the war would have ended much sooner. "The historian would have never heard of San Jacinto. Fannin and his men would have been saved, the butchery of Goliad averted and the 'Napoleon of the West' would have found his Waterloo somewhere between Bexar and the 'Lexington' of Texas [Gonzales]. The comrades who assembled at Gonzales went there to *fight*, not to run."

In another army, the scorn of his men might have been a lesser problem. But in the Texas army, where soldiers served at their own discretion and for their own purposes, the disrespect for Houston threatened to sabotage the revolution. A Texas agent at New Orleans cautioned the members of the interim government not to fool themselves about the motives of new recruits. "The declaration of independence will have a very powerful influence in your favor," he said, "but you will find that nine out of ten who may emigrate to Texas

hereafter will go there not to fight its battles, but to profit by its necessities." The volunteers had brought themselves to Texas, and they
might take themselves away from Texas. They treated orders as advice
and heeded their commander chiefly when they agreed with his decisions.

If Houston had had the nerve of Andrew Jackson—or if he had
been in the United States, a country with laws that could be enforced—he might have had his insubordinates shot. On occasion he
threatened to do just that. Two privates were accused of mutiny and
desertion; a court-martial convicted and sentenced the pair to death.
Houston let the lesson sink in for a while. But then he found reasons
to reprieve the two.

Whatever the prudence of retreat, the decision to fall back unnerved
the populace, which had been counting on Houston to hold the line at
the Guadalupe. Creed Taylor described the sudden change in mood
when word got out that Houston wouldn't fight. For days men had
been passing his mother's house, heading toward Gonzales, where
they expected to battle the invaders. They spoke confidently of how
they would thrash Santa Anna, and their confidence raised the hopes
of the locals. "Then on a day there was a lull, and the tide turned. . . .
As they returned they were greatly excited, halting only long enough
to shout, 'The Mexicans are coming! Houston is making for the Trinity, the Sabine! Flee for your lives!' "

Things got worse. News arrived of the disaster at the Alamo; this
was followed by wild rumors of massacres of men, women, and children along the Guadalupe. Panic seized the entire populace. "The
first law of nature, self-preservation, was uppermost in the minds of
the settlers," Taylor wrote. "And thus the great exodus began."

The exodus was rendered more difficult, and the panic intensified, by the fact that the flight occurred in late winter. One of the attractions of Texas was that farmers didn't have to feed their livestock during the winter; the horses and cattle could graze year-round. But from the first hard freeze of December or January till spring greened the pastures, the pickings were often slim, and the stock grew gaunt and weak. The strongest animals could pull wagon and carts but not swiftly or far. Beyond this, late winter was the mud season, when roads turned to gumbo, especially under heavy traffic. Finally, many of the settlers lacked efficient wheeled transport; clumsy, homemade carts were common, straining the draft animals all the more.

In the case of the Taylor family, the sole vehicle was an oxcart with solid wheels cut from a log. Mrs. Taylor intended to hitch the cart to two yoke of her best oxen, which were none too good at the time. Creed and his brother talked her out of this plan. "We explained to mother that if we depended on these slow oxen, we could not hope to outrun the Mexican army, and that we might as well stay where we were and take our chances." She wanted to leave that very night, but they persuaded her to wait till morning, when they would scout the range for the best horses they could find—again, a relative distinction—which they would load with packs for a faster getaway.

Catching the horses took longer than expected, as did packing the family's few movable possessions—bedding and personal items—onto the horses. The fruit of years of labor had to be abandoned. "There was a little corn left in the crib, a large supply of nicely cured bacon in the smokehouse, and the yard was full of chickens, turkeys, geese and ducks, besides a good stock of hogs. All of these we left to the invaders." The younger children cried upon leaving the only home they had ever lived in. Mrs. Taylor's reaction was different. "If mother shed a tear, I never knew it, though there was an unusual huskiness in her voice that day. Mother was brave and resolute, and I

heard her say to a lady while crossing the Brazos, under great difficulties, that she was going to teach her boys never to let up on the
Mexicans until they got full revenge for all this trouble."

As it happened, the family's sacrifices in the service of swifter
travel came to naught. After only an hour on the road the Taylors
overtook a family from farther up the Guadalupe, traveling with an
oxcart. Despite their slow pace, they talked the Taylors into traveling
with them, for mutual protection. Before long the crowds on the road
forced all to move at the pace of the slowest. "People were trudging
along in every kind of conveyance, some on foot carrying heavy
packs," Creed Taylor said. "I saw every kind of conveyance ever used
in that region . . . hand-barrows, sleds, carts, wagons, some drawn
by oxen, horses, and burros. Old men, frail women, and little children, all trudging along." Taylor later fought in the Mexican War, but
he believed the Runaway Scrape—as Texans later called the flight of
1836, with the relieved humor of having survived it—was as bad as
anything he ever saw. "I have never witnessed such scenes of distress
and human suffering. True, there was no clash of arms, no slaughter
of men and horses, as on the field of battle; but here the suffering was
confined to decrepit old men, frail women, and little children. . . .
Delicate women trudged alongside their pack horses, carts, or sleds,
from day to day until their shoes were literally worn out, then continued the journey with bare feet, lacerated and bleeding at almost every
step. Their clothes were scant, and with no means of shelter from the
frequent drenching rains and bitter winds, they traveled on through
the long days in wet and bedraggled apparel, finding even at night little relief from their suffering, since the wet earth and angry sky offered no relief."

Predictably, disease descended on the refugee columns.
Measles and other contagions laid many low and carried the weak
away. The dying received no shelter, succumbing beneath the heed-

less sky at the edge of the road, where they were buried in hasty graves and forgotten by all but their kin.

Yet at times the exodus brought out the best in the living. A woman with four children had lost her husband in the Alamo; she became a mother for the fifth time just as her party was crossing the Colorado. "A family having a rickety open wagon drawn by two lean ponies gave the helpless mother bed and transportation by throwing part of their belongings from the wagon to make room for a woman they had never seen before," Taylor recalled. "During rains, by day or night, willing hands held blankets over the mother and babe to protect them from the downpours and chilling storms."

Many men from the army, like the Taylor boys, had abandoned their soldierly duties to help with the evacuation, but enough stayed with Houston to make the flight an affair mostly of women, children, and old folks. "It was no uncommon sight to see women and children without shoes, and otherwise thinly clad, wading in mud and chilling water almost to their knees," Taylor said. "When a cart or wagon became mired—which was an hourly occurrence east of the Brazos—there was no dearth of helping hands. But in proportion the men were few, and so the women and children were forced to perform most of the labor. Thus these half-clad, mud-besmeared fugitives, looking like veritable savages, trudged along."

Houston's retreat was better organized and slower than that of the refugees but not much less inexorable. Hard upon the report of the Alamo's fall, Houston learned that the enemy was hastening toward Gonzales. "The army of Santa Anna had encamped on the Cibolo on the night of the 11th inst., after a march of twenty-four miles that day," Houston informed James Collinsworth, the chairman of the

Texas government's military affairs committee. "The army was to en-
camp on the 12th at Sandy, and proceed direct to Gonzales." Santa
Anna's numbers couldn't be calculated precisely but were estimated
as "exceeding two thousand infantry." Against Houston's 374 men,
this made for an impossible Texan disadvantage and dictated a Texan
retreat. "I deemed it proper to fall back and take a post on the Colorado, near Burnham's." Subsequent intelligence suggested that
Mexican forces in Texas totaled five or six thousand, although a few
estimates ran much higher. "Some say thirty thousand! But this can
not be true." It was partly to stifle rumors like this that Houston tried
to prevent the men still in camp from following the lead of the deserters. "They have disseminated throughout the frontier such exaggerated reports that they have produced dismay and consternation
among the people to a most distressing extent." The truth was bad
enough. "Gonzalez is reduced to ashes!"—burned by the Texans to
prevent its provisions' falling into enemy hands.

Houston's army reached the Colorado the same day Fannin
abandoned Goliad. Houston still anticipated a rendezvous with Fannin, which, if accomplished, would have augmented his force substantially. But even without Fannin the army began to grow.
Volunteers arrived from the east, their journey shortened by Houston's own progress in that direction. Though Santa Anna still pursued
him—"The Mexican army will not leave us in the rear," Houston
said—the Texan commander was more hopeful than he had been in
weeks. "The force of Santa Anna has been greatly overrated. He must
have lost one thousand, or perhaps more, at the Alamo. It is said the
officers have to whip and slash the soldiers on the march. And, if they
should advance to the Colorado, it will be some time, as there is such
scanty subsistence for animals." The critical question was whether
Texans, as a group, would rise to the challenge their country faced.
"Our own people, if they would act, are enough to expel every Mexi-

can from Texas. . . . We can raise three thousand men in Texas, and fifteen hundred can defeat all that Santa Anna can send to the Colorado. We would then fight on our own ground, and the enemy would lose all confidence from our annoyance." But time was short and growing shorter. "Let the men from the east of the Trinity rush to us! Let all the disposable force of Texas fly to arms! If the United States intend to aid us, let them do it now! . . . Send all the good horses you can get for the army. . . . Send ammunition for fifteen hundred men; but first send eight hundred men." Whatever might happen, Houston vowed to do his part. "If only three hundred men remain on this side of the Brazos, I will die with them, or conquer our enemies."

Houston had always been emotional, but the strain of the flight from Santa Anna pushed him to the edge, causing some to assume, perhaps correctly, that he was still on the bottle. From exhilaration one day he plunged to despair the next. "I am not easily depressed," he wrote Thomas Rusk from the Colorado, "but, before my God, since we parted, I have found the darkest hours of my past life!" The enemy was close behind, and the army unready to meet it. "My excitement has been so great that, for forty-eight hours, I have not eaten an ounce, nor have I slept. I was in constant apprehension of a rout; a constant panic existed in the lines."

The panic in the lines increased the panic in the population. Deserters from Houston's army rationalized their flight by exaggerating the Mexican threat, prompting civilians to believe they wouldn't be safe west of the Sabine. Houston tore his hair in frustration. "All would have been well, and all at peace on this side of the Colorado, if I could only have had a moment to start an express in advance of the deserters," he wrote. "But they went first, and, being panic struck, it was contagious, and all who saw them breathed the poison and fled."

Houston's spirits sank further on hearing that Fannin had been surrounded on the retreat from Goliad. Houston didn't yet know the outcome of the battle, but he had to assume that Fannin wouldn't be joining him after all, which added another grim element to his situation. "If what I have heard from Fannin be true," Houston wrote, "I deplore it, and can only attribute the ill luck to his attempting to retreat in daylight in the face of a superior force." Speaking better than he knew, Houston added, "He is an ill-fated man."

Houston learned at the Colorado that the interim government, seized by the same panic that afflicted the whole populace, had abandoned Washington-on-the-Brazos. Although the squabbling among the politicians during the previous months had led him to expect nothing good from the governing class of Texas, he thought this decision revealed a particular want of character, besides making his job harder. "The retreat of the government will have a bad effect on the troops," he predicted.

Amid the gloom, Houston grasped at any cause for hope. His scouts captured two Mexican spies, who revealed that Santa Anna's forces were smaller than Houston had thought. The arrival of some fresh recruits, followed by word that more were coming, suggested that the panic might be easing. "Men are flocking to camp," Houston wrote on March 24, with suddenly renewed optimism. "And I expect, in a day or two, to receive two hundred volunteers and regulars. Forty-eight muskets and a supply of ammunition came opportunely last night. In a few days my force will be highly respectable."

For obvious reasons, the strategies of opposing generals in war tend to be inverse images of each other. Thus it was with Santa Anna and Houston. Where the Texan leader wished to avoid battle, to give space and get time, Santa Anna aimed to provoke battle, to save space and steal time. Any general in Santa Anna's position would have adopted the same strategy, for Houston's army would only get stronger the nearer it got to the heavily settled regions of Texas, and the closer it drew to the United States.

Yet Santa Anna had special reason for wanting to end the Texas war quickly. As important as Texas was to the Texans, it was only a small part of Mexico, and was perhaps less important than its size suggested. However apt or inaccurate Santa Anna's identification with Napoleon may have been, the Mexican president-general shared a signal liability with the French emperor-general: neither could leave his capital for long without worrying that his enemies were conspiring against him, and hence neither could afford an extended distant campaign. From the moment Santa Anna set out for Texas in December 1835, he reckoned how he might bring the war against the rebels to a rapid close. A patient man, or merely a general who wasn't also president, could have taken the time to consolidate his victories over the Texans, to secure his lines of communication, and to drive Houston and his untrained troops across the Sabine and out of Texas, as other filibusters had been driven out before. By the same token, a president who didn't owe his political position to his prowess at arms could have risked leaving the war in Texas to a subordinate. But Santa Anna couldn't stand to let an underling wear the laurels that would come to the general who preserved the integrity of Mexico. The hero of Tampico must be the hero of Texas.

Through the end of March 1836, the hero's campaign was on track. "The capture of the Alamo, in spite of its attendant disasters, and the quick and successful operations of General Urrea gave us a prodigious moral prestige," Santa Anna declared. "Our name terrified the enemy, and our approach to their camps was not awaited. They fled disconcerted to hide beyond the Trinity and the Sabine. . . . The attainment of our goal was now almost certain."

In some respects the war was going *too* well. As the Mexican forces marched east, the only sign that a rebellion even existed was the ruin in which the rebels left the countryside. Like the Russian army that had opposed Napoleon, the Texan army burned the towns from which it retreated, the fields through which it marched, and the supplies it couldn't carry. It was a harsh policy, but it had the desired effect, rendering an occupation of Texas by Santa Anna's army difficult and unattractive. The president-general admitted as much, regarding his hunt for Houston: "It was then, with sorrow on the part of the troops, that thought was given the need of garrisoning that vast territory in order to hold our conquest; and the mere idea of remaining in Texas dismayed the triumphant soldier more than defeat. Our campaign was a military parade; but to remain in Texas, perhaps forever, what a misfortune!"

José de la Peña judged the dismay of the Mexican soldiers to be the work of their own officers as much as that of the Texans. The Texans didn't succeed in destroying all the crops and livestock of the district they abandoned. "There was a great abundance of pigs and chickens," de la Peña wrote regarding the vicinity of Gonzales. But through mismanagement, corruption, or simply the arrogance of the ruling class, the officers withheld the best for themselves and let the rank and file suffer. "At the Colorado the soldier's half-rations of corn tortilla terminated, and his total diet was reduced to one pound of meat and a half-ration of beans." Hunger makes everything harder, and it made the Mexican soldiers, confronting the privations of an army long in the field, utterly miserable. "Think of the soldier so poorly fed, clothed and shod even worse, sleeping always in the open, crossing rivers and swamps, exposed to hours of burning sun, at other times to heavy downpours, and even during hours of rest having to protect his firearms from the rain, as he had no protective covers for them, though the campaign required crossing wilderness."

The hungry soldiers were told to guard bags of corn reserved for the senior officers. They did so without open complaint, but not without resentment that became manifest in their behavior. "When by accident a sack would tear, we have had the unpleasant experience of seeing the soldiers and the women who accompanied them gather around like chickens in order to pick up the last grain." Absorbing insult after injury, the soldiers were charged for their rations even when they received none.

To de la Peña, the worst aspect of the war was its wanton destructiveness. The fleeing rebels put the torch to the products of the Texans' labor as they left; the Mexican soldiers and camp followers ravaged much of what the rebels didn't ruin. "I found one house still standing and others that had been burned, among which there were indications that one had been a large one and that another cotton gin had been lost during the fire," de la Peña wrote after investigating a neighborhood recently abandoned by the rebels. "There was also a medium-sized barn full of cotton bales, many of which had apparently been used for a trench, all scattered along the bank of the river. . . . It was really sickening to see so many of these destroyed." One resident woman, a Tejana who hadn't fled, told de la Peña that the cotton losses alone tallied more than ten million pesos. In a bitter tone she explained that the rebels had disseminated tales of terror that frightened even the law-abiding into leaving. Often the latter burned their property on the way out; when they didn't, the rebels lit the match.

The experience caused de la Peña—a professional soldier—to question the whole enterprise of the war. He conceded nothing to Santa Anna in love of Mexico or desire to defend it, but he thought the war disgraceful. "No one would disagree with me that provisions should have been made to prevent the war, or that, once begun in order to vindicate an injured nation, it should have been carried out in a less disastrous fashion."

While de la Peña decried the destructiveness of the war, Houston and Santa Anna did their best to extend it. Destruction was an essential part of both generals' war means. Each embraced a strategy of scorching the earth, although for different reasons. Houston wanted to deprive Santa Anna of sustenance for his Army of Operations, which to be successful, Houston knew, had to become an army of occupation. Houston guessed that he could supply himself from the east, from his rear, longer than Santa Anna could supply himself from the west, from *his* rear. And by burning whatever his men or the refugees couldn't carry, Houston would prevent Santa Anna from living off the land. Santa Anna sought not to starve Houston but to terrorize the Texans into abandoning their rebellion. This strategy dictated the no-quarter policy on the battlefield; applied to the countryside at large, it called for laying waste to whatever the Texans had wrought for the good during the previous decade.

All this was obvious—often painfully so—to observers on both sides. What was not obvious was Houston's second strategy, a secret alternative designed to guarantee victory even if the Texans didn't win another battle, which appeared entirely possible. Not for nothing had Houston cultivated Andrew Jackson, and vice versa, all those years; not without cause, and consequence, had Houston huddled with America's foremost expansionist in Nashville en route to Texas; not without reason had Houston posed as an Indian agent on arrival and renewed his Indian acquaintanceships even while the siege tightened around the Alamo. When Houston spoke of falling back to the Sabine if necessary, he did so with confidence that help waited there in the form of U.S. troops. Old Hickory's impatience with border troubles that threatened American territory was a matter of historical record, as Florida-less Spain could have told anyone in Mexico (and probably did, now that Spain was speaking to Mexico again). Jackson's desire to add Texas to the Union was also a matter of record. Jackson claimed the Neches River, rather than the Sabine, as the southwestern border of the United States, and the fact that almost nothing in diplomacy or prior usage supported this claim revealed it as the ruse, or rationale, it almost certainly was. Very little imagination was required to envision a scenario in which Santa Anna chased Houston toward the Sabine and sent a flood of Texas refugees into Louisiana, creating chaos that would trigger a clash between Mexican and American forces. American soldiers would be killed on what the American president would assert to be American soil; an outraged Congress would declare war on Mexico; a conflict would ensue in which the United States would seize Texas and perhaps additional territory.

Major General Edmund Gaines was the commanding officer of the Western Department of the U.S. Army, with responsibility for the defense of Louisiana and the southwestern frontier of the United States. Perhaps Gaines had studied the career of Jackson; certainly he knew Jackson's reputation as the scourge of Spain and Britain. And Gaines was very much the man to make the most of whatever opportunities crossed his path. In the last week of March 1836, while Houston was retreating east, the American general informed War Secretary Lewis Cass of the measures he was taking to secure the border of Louisiana. He said he had checked his arsenals for adequate arms and ammunition, that he might carry out the duties assigned to him—

"duties which derive great importance from the recent accounts of the sanguinary manner in which the Mexican forces seem disposed to carry on the war" currently raging across the border. So far he had kept aloof from the conflict, but perhaps not for much longer. "I take leave to suggest whether it may or may not become necessary, *in our own defense*, to speak to the contending belligerents in a language not to be misunderstood—a language requiring *force* and military supplies that shall be sufficient, if necessary, for the protection of our frontier." Because the United States maintained correct relations with Mexico, communications from Washington to Gaines nearly always spoke in terms of defending the border against Indians, which was expressly allowed by treaty between the United States and Mexico. Gaines, writing in the other direction, included Indians in his threat assessment but more candidly mentioned Mexico. "Should I find any disposition on the part of the Mexicans or their red allies to menace our frontier," he declared, "I cannot but deem it to be my duty not only to hold the troops of my command in readiness for action in defense of our frontier, but to anticipate their lawless movements, by crossing our supposed or imaginary national boundary."

Gaines recommended raising a force substantially larger than Santa Anna's army. He said he had taken the liberty of applying to New Orleans to borrow that city's legionary brigade, which had answered in a way that signaled its leaders' understanding of what was required. "The officers of the legion, with the gallant general at their head, cordially responded that they would, whenever it might be deemed necessary, promptly repair to the frontier, delighted with the opportunity of carrying into effect the wishes of the President, under whose immediate command many of the officers had distinguished themselves in the defense of their city and state in the memorable triumphs of December 1814 and January 1815." Gaines addressed this letter to Cass, as protocol required. But his intended audience was made obvious by his closing: "All which is submitted for the information of the President of the United States, with profound respect."

Gaines and Houston weren't the only ones looking to Jackson. Samuel Carson was the Texas secretary of state; whether from conversations with Houston or on his own, he concluded that American intervention might be the salvation of the infant republic. "News—good news," he reported to Texas president David Burnet in early April from East Texas. "I have just heard through a source . . . that a company or battalion of U.S. troops left Fort Jessup [on the American side of the Sabine] eight or ten days since, crossed the Sabine, and were marching toward the Neches. I believe it to be true." In fact, it wasn't true yet. But even if premature, the report persuaded Carson that help was in sight. "Jackson will protect the neutral ground, and the beauty of it is, he claims to the Neches as neutral ground."

General Gaines knew better than to expect explicit endorsement from Washington of his forward policy, but in the absence of contradictory orders, he proceeded with his planning. He relocated his headquarters to Natchitoches, to be closer to the front, and he filed reports to Washington that painted the threat to American territory—and to American standards of decency—in increasingly lurid colors. Portions of several Indian tribes had crossed over from Louisiana into Texas, he said. "When to this fact is added the reports daily received at this place, that the army of Mexico, commanded by the President, St. Anna, in person, is rapidly approaching in this direction, through the center of Texas; that his plan is to put to death all he finds in arms, and all who do not yield to his dictation; that as soon as he comes to the section of country occupied by the Indians in question, on the waters of the Trinidad, or Trinity, river, they will unite with him in his war of extermination; and that no boundary line, save such as that they find properly guarded with an efficient force, will be sufficient to arrest the career of these savages, I cannot but deem it my duty to prepare for action."

In a circular letter to the governors of Louisiana, Mississippi, Alabama, and Tennessee, Gaines went on to say that he had heard that a Mexican national named Manuel Flores had been traveling among the Indians of the borderlands, apparently at the behest of the Mexican government, urging the aborigines "to join them in the war of extermination now raging in Texas," as Gaines described it. The general asked rhetorically "whether I am to sit still and suffer these movements to be so far matured as to place the white settlements on both sides of the line wholly within the power of these savages." He concluded that he was not. This was why he was writing the governors: to request reinforcements, in particular mounted troops, the only kind that would "enable me to interpose an effectual check on the daily increasing danger." Gaines went on to say that additional federal troops would take too long to reach the frontier; he didn't mention—but must have thought—that additional federal troops would require positive action from Washington, which wanted to stay at arm's length from whatever occurred on the border.

Sam Carson met Gaines at Natchitoches "and had with him a full and satisfactory conversation," as the Texas secretary of state reported to President Burnet. Gaines had to be careful what he told Carson. "His position at present is a delicate one and requires at his hands the most cautious movements," Carson said. Gaines's reticence kept Carson from predicting definitively how the general would act. "But one thing I think I may say, that should he be satisfied of the fact that the Mexicans have incited any Indians who are under the control of the United States to commit depredations on either side of the line, he will doubtless view it as a violation of the treaty. . . . Be assured that he will maintain the honor of his country and punish the aggressor, be him whom he may." Speaking for himself, Carson said he believed the Mexicans did have some Caddos, Cherokees, and other tribesmen with them. "It is only necessary, then, to satisfy General Gaines of the facts, in which case be assured he will act with energy and efficiency." The general was preparing to march to the Sabine. "The proofs will, I have no doubt, be abundant by the time he reaches the Sabine, in which case he will cross and move upon the aggressors." Carson concluded this message to Burnet by saying: "I shall write General Houston and advise him fully upon this subject."

Gaines in fact advanced to the Sabine, to await further developments and instructions. Among the latter was a message from Secretary Cass explaining President Jackson's position. "It is not the wish of the President to take advantage of the present circumstances, and thereby obtain possession of any portion of the Mexican territory," Cass disclaimed. He then went on: "Still, however, the neutral duties, as well as the neutral rights, of the United States will justify the Government in taking all necessary measures to prevent a violation of their territory. Recent events induce the belief that the Mexican forces, as well as the inhabitants of Texas, must be in a high state of excitement." Cass said that the government at Washington had reason to believe that the Mexicans were provoking the Indians against the Texans, as General Gaines had indicated. "It may, therefore, well be, as you anticipate, that these various contending parties may approach our frontiers, and that the lives and property of our citizens may be placed in jeopardy. Should this be the case"—and now came the words Gaines had been waiting for—"the President approves the suggestion you make, and you are authorized to take such position, on either side of the imaginary boundary line, as may be best for your defensive operations." In what parsed as a constraint but, in the context of this authorization, served as permission, Jackson added, speaking through Cass: "You will, however, under no circumstances advance farther than old Fort Nacogdoches, which is within the limits of the United States, as claimed by this Government."

Chapter 18

A People in Arms

At the beginning of April 1836, Santa Anna felt victory over the Texas rebels to be within his grasp. "The capture of the Alamo, in spite of its attendant disasters, and the quick and successful operations of General Urrea gave us a prodigious moral prestige," the president-general recalled. "Our name terrified the enemy, and our approach to their camps was not awaited. They fled disconcerted to hide beyond the Trinity and the Sabine. . . . The attainment of our goal was now almost certain."

Santa Anna's sole problem was the result of his brilliant success—the very terror and disconcertion of the enemy. The president-general had hoped to crush Houston and the rest of the insurgents as he had crushed their comrades at Béxar and Goliad. But Houston knew only how to run. "The enemy was not undertaking a retreat but was in full flight."

Chasing Houston further might be futile and even counterproductive. A rabble in flight traveled faster than any army could advance in decent order. And though Santa Anna couldn't know the intentions of General Gaines on the Sabine, he could guess. Andrew Jackson's scorn for international boundaries and the niceties of law was patent; Santa Anna saw no reason to give the American president—the father of filibusters—an excuse to invade Mexico.

That left two alternatives. The Army of Operations could transform itself into an army of occupation and remain in Texas indefinitely. Santa Anna found this personally distasteful (where was the glory in occupation?) and politically prohibitive (who would pay to keep the soldiers so far from home? How would the rest of Mexico be defended?).

The other alternative was to decapitate the rebellion by seizing the rebel government. Santa Anna learned that the ringleaders of the insurgency had abandoned Washington-on-the-Brazos, heading toward the coast. "Through some of the colonists taken, among them a Mexican, I discovered that the heads of the Texas government, Don Lorenzo Zavala, and other leaders of the revolution were at Harrisburg, twelve leagues distant on the right bank of Buffalo Bayou." Because Houston had gone in the other direction—north, toward Groce's Crossing of the Brazos—the rebel government was undefended. "Their arrest was certain if our troops marched upon them without loss of time."

This was the opening Santa Anna had been looking for. With typical audacity and decisiveness, and "without confiding in anyone," he staked the outcome of the war on a gamble. Conventional wisdom dictated keeping his army together, lest he lose his most important advantage over the rebels. But like Napoleon, Santa Anna disdained convention. To deliver his coup de grace, he pulled some 750 dragoons, grenadiers, and riflemen out of their regiments. "I started with these forces toward Harrisburg the afternoon of the 14th."

By then Houston had nearly lost control of the Texan army. During the final weeks of March and the first weeks of April, he continued to retreat, believing that his force was no match for Santa Anna's and hoping to draw the Mexican general toward the border and a collision with General Gaines and the U.S. Army. But as Santa Anna pressed forward and the refugee stream of Texas settlers swelled into a terrified torrent, demands that Houston stand and fight became shriller and more insistent. Sam Carson wrote to David Burnet from the banks of the Trinity River in early April, describing a scene unlike any he had ever imagined. "The panic has reached this place," Carson said. "Destruction pervades the whole country." Three hundred people were crowded to the river's edge, hoping to get across, but the spring rains were raising the river and soon they all would be trapped. "Never till I reached the Trinity did I despond," Carson explained. The fear and flight were uncontrollable, short of a victory in the field by Houston. "Nothing can stop the people unless Houston is successful." Houston simply must fight. A single victory could change everything. "If under the providence of almighty God he has whipped them, the panic can be allayed and the people will return and drive the enemy out of the country. But should it be otherwise . . ." Carson shuddered and declined to speculate.

David Burnet agreed. "Our friend the commander-in-chief has heavy responsibilities resting upon him," the Texas president told War Secretary Rusk. "It were perhaps hyperbolical to say 'the eyes of the world are upon him,' but assuredly the people of Texas are looking toward him with an ardent and anxious gaze. They regard his present conduct as decisive of the fate of their country." Burnet asked why Houston's army should be retreating before a "contemptible Mexican force" of a mere thirteen hundred men. "Have we so far forgotten our wonted boasts of superior prowess as to turn our backs to an equal number of a foe that has given us every imaginable incentive to action—vigorous, prompt, daring action? I hope it will not be." The people of Texas were crying for a battle, and Burnet shared their feel-

ing. "A further retreat without a fight would be infinitely disastrous. . . . For our country's sake, let something be done, something
that will *tell* upon our enemies and upon ourselves."

To Houston himself, Burnet was even blunter. In a letter carried
by Rusk to Houston's camp, the Texas president declared:

> Sir: The enemy are laughing you to scorn. You must fight
> them. You must retreat no farther. The country expects
> you to fight. The salvation of the country depends on you
> doing so.

Houston bridled at the criticism from persons not even in the
field. "Taunts and suggestions have been gratuitously tendered to
me," he complained, "and I have submitted to them without any disposition to retort either unkindness or imputation." But a man could
tolerate only so much. "What has been my situation? At Gonzales I
had three hundred and seventy-four efficient men, without supplies,
even powder, balls, or arms. At the Colorado, with seven hundred
men, without discipline or time to organize the army. Two days since,
my effective force in camp was five hundred and twenty-three men."
And with this he was supposed to defeat a Mexican force of thousands? "I have, under the most disadvantageous circumstances, kept
an army together . . . but I can not perform impossibilities."

The carping of his troops was harder to ignore. Throughout the
retreat, grumblers asserted that they ought to be marching west
rather than east, that in a real war real men wanted to fight. The first
serious trouble surfaced at San Felipe, when it became clear that
Houston wouldn't defend Austin's capital. Wiley Martin had fought
under Jackson at Horseshoe Bend, where he outranked Houston, and
he had emigrated to Texas long before Houston, as part of Stephen
Austin's original three hundred. On both grounds he chafed at taking

orders from Houston, and at San Felipe he decided he wouldn't do so any longer. When Houston ordered the town evacuated, Martin simply refused, and he became a focus of resistance to Houston and the strategy of retreat.

Mosely Baker was another objector. Baker had run afoul of Houston at Nacogdoches, and he would remain at odds with Houston for the rest of their careers. Yet the nadir of their relationship occurred during the campaign of 1836. Even years later, Baker boiled to think about that trying period. "By your retreat you abandoned the whole country west of the Colorado to the enemy," he accused Houston. "But what was still more disastrous than all, you infused a feeling of terror and dismay into the minds of the people." At the time of the declaration of Texas independence, Baker said, the people of Texas were eager to fight the Mexicans and were confident they could win. "So soon, however, as it was found out that you were retreating, a new face was given to the whole matter." The farther Houston retreated, the further public confidence fell. "So soon as you crossed the Colorado, the families all to the west side of that river hurried away to the settlements on the east side, and by the dreadful accounts given in their terror the feeling became general, and universal consternation seized the country." With many others, Baker had expected Houston to make a stand at the Brazos; when the commander ordered San Felipe abandoned, Baker revolted. Like Martin, he insisted he would stay.

Houston faced a dilemma, either horn of which might gore him and eviscerate the revolution. To treat the Baker-Martin challenge as the mutiny it was risked rending the entire army; for all he knew, half his men would side with Baker and Martin against him. On the other hand, to acquiesce in their insubordination would certainly make discipline an even greater problem in the future.

Houston adopted the course of lesser resistance. If Baker and

Mosely wanted to draw a line at the Brazos, he would let them. But to save face, he made permission mandatory: he *ordered* them to defend the Brazos. Baker and one company would guard the crossing of the Brazos at San Felipe, Martin and another company the crossing at Fort Bend, twenty-five miles downstream. Meanwhile Houston would take the balance of the army, about five hundred men, upstream to Groce's plantation.

As he guessed it would, Houston's refusal to confront this challenge to his authority merely borrowed time. The army spent two weeks at Groce's, during which Houston rested and trained the men and allowed the sick to recuperate. The time also allowed the malcontents to mutter that the army needed a new general. A principal among the complainers, Alexander Somervell, a lieutenant colonel of the volunteers, tested sentiment in favor of deposing Houston. "He came to the tents of the company to which I belonged, and talked with the men, expressing himself strongly," recalled J. H. Kuykendall, the youngest of three Kuykendall brothers in the rebel army. "Should General Houston persist in avoiding a conflict with the enemy, and continue to march to the eastward, as it was generally believed he intended to do, he said he was in favor of depriving him of the command and supplying his place with a more belligerent leader, and wished to know whether our company favored such a course and would *take* it, should it become necessary. He was assured by both officers and men that he might rely upon their cooperation." Somervell and his sympathizers then queried the rest of the army and apparently got much the same reply. What surprised Kuykendall was the openness of the insubordination. "There was no injunction of secrecy; no one disguised his sentiments; and General Houston could not have been ignorant of what was in agitation."

Houston indeed was aware of the incipient mutiny. Nicholas Labadie, a French Canadian who had come south to fight the Mexicans, and a member of the Liberty company of volunteers, identified Sidney Sherman as the one the mutineers looked to. "Col. Sidney Sherman had been elected colonel of the Second Regiment, to which the Liberty Company belonged," Labadie said, "and while all were saying it was time to be doing something besides lying in idleness and getting sick, upon hearing this challenge it was declared to be necessary that the army should have another commander, and Colonel Sherman was pointed out as the man best calculated to meet the emergency."

Sherman did nothing to stop the talk, but Houston did. "This came to the ears of General Houston, who at once caused notices to be written and stuck on trees with wooden pegs, to the effect that the first man who should beat for volunteers should be courtmartialed and shot. One of these notices was pinned to a hickory tree not six feet from the tent of the Liberty Company." The notes had a marginally sobering effect on the disgruntled, but what seems to have kept the mutiny in check at this point was a backfire rumor Houston started that the army would be marching soon.

Given the discontent in the Texas army during the retreat, and in light of the broad disdain for authority that characterized many of those drawn to Texas before and during the revolution, the surprising thing wasn't that the army was constantly on the verge of falling apart, but that it held together as long as it did. This cohesiveness, such as it was, reflected a common desire to defeat the enemy, but it also reflected the charisma of the commander. As exasperated as the men became with Houston, many of them grew to love him. Frank Sparks, a teenager from Mississippi, remembered that Houston wasn't above the practical jokes the men—especially the younger men like Sparks—

played on one another. A new recruit had an old flintlock rifle that needed repair; he asked Sparks and some friends where he could find a blacksmith in camp. One of the friends pointed to Houston's tent. "The blacksmith is there," he said. The new man nodded gratefully and presented his gun to Houston, whose dress and demeanor revealed nothing of his rank. "I want you to fix my gun," the fellow said. "The lock is out of order; it won't stand cocked." Houston, not recognizing the newcomer, guessed what was afoot and went along. "Set her down here," he told the rifleman, "and call in an hour." Houston cleaned the lock, and when the man returned, his rifle worked perfectly. The others weren't through with their tricks. They now revealed Houston's identity to the newcomer and told him that the general was angry at having been insulted and planned to have the new man shot. They let him sweat while he pleaded for help in finding a way out of his fix. Finally they told him to throw himself on the commander's mercy, which he did. Houston laughed and told the fellow to put his gun to good use against the enemy.

Houston shared the hardships and annoyances that vexed the army. When mud bogged the wagons, he waded in with the others and heaved harder than most. One night he wandered out past the picket lines; on returning he was stopped by a sentry, a recruit who hadn't met the general. Houston explained who he was, but the sentry replied that he had orders to let no one pass without authorization. Houston answered that orders were orders, and he waited patiently till another officer arrived and confirmed his identity.

Although he stressed the need for discipline, Houston occasionally collaborated in rule bending. He commandeered cattle from farms along the route but gave strict orders for the men not to touch pigs and chickens, which, unlike the wild bovines, were the cherished personal property of families. Frank Sparks wanted a break from beef and, discovering an abandoned barnyard full of chickens

and hogs and a smokehouse packed with bacon, told several friends
he was going to cook a regular dinner. They warned that Houston
would punish them; he responded that he'd accept the blame.

> I went to work and killed twelve grown chickens, dressed
> them, and put them in a large wash pot. I also put in some
> sliced bacon. I then made an oven and a large skillet of
> cornbread. I took six of the chickens and put them in a
> dinner pot, with at least half a gallon of rich gravy, and set
> it away, together with the oven of bread. . . . I called the
> men to come to dinner. The yard was covered with feath-
> ers, and the men said to me, "Ain't you afraid Houston will
> punish you if you don't take those feathers away?" I said,
> "No." Well, we all did justice to that dinner.

The commander in chief and several other officers, including
Thomas Rusk (who had joined the army), rode up not long after the
men finally put down their knives. Sparks was sitting on a rail fence
in the yard.

> I opened the gate and said, "Gentlemen officers, I wish to
> see you in the house." I led the way, and they all followed
> me in. I saw Houston knit his brows when he saw the
> feathers in the yard. When they were all in, I closed the
> door, and addressed General Houston in the following
> way: "General Houston, I have disobeyed orders. When we
> arrived here, I found everything deserted and we were
> hungry, for we have had nothing to eat except beef; so I
> killed some chickens and baked some bread, and we had a
> good dinner."
>
> He looked at me as if he were looking through me,

and said, "Sparks, I will have to punish you. You knew it was against orders; I will have to punish you."

I said, "General, I saved you some." And I took the lids off the vessels that contained the chicken and the bread, and told them to help themselves. Rusk drew his knife first, and all the others followed suit, except Houston, who had not taken his eyes off me all this time. Finally he said, "Sparks, I hate to punish you. You have been a good soldier, never shirking your duty. But I will have to punish you."

I said, "General, I will submit to whatever you put upon me."

Rusk said, "General, if you don't come on we'll eat all the dinner. . . . Sparks is a good cook."

Then the general drew his knife and attacked the dinner. After he had eaten a short time, General Rusk said, "General Houston, it is a maxim in law that 'he who partakes of stolen property, knowing it to be such, is guilty with the thief.' "

General Houston replied, "No one wants any of your law phrases."

After the meal, General Houston said, "Sparks, I'll not punish you for this offense, but if you are guilty of it the second time I'll double the punishment."

Santa Anna's flying regiment reached Harrisburg thirty hours after setting out. But the news of his coming had traveled even faster. "I entered Harrisburg the night of the 15th, lighted by the glare of several houses that were burning, and found only a Frenchman and two

North Americans working in a print shop," the president-general wrote. These laggards explained that the rebel leaders had fled for Galveston Bay. Santa Anna resumed the chase, which ended, for the moment, at New Washington, on the shore of the bay, just moments after David Burnet and other Texas officials cast off in rowboats from the shore. In one of the rare displays of gallantry in all the bitter war, the Mexican vanguard held its fire upon the insurgent boats on account of women aboard. Though Santa Anna was disappointed at having failed again to capture the rebel chiefs, he took solace from having driven them off the mainland, to Galveston Island. Containing the rebels there, and eventually eliminating them or expelling them from the country, would be no great chore.

Houston, however, remained at large. Santa Anna's spies informed him of the movements of the rebel army. "Due to the reports which I have gathered at this point," he told General Filisola, "I have no doubts that the entitled General Houston, who was at Groce's Crossing with a force of five to six hundred men, has moved toward Nacogdoches and should have left yesterday in that direction." Santa Anna wasn't worried about Houston's head start toward the border. "Since he is escorting families and supplies in ox-drawn wagons, his march is slow. The Trinity River, moreover, should detain him many days." Santa Anna expected to catch Houston at the Trinity and to destroy his army before it reached the contested region between the Neches and the Sabine.

Everything in Houston's actions till mid-April suggested that Santa Anna was right: that the rebel general intended to continue east to the Trinity and beyond. If he had wanted to fight he would have done so at the Guadalupe or the Colorado or the Brazos. Any one of those rivers, especially with spring's high water, would have helped even the odds between the rebels and the Army of Operations. And had Houston made a stand, he would have rallied the settlers behind him, evening the odds still more. But he chose to retreat, to draw Santa Anna closer and closer to the trap he had laid with Jackson and General Gaines.

And then, suddenly, he changed his mind. Santa Anna contributed to Houston's new thinking, but Houston's men contributed more. Not least because Houston's route toward the Trinity traced the road Santa Anna had already followed to Harrisburg, the rebel general learned of Santa Anna's gamble shortly after the Mexican chief rolled the dice. Houston couldn't tell just how many troops Santa Anna had taken to Harrisburg, but the number was obviously far smaller than the Mexican total. After being outnumbered all spring, Houston discovered to his surprise that he now commanded a larger force than his rival. And after weeks of being scolded from above and taunted from below for his failure to fight, he now had a chance to prove his critics wrong.

Perhaps he would have seized the chance unaided, but his men ensured that he did not let it slip. There were few secrets in the rebel camp; the officers and men learned of Santa Anna's isolation from the rest of the Mexican army about the same time Houston did. This knowledge made mutiny all but inevitable should Houston stick to his strategy of retreat.

During the course of the march from the Guadalupe, Houston had cited the Mexican superiority in artillery as a reason for avoiding a clash. Before leaving Groce's, the army received two cannons, sent from Cincinnati via New Orleans and Galveston and dubbed the "Twin Sisters" after the twin daughters of a Texas immigrant on the same ship. Many of the rebels took the cannons' arrival as reason to attack, and when Houston gave no sign of doing so, their former restiveness resurfaced. Wiley Martin's company deserted en masse. "General, I have brought but my sword," Nicholas Labadie recalled Martin saying. "My company has disbanded. On hearing that you were retreating to Nacogdoches, they declared they would no longer bear arms, but would protect their families, and they have therefore all dispersed." Mosely Baker, likewise returned to the main column, swore he'd retreat no further. Labadie related: "I was then standing within four or five steps of Gen. Houston, and I asked Capt. Baker if his company was on the road to Robbins' Ferry"—the Trinity cross- ing. " 'They are on that road,' said he. 'But,' said I, 'are you and your men willing to retreat there?' . . . 'No, never! never!' said he, 'for if Gen. Houston will not take us to meet the enemy, we will elect a com- mander who will.' "

Houston got the message. Tempted by Santa Anna's gamble, he let the men have their way. The road to the Trinity and the road to Harrisburg coincided as far as the farm of a man named Roberts; there it forked, with the left branch leading to the Trinity and the right to Harrisburg. As the column approached the fork, everyone wondered which branch they would take. Farmer Roberts had his own view on the subject, and when Houston drew near, Roberts pointed to the right and shouted so loudly that none could not hear: "That right hand road will carry you to Harrisburg just as straight as a compass." The marching men took up the cry: "To the right, boys, to the right!" And all proceeded to the right, with Houston saying not a word.

In no regular army could such a critical decision have been made by what amounted to a vote of the rank and file. But the Texan army—as Stephen Austin and Edward Burleson and Sam Houston long before now had learned—was no regular army. It was an oxy- moron: a democratic army, one that indeed made its own decisions.

Houston's insight, at the crucial moment, was to recognize this fact, and put it to use.

★

"This morning we are in preparation to meet Santa Anna," Houston wrote a friend on April 19. "It is the only chance of saving Texas." He lamented that the country hadn't rallied to the cause more enthusiastically. "Texas could have started at least four thousand men. We will only have about seven hundred men to march with, besides the campguard." In an allusion to the troops' role in his decision for battle, Houston said, "It is wisdom growing out of necessity to meet the enemy now. No previous occasion would justify it." He still wasn't sure it was a good idea. "The odds are greatly against us." But he was willing to take a gamble himself. "The troops are in fine spirits, and now is the time for action. . . . We go to conquer."

The Texan army crossed Buffalo Bayou to pin Santa Anna in the triangle between the bayou and the San Jacinto River. The crossing, accomplished on a makeshift raft and a flimsy rowboat, filled most of the day. Houston then ordered a march south and kept the men moving till midnight, when he finally allowed them to slump by the road. Only a few hours later he rolled them out and drove them hard again, to Lynch's Ferry, near the confluence of Buffalo Bayou and the San Jacinto, to prevent Santa Anna's slipping away. They reached the ferry in the late morning and deployed among the dense oaks that lined the banks of the bayou.

Santa Anna didn't intend to slip away. He was more eager to fight than Houston, and as soon as he learned that the rebels were bound not for the Trinity but for him, his excitement got the better of him—and, in a different manner, of his troops. "At about eight o'clock A.M., everything was ready for the march," wrote Pedro Delgado, a colonel of artillery, regarding the Mexican departure from New Washington. "We had burnt a fine warehouse on the wharf, and all the warehouses in the town, when Captain Barragan rushed in at full speed, reporting that Houston was close on our rear." The troops had begun filing up a narrow lane that led through a wood; Santa Anna was still in his tent. "Upon hearing Barragan's report, he leaped on his horse and galloped off at full speed for the lane, which, being crowded with men and mules, did not afford him as prompt an exit as he wished. However, knocking down one and riding over another, he overcame the obstacles, shouting at the top of his voice, 'The enemy are coming! The enemy are coming!' The excitement of the General-in-chief had such a terrifying effect upon the troops that every face turned pale, order could no longer be preserved, and every man thought of flight or of finding a hiding place, and gave up all idea of fighting." (Santa Anna remembered things differently: "All of the members of the division heard of the approach of the enemy with joy, and in the highest spirits continued the march.") Reining in their fear (or their joy), the Mexican troops formed an attack column and proceeded toward the juncture of Buffalo Bayou and the San Jacinto.

"It was two o'clock P.M. when we descried Houston's pickets at the edge of a large wood, in which he concealed his main force," Delgado wrote. "Our skirmishers commenced firing; they were answered by the enemy, who fell back in the woods." Thus began the battle Santa Anna had been trying to provoke and Houston, till lately, to avoid. Santa Anna was more eager than ever and wanted to attack in force at once. But Houston kept to the woods, leaving Santa Anna to puzzle how to draw him out. Meanwhile the Mexican commander ordered Delgado to open cannon fire in the direction of the Texans, whose Twin Sisters responded with grapeshot that severely wounded Captain Urizza, the officer from the battle of the Alamo. For his part,

Delgado wounded James Neill, the Texan artillery chief who had commanded the Alamo before Travis.

Houston was content, for the moment, to have engaged and bloodied the enemy, but his men demanded more. Sidney Sherman loudly declared that a cavalry charge would scatter the Mexicans and carry the day. Houston thought Sherman a fool; the Texans didn't have proper cavalry, only riflemen with horses, which principally provided larger targets for Mexican cannons and muskets. But Sherman paid no more attention to Houston than Baker and Martin had, and he quickly gathered sixty eager horsemen, including War Secretary Rusk. Again feigning control, Houston belatedly blessed the foray but ordered Sherman merely to reconnoiter and under no circumstances to engage the enemy in force.

Sherman ignored the order and on first contact with Mexican troops launched a charge. Santa Anna, who recognized courage when he saw it, was impressed. "About one hundred mounted men"—Santa Anna's war stories, like many of the genre, inflated enemy strength—"sallied forth from the woods and daringly threw themselves upon my escort placed on our left. For a moment they succeeded in throwing it into confusion and seriously wounding one of the dragoons." But the Texans' moment passed. Forced to dismount to reload, they were vulnerable to a charge by the real cavalry of the Mexicans. Soon they were surrounded and fighting for their lives. Sherman signaled frantically to Houston for reinforcements.

This was precisely what Houston had wanted to avoid. He had known that his men could fight from the trees, but he doubted they could stand up to the Mexican dragoons in the open field. Sherman's sally had proved him right, and he had no intention of sending the rest of the army out to meet a similar fate.

But the army, as before, had a mind of its own. Jesse Billingsley, a two-year Texan from Tennessee who commanded a company of volunteers mustered into the regular army, refused to let Sherman and his followers be massacred by the Mexicans. "Seeing him under a heavy fire and receiving no orders from General Houston to go to his support," Billingsley remembered, "I determined to go voluntarily, and accordingly led out the first company of the first regiment." The remainder of the regiment followed, and all began marching toward the field where Sherman and the others were battling desperately.

Houston was outraged at the insubordination but unable to prevent it. "He ordered us to countermarch," Billingsley recalled. "This order the men treated with derision, requesting him to countermarch himself, if he desired it." The arrival of the regiment distracted the Mexicans long enough to let Sherman and the others retire to the trees with the rest of the Texans.

Miraculously, only two men were wounded in this escapade, besides several horses killed. Thomas Rusk had a narrow escape, made possible by the timely intervention of a late recruit, Mirabeau Lamar, who rode down a Mexican dragoon about to dispatch the secretary of war. Lamar also rescued a teenage Irish volunteer dazed in falling from his mount. So daring were Lamar's horseback exploits that some of the Mexican cavalrymen spontaneously burst into applause.

If Houston expected Sherman to be chagrined at having hazarded several dozen men to no good purpose, he was mistaken. Sherman showed not the least repentance but rather berated Houston for not throwing the entire army into the battle and having it out with the Mexicans then and there. Houston tongue-lashed Sherman for stupidity and insubordination, but the rebuke had little effect beyond embittering Sherman against Houston permanently.

As night fell, Houston worried about the day ahead. Santa Anna was precisely where Houston wanted him, and the Texan troops were itching to take on the Mexicans. But almost none of the Texans had seen genuine battle, and their lack of discipline—meaning not just their willingness to withstand fire but their ability to follow orders under pressure and act in unison—was frightening. They could probably skirmish with the best of irregulars, but could they stand up to regular soldiers in a pitched fight? General Gaines's men presumably could, which had been one of their attractions all along. Houston wondered, even now, whether he should have continued to retreat. But the decision had been made, and soon he would discover whether it was the wrong one. He wasn't sure his men could win the war in a day; there were thousands of Mexican troops besides Santa Anna's in the field. But because these were the only troops Texas had, a day might suffice to lose the war.

Exhausted from worry and exertion, Houston was still sleeping the next morning when General Cos unexpectedly arrived at Santa Anna's camp with a contingent that doubled the Mexican force. Many of Houston's officers and men took this as additional evidence of their commander's incapacity to lead. If the battle had been the day before, they could have fought Santa Anna and Cos separately; now they would have to fight the two Mexican generals together.

Houston had been reluctant to attack before Cos's arrival, and he was more reluctant after. He liked his position and preferred to let Santa Anna assume the danger of the initiative. As John Swisher recalled, the Texans' position had much to recommend it.

It would be difficult to select anywhere better ground for an impregnable camp than that now occupied by our army. It was about two or three feet above the water's edge and ran back from fifty to one hundred yards on a level, cov-

ered with trees, but with little or no undergrowth, to a second bank about ten feet high. This last bank was not so
steep that the troops could not easily walk to the top, deliver their fire, fall back, load, advance and fire again.

The Mexican position was far less attractive. "We had the enemy
on our right, within a wood, at long musket range," Pedro Delgado
explained. "Our front, although level, was exposed to the fire of the
enemy, who could keep it up with impunity from his sheltered position. Retreat was easy for him on his rear and right, while our own
troops had no space for maneuvering. We had in our rear a small
grove, reaching to the bay shore, which extended to our right as far as
New Washington. What ground had we to retreat upon in case of a reverse? From sad experience, I answered: None!"

Delgado related his fears to General Castrillón, who shared
them. "What can I do, my friend?" Castrillón said. "I know it well, but
I cannot help it. You know that nothing avails here against the
caprice, arbitrary will and ignorance of that man." The reference, of
course, was to Santa Anna, for whose ears Castrillón intended his
criticism. "This was said in an impassioned voice," Delgado remarked, "and in close proximity to His Excellency's tent."

Yet His Excellency saw merit in the Mexican position. "I shut
the enemy up in the low marshy angle of the country where its retreat
was cut off by Buffalo Bayou and the San Jacinto," Santa Anna said.
"Their left was opposed by our right, protected by the woods on the
banks of the bayou; their right covered by our six-pounder and my
cavalry; and I myself occupied the highest part of the terrain."

Whoever had the better of the terrain, Santa Anna now had the
edge in numbers. But the troops that came with Cos weren't ready for
battle. They had been on the road all night and required food and
rest. Santa Anna assumed that if the rebels were going to attack, they

would have done so at dawn; since they hadn't, he didn't think they would before the next day. He ordered the new arrivals to stack their arms and take a nap in the grove by the bayou. As he himself had gone without sleep while supervising the erection of breastworks, he too lay down to rest.

Santa Anna's assumption might have been right as it related to Houston. The Texan general remained cautious and wouldn't lightly abandon his strong defensive position for the hazards of an assault across open ground. But Santa Anna's assumption didn't apply to Houston's men, who again forced their commander's hand. Accounts differ regarding the degree of unrest in the Texan camp. Nicholas Labadie portrayed Houston as continuing to dither till John Wharton (the brother of Stephen Austin's fellow envoy to the United States) brought the issue to a head. "Col. Wharton visited every mess in camp," Labadie said, "and slapping his hands together, he spoke loud and quick: 'Boys, there is no other word today but fight, fight! Now is the time!' Every man was eager for it, but all feared another disappointment, as the commander still showed no disposition whatever to lead the men out." Wharton persisted, and the men began to respond, till finally Houston declared, "Fight, and be damned!"

Houston remembered things otherwise. He said that at a noontime war council the demands to attack were confined to two junior officers. Their four seniors—not including Houston but including Rusk—cautioned against ordering the untested Texan troops across an open field against the Mexican defenses. Better to let the enemy do the attacking. "Our situation is strong; in it we can whip all Mexico," Houston paraphrased the majority.

If the two versions reveal a difference, it was chiefly about timing. Houston knew he couldn't delay long, given the belligerence of his troops and the inevitable approach of the rest of the Mexican army (which he tried to slow by ordering the destruction of the bridge over which Cos had come). The Texan commander might wait a day, maybe two, but he couldn't wait longer than that without losing all hope of victory.

In fact he didn't wait even a day. Driven for years by his ambition, goaded for weeks by his men, presented just now by Santa Anna with an unprecedented opportunity, Houston on the afternoon of April 21 took the fateful step. At three-thirty he ordered the Texans to form up. "Our troops paraded with alacrity and spirit, and were anxious for the contest," he recalled, in what was a substantial understatement. Though less than a mile from the Mexican camp, the Texans moved forward undetected, concealed by a small hill, by tall grass, by the Mexicans' fatigue, and by Santa Anna's conclusion that the rebels wouldn't attack that day.

As he sent the men into battle, Houston still worried that their ranks would splinter under fire. He was right to worry. "Our regiments were volunteers, and knew nothing whatever about drilling," Frank Sparks admitted. If they could keep one thought in mind, to hold their fire as long as possible, Houston would be lucky. "We were ordered not to fire until we could see the whites of the enemies' eyes," Sparks said.

The advance proceeded quietly until the Texans were within a quarter mile of the Mexican camp. Two columns of infantry, totaling some six hundred men, pushed ahead of the artillery, which consisted chiefly of the Twin Sisters. The Texan cavalry—a few dozen mounted riflemen under the newly promoted Mirabeau Lamar—circled to the Mexican left. Houston, astride a white stallion acquired for the occasion, rode amid and around the troops. At his order the cannons opened fire with grape and canister, the cavalry galloped forward, and the infantry charged, screaming, "Remember the Alamo! Remember Goliad!"

The surprise attack stunned Santa Anna and the Mexicans. "I was in a deep sleep when I was awakened by the firing and noise," Santa Anna said. "I immediately perceived we were attacked, and had fallen into frightful disorder." The disorder deepened as the Texans surged forward. "The utmost confusion prevailed," Pedro Delgado remembered. "General Castrillón shouted on one side; on another, Colonel Almonte was giving orders; some cried out to commence firing; others, to lie down to avoid grape shots. . . . I saw our men flying in small groups, terrified, and sheltering themselves behind large trees. I endeavored to force some of them to fight, but all efforts were in vain—the evil was beyond remedy: they were a bewildered and panic-stricken herd."

The Mexican officers were unable to stem the panic. Delgado remembered that Santa Anna was completely nonplussed. "I saw His Excellency running about in the utmost excitement, wringing his hands, and unable to give an order." Other officers were incapacitated by the enemy fire. "General Castrillón was stretched on the ground, wounded in the leg. Colonel Treviño was killed, and Colonel Marcial Aguirre was severely injured." With the officers down or undone, the rank and file—reluctant conscripts, hungry and far from home—were a lost cause.

Confusion turned to rout. "On the left, and about a musket-shot distance from our camp, was a small grove, on the bay shore," Delgado wrote. "Our disbanded herd rushed for it, to obtain shelter from the horrid slaughter carried on all over the prairie by the blood-thirsty usurpers." The Mexican troops fled for their lives, only to be pinned at the edge of the bayou. "The men, on reaching it, would helplessly crowd together, and were shot down by the enemy, who was close enough not to miss his aim. It was there that the greatest carnage took place."

All accounts of the battle agree that the carnage was indeed very great. The anger that had been building among the Texans since the Alamo and Goliad burst forth in a bloodbath that matched the former for ferocity and the latter for numbers killed. Frank Sparks left one of the less gruesome accounts. "We charged with such fury that the Mexicans fled in a very short time," he said. "The rout was general and a great slaughter of Mexicans took place within four hundred yards of their breastworks. . . . About ten acres of ground was literally covered with their dead bodies." Ramón Martínez Caro, Santa Anna's secretary, surveyed the field after the battle under the guard of one of Houston's lieutenants. "He led me to the entrance of the road taken by our troops in their flight," Martínez Caro wrote, "and there I saw, both to the right and to the left, as far as the eye could see, a double file of corpses, all men from our force. Moved by this sad spectacle—would that it had been the last—I still had the more bitter sorrow of being conducted a short distance to the left, where there was a small creek, at the edge of the woods, where the bodies were so thickly piled upon each other that they formed a bridge across it."

Most of the killing occurred in the battle proper. Martínez Caro's guide, pointing to the bridge of bodies, explained, "At this place, they rushed in such confusion and in such numbers that they converted the crossing into a mud hole, obstructing the way, and our soldiers in the heat of battle massacred them." The Texans shot hundreds of the Mexicans. "It was nothing but a slaughter," said W. C. Swearingen, regarding the scene at the bayou. "They at first attempted to swim the bayou but they were surrounded by our men and they shot every one that attempted to swim the bayou as soon as he took the water, and them that remained they killed as fast as they could load and shoot them until they surrendered."

Yet surrender didn't end the killing. Nicholas Labadie described the execution of a prisoner.

> I pursued a fresh trail into the marsh, and came upon Col. Bertrand, who had bogged, and on his knees he begged for his life. Supposing myself alone, I extended my left hand to raise him up, but was surprised to hear a voice behind me saying, "Oh! I know him; he is Col. Bertrand of San Antonio de Bexar. General Teran made him colonel." This was said by one Sanchez, a Mexican, in Capt. Seguin's company, composed of some thirty Mexicans [Tejanos] fighting on our side. He had scarcely done speaking when I observed three others coming up with levelled guns. I cried out to them: "Don't shoot, don't shoot; I have taken him prisoner." These words were hardly spoken, when bang goes a gun, the ball entering the forehead of poor Bertrand, and my hand and clothes are spattered with his brains, as he falls dead at my feet.

Dismay at the actions of his comrades caused Labadie to draw a curtain at this point in his narrative; he added only that he "shortly after witnessed acts of cruelty which I forbear to recount."

Moses Bryan, nephew of Stephen Austin, told a similar tale.

> The most awful slaughter I ever saw was when the Texans pursued the retreating Mexicans, killing on all sides, even the wounded. . . . I came upon a young Mexican boy (a drummer, I suppose) lying on his face. One of the volun-

teers brought to Texas by Colonel Sherman pricked the
boy with his bayonet. The boy grasped the man around the
legs and called in Spanish: *"Ave Maria purissima, por Diós
salva me vida!"* ["Hail Mary most pure, for God's sake, save
my life!"]. I begged the man to spare him, both of his legs
being broken already. The man looked at me and put his
hand on his pistol, so I passed on. Just as I did, he blew out
the boy's brains.

The murdering frenzy almost claimed some of the Texans' own
wounded. Nineteen-year-old Alphonso Steele had been shot in the
head, but not fatally. Yet the blood ran down in his eyes and nearly
blinded him.

I could hardly see anything and I sat down on a dead Mexican. While I was sitting there some of Millard's regulars,
who'd stayed at the breastworks and were busy sticking
their bayonets through wounded Mexicans, came along.
And one of them had his bayonet drawn back to stick
through me when Tom Green of our artillery corps
stopped the regular from killing me.

Houston made a halfhearted effort to stanch the bloodletting,
but the men obeyed as poorly now as before the battle. Nicholas
Labadie encountered the Texan commander as the Mexican resistance was ending and the slaughter was beginning. Houston had been
in the thick of things from the start, and showed it.

I observed Gen. Houston on a bay pony, with his leg over
the pommel of the saddle. "Doctor," said he, "I am glad to
see you; are you hurt?" "Not at all," said I. "Well," he re-

joined, "I have had two horses shot under me, and have received a ball in my ankle, but am not badly hurt." "Do you wish to have it dressed?" said I. "Oh, no, not now, but I will when I get back to the camp. I can stand it well enough till then."

He then faces his horse about, and orders the drum to beat a retreat. But the men, paying no attention to the order, shouted with expressions of exultation over the glorious victory, and it was difficult to hear anything distinctly. . . . Then while I was within ten feet of him, he cries out, as loud as he could raise his voice: "Parade, men, parade!" But the shouts and halloing were too long and loud; and Houston, seeing he could not restore order, cries at the top of his voice: "Gentlemen! Gentlemen! Gentlemen! (a momentary stillness ensues) Gentlemen! I applaud your bravery but damn your manners."

Robert Hunter observed a more specific reaction to Houston's entreaties. "General Houston gave orders not to kill any more but to take prisoners," Hunter recalled. "Capt. Easlen said, 'Boys, take prisoners—you know how to take prisoners. Take them with the butt of your guns, club guns,' and said, 'Remember the Alamo, remember La Bahía [Goliad], and club guns, right and left, and knock their brains out.'" Hunter added, "The Mexicans would fall down on their knees and say, 'Me no Alamo, me no La Bahía.'" But it did them little good. Many ran for a lagoon behind the battlefield. "Man and horse went in head and ears to the bottom. . . . That lagoon was full of men and horses for about twenty or thirty feet up and down it, and none of them ever got out. I think their bones are laying there yet."

PART FOUR

Lone Star and Union (1836–1865)

Victors and Vanquished

On the day after the battle, Sam Houston and Santa Anna met for the first time. Houston had spent the night in pain from his ankle injury, but otherwise he blessed his good fortune and congratulated his comrades in arms. Santa Anna's wounds were to pride and ambition, and he cursed his evil fate and the incompetents who had failed him at what should have been his hour of triumph. The Mexican general's escape from the battlefield was hardly the stuff of honor and glory; rather than rally the troops or attempt a surrender, he flew from the fighting with personal safety first in mind. Doubtless he rationalized that no one was more important to Mexico than he, holding the highest offices his country could bestow, and that the national interest required that he not be killed or captured. Probably he inferred from the slaughter around him that capture might not have been an option till the Texans satisfied their blood lust. In any event, he seized a horse from an aide and galloped west, in the direction of General Filisola and the main body of the Army of Operations. He shortly saw that the Texans had destroyed the bridge over Buffalo Bayou that was to be his escape route. Confused, disoriented, and in understandable fear for his life, he floundered in the mud along the bayou till night fell, whereupon he took shelter among the pines that bordered the stream. At daybreak he discovered a cabin, empty of inhabitants but containing some civilian clothes; partly for comfort but equally for disguise, he exchanged his soaking, soiled general's uniform for a pair of plain trousers and a blue cotton jacket. He struck off again, on foot now, and managed a few miles before being sighted by a band of Texans hunting for Mexicans who had somehow escaped the killing of the previous day. He tried to hide but to no avail, and the Texas horsemen surrounded him.

They had no idea who he was, and he didn't enlighten them. They took him prisoner and continued their mission. Only one of the Texans, Joel Robison, spoke much Spanish. Robison asked the prisoner if he knew where Santa Anna and Cos were. "He said he presumed they had gone to the Brazos," Robison recalled. Robison accepted the answer, and the group moved on, with the Texans riding and the prisoner walking. Santa Anna wasn't used to walking; he tired and asked to rest. Some of the Texans, assuming he was harmless, proposed to let him find his own way to the camp of prisoners. But one said he'd shoot him before he'd let him go. So Robison hauled Santa Anna up behind him on his horse. The young rebel and the defeated general conversed about the battle. Santa Anna asked how many soldiers the Texans had. Less than eight hundred, Robison answered. "He said that I was certainly mistaken, that our force was surely much larger." Robison affirmed that the number was correct, embarrassing Santa Anna into reflective silence. The group reached the camp of prisoners, where, to the astonishment of Robison and the others, the Mexicans greeted the new arrival with shouts of "El Presidente! El Presidente!"

At once Santa Anna was taken to Houston, who lay beneath an oak tree resting his ruined ankle. Between Houston's pain and Santa

Anna's chagrin and fear—news of his capture had raced through the Texan camp and drawn the angry and curious to witness the encounter between the opposing commanders, with most of the Texans clamoring for vengeance—the interview was strained. If Houston was tempted to yield to the popular judgment, he resisted the temptation. His was not a vindictive personality; besides, he reckoned that Santa Anna would be more useful alive than dead. And anyway, as one who had spent the last two months trying to impress his army with the need for discipline and observance of military forms, he insisted on hewing to protocol in dealing with his defeated enemy.

Nicholas Labadie, present at the interview on account of being a doctor and able to speak Spanish, recalled Houston asking, "General Santa Anna, in what condition do you surrender yourself?"

Santa Anna responded, "A prisoner of war."

Houston said, "Tell General Santa Anna that so long as he shall remain in the boundaries I shall allot him, I will be responsible for his life."

Santa Anna's spirits revived at learning he'd live another day. And with his reviving spirits he regained some of his characteristic audacity. "Tell General Houston that I am tired of blood and war, and have seen enough of this country to know that the two people can not live under the same laws," he said. "And I am willing to treat with him as to the boundaries of the two countries."

Houston must have smiled inwardly at this boldness. Until the day before, Santa Anna had held that the Texans were nothing but pirates, to be lawfully exterminated by any means possible. Now he declared himself weary of war and convinced that the Texans must have their own country. How much of Santa Anna's history Houston knew is open to question; the Texan general might or might not have been aware of Santa Anna's battlefield conversion to Mexican nationalism in 1821 or his sudden embrace of republicanism two years later. But Houston certainly entertained doubts about the sincerity of Santa Anna's belief that Texas must be independent.

So he put Santa Anna off. He explained that he was a military commander and nothing more; it was for the civilian government to negotiate treaties.

What Houston didn't say but certainly realized was that Santa Anna couldn't speak for the Mexican government. Or more precisely, he might speak for the Mexican government but the government wouldn't have to listen. Captured commanders, by virtue of their capture, lose their commands. Whether the same principle applied to captured dictators, Houston couldn't say. But he required little imagination to suppose that the Mexican government would disavow any agreement made by Santa Anna under duress, or that the middle of the rebel camp, with the Texan rank and file screaming for his head, counted as duress.

Even so, Santa Anna could provide something more valuable than paper assent to Texas independence. The bulk of the Army of Operations remained in the field. General Filisola's command was the closest and might arrive at San Jacinto in a day or two. General Gaona was approaching from the northwest. Farthest but largest was General Urrea's force. Houston appreciated that catching Santa Anna's army asleep had been a stroke of luck, one he couldn't count on repeating. But with the hostage's help, he might not have to. Santa Anna was probably egocentric enough to believe that no other Mexican general could win where he had lost. Or perhaps he was insecure enough not to want the experiment made. In any case he understood, without Houston's saying it, that his life would be forfeit in the event of an attack.

Santa Anna's thoughts seem to have anticipated Houston's. When Thomas Rusk, also present, pointed out that Filisola was drawing near and the Texans would soon have to fight him, Santa Anna responded, "No, I will order him to return."

Rusk had a better idea. "Order him to deliver up himself and his army as prisoners of war."

"Ho!" said Santa Anna (again according to Labadie's recollection and translation). "He will not do it. He will not do it. You have whipped me. I am your prisoner. But Filisola is not whipped. He will not surrender as a prisoner of war. You must whip him first. But if I give him orders to leave the limits of Texas, he will do it."

Houston judged that Santa Anna was right. Surrender was too much to ask of Filisola and the others, but withdrawal wasn't. Houston listened carefully as Santa Anna dictated a dispatch. "Since I had an unfortunate encounter with the small division operating in my vicinity, as a result I am a prisoner of war of the enemy," Santa Anna explained to Filisola. "In view of this, I command Your Excellency to order General Gaona to countermarch to Béxar to await my orders, which Your Excellency will also do with the troops under your command. Likewise direct General Urrea to withdraw his division to Guadalupe Victoria." In a separate letter to Filisola that complemented this order, Santa Anna asserted that much depended on the general's swift compliance. "I recommend to you that as soon as possible you carry out my order concerning the withdrawal of the troops since this is conducive to the safety of the prisoners, and in particular that of your most affectionate friend and companion who sends you his deepest regards, Antonio López de Santa Anna."

★

Santa Anna's order placed Filisola in a quandary. By no stretch of military custom was he bound to obey an order dictated from captivity. But Filisola had to assume that Santa Anna would eventually be released; if the Texans had intended to kill him, they probably would have done so by now. To disobey would put Filisola on the wrong side of a man not known for forgiveness. At the same time, though the news of the San Jacinto debacle hadn't reached the Mexican capital yet, when it did it doubtless would inspire Santa Anna's enemies there, who would ask searching questions of a general who abandoned the Texas campaign simply because his superior lost one battle.

The prospect of retreat appealed to some in the Mexican army but angered others. "A few hours before, we thought only of flying to avenge our companions and our general-in-chief," José Urrea wrote. "And now the first rumors of turning our back upon them in their misfortune began to be heard. Such a sudden change could not but arouse extreme feelings of despair and dismay, of shame and indignation." The idea of retreat struck Urrea as bizarre. "My division at that time was in the finest condition. Each soldier could hold up his head proudly, for up to then they had met only victory in every encounter with the enemy. . . . Everyone, even to the last soldier, was convinced of our superiority and of the worthlessness of the enemy." To be sure, Houston had beaten Santa Anna. But in doing so he had given away his location. "Everything seemed to point, therefore, to a concentration of our forces in order to march upon him and repair the defeat suffered by our vanguard."

José de la Peña agreed, as did a majority of the junior officers. De la Peña and the others hoped Urrea would act on his anger. "Most of the army would have followed him gladly to rectify the disaster at San Jacinto, had he wanted to place himself at their head," de la Peña wrote. "Several of us officers, indignant to learn that our disgrace was to be consummated, invited him to do so." De la Peña recalled the dictum of Napoleon (the real one) that retreat almost always cost more than advance, that steadfastness was the surest route to victory. De la Peña was certain that victory still awaited Mexican arms. "Doubtless we would have achieved it, had there only been a commander who would have led us into it and who could have appraised the advantages to be gained by not showing the enemy our backs. We would have conquered had there been among those in charge a single one desiring glory, who could have foreseen the renown that would have been his if he had taken that resolution, for which no great heroism was necessary. General Urrea seemed destined to play this brilliant role, and everyone pointed to him as the best suited to carry it out."

But Urrea let the laurels pass. When Filisola made clear that he would comply with Santa Anna's order, and the other generals fell in line, Urrea swallowed his indignation and did so, too.

Politics played the largest part in Filisola's decision, but logistics entered as well. Lacking Santa Anna's political and emotional investment in the Texas campaign, Filisola felt more acutely the problems of supply that confronted the Army of Operations. His lines of communication and transport were stretched long and thin, and, especially with the boost in rebel confidence from the victory at San Jacinto, they were alarmingly vulnerable to enemy attack. Moreover, though Houston's scorched-earth strategy hadn't prevented Santa Anna from pressing forward with his regiment of hundreds, it severely hampered Filisola's army of thousands. He wondered if he could even make it back to Mexico, let alone sustain himself in Texas. Finally, Filisola couldn't ignore the prisoners of war, including Santa Anna, who remained at the mercy of the rebels. To resume the attack risked six hundred lives.

Afterward, when the Mexican government called him to account for his conduct in Texas, Filisola defended his decision to retreat.

"Should it become necessary that I forfeit my life," he said, "I shall deem myself more than fully repaid by having been instrumental in saving the lives of 600 unfortunate prisoners and perhaps that of 2,500 other companions-in-arms who would very likely have perished, if not at the hands of the enemy, as a result of the rigors of the climate, the season, and hunger."

Filisola's retreat hardly settled the issue of Texas independence. The rebels had won the latest battle, but the war continued. Until Mexico conceded defeat, the Texans must prepare for further invasions.

Yet Filisola's retreat bought the rebels breathing space, which was more than Houston had enjoyed for months, and he made the most of it. The Mexican ball that blasted his ankle left shards of bone embedded in the flesh; these invited infection, which spread up his leg and threatened gangrene or septicemia. No surgeon in Texas possessed the skill and equipment to perform the operation that would save Houston's life. Labadie and the other medics told Houston he'd better get to New Orleans. In mid-May he sailed from Galveston.

Santa Anna hoped to leave for Mexico shortly thereafter. The Mexican general's charm never served him so well as in the weeks following his defeat. It kept him alive in Houston's camp, and it caused the Texas government to promise his release. President Burnet and Santa Anna signed a treaty by which the latter, "in his official character as chief of the Mexican nation," acknowledged "the full, entire, and perfect Independence of the Republic of Texas." The Mexican army would retire across the Rio Grande, and Santa Anna, on his "inviolable parole of honour," would not resume hostilities against Texas. In exchange, Burnet and the Texas government guaranteed Santa Anna's life and agreed to transport him to Veracruz, "in order that he may more promptly and effectually obtain ratification of this compact." Commissioners from Texas to Mexico would negotiate final terms of peace and a treaty of amity and commerce.

Burnet had little besides Santa Anna's word that he would do what he promised once he reached Mexico. And in fact Santa Anna had no intention of making more than a pro forma effort, if that, on behalf of his agreement with the Texans. "I did promise *to try* to get a hearing for the Texas commissioners," he said later. "But this in itself did not bind the government to receive them, nor if they were received did it have to accede to all their pretensions. . . . I offered nothing in the name of the nation. In my own name I pledged myself to acts that our government could nullify."

Yet Santa Anna had a knack for making the unlikely plausible. He avowed that he'd learned his lesson in Texas and wished, for himself and his country, to move on. Anyway, he argued, he was the only one who could make peace stick in Mexico. No one else had the stature to acknowledge defeat. Whether or not it was in his own interest to return to Mexico, it was in the interest of Texas for him to do so.

Unfortunately for Santa Anna, his persuasiveness didn't reach beyond his voice and personal presence. Burnet prepared a boat to take him south, but even as he did so, volunteers from the United States continued to arrive in Texas. Two hundred reached Velasco on the very day that Santa Anna was embarking. Frustrated to learn that the fighting was over—which, among other consequences, jeopardized the land bounty they had been promised—the volunteers vented their anger by crying for the blood of the beast of the Alamo and Goliad. Burnet, who hoped to continue in Texas politics, acceded to the popular will so far as to order the prisoner ashore.

Santa Anna was stunned. He had already composed a farewell letter to the Texans. "My Friends," he said, "I have been a witness to your courage in the field of battle, and know you to be generous. Rely with confidence on my sincerity, and you shall never have cause to regret the kindness shown me. In returning to my native land, I beg you will receive the thanks of your grateful friend." Now it appeared his "friends" were going to kill him. From the baying on the beach, he was sure his time had come. "I immediately wrote to Mr. Burnet an official communication which I concluded by saying *that I was determined not to leave the ship alive*," he recalled. Better to die by his own hand, he reasoned, or by a swift bullet aboard than to be torn asunder by the mob. Only on receiving assurance that his person would be respected and his confinement continue no more than a few days did he allow himself to be taken off.

He survived the landing, but his imprisonment stretched from days to several weeks. Nor was he safe behind bars. "Every private felt called to assassinate me," he remembered. "On the 27th of June a pistol was fired at me through a window near my bed and almost caused the death of Colonels Almonte and Nuñez. Finally, on the 30th of June, orders were issued for our removal from Columbia"—to which the prisoners had been taken lest they be seized by lynchers on the coast—"to Goliad where we were to be executed in the place that Fannin and his men had been shot."

★

Houston had saved Santa Anna after the battle of San Jacinto; now it was Stephen Austin's turn. On July 1 Austin arrived back from the United States. Following its promising start in the Mississippi and Ohio Valleys, Austin's diplomatic mission had stalled on the Atlantic seaboard. The Texans' long delay in declaring independence deterred

Congress and the Jackson administration from supplying official support, and the grim news from the Alamo and Goliad frightened bankers and others who might have tendered financial backing. The bad tidings also discouraged Austin personally. "Desolation it seems is sweeping over Texas," he wrote. "My heart and soul are sick." Yet having come so far—in time, distance, and effort—he refused to surrender hope. "My spirit is unbroken. . . . Texas will rise again." When Austin learned that Texas had indeed risen at San Jacinto, sooner than expected, he hailed the victory as a sign from heaven and immediately turned west. "Much more now depends on a correct course and union at home, than on any thing else," he wrote Mary Holley. "Nothing shall induce me to leave home again until all is settled there."

The first thing to settle was the war. Austin had dealt with the Mexican government during the entirety of its existence, and he knew how hard it was to get a decision out of Mexico City. Guessing that recognizing Texan independence would be more difficult than anything Mexico had ever done, Austin reasoned that something novel was necessary to spur Mexican decision making. He arranged for Santa Anna to approach Andrew Jackson. The American administration still hadn't recognized Texas and so wouldn't treat officially with its representatives, but it might treat with Santa Anna on Texas's behalf. Santa Anna, by making himself thus useful, could escape his appointment with the firing squad. Santa Anna explained how he learned of the scheme: "Stephen F. Austin, whom I had befriended in Mexico, moved by my unfortunate condition, told me that *if I would write a letter to General Jackson flattering the hopes of the Texans, even if I only used courteous phrases, the very name of that official, from whom Texans expected so much and whom they heard with the greatest respect, would restrain popular fury and facilitate my salvation.*"

Austin helped Santa Anna draft a letter to Jackson. Santa Anna wrote that his expedition to Texas had been "in fulfillment of the duties which a public man owes to his native country and to honor." The American president could certainly understand this. The fortunes of war, however, had prevented Santa Anna's doing justice to country and honor, instead delivering him as prisoner to Jackson's protégé, "Don Samuel Houston." Santa Anna gratefully acknowledged the respect Houston had accorded him, and he recounted how he and Houston had agreed on the withdrawal of Mexican forces. He explained that he had been on the verge of departing for Veracruz to pursue a definitive settlement when "some indiscreet persons raised a tumult, which obliged the authorities forcibly to land me and again to place me in close confinement." This setback had revived the war spirit in Mexico, with the result that General Urrea—as Santa Anna and the Texans had lately learned—was returning north with a fresh army.

All this prefaced the main point of the letter: "The duration of the war and its disasters are therefore necessarily inevitable unless a powerful hand interpose to cause the voice of reason to be opportunely listened to. It appears to me, then, that it is you who can render so great a service to humanity by using your high influence to have the aforesaid agreements carried into effect." Santa Anna asked Jackson to join him in negotiating a settlement of the Texas war. "Let us establish mutual relations, to the end that your nation and the Mexican may strengthen their friendly ties and both engage amicably in giving existence and stability to a people that wish to figure in the political world." With Santa Anna's help, President Jackson and America could rely on Mexico. "The Mexicans are magnanimous when treated with consideration. I will make known to them, with purity of intentions, the reasons of conveniency and humanity which require a frank and noble conduct, and I do not doubt they will adopt it when conviction has worked upon their minds."

Jackson would have given this remarkable letter a closer reading had he not already received notice from Mexico City that Santa
Anna had been deposed in absentia. If Jackson had shown Santa
Anna's letter to the Mexican minister in Washington, the Mexican
government might well have indicted the ex-dictator for treason in
seeking the detachment of Texas from Mexico. Jackson had never
been a stickler for form, but in the last months of his presidency he
declined to provoke Mexico by accepting Santa Anna's unauthorized
offer of mediation. Better, he judged, to work with the regime that actually ruled in Mexico City. "Until the existing Government of Mexico ask our friendly offices between the contesting parties, Mexico
and Texas, we cannot interfere," Jackson answered Santa Anna. "But
should Mexico ask it, our friendly offices will, with pleasure, be afforded to restore peace and put an end to this inhuman warfare."

Jackson wrote in the same vein to Sam Houston, now returned
to Texas. He went on to advise his old friend to hold on to Santa Anna,
neither freeing nor executing him.

I have seen a report that General Santa Anna was to be
brought before a military court, to be tried and shot.
Nothing *now* could tarnish the character of Texas more
than such an act at this late period. It was good policy as
well as humanity that spared him—it has given you possession of Goliad and the Alamo without blood or loss of the
strength of your army. His person is still of much consequence to you. He is the pride of the Mexican soldiers and
the favorite of the priesthood, and whilst he is in your
power the priests will not furnish the supplies necessary
for another campaign, nor will the regular soldier *voluntarily* march when reentering Texas may endanger or cost
their favorite general his life. . . . Let not his blood be

shed, unless it becomes necessary by an imperative act of just retaliation for Mexican massacres hereafter.

Houston agreed with Jackson regarding Santa Anna's value but explained it slightly differently. "While Santa Anna was held a prisoner," Houston said afterward, "his friends were afraid to invade Texas because they knew not at what moment it would cause his sacrifice. His political enemies dared not attempt a combination in Mexico for a Texas invasion, for they did not know at what moment he might be turned loose upon them."

In terms of popular reaction, Stephen Austin's return to Texas after six months in the United States stood in sharp and discouraging contrast to his earlier return after eighteen months in Mexico City. Then he had been hailed as a savior, the unifier who would bring together the contending parties in the struggle for Texas's future. Now he was hardly noticed. The hero of the hour was Houston, limping on his bad leg but walking taller for the infirmity. The founder, the one who had made Houston's victory possible by making Texas what it became, was all but forgotten amid the praise for the liberator.

Texans, most of whom by now owed nothing directly to Austin, tossed him aside casually but definitively two months after his arrival. Elections to replace provisional president Burnet with a permanent chief executive were scheduled for September. Austin, hoping to reclaim his role as paterfamilias of Texas, announced his candidacy. For several weeks he had reason for optimism, as his principal opponent was Henry Smith, who remained as controversial as when the general council impeached him. Yet at the last moment

Houston entered the race, and the liberator overwhelmed the founder by a margin of nine to one.

Austin publicly congratulated Houston but privately railed at the ingratitude of those who followed the man on the horse. "Many of the old settlers who are too blind to see or understand their interest will vote for him," Austin said of Houston as the election approached. Upon Austin's defeat he told James Perry, "I once believed all men honest until the reverse appeared. I now think all the reverse until I see them tried."

Austin had to sit aside while Houston took the oath of office and delivered the first inaugural by an elected Texas president. Houston was visibly moved by the occasion. After congratulating his compatriots and comrades in arms for their valor and resolve, and after warning that the work of independence was not yet finished ("We must keep all our energies alive, our army organized, disciplined, and increased agreeably to our present necessities"), he presented to the people of Texas his sword of command. An eyewitness described the feelings—"more eloquently impressive than the deepest pathos conveyed in language"—that surged through Houston as he gave up his weapon: "The President was unable to proceed further; but having firmly clinched it with both hands, as if with a farewell grasp, a tide of varied associations of ideas rushed upon him in the moment; his countenance bespoke the workings of the strongest emotions, his soul seemed to have swerved from the hypostatic union of the body, and to dwell momentarily on the glistening blade." As Houston handed over the sword, he said, "I have worn it with some humble pretensions in defense of my country, and should the danger of my country again call for my services, I expect to resume it, and respond to that call, if needful with my blood and life."

Austin must have reflected that against such a performance, and against the martial prowess it supposed, he had no hope to hold the love of Texans. With prescience he had written earlier that the warrior always won out over the pioneer. "A successful military chieftain is hailed with admiration and applause, and monuments perpetuate his fame. But the bloodless pioneer of the wilderness, like the corn and cotton he causes to spring where it never grew before, attracts no notice. . . . No slaughtered thousands or smoking cities attest his devotion to the cause of human happiness, and he is regarded by the mass of the world as a humble instrument to pave the way for others." Watching Houston, Austin knew that the warrior had won and this pioneer must yield.

Houston gracefully brought Austin into his cabinet as secretary of state, but the office was hardly what Austin had hoped for and considered his due. Ill health added to his distress. "Since my return from the U.S. I have been confined much of the time with sickness and am now barely able to get about," he told Mary Holley. Austin's mental state reflected his condition of body. His enemies, he complained, accused him of reneging on promises. "This has mortified me very much, for I do not merit it." He had exhausted himself in the service of Texas while others reaped the benefits of his labors. "I have no house, not a roof in all Texas, that I can call my own. The only one I had was burnt at San Felipe during the late invasion of the enemy. I make my home where the business of the country calls me. . . . I have no farm, no cotton plantation, no income, no money, no comforts. I have spent the prime of my life and worn out my constitution in trying to colonize this country."

Another man might have grown terminally bitter at the unfairness of it all. Austin nearly did. But one thing, one final task to crown his labors in Texas, remained to give meaning to his life. A referendum conducted with the September elections revealed overwhelming support for annexation to the United States. Austin, as Texas's chief diplomat, assumed the responsibility of guiding Texas to that safe harbor.

For assistance he again turned to Santa Anna. "*Suppose* that Santa Anna should go to Washington city and have an interview with the President of the U.S.," Austin mused in early November. By now the threat of another Mexican invasion had eased, diminishing the hostage value of the general. "Santa Anna is useless to Texas so long as he is detained as a prisoner here," Austin said. Indeed, Santa Anna had become a hazard. "Both parties in Mexico would be well satisfied if he were to be shot, and either would make hostile demonstrations against Texas if by doing so his life would be jeopardized." On the other hand, as one who retained the respect of certain influential groups in Mexico, Santa Anna might yet serve a useful intermediary purpose. "He distinctly and positively declares that the basis on which he will act is to terminate the Texas war, because this country is lost to Mexico and consequently the true interests of the latter require that the dispute should end without more delay or more sacrifices." The United States government could facilitate peace by encouraging Mexico to abandon claims to Texas in exchange for a monetary payment; and though the Mexican government would never solicit such a deal, if an American offer were delivered by a person not officially connected to either government—Santa Anna, for example—Mexico might listen. Anyway, when Santa Anna delivered the American offer to Mexico, one of two things would happen. The Mexican government would accept the offer, leading to swift annexation by the United States, or Mexico would be plunged once more into turmoil, rendering a resumption of the Texas war impossible.

Houston endorsed Austin's scheme, and the Texas president and the secretary of state launched Santa Anna on one of the unlikelier diplomatic missions of the period. The defeated general started for Washington in the company of Colonel Almonte and an escort of Texas officers. Delighted to be out of prison and away from the angry Texans, Santa Anna enjoyed the trip immensely. High water rendered the first leg of the journey, by horseback to the Mississippi River, difficult and time-consuming. Santa Anna joked with Barnard Bee, the Texan officer in charge of the group, that they would have made faster progress by boat. From Vicksburg, Bee wrote to Houston, "General Santa Anna is in fine spirits and speaks of you often. Your kindness to him, you may be assured, will not soon be forgotten." The party drew large crowds all along the route; gawkers typically came hating the murderous tyrant but left liking the charismatic don. One observer described him as "pleasant of countenance and speech (which is exclusively Spanish), very polite, and using stately compliments." At Frederick, Maryland, Santa Anna met General Gaines, into whose clutches Houston had hoped to deliver him. The details of the interview have been lost; doubtless the two soldiers sized each other up.

By the time Santa Anna reached Washington, he was a celebrity. "General Andrew Jackson greeted me warmly and honored me at a dinner attended by notables of all countries," Santa Anna remembered. On the day after the dinner, the two men—each epitomizing his era in the history of his nation—met privately. Jackson could be blunt, but he could also be diplomatic; Santa Anna was always artful. The pair danced around the issue of transferring Texas to the United States. Jackson, though knowing the wishes of Houston and Austin, couldn't speak for Texas, while Santa Anna, despite believing that he still embodied the interests of the Mexican people, even if they didn't realize it, couldn't speak for Mexico. According to Santa Anna's recollection, Jackson finally raised the issue of a transfer and an American payment. "President Jackson was keenly interested in the outcome of the war with Mexico. He told me, 'If Mexico will recognize the independence of Texas, we will indemnify your country with six million pesos.' " Santa Anna demurred, saying, "To the Mexican Congress solely belongs the right to decide that question."

In Jackson's version it was Santa Anna who broached the issue of a transfer of Texas to the United States for a "fair consideration." And it was Jackson who demurred. "Until Texas is acknowledged independent, we cannot receive her minister or hold any correspondence with her as a nation." Moreover, any American dealings with Mexico must be through established channels. "We can only instruct our minister at Mexico to receive any proposition her government may make on the subject. Until we hear her views, we cannot speak to Texas."

But Santa Anna hadn't come all the way to Washington simply to be told that the American government wouldn't talk to him. Jackson intimated that Mexico might wish to settle the Texas affair as part of a larger package, one including California. In exchange, Jackson was prepared to pay $3.5 million. "But before we promise anything," Jackson added, "General Santa Anna must say that he will use his influence to suspend hostilities."

Santa Anna's influence was the crux of the issue. Jackson and Santa Anna both understood that the latter didn't currently represent Mexico, but both anticipated that he might do so in the future. Santa Anna again disavowed designs on Texas. "He said he was satisfied that it was for the interest of Mexico and Texas that there should be an immediate peace between them," wrote William Wharton, Stephen Austin's former partner as commissioner to the United States, now serving alone in that capacity. Wharton debriefed Santa Anna after the White House meeting and summarized the Mexican general's reasoning and remarks. "He knew from his own observation that Mexico could never conquer Texas, and that if she succeeded in temporarily overrunning the country, she could not hold it without standing garrisons of 20,000 soldiers, which Mexico could not raise, nor support if raised." Santa Anna acknowledged that Texans might reasonably suspect his motives. But they should look beyond motives to interests. "He further said that, granting he was the perfidious and ungrateful monster he was so often represented, granting he would do nothing on account of gratitude or love for the Texians, yet that his own and his country's interest palpably dictated his intended course of future action." Santa Anna knew that some Texans might object (as Wharton did indeed object) to negotiations between the United States and Mexico regarding the fate of Texas. But he encouraged Texas to be flexible. "He concluded by jocularly saying that the United States had an overflowing treasury, about which there was much debate and squabbling, and he hoped that I as minister of Texas would not oppose any obstacles to his obtaining a few millions from this government for a quit claim to Texas."

Wharton had been an early distruster of Santa Anna, and the events of the war added to his distrust. But his skepticism faded before Santa Anna's charm. "He spoke with a great deal of feeling and apparent candour throughout," Wharton said of the interview.

Jackson was harder to charm, but he concluded that the man who had been the foremost obstacle to Texan independence might become its indispensable agent. The president took the extraordinary step of directing an American warship to carry the general back to Mexico. "He placed at my disposal for my voyage to Vera Cruz a battleship, whose commander attended me with great respect," Santa Anna recalled. In fact it was a frigate that took the former Mexican president home, and it wasn't respect for Santa Anna's person that motivated Jackson but the American president's desire to culminate his own career of expansionism by adding Texas and perhaps California to the empire of American democracy. War makes strange bedfellows, but rarely stranger than Old Hickory and the Napoleon of the West, now allied by the odd twists of the war for Texas.

★

Stephen Austin would have applauded Jackson's reinjection of Santa Anna into Mexican politics had he lived to observe it. Austin's forty-third birthday, November 3, 1836, revealed a man who seemed far older than his years. His face was drawn, his strength exhausted. His broken finances constrained him to rent an unheated room at the back of a small house in Columbia, which served as the republic's temporary capital. Winter began in late November that year, and each norther that pounded south set Austin coughing. A December cold became pneumonia. Opium helped him sleep but aggravated his lung condition by shortening his breath. He tried to clear his airways by sitting up; this wearied him more than ever. At times he knew where he was; at times he drifted and dreamed, perhaps of the rosy bower and the warm circle of friends he had sketched, years before, to Mary Holley. At noon on December 27 he died.

Sam Houston issued a mournful proclamation. "The Father of Texas is no more!" the president said. "The first pioneer of the wilderness has departed!" If Houston remained ambivalent about Austin, if anything persisted of the scorn he had felt for the empresario, he cast such feeling aside in the face of death. "As a testimony of respect to his high standing, undeviating moral rectitude, and as a mark of the nation's gratitude for his untiring zeal and invaluable service, all officers civil and military are required to wear crape on the right arm for the space of thirty days." Garrisons would fire salutes of twenty-three guns, one for each Texas county, and would hang black for the "illustrious deceased."

Slavery and Freedom

Austin might have reflected, in his final moments, that it was a family curse to falter with the promised land in view. Moses Austin had conceived the Texas colony but succumbed before it was born; Stephen delivered Texas to the American doorstep but died before the child was taken in.

If pneumonia—the same malady that felled his father—hadn't killed Stephen, the fight for annexation might have. At least it would have broken his heart, for it revealed that whatever Austin's purpose in founding a colony in Texas, others had turned the founding to their own ends. For Austin, slavery had been the price of attracting colonists to Texas, an evil currently necessary but perhaps not always so, and certainly not essential to his larger vision of putting ordinary people on the extraordinary land of Texas. But for those who fought over annexation, slavery was the crux of the issue. Texas—Austin's Texas, Austin's promised land of opportunity—became a symbol in American politics not of personal freedom but of chattel slavery.

★

John Quincy Adams never forgave Andrew Jackson for the war Old
Hickory and his partisans, including Sam Houston, had waged upon
Adams's presidency. Nor did he ever accept the democratic revolution that sent the Tennesseean to the White House and himself home
to Massachusetts. The rapid spread of the democratic disease was
shocking; it touched even Adams's alma mater, which awarded an
honorary degree to Jackson. "I *could not* be present to see my Darling
Harvard disgrace herself by conferring a Doctor's degree upon a bar-
barian and savage who could scarcely spell his own name," Adams
told his cousin, who happened to be Harvard's president.

Like most of the Adams men (and more than a few of the Adams
women, including his mother, Abigail), John Quincy Adams could be
crotchety, even misanthropic. And he grew testier with age and political disappointment. But enough of the family's proprietary feeling
for the republic remained, and enough of Adams's desire to thwart
the demons of democracy, that he eschewed retirement and instead
offered himself as a candidate for Congress. And sufficient respect
for the Adams name persisted in Massachusetts, and sufficient Yankee determination to stem the tide that was draining political influence from New England to the West and South, that Adams's
constituents returned him to Washington.

Adams took his seat in the House of Representatives midway
through Jackson's first term. He endorsed the president's strong
stand against the nullifiers of South Carolina but otherwise found little to like in Jackson's approach to governance. The president's popularity was simply further testimony to the ignorance of the masses.
Adams's own isolation in Congress, an isolation that grew by the year,
he took for righteousness. "To withstand multitudes is the only un-
erring test of decisive character," he said.

The multitudes most needed withstanding, Adams believed, on

the subject of slavery. Before he entered Congress, Adams had given slavery little thought. He didn't approve of the institution, but neither did he deem it especially dangerous to republican virtue. Yet events of the 1830s convinced him that slavery placed America in mortal danger. Foremost of these events was the war for Texas.

With the rest of America, Adams had observed the emigration to Texas swell from a trickle to a flood. He had long applauded westward expansion; treaties he negotiated as secretary of state gave America its first solid claim to the Pacific shore. But the expansion he sought had been an expansion of American liberty, and when he learned that the emigrants to Texas were re-fixing slavery upon that Mexican province, in the face of Mexican law, his enthusiasm for Texas evaporated.

Adams wasn't alone in seeing slavery in a new light. The age of democracy was also the age of a growing opposition to slavery. As the ideology of the everyman took hold across the country, the existence of a large class permanently beyond the pale obtruded on the American conscience. Northerners had shed slavery as part of the democratizing trend; now they felt free to criticize the South for failing to do the same. Some went so far as to embrace abolitionism, which, while nowhere a majority view, nonetheless set the moral tone for much of the antislavery movement. And the tone grew shriller with time. William Lloyd Garrison, the noisiest of the abolitionists, damned not only slavery but a political system that allowed the slaveholders to indulge their wickedness. Garrison burned a copy of the Constitution, which he called "a covenant with death and an agreement with Hell."

Southerners viewed the abolitionists with scorn. It was easy to be moral, they said, when the economy of one's region didn't depend on slave labor. And by dishonoring the Constitution, the abolitionists brought upon themselves blame for the demise of the Union, should matters come to that. Defensive southerners responded by taking the offensive, celebrating slavery as an instrument for good, for the civilizing and Christianizing of benighted and heathen Africans. Slavery was proclaimed a fundament of southern life, a keystone of a superior culture.

Because the Constitution seemed to protect slavery in the states, much of the debate over the future of the institution was hypothetical and anticipatory, an argument about what would happen as the Union expanded into new territories. Texas made the debate real and immediate. The outbreak of fighting there alerted advocates of slavery and opponents alike that Texas might soon be a candidate for admission to the Union. Both sides deemed Texas a test of the political viability of their views. If the opponents of slavery could block annexation, they might contain the noxious institution. If slavery advocates could win the admission of Texas, new horizons opened in the Southwest.

John Quincy Adams launched the annexation debate in Congress with a thunderous salvo. In the final week of May 1836, while Americans were absorbing the news of San Jacinto, Adams digressed from discussion of an Alabama relief bill to declare preemptive war on what he deemed the conspiracy to foist slave Texas on the American republic. The conspiracy, Adams said, had been years in the making. President Jackson had tried to pry Texas from Mexico by money and threat. The effort had failed and poisoned relations between the United States and Mexico. "A device better calculated to produce jealousy, suspicion, ill will, and hatred could not have been contrived." The motives of the administration became clear in the denouement. "This overture, offensive in itself, was made precisely at a time when a swarm of colonists from the United States were covering the Mexican border with land-jobbing, and with slaves introduced in defiance of Mexican laws, by which slavery had been abolished throughout that republic." The attempt continued. "The war now raging in Texas is a Mexican civil war, and a war for the reestablishment of slavery where it was abolished." Into this civil war the conspirators were attempting to thrust the United States. Adams knew of the movements of General Gaines along the Sabine. And as the one who, as secretary of state, had made the Sabine the border between the United States and Mexico, he knew that Jackson's claim to the Neches was insupportable by law or custom. The only explanation for Gaines's actions was that the administration wanted an excuse to enter the disgraceful war—the "war between slavery and emancipation"—under way in Texas. "Every possible effort has been made to drive us into the war, on the side of slavery."

Adams demanded to know whether the members of the House understood what a war for Texas would entail, and he proceeded to tell them. "Your war, sir, is to be a war of races—the Anglo-Saxon American pitted against the Moorish-Spanish-Mexican American, a war between the northern and southern halves of North America, from Passamaquoddy to Panama. Are you prepared for such a war?" What would be America's cause in this war? "Aggression, conquest, and the re-establishment of slavery where it has been abolished. In that war, sir, the banners of freedom will be the banners of Mexico; and your banners, I blush to speak the word, will be the banners of slavery."

What if America won the war? Would the slave conspiracy be satisfied? By no means! "Suppose you should annex Texas to these United States; another year would not pass before you would have to engage in a war for the conquest of the island of Cuba." The powers of Europe would not stand idly by. Spain, of course, would defend Cuba, while Britain would resist the expansion of American influence—and American slavery—toward Central America and the Caribbean. Britain had abolished slavery in her own empire, and for reasons of conscience and mercantile competitiveness she would oppose its spread under the American flag. A war against Britain was a real possibility. A more ignominious struggle was hard to imagine. "Sir, what a figure, in the eyes of mankind, would you make, in deadly conflict with Great Britain, she fighting the battles of emancipation, and you the battles of slavery; she the benefactress, and you the oppressor, of human kind!" Nor would the wars that followed the taking of Texas be solely against foreign foes. Only the foolish or willfully blind could not see the "inevitable consequence of them all: a civil war."

Adams's antislavery, anti-Texas views resonated across the North. Benjamin Lundy, an itinerant abolitionist and editor who claimed the distinction of having converted William Lloyd Garrison to abolition, published a series of tracts entitled, first, *The Origin and True Causes of the Texas Revolution Commenced in the Year 1835*, and, subsequently and more descriptively, *War in Texas, a Review of Facts and Circumstances, Showing that this Contest is a Crusade against Mexico, Set on Foot and Supported by Slaveholders, Land-Speculators, &c., in Order to Re-Establish, Re-Extend, and Perpetuate the System of Slavery in the United States*. Lundy reprinted Adams's House speech against Texas, along with anti-Texas editorials from such journals as the New York *Sun*, which asserted that the annexation of Texas would "inevitably DISSOLVE THE UNION." The *Sun* elaborated: "The slave states having this eligible addition to their land of bondage, with its harbors, bays, and well-bounded geographical position, will ere long cut asunder the federal tie which they have long held with ungracious and unfraternal fingers, and confederate a new and distinct slaveholding republic, in opposition to the whole free republic of the North." Lundy, speaking in his own voice, demanded: "CITIZENS OF THE FREE STATES!—Are you prepared to sanction the acts of such freebooters and usurpers? . . . Are you willing to be MADE THE INSTRUMENTS of these wanton aggressors? . . . PEOPLE OF THE NORTH! WILL YOU PERMIT IT?"

The opposition of Adams, Lundy, and the others had little effect on Andrew Jackson. The president deferred recognition of Texas for several months, hoping Santa Anna might succeed in persuading the Mexican government to accept a treaty transferring Texas and California to the United States. Recognition would ruin the chances for any such treaty. But as his days in office dwindled and nothing hopeful came from Mexico City, Jackson decided to go ahead. He invited William Wharton to the White House to share the good news and a glass of wine. Upon leaving, Wharton wrote to friends in the Texas government: "I have at length the happiness to inform you that President Jackson has closed his political career by admitting our country into the great family of nations."

If Jackson had had six months more in office, he might have taken the next step to annexation. Mexico had been his stumbling block, and, having given up on Mexico, he would gladly have confronted the American opponents of annexation, starting with Adams, whom he despised as much as ever. But time ran out, and he retired to the Hermitage with his Texas dream unfulfilled.

His successor, Martin Van Buren of New York, lacked Jackson's courage, determination, and popularity. Van Buren's political influence rested on an unstable coalition of northern and southern interests; to reach for Texas risked pulling the northern prop from under himself. And when his first year in office produced the worst financial panic since the depression that had helped populate the Austin colony in the early 1820s, Van Buren lost all desire to court more controversy than he had to. Texas he would leave to future presidents.

★

And to the Texans themselves. Spurned by the United States, still claimed by Mexico, Texas reluctantly embarked on a career as independent republic. Though hindsight would hallow the years of Texas nationhood—Texas schoolchildren would be taught to cherish the fact that their state, alone of the eventual fifty, had once been a separate republic—to those who lived through them, they were fraught with danger and confusion.

The gravest danger was the one that had prompted Spain and then Mexico to grant Moses and then Stephen Austin permission to found their colony. If anything, the threat from the Comanches and other Indian tribes grew during the Texas revolution. The Texas rebels broke Mexico's power without replacing it with their own, and the Indians lost no time in taking advantage of their opportunity. "Bastrop county suffered more from Indians during the year 1836 than for any other year of its history," Noah Smithwick remembered. "I could mention numbers of its best men who were killed during that year." Bastrop County served as an instructive example of the Indian troubles, and Smithwick was an informed witness. At the northern edge of Austin's colony, Bastrop bordered the region the Comanches still claimed for their own, and with many of the American men gone to fight the Mexicans, the Indians raided far down into the colony. Smithwick took leave of the anti-Mexican army to enlist in a ranger company established to hold the northern frontier against the native warriors. From January 1836 he rode up and down the Colorado River chasing Indians, recapturing livestock, reclaiming captives, and generally conducting a war that paralleled the war against Mexico. The casualties in this war were fewer than those in the struggle against Mexico, but the engagements were no less brutal in their smaller way. Raid and reprisal, stalking and ambush, scalping and mutilation characterized the tactics of both sides. The fighting continued long past San Jacinto and the withdrawal of Mexican forces from Texas, with neither Indians nor Anglos having a clear advantage.

Upon his inauguration as Texas president, Sam Houston tried to end the Indian war. This suited Smithwick and most of those he knew. "The white people, weary of the perpetual warfare which compelled them to live in forts and make a subsistence as best they might, hailed the proposition for a treaty with delight," Smithwick wrote. The Comanches along the Colorado were also tired of the fighting, and they agreed to negotiate. They spoke no English, and the Anglos no Comanche, but the Indians knew some Spanish, as did Smithwick, who accordingly became a treaty commissioner for the Texans. The Comanches insisted that Smithwick travel to their camp, to negotiate on their own turf. His comrades warned him not to go, but he decided to chance it. "Knowing that there is a degree of honor even among Indians touching those who voluntarily become their guests, I yielded to the stress of circumstances and agreed to accompany them back to their camp."

Along with nearly every other Anglo in Texas, Smithwick considered the Indians savages, and as a ranger he had battled them fiercely. But he appreciated their better points, and he approached their camp with a relatively open mind. First to catch his eye were the captives: one Anglo woman and two Anglo boys, and one Mexican woman and two Mexican boys. Of the six, the Mexican woman was the only one who indicated any desire to leave the Comanches. She had been captured as a grown woman and was homesick. But the others had been taken young, had grown up among the Comanches, and considered themselves Comanches. One, an Anglo lad of about eighteen, in fact had been captured twice by Smithwick's rangers, but each time escaped and returned to his adoptive people. The Comanches also had a captured Waco child. One of Smithwick's hosts, Chief Quinaseico, explained that his band of Comanches had surprised a camp of Wacos and killed them all, except that one boy. "After the fight was over I went into a lodge and found this boy, about two years old, sitting beside its dead mother crying," Quinaseico explained to Smithwick. "My heart was sorry for him, and I took him up in my arms and brought him home to my lodge and my wife took him to her bosom, and fed him, and he is mine now."

Smithwick spent several weeks with the Comanches. Various aspects of their lives and customs struck him as noteworthy. They were entirely carnivorous, subsisting on buffalo and other game. This gave them an advantage over tribes that grew corn and squash or gathered pecans and tubers, for they had no particular territory they had to defend. Unlike most tribes, the Comanches eschewed alcohol, which gave them another advantage, especially in dealings with whites, who relied on liquor in Indian diplomacy. Though terrible against their enemies, the Comanches were quite orderly among themselves. "They were the most peaceable community I ever lived in," Smithwick said. "Their criminal laws were as inexorable as those of the Medes and Persians, and the code was so simply worded there was no excuse for ignorance. It was simply the old Mosaic law, 'an eye for an eye and a tooth for a tooth.' . . . In cases of dispute, a council of the old men decided it, and from their decision there was no appeal." While the Comanches merrily tortured enemies who fell alive into their hands, they treated each other with kindness and respect. "I never saw a woman or a child abused. The women, as in all savage tribes, were abject slaves, but their inferiority was their protection from the chastisement which 'civilized' husbands sometimes visit on their wives. An Indian brave would have felt it a burning disgrace to strike a woman."

Smithwick's sojourn included conversations about the relative claims of Indians and Anglos to Texas. "I had many long, earnest talks with those old Comanche chiefs, and I could not but admit the justice of their contention," Smithwick said. "The country they considered theirs by right of inheritance; the game had been placed there for their food." A chief named Muguara put the aboriginal case most suc-cinctly:

> We have set up our lodges in these groves and swung our children from these boughs from time immemorial. When game beats away from us we pull down our lodges and move away, leaving no trace to frighten it, and in a little while it comes back. But the white man comes and cuts down the trees, building houses and fences, and the buf-faloes get frightened and leave and never come back, and the Indians are left to starve, or, if we follow the game, we trespass on the hunting ground of other tribes and war en-sues.

Smithwick asked if the Comanches would agree to settle down and become farmers. "No," Muguara answered, "the Indians were not made to work. If they build houses and try to live like white men they will all die." So what *was* the solution? Muguara put it simply: "If the white men would draw a line defining their claims and keep on their side of it, the red men would not molest them."

Smithwick thought this a good idea, and he took it to Sam Hous-ton. The Texas president agreed in principle. But he discovered that the Texas legislature, like Texans generally, held a different view. Houston had negotiated a treaty with his old friends the Cherokees, designed to secure their rights in the new republic, only to have the legislature reject it. Houston was fairly certain that what was withheld from the Cherokees would never be offered to the more warlike Co-manches. As he sadly told Smithwick, "If I could build a wall from the Red River to the Rio Grande, so high that no Indian could scale it, the white people would go crazy trying to devise means to get beyond it."

Houston was right, as his successor demonstrated. The Texas constitution forbade consecutive terms for president, and Houston was followed in 1838 by Mirabeau Lamar, the dashing horseman of San Jacinto (who won election by default after both his principal rivals committed suicide). Lamar launched an aggressive campaign to drive the Comanches north of the Red River. The bloody symbol of Lamar's approach was the "Council House fight," an 1840 incident in which a large delegation of Comanches visiting San Antonio to arrange a peace settlement was seized by Texas authorities, triggering gunfire that killed thirty-five Comanches, including a dozen chiefs and several women and children, and seven Texans. The affair sparked a summer of raids and reprisals that reciprocally ravaged Texas towns and Comanche villages, killed scores of fighters and noncombatants on both sides, and thoroughly unsettled the frontier. At great and unsustainable expense, the Texans forced the Comanches north. But only the wishful among the Texans imagined that the Comanches' tactical retreat terminated the historic contest for control of the vast Texas plains.

The vulnerability of Texas to Indian attack from the north was mirrored by its vulnerability to Mexican attack from the south. Mexico's long revolution, which had begun in 1810 and lately spun off the Texas revolution, continued to convulse the country. During Santa Anna's detention in Texas, his rivals quarreled for primacy in Mexico City, while federalists in various provinces agitated for local autonomy. The government lacked resources to pay its debts or defend the country from those foreigners who insisted on collecting what was owed to them. The French exploited an incident in which one of their nationals saw his bakery burned, and launched what was called "la guerra de los pasteles" (the Pastry War), ultimately landing French marines at Veracruz.

Santa Anna had retired to his hacienda after returning from the north, but he recognized an opportunity to reprise his role at Tampico nine years before. He rushed to the coast to defend Mexico's honor. Although he succeeded in repulsing the invaders, his leg was badly injured by French cannon fire. Doctors debated treatment, leaving the general to issue a poignant message to his countrymen: "Probably this will be the last victory that I shall offer my native land. . . . From this day forward the most unjust of Mexican enemies shall not dare to place their feet on our soil. . . . May all Mexicans, forgetting my political mistakes, not deny me the only title which I wish to leave my children, that of a good Mexican."

Santa Anna's dying request was published as a poster that circulated throughout the country. When its publication was followed by news that the hero hadn't died after all, but survived a grim amputation, his reputation was remade. He traveled slowly to Mexico City, reveling in his popularity and worrying his rivals. He might have seized power upon reaching the capital, but he contented himself with the title of interim president, bestowed by a grateful congress, and retired to his hacienda once more, to allow matters to ripen further. They soon did, and when he returned again to the capital, in the autumn of 1841, it was as though his troubles in Texas had never occurred.

Indeed, he soon turned those troubles to his own benefit. Ignoring everything he had told the Texans and the Americans about Texas being lost to Mexico, Santa Anna distracted his compatriots from their domestic problems by reopening the Texas war. In the spring of 1842 he sent General Rafael Vásquez against San Antonio with seven hundred men. Vásquez captured the town with little difficulty, but he remained only a few days before returning south with such valuables as could be readily carried. Several months later a more serious offensive, under General Adrian Woll, took San Antonio again. Woll lingered to tangle with a force dispatched by Sam Houston, who had been elected president once more; in the clash some hundred soldiers, counting both sides, were killed. Woll retreated toward the Rio Grande with the Texans in pursuit. The Texans chased Woll across the river, but then three hundred of them—forgetful of the fate of the Matamoros expedition of 1836—descended on the Mexican town of Mier, seeking booty. They were captured after sharp fighting and were sent south as prisoners. On the road they escaped and fled into the mountains. Some starved there, and some found their way back to Texas, but the majority were retaken. Santa Anna ordered that every tenth prisoner be shot. A jar of beans was passed among them, containing black and white beans in the ratio of one to ten. The prisoners blindly drew the beans, and the seventeen with black were executed.

Andrew Jackson Dies Happy

Had the Texas republic otherwise thrived, it might have weathered the Indian wars and Mexican invasions with little damage to the collective psyche. But the hard times that hit the United States with the Panic of 1837 spilled across the Sabine, complicating the creation of all the institutions of government and society the new country required. Texas finance was a bad joke. Until the panic summer, bank notes issued in Louisiana and Mississippi circulated in Texas, albeit discounted for distance from the banks of issue. Specie—gold and silver—immigrated in the pockets of the people who came. But as the banks behind the paper crumbled, the metal money went into hiding and Texans were reduced to barter. "Horses were generally considered legal tender," Noah Smithwick recalled. "But owing to the constant drain on the public treasury by the horse-loving Indian, that kind of currency became scarce, so we settled on the cow as the least liable to fluctuation."

Land scrip and government promissories served as a substitute for money. Yet these inspired speculation, with strapped holders selling them at far below face value to persons willing to bet on the rise. A visitor to the town of Houston, which sprang up on Buffalo

Bayou not far from the San Jacinto battle site, described how speculators turned distress to profit.

> Some were engaged in purchasing the discharges of the
> soldiers, each of whom is entitled, beyond his pay of eight
> dollars a month in government paper, to six hundred and
> forty acres of land for each six months' service and in pro-
> portion for a less period. For this he gets a certificate from
> the government. The discharged soldier comes to Hous-
> ton, hungry and next to naked, with nothing but his claims
> upon the government, which his situation compels him to
> sell. If he gets ten per cent for his money scrip and fifty
> dollars for a six months' discharge, he receives quite as
> much as these claims were selling for during the summer.

Beyond the effects of such transactions on the economy, they badly
sapped morale. "When the storm beaten soldier thus sees the reward
of all his sufferings reduced to a few dollars, he has too much reason
to lament over the time which he has worse than thrown away and often in despair gives himself up to total abandonment."

In time the government issued proper currency to redeem the
warrants. This suited the speculators but, because nothing substantial backed the currency, merely deferred the day of reckoning.
Smithwick described the system in action.

> When the first issue of treasury notes came to take the
> place of the land scrip and military scrip, the sporting fra-
> ternity hailed the change with delight; but, when . . . the
> treasury notes ran down till it took a mountain of them to
> represent a small stake, the gamblers grew discontented.
> Their distress was relieved when the exchequer bills re-

placed the dishonored redbacks, as the treasury notes were called. But again the currency depreciated till a small jack-pot could not accommodate the bulk of paper. Then they began talking about the advisability of "a new ish" [issue], and, that hope of relief failing, some of them went off and joined the army. Sowell tells of one who drew a black bean [after the Mier debacle] and went to his death with a smile. I have heard the story often.

The financial woes of the republic reflected the lack of experience of its leaders and their democratic distrust of banks and bankers. Andrew Jackson had killed the Bank of the United States (and in doing so helped touch off the Panic of '37), and Sam Houston wasn't about to saddle Texas with anything similar. But a deeper problem was the underlying insecurity of the republic. As long as Mexico refused to recognize Texan independence, and as long as it could send troops across the Rio Grande, even if only sporadically, Texas had to prepare for war. This bled the treasury and discouraged the investment that would have put Texas on a more solid fiscal footing.

It also gave life in republican Texas a peculiar air. Soldierly types—young men looking for trouble, with time on their hands—were overrepresented in the Texas population. They frequented saloons and gambling houses, astonishing visitors with their capacity for drink and riotous behavior. A traveler from Ohio was told that the Texas climate required regular consumption of alcohol. He wasn't convinced but couldn't deny the prevalence of the view. "While I hesitate to admit that there is something relaxing in the climate that makes it necessary for all to indulge in the use of some kind of stimulus to some extent to keep up the spirits, I must acknowledge that there were few who did not give ear to the doctrine." The Texans crowded the saloons every day of the week and most nights, striving to satisfy their insatiable thirst. "The extent to which this vice was carried on exceeded all belief. It appeared to be the business of the great mass of the people to collect around these centers of vice and hold their drunken orgies, without seeming to know that the Sabbath was made for more serious purposes and night for rest. Drinking was reduced to a system and had its own laws and regulations. Nothing was regarded as a greater violation of established etiquette than for one who was going to drink not to invite all within a reasonable distance to partake, so that the Texians being entirely a military people not only fought but drank in platoons."

The Texans gambled even more than they drank. So egregious did the gaming become that the legislature felt obliged to curb the cards and dice. "But as those who passed the law were the most active in breaking it," the Ohio traveler noted, "the law itself was of little consequence any further than it afforded the gambler the double satisfaction of knowing that he was breaking the laws of God and those of man at the same time."

Drinking and gambling naturally gave rise to fighting. "Some of the disturbances which took place during my stay at Houston were of the most revolting description," the Ohioan said, "and one or two encounters occurred which were attended with mortal consequences, under circumstances of peculiar horror. Some of the scenes which took place in the streets exceeded description and afforded a melancholy proof to what a point of degradation human nature may descend."

As in many frontier societies, the institutions of public order lagged behind the causes of social disorder. The problem was aggravated in Texas by the continuing state of war, with its expense and its appeal to the violence-prone. During the whole period of the republic, crime—lethal and lesser—was a major problem. In 1843 a minister at Houston devoted a sermon to the subject:

> God has said, *Thou shalt do no murder*. This people have reversed the command. I do not here speak of that fashionable mode of taking life, according to an imperious code of *self-styled* honor [dueling deserved a separate sermon, being a plague unto itself]. But I speak of *wanton, barbarous outrages*, in violation of all law human and divine, which find among this people, not simply apologists, but everywhere bold defenders. Go through this land, and point me to a single town which has not been the scene of some deadly affray . . . and then tell me of an instance where the murderer has been arraigned by the proper authorities and made to suffer the penalty due to his crime. Nay, men swear each other's death, and that too openly—and from day to day walk the streets with deadly weapons, and no effort is made to put a stop to their murderous intentions— and when at last one has fallen, how often is heard the comment—"It is all right, he ought to have died long ago."

In parts of the republic, individual crime escalated to irregular warfare. The Redlands of East Texas were as lawless as in the bad old days of the Neutral Ground; rival gangs of land cheats, extortionists, arsonists, and horse thieves organized themselves as "Regulators" and "Moderators" and intimidated or enrolled local officials. Dozens of people died, and for years the region raged beyond the control of the government of the republic.

Yet the troubles in Texas didn't prevent people from wanting to move there. On the contrary, Texas was even more desirable as a destination than it had been before the revolution. Land remained cheaply available, and immigrants no longer had to worry about restrictions on religion or slavery. Being a separate country from the United States, it continued to attract those who wished to leave wives, debts, and indictments behind. As the ruckus in the Redlands and on the streets of most Texas towns demonstrated, not all the immigrants became upstanding citizens on arrival. But even if they had, the sheer numbers of the immigrants—the population of Texas more than doubled during the years of the republic, from about 50,000 to around 125,000—would have tested the ability of the new country to absorb them. An orderly immigration would have strengthened the republic; the disorderly immigration it actually experienced made things more unsettled than ever.

Texans weren't the kind to worry excessively. Most accepted a certain chaos as a cost of living in the new land. But amid the Indian attacks, the Mexican invasions, the financial implosion, and the spontaneous and organized crime, even the optimistic wondered what was becoming of Texas. "A general gloom seems to rest over every section of the Republic," a widely read newspaper observed in 1842, "and doubt and sorrow are depicted on almost every brow."

The republic required help, which certain foreign governments were willing to provide. As France's meddling in Mexico suggested, the French government saw opportunity in the troubles surrounding the Texas revolution. French merchants coveted access to Texas markets, French spinners to Texas cotton. King Louis-Philippe wanted to reclaim a role for France in the New World and thought the contested coast of the Gulf of Mexico a likely place to start. France recognized the independence of Texas in 1839 and spent the next several years inflating Texan egos and ambitions, especially vis-à-vis the United States.

But it was Britain that caught the eye of Texans. Where France dreamed of a New World sphere of influence, Britain already had one. In the quarter century since Spain's Latin American empire had fallen apart, the British had been busy reconfiguring the pieces into a Latin American empire of their own. This British empire mostly lacked formal trappings, being a realm in which trade rather than territory was the goal. British diplomats and merchants negotiated and exploited pacts that opened markets throughout Spain's former realm to British commerce and investment. In exchange, Britain's own markets were made available to Latin American exports—at a time when most other countries, including the United States, restricted goods from abroad. The British navy kept competitors away from Britain's new friends.

From the start of the Texas troubles, Britain registered interest in the emergence of another republic from the Spanish ruins. By the 1830s British textile mills had grown alarmingly dependent on American cotton; Texas offered a separate source of the fluffy stuff. That an independent Texas might block the expansion of the United States to the southwest made the prospect still more appealing. Britain had fought two wars with the United States since 1776, and sufficient points of friction remained—along the border with Canada, for instance, and in the Oregon country—that a third conflict (as John Quincy Adams warned) was hardly inconceivable. Whatever impeded American expansion suited Britain.

One small matter, however, limited British enthusiasm for Texas independence. Having decided that slavery was bad for themselves and their empire, the British concluded—from a mix of altruism and competitiveness—that it was bad for the world. They sought to suppress the slave trade and avoided consorting conspicuously with governments that hadn't seen the light that dawned on Britain in 1833.

Yet British leaders believed that the purposes of humanity and Britannia alike could be served by adept diplomacy toward Texas. The Texans might be moved to emancipate their slaves, perhaps in exchange for a British loan to rescue their failing treasury. Or the British government might simply buy all the Texas slaves and manumit them. Either way, Texas would grow closer to heaven and to Britain.

But the prerequisite for any such plan was that Texas remain distinct from the United States. An independent Texas might yield to British blandishments; a Texas attached to the United States would never do so. From the moment of Texas independence, British leaders did their best to frustrate American annexation. British foreign minister Lord Palmerston, with the sort of understatement on which the British ruling classes prided themselves, told the House of Commons in August 1836 that the prospect of American annexation "would be a subject which ought seriously to engage the attention of that House and of the British public."

For the first few years of independence the Texans kept their distance from Britain. Sam Houston and other veterans of the War of 1812 had difficulty seeing the British as other than enemies; nearly all Texans preferred, and many still hoped for, the embrace of the United States.

But when that embrace was slow in coming, and when the Mexican attacks of 1842 underscored the vulnerability of the Lone Star republic, British protection appeared more promising. In November 1842 Houston wrote to the British chargé d'affaires in Texas, Charles Elliot, describing his "intense anxiety for peace with Mexico" and suggesting that the British diplomat might facilitate it. "I know of no gentleman whose agency, in my estimation, would go farther in the attainment of the object than your own." After this first feeler elicited little response, Houston put the point more directly. "If England produces a pacification between this country and Mexico, she will thereby secure a friend on the gulf whose contiguity to the United States, in the event of war, would not be desirable to that country." Houston acknowledged that his offer—to side with England in a conflict against the United States—marked a reversal of long-standing attitudes in Texas. But the United States had brought the shift on itself. "Texas once evinced a willingness, amounting to unexampled unanimity, to become annexed to the United States. We sought the boon with humble supplications. In this posture we remained on the outer porch of their Capital for many months. Our solicitations were heard with apathy. Our urgency was responded to with politic indifference." So now Texas was looking elsewhere.

Houston's angling in English waters was intended to attract the attention of the United States. It achieved its purpose, inspiring President John Tyler to propose a treaty of annexation, which Houston accepted. But this was the easy part, as anyone familiar with American politics knew; much harder was to persuade the Senate to accept the treaty. Houston guessed that the job was too big for Tyler, America's first accidental president (following the pneumonic death of William Henry Harrison). So he called on his old commander, the hero of New Orleans.

Andrew Jackson's health had declined dramatically since he left the White House. He suffered from insomnia, vertigo, dropsy, shortness of breath, and constant pain in head and body. Yet he was still the most formidable figure in American politics: the old lion of the

nation's oldest party, the embodiment of the people's will. His enemies detested him as much as ever but kept a wary distance. His
friends still loved him and hung on his—fewer and fewer—public
words.

Houston knew that Jackson had followed the annexation debate
and that he remained committed to its positive outcome. In a letter of
February 1844, Houston assured the old general they were in perfect
agreement on the issue. "I am determined upon immediate annexation to the United States," Houston said. Yet many Texans were wary,
in light of their prior experience with the United States. Much was
riding on the action of the Senate, and much would be lost if the
treaty failed.

> My venerated friend, you will perceive that Texas is pre-
> sented to the United States as a bride adorned for her es-
> pousal. But if, now so confident of the union, she should
> be rejected, her mortification would be indescribable. . . .
> Were she now to be spurned, it would forever terminate
> expectation on her part, and it would then not only be left
> for the United States to expect that she would seek some
> other friend, but all Christendom would justify her in a
> course dictated by necessity and sanctioned by wisdom.

Jackson rose to Houston's challenge. The old general launched
his final campaign. He issued instructions to his lieutenants Francis
Blair and William Lewis to mobilize the troops in the Senate. Texas,
he told Blair, was "all important to the security and the future peace
and prosperity of our Union." He added, "I hope there are a sufficient
number of pure American democrats to carry into effect the annexation of Texas." To Lewis he wrote, "I hope this golden moment will be

seized to regain Texas." (With other Democrats, Jackson held that Texas had been part of Louisiana till bargained away by John Quincy Adams in 1819. For this reason they often spoke of "regaining" or "reannexing" Texas.) Should the present opportunity be squandered, Jackson contended, Britain would capitalize on America's failure and weld Texas into an alien empire blocking American expansion. The United States would break up that empire sooner or later, but doing so "would cost us more blood and treasure . . . than we have spent in gaining our independence and our last war with Great Britain." In another letter to Lewis, Jackson made this point more emphatically: "Houston and the people of Texas are now united in favor of annexation. The next President of Texas may not be so. British influence may reach him, and what can now be got from Texas, freely and peaceably, may evade our grasp and cost us oceans of blood and millions of money to obtain."

To the argument that annexation might provoke a war with Mexico, Jackson rejoined that Mexico had been attacking Texas these eight years, and it was time for America to make it stop. "The United States having been the first nation that acknowledged Texian independence, are we not bound to be the first to boldly step forward to put an end to this savage, marauding war?" Opponents worried that Britain would fight to prevent annexation; the victor of New Orleans refused to be cowed. "I say for one, ratify the treaty and take all the consequences." Texas must be American, sooner or later. "Can there be any prospects of a more favorable time? I answer no."

By this point Henry Clay, the leading candidate among the Whigs for the 1844 presidential nomination, had announced against annexation. Martin Van Buren, the favorite among the Democrats, was waffling on the issue. Because Van Buren had been Jackson's vice president and personally anointed successor, many in America wondered whether he spoke for Old Hickory. Jackson made clear that Van

Buren did not. Jackson defended the restraint of his own administration and Van Buren's on the Texas question but said that the time for restraint was past. Texas had shown its ability to stand on its own. "Eight years have elapsed since the memorable battle of St. Jacinto, and there has been no serious attempt by Mexico to occupy the country, and it is certain none can be made with any chance of success." Texas offered herself for annexation and was entirely within her rights in doing so. But she might not do so again. If rejected by the United States, she must turn to Europe for assistance. "What would then be our condition? New Orleans and the whole valley of the Mississippi would be endangered. The numerous hordes of savages within the limits of Texas and on her borders would be easily excited to make war upon our defenseless frontier." Annexation would serve Texas, but would serve the United States even more. "She is the key to our safety in the South and the West. She offers this key to us on fair and honorable terms. Let us take it and lock the door against future danger."

Jackson didn't say so in public, but he knew that the fight for annexation was his last battle. And it might be his most important, for on Texas turned everything he had struggled decades to achieve. "The subject has carried me on until I am gasping for breath," he wrote William Lewis. "It is a subject that involves a magnitude of interest in it for weal or for woe to the United States. . . . My dear Major, although I know my time is short here below, I love my country, and this subject involves its best interest—*the perpetuation of our republican system, and of our glorious union.*"

✦

Jackson's foe in his final contest was his longtime enemy, John Quincy Adams. In the eight years since the Texas revolution, Adams

had identified himself ever more closely with abolition. He successfully defended the slave-mutineers of the Spanish *Amistad*, who
seized their vessel and sailed for freedom only to be tried for piracy.
"Extraordinary," noted Justice Joseph Story of Adams's summation
before the Supreme Court. "Extraordinary for its power and its bitter
sarcasm, and its dealing with topics far beyond the record and points
of discussion." Adams led the opposition, so far unsuccessful, to the
"gag rule," which stifled debate in the House on slavery. For his pains
he was subjected to death threats and innumerable slanders and li-
bels. "Yet my conscience presses me on," he wrote in his diary. "Let
me but die upon the breach."

Adams wasn't surprised that the Democrats would stoop to saying he had given away Texas, but neither was he going to let their
mendacity go unchallenged. When Jackson joined the chorus of condemnation of the 1819 treaty and denied foreknowledge of its terms,
Adams demonstrated that Jackson had in fact approved the treaty in
advance, and he denounced as "bold, dashing, and utterly baseless
lies" Jackson's claims to the contrary. Adams warned the people of
the North: "Your trial is approaching. The spirit of freedom and the
spirit of slavery are drawing together for the deadly conflict of arms.
The annexation of Texas to this union is the blast of the trumpet for a
foreign, civil, servile, and Indian war. . . . Burnish your armor, prepare for the conflict. . . . Think of your forefathers! Think of posterity!"

Adams's warning fell on ears attuned to a different siren.
Though Jackson's lobbying failed to get the Texas treaty past the Senate, it ruined the candidacy of Van Buren and enhanced the prospects
of another Jacksonian, James Polk, the engineer of the defeat of
David Crockett, and an ardent annexationist. Polk was a dark horse
going into the Democratic convention, but he won the nomination on

the strength of his Jacksonian connections and his expansionist promises. He captured the general election by the same means, leaving Clay stuck in a straddle between his southern roots and his northern aspirations.

John Tyler could interpret the election results as well as anyone. With little to show for his tenure as president till now, he determined to place his mark on the American map by annexing Texas before leaving the White House. America had never annexed another country, and politicians and constitutional scholars puzzled as to how it might be done. A treaty, requiring two-thirds in the Senate, remained an impossibility, so Tyler turned to a joint resolution, which needed a simple majority in each house.

John Quincy Adams made his last stand in the lower chamber. He cited his record as secretary of state and president to prove that he had nothing against expansion per se. Only slavery and a decent respect for America's neighbors prevented him from endorsing the annexation of Texas. "If slavery were totally abolished forever in Texas, and the voluntary consent of Mexico could be obtained, I would vote for the annexation of Texas tomorrow." But under current conditions he couldn't approve any such thing. As the momentum for annexation grew, Adams foresaw only disaster. "The Union is sinking into a military monarchy, to be rent asunder like the empire of Alexander or the kingdoms or Ephraim and Judah. . . . The prospect is deathlike."

The prospect grew even grimmer, in Adams's view, when the House joined the Senate in approving annexation. Three days before leaving office, Tyler affixed his signature to the joint resolution.

Jackson was dying by now. He received the good news from Francis Blair. "I congratulate you, dear General, on the success of the great question which you put in action," Blair said. Jackson, his thin body become a wraith, his burning eyes finally clouded, responded softly, "I not only rejoice, but congratulate my beloved country. Texas is reannexed, and the safety, prosperity, and the greatest interest of the whole Union is secured."

Chapter 22

The Trial of Sam Houston

In March 1861, the governor of Texas sat quietly in the house the state had built for its chief executives in the city named for his only equal in the pantheon of Texas heroes. Night had fallen across Austin, but more than night was falling across America, and Sam Houston waited to hear the latest ill tidings. He had just passed his sixty-eighth birthday, and he felt every one of those years. His San Jacinto ankle had never healed properly, and it reminded him at each step of his day of triumph. His arrow wound from the Horseshoe Bend still suppurated, recalling his time with General Jackson. Between the ooze and the limp—the first a mark of his service to the United States, the second to Texas—he did better sitting than standing these days.

He had outlived most of his peers from those earlier times. Stephen Austin, of course, died in the year of Texas independence. Andrew Jackson died in the year of annexation. John Quincy Adams collapsed and died in the House in 1848, still declaiming against slavery, still convinced that Texas foretold the wreck of the Union. Santa Anna survived, but he had more lives than a cat.

Houston hadn't believed it then, and he hated to admit it now, but Adams—not Jackson—had been right about Texas and the Union.

As soon as the American Congress offered annexation, Houston had thrown over the British. "Supposing a charming lady has two suitors," he explained to an audience wondering at his apparent change of heart.

> One of them she is inclined to believe would make the better husband, but is a little slow to make interesting propositions. Do you think if she was a skillful practitioner in Cupid's court she would pretend that she loved the other "feller" the best and be sure that her favorite would know it? [Laughter and applause.] If ladies are justified in making use of coquetry in securing their annexation to good and agreeable husbands, you must excuse me for making use of the same means to annex Texas to Uncle Sam. [Laughter and cheers.]

The laughter faded, however, when annexation and a consequent dispute over the boundary of Texas triggered the war with Mexico that Adams had predicted. The conflict suited James Polk, who employed it to acquire California and round out the American Southwest. It also suited Santa Anna, in a different way. In the year of Texas's annexation to the Union, the Mexican leader had again overreached himself and thereby united disparate elements of the opposition; these combined to force him from power and from the country. "Mexicans!" he declared as he embarked for Cuba. "In my old age and mutilated, surrounded by a wife and innocent children, I am going into exile to seek a resting place among strangers. Mercifully forgive the mistakes I made unintentionally, and believe me, in God's name, that I have labored sincerely that you should be independent, free and happy."

He wasn't gone long, though, before Polk conspired to send him back to Mexico. On the theory previously endorsed by Houston and Jackson, Polk judged that Santa Anna would make mischief in Mexico upon reentry, and no sooner had the second war for Texas begun— with fighting along the Rio Grande—than the American president directed U.S. naval commanders in the Caribbean to let Santa Anna through their blockade of the Mexican coast.

Polk's thinking proved as wishful as Houston's and Jackson's on the same subject. Santa Anna rallied Mexican forces against the American invaders, dashing to meet Zachary Taylor at Buena Vista in the north, then racing to cut off Winfield Scott at Cerro Gordo on the road from Veracruz. The hero was again in his element defending Mexico from invasion, and between his battlefield bravery (he led from the front and had horses killed beneath him) and his stirring speeches ("Mexicans! You have a religion: protect it! You have honor: free yourselves from infamy! You love your wives, your children: liberate them from American brutality!") he inspired his countrymen to resist the invaders with surprising effectiveness. Yet he couldn't overcome the backbiting and suspicion that had characterized Mexican politics since 1810 (to which, of course, he had contributed his full share), and he couldn't keep Scott and the Americans from capturing the Mexican capital in the summer of 1847. He tried to arrange a surrender, but the Mexican congress couldn't bring itself to face defeat, and his efforts earned him another exile. He narrowly escaped capture by Texas Rangers serving under the American flag but bent on avenging the Alamo and Goliad; only a safe-conduct issued by the U.S. commander of the Jalapa district allowed him to pass through the Ranger ranks, while the Texans gnashed their teeth and longed for the days under Houston when they ignored orders at pleasure.

The war ended in what appeared a brilliant victory for the United States, with Mexico accepting American control of Texas and additionally ceding California and New Mexico to the United States.

And the victory seemed even more brilliant just months after the Treaty of Guadalupe Hidalgo, when word arrived that a carpenter in California digging a race for a sawmill had discovered gold. By 1848 the spirit of "manifest destiny" infused American politics, and many Americans found it easy to believe that heaven had anointed them to take and civilize the whole of North America. But nothing seemed such patent proof of the destinarian case as the gold discovery. For a quarter millennium the gold of California had been hidden from the Spanish, for a quarter century from the Mexicans; but it hadn't eluded the Americans for a quarter year. Polk and the expansionists had expected the Mexican War to pay for itself in the long run; to see it pay so soon—and in gold, no less—was enough to convince the most skeptical that God was an American.

Yet the golden lining came with a cloud. Although Texas had entered the Union as a slave state, the condition of the rest of the Mexican cession vis-à-vis the peculiar institution had to be determined. Until the gold discovery, most observers assumed that whatever arrangements needed to be made could be made slowly, as the newly acquired territory—mostly desert or mountains, and dauntingly distant from the populated areas of America—filled slowly with people. The Louisiana Purchase, to cite the obvious precedent, was still half empty a half century after Jefferson acquired it. But the gold rush to California overturned all expectations. By the middle of 1849 California had more than enough people to qualify for statehood; by the end of that year those people had written a constitution and sent it to Washington, with emissaries who demanded California's admission to the Union.

★

Sam Houston was there to greet them. To no one's surprise, Houston had been chosen to represent Texas in the U.S. Senate upon annexation. That he accepted the office, however, wasn't a foregone conclusion. Houston had remarried (after a belated divorce from Eliza), and his new wife, Margaret, didn't want him to leave Texas. She hoped his retirement from the Texas presidency in December 1844 would bring him home to her for good. A poet, she put in verse her vision for him and the family they were creating:

> This task is done. The holy shade
>> Of calm retirement waits thee now.
> The lamp of hope relit hath shed
>> Its sweet refulgence o'er thy brow.
>
> Far from the busy haunts of men,
>> Oh! may thy soul each fleeting hour
> Upon the breath of prayer ascend
>> To Him who rules with love and power.

It was a fond hope, but Margaret could have guessed her husband wouldn't find contentment communing with God. He heeded Margaret sufficiently not to seek public office, but he couldn't—or wouldn't—decline an office that sought him. When the people of Texas, speaking through the Texas legislature, insisted that he serve them in the Senate of the United States, he didn't say no.

Houston's return to Washington excited great comment. His appearance was more striking than ever. He walked with the limp from San Jacinto, but still he towered over ordinary men. His mane and side whiskers were silver now, topped by a white beaver hat and set against a multicolored Cherokee blanket draped over his dress coat. President Polk might have been the political heir of Jackson, but Houston was Old Hickory's spiritual heir and first scion in the line of democratic descent. It was Houston, rather than Polk, who had has-tened to Jackson's deathbed in Nashville, only to arrive moments late. He instructed his young son, the eldest of eight children he would have with Margaret, to mark the moment. "My son," he said, "try to remember that you have looked upon the face of Andrew Jackson." As Polk's presidency wound down, many in Washington thought the magnificent Texan—the conqueror of Santa Anna, the George Washington of the Lone Star republic—ought to assume Jackson's political mantle. Returning from a White House reception that saw Polk off, Houston wrote to Margaret: "I suppose that not less than one hundred persons of both sexes spoke to me on the subject of bringing you to the White House, and living there! It may be so!!"

While Margaret prayed to be spared such a fate, Houston dreamed of this stunning conclusion to his remarkable career. But any aspirant to the American presidency in the mid-nineteenth century had to negotiate the narrowing channels of slavery politics, which tightened treacherously upon California's application to the Union. Henry Clay, returned to the Senate after losing the presidency to Polk, proposed to wrap California in a package acceptable to North and South alike. The North would get a free California (the California constitution barred slavery) and an end to the slave trade in the District of Columbia, while the South would get a stiffened fugitive slave law and the possibility of slavery in the rest of the Mexican cession. To sweeten the deal for Texas, the federal government would assume the former republic's crushing debts.

Clay's compromise bill elicited the greatest Senate debate in American history. Clay himself spoke for days on behalf of his measure. John Calhoun, too weak to address the Senate in his own voice, and coughing blood from the tuberculosis that would kill him before the debate ended, had an associate read a rebuttal that was as incendiary as anything the old nullifier had ever written. Daniel Webster riposted that such sentiments as Calhoun's were irresponsible and incipiently treasonous.

Sam Houston had special standing in the affair, hailing from the state that had set the whole crisis in motion. He sided with Calhoun and most of the South in holding that Congress had no right to speak on slavery in the admission of new states. Under the Constitution, Congress could—and must—insist that the states applying for admission have republican governments, but beyond that, Houston said, Congress could not go without trampling the rights of the people. "The Congress of the United States does not possess the power to legislate upon the subject of slavery, either within the Territories or in any other section of the Union. . . . In the formation of their constitutions, under which they ask admission, the people of the Territories have the right to give their own form to their own institutions, and in their own way."

Yet Houston's democratic faith in the people didn't prevent him from denouncing those people who spoke of extreme measures in the event their side didn't get everything it wanted in the present debate. Northern abolitionists were "a contemptible minority," he said, while southern secessionists were "ultras" blind to the danger of the course they advocated. This danger was nothing less than "a war of dissolution, the worst of all wars; a war not of race, a war not of language or of religion, but a war of brothers, the most sanguinary of mortal strife." Houston urged his colleagues to set aside sectionalism and seek the national interest. "I call upon the friends of the Union from every quarter to come forward like men and to sacrifice their differences upon the common altar of the country's good, and to form a bulwark around the Constitution that cannot be shaken." In the current climate, this was no small request. "It will require manly efforts, sir, and they must expect to meet with prejudices growing up around them that will assail them from every quarter. They must stand firm to the Union, regardless of all personal consequences." Houston acknowledged that he wasn't a religious man, but he almost wished he was, that he might request the aid of the Almighty. "I cannot offer the prayers of the righteous that my petition might be heard. But I beseech those whose piety will permit them reverently to petition, that they will pray for this Union and ask that He who buildeth up and pulleth down nations will, in mercy, preserve and unite us. For a nation divided against itself cannot stand." Beyond this, Houston's one request was that in the event that prayers and the wisdom of the people proved unavailing, he not live to see the result. "I wish, if this Union must be dissolved, that its ruins may be the monument of my grave and the graves of my family. I wish no epitaph to be written that I survive the ruin of this glorious Union."

He didn't get his wish. The decade after the Compromise of 1850, as Clay's ultimately successful omnibus measure was called, witnessed the fulfillment of the fears of every friend of the American Union. The Fugitive Slave Act outraged the North by compelling complicity in the return of escaped bondsmen (and others merely alleged by interested parties to have escaped), while the admission of free California continued to rankle the South. The Kansas-Nebraska Act of 1854 repealed the Missouri Compromise of 1820 and opened those two territories to slavery should settlers there choose it; in the process the act provoked a guerrilla war in "bleeding Kansas" and furnished recruits to the new, antislavery Republican party. The Supreme Court declared in the 1857 Dred Scott case that Congress had no authority to bar slavery from the territories, a decision that appeared to corroborate the slaveholder-conspiracy theories of abolitionists and other northerners, with slaveholding Chief Justice Roger B. Taney cast as arch-conspirator. John Brown's botched but bloody effort to start a slave rebellion at Harpers Ferry, Virginia, in 1859, and the reverence accorded the convicted murderer on his way to the gallows, convinced southerners that the real conspiracy was in the North. Abraham Lincoln's 1860 election, with solely northern support, made the perfection of the antislavery conspiracy seem merely a matter of time.

Houston watched the descent toward dissolution with sickening dread. He called the Kansas-Nebraska bill "an eminently perilous measure" and urged the South not to repeal the Missouri Compromise. Repeal, he said, would provoke the North and unsettle the Union. "Maintain the Missouri Compromise! Stir not up agitation! Give us peace!"

He stayed in the Senate another half decade but, as a southern Unionist, found himself increasingly isolated. His cachet in the country as a whole continued to be formidable; Democrat Andrew Johnson of Tennessee asserted, as his party surveyed its presidential prospects, "All agree that if Sam Houston could receive the nomination that he would be elected by a greater majority than any other person." But as the Democrats' center of gravity drifted from West to South, from the land of Jackson to that of Calhoun, an outspoken Unionist stood no chance of being nominated. In the late 1850s secessionist sentiment seized the Texas legislature, and in 1859 it forced Houston from the Senate.

Yet the ordinary people of Texas still responded to the hero of San Jacinto, and Houston had hardly returned from Washington before they elected him governor. Meanwhile his supporters outside the state persisted in hoping for a Houston presidency. After the Democratic party split in the summer of 1860, Houston's friends put his name forward at the convention of the Constitutional Union party. He narrowly lost the nomination to John Bell of Tennessee.

Passion drove politics that season, and the secessionist fever rose by the week. Houston tried to talk it down, with a passion of his own. To a crowd in Austin he spoke of what he had hoped to accomplish in his long public life, and what the secessionists endangered. "Upward of forty-seven years ago," he said of his service with Andrew Jackson, "I enlisted, a mere boy, to sustain the national flag and in defense of a harassed frontier." A belief in the Constitution and the Union had motivated him then, as it motivated all who joined him in those parlous times. "And when again, in 1836, I volunteered to aid in transplanting American liberty to this soil, it was with the belief that the Constitution and the Union were to be perpetual blessings to the human race, that the success of the experiment of our fathers was beyond dispute, and that whether under the banner of the Lone Star or that many starred banner of the Union, I could point to the land of Washington, Jefferson, and Jackson as the land blest beyond all other lands, where freedom would be eternal and the Union unbroken." Houston had watched the Union grow and prosper. "I have seen it extend from the wilds of Tennessee, then a wilderness, across the Mississippi, achieve the annexation of Texas, scaling the Rocky Mountains in its onward march, sweeping the valleys of California, and laving its pioneer footsteps in the waves of the Pacific." This empire of liberty and prosperity was what the secessionists were determined to destroy.

Houston summoned the spirit of Old Hickory to oppose the wreckers. "I invoke the illustrious name of Jackson and bid you not to prove recreant to his memory. . . . To the national men of long service, to the young men who have been reared to love that name, I appeal. The same issue is upon you that was upon him. He stood with the Constitution at his back and defied disunion." Jackson's example should strengthen his followers against sectionalists of all parties.

"Let the people say to these abolition agitators of the North, and to the disunion agitators of the South, 'You cannot dissolve this Union. We will put you both down; but we will not let the Union go!' "

Houston hoped reason would prevail but feared it would not. And he wished again, if it did not, to be spared the sight of the rending of everything he had struggled to achieve. "It has been my misfortune to peril my all for the Union, so indissolubly connected is my life, my history, my hopes, my fortunes with it. And when it falls, I would ask that with it might close my career, that I might not survive the destruction of the shrine that I had been taught to regard as holy and inviolate since my boyhood. I have beheld it, the fairest fabric of government God ever vouchsafed to man, more than half a century. May it never be my fate to stand sadly by gazing on its ruin!"

And now, five months later, he awaited a delegate from the convention that had decreed Texas secession. The election of Lincoln had prompted several southern states to make good their threat to leave the Union. Texas moved more slowly than the rest, in no small part because Houston employed every device he could think of to frustrate what was clearly a majority sentiment among Texas voters. He refused to call a special session of the legislature or summon a convention to consider secession, as had been done in other states; when a convention gathered over his objection, he belatedly brought the legislature into session, to muddy the political waters. But his obstructive efforts failed. The convention endorsed secession, and a popular referendum ratified it. The convention then drafted a new constitution for Texas, attaching the state to the Confederacy and requiring Texas officials to swear allegiance to the Confederate government.

Houston watched all this from the governor's house on a hill across from the state capitol. Now he waited for the convention's emissary, who would formally notify him of the convention's action and of his new duty.

George Chilton arrived at eight. He advised the governor that the convention required his oath at once; should he fail to comply, he would be removed from office.

Chilton wasn't half Houston's age, having been a child at the time of San Jacinto. And his service to Texas paled beside the decades Houston had devoted to his adopted country and state. Consequently Chilton could hardly object when Houston requested more time to consider his response to the convention's demand. By noon the next day, Houston said, the convention would have its answer.

That night was the longest of Houston's life. Past twelve and far till dawn, he struggled with his conscience, with what was left of his ambition, and with history. The irony of his predicament must have forced a wry smile to his face even as it banished sleep from his brain. He, the man who had done more than any other to attach Texas to the Union, was now required to approve the severing of Texas from the Union. Each weary step as he paced the pine boards of the mansion recalled the personal price he had paid; his ankle hurt more on some steps, his thigh on others. To choose between Texas and the Union was to deny the meaning of half the pain he had suffered to bring them together.

The irony was personal, but it was more than that. Houston had fought a war, risking life and reputation, to free Texas from Mexico and make Texas part of the American Union; yet the very success of that war had taught Texas and the South how to dismantle the Union. The secession of Texas from Mexico in 1836 supplied a model for the secession of the South from the Union a quarter century later. In each case secession was defended in terms of states' rights, said to have been traduced by an overweening central authority. Santa Anna had destroyed the Mexican constitution of 1824 by a few swift blows; the North and the Republicans, southerners asserted, had been undermining the American constitution of 1787 for decades. In each case slavery played a role. In Texas in the 1830s slavery was one concern among several; in the South in the early 1860s it was the defining grievance of the Confederacy. Many southern secessionists in 1861 doubted that the North would fight, or if it did that its efforts would avail any better than those of Mexico against Texas in 1836. Hadn't a handful of Texans defeated the hosts of Santa Anna? With such inspiration, did it matter that the North outnumbered the South?

But there was a deeper irony. Houston, like Jackson and all who won political distinction in the age of democracy, placed his confidence in the people. "The people are always right: that is the dogma of the republic," Alexis de Tocqueville had scribbled in the same notebook in which he marveled at the election of David Crockett. Houston agreed, regarding both the phrase being the dogma and the people being right. The people could be unruly and intemperate, as his soldiers were unruly and intemperate during the retreat across Texas in 1836. But eventually the people got it right, as his men got it right at San Jacinto, and as the people of Texas got it right—if he did say so himself—in conferring on him the highest offices at their command.

The people were a tide nothing could resist for long. They had broken down the barriers to voting in the United States in the early nineteenth century. They had swarmed into Texas against the wishes of the Mexican government. They had made the independence of Texas inevitable, seizing that province in fact before they seized it in name. They had demanded the annexation of Texas to the United States and ultimately compelled Congress to take Texas in.

During all that time Houston had seen the people as a progressive force. Democracy could be rough; no one who knew Indians and loved many of them as Houston did could be other than dismayed at what American democracy had done to them. But on balance the expansion of democracy, the growth of the American Union, had been a blessed thing. Democracy delivered opportunity; it meant better lives for more ordinary men and women than had ever enjoyed such opportunity in other times or places.

Yet now democracy was destroying the Union. Houston had held out against secession until the people of Texas spoke; he had hoped against reason and evidence that they would see the error of their intended ways. He didn't doubt that secession would lead to war—and not a war like that against Santa Anna but a conflict so violent as to make the Alamo and San Jacinto seem mere skirmishes.

It was a bitter draft for Houston to swallow: that the people could be so wrong. And it left him at a loss. The people of Texas had chosen disunion, and the representatives of the people now demanded that he swear allegiance to the secessionist confederacy. During his sleepless night, hobbling on his Texas ankle, rubbing his Union wound, he pondered his alternatives. The voice of the people, or the voice of his conscience? Texas or the Union?

In the dark, cold hours of dawn he reached his decision. The convention wanted his answer; instead he addressed it to a higher authority: the people.

Fellow citizens:
In the name of your rights and liberties, which I believe
have been trampled upon, I refuse to take this oath.
In the name of the nationality of Texas, which has been
betrayed by this convention, I refuse to take this
oath.

In the name of the constitution of Texas, which has been
trampled upon, I refuse to take this oath.
In the name of my own conscience and manhood, which
this convention would degrade by dragging me be-
fore it, to pander to the malice of my enemies . . . I
refuse to take this oath.

Houston understood the consequences of his refusal. "I am ready to be ostracized sooner than submit to usurpation. Office has no charm for me, that it must be purchased at the sacrifice of my conscience and the loss of my self-respect."

It was the saddest moment of his life. "I have seen the patriots and statesmen of my youth, one by one, gathered to their fathers, and the government which they had created rent in twain; and none like them are left to unite it once again. I stand the last almost of a race, who learned from their lips the lessons of human freedom."

Houston died in 1863, in the month of the battle of Gettysburg. He lived long enough to see his dire forecasts of the horrors of civil war come true, but not long enough to see the Union survive its greatest trial, nor to see Texas re-joined to the land of his birth. Though he mourned the losses Texas suffered during the war (his son was gravely wounded at Shiloh), he would have believed that democracy won in the end, as the American people secured popular government against the forces of particularism and disunion. And he would have been gratified to know that the two causes closest to his heart—the Union and Texas—could cohabit again in peace.

He had always thought that Texas and the Union were cut from the same cloth, that the republican principles of 1836 were indeed those of 1776. The lesson of both fateful years was that people must govern themselves, even if—or especially if—self-government required rebellion against forms and institutions received from the past, and even if the people were far from saints. Houston couldn't speak from personal acquaintance of the patriots of '76, but he would have been the first to acknowledge the imperfect pedigrees and mixed motives of those who fought beside him in the Texas revolution. Stephen Austin might have been above reasonable reproach, having lived as a loyal citizen of Mexico till Santa Anna overturned the Mexican constitution and drove him to revolt, but nearly everyone else was an opportunist of one sort or another. William Travis had abandoned his debts and pregnant wife to come to Texas, where he made trouble for the Mexican authorities as a way of making the reputation he had always coveted. James Bowie, having swindled himself into a corner in Louisiana, crossed the Sabine to continue his swindling on Mexican soil. David Crockett hoped to recover in Texas the political career he had lost in Tennessee. And of course Houston himself, crushed by love and dazed by drink, had traveled to Texas to find the man he had been before Eliza broke his heart.

But none of these, nor even most of the latecomers who arrived in response to the bounties promised to volunteers in the Texan army, were *merely* opportunists. They believed in liberty, as they understood the term. They believed in the rule of law and the right of people to govern themselves. Their victory was a victory for democracy, in the dawning age of democracy. If it was also a victory for slavery, this aspect of the triumph proved passing when democracy defeated slavery in the Civil War.

Houston was not religious, placing his faith in the people rather than in heaven. Yet he was forced to concede that the people, no less

than heaven, sometimes worked in mysterious ways. The events culminating in the Texas revolution transcended morality, in the ordinary sense. Tens of thousands of Americans came to Texas to seek a
better life. Some came legally, many others illegally. No force short of
an army at the Sabine could have stopped them, so long as the opportunities in Texas were far greater than those at home. Certainly few of
them felt any compunction about bending or dodging Mexican law in
pursuit of their dreams. And after making Texas theirs by occupation,
they saw no reason not to make it theirs by revolution.

Were they justified in doing so? Sensitive souls—the John
Quincy Adamses of the era—complained that they were stealing land
from Mexico. And maybe they were. But these were Americans, a
people who were in the process of taking far more land from the native peoples of North America than the Texans took from Mexico
(which itself, of course, was trying to take Texas from the Indians). If
the Texans were guilty of theft, the people from whom they sprang
were much guiltier. In any event, the sensitive souls who fretted
about such things didn't frequent the frontier, where questions of
survival took precedence over nuances of law.

For better and worse, Texas was very much like America. The
people ruled, and little could stop them. If they ignored national
boundaries, if they trampled the rights of indigenous peoples and of
imported bondsmen, if they waged war for motives that started from
base self-interest, all this came with the territory of democracy, a
realm inhabited by ordinarily imperfect men and women. The one
saving grace of democracy—the one thing that made all the difference
in the end—was that sooner or later, sometimes after terrible strife,
democracy corrected its worst mistakes. For a generation after San
Jacinto, even the most ardent supporters of the Texas revolution had
difficulty contending that the victory of Houston's ragged band had

actually enlarged the area of human liberty. But when the Civil War terminated slavery, and as the American Southwest filled with people pursuing their own versions of the democratic dream, it was hard not to accept Houston's faith that the people ultimately got things right, and that the victory of the Texans was a victory for America.

Notes

The notes below cite sources of direct quotations and specific information that is not available in standard reference works. More general descriptions of events and personalities have been drawn from the manuscripts, books, and articles listed (and in many cases annotated) in the Bibliography.

Abbreviations

AP: Austin Papers
CAJ: Correspondence of Andrew Jackson
DCRT: Diplomatic Correspondence of the Republic of Texas
PCSH: Personal Correspondence of Sam Houston
PTR: Papers of the Texas Revolution
SWHQ: Southwestern Historical Quarterly
WSH: Writings of Sam Houston

Part One : The Banks of the Brazos (to 1828)
1. The Promised Land

5. "As to business": Gracy, 27.
6. "The metal is mixed": Jefferson, 150.
7. "on the Spanish side": ibid., 151.
8. "abominably bad . . . Milk and Honey": M. Austin, 524–26.
10. "None but those . . . more agreeable": ibid., 527–33.

11. "It is fast improving . . . I have ever seen": ibid., 535–40.
13. "In 1802": Wooten, 1:441.
14. Eight hundred thousand pounds . . . $190,000: Gracy, 110, 128.
15. "What have I done": ibid., 102.
16. "Would to God": *AP*, 1:333.
16. "To remain in a country": ibid., 1:385.
22. "the agent of three hundred . . . orders given them": Hatcher, 354–55.
22. "The proposal which he is making": McClean, 1:301.
23. "a mere skeleton": Gracy, 205.
23. "full confidence . . . to the Colorado": *AP*, 1:379.
24. "I returned from St. Antonio": ibid., 1:384.
24. "I flattered myself": ibid., 1:394.
24. "His fever was higher . . . he had commenced": ibid., 1:409–10.

2. El Camino Real

27. "From this employment": Cabeza de Vaca, 85.
27. "The food is poor . . . having no hunger": ibid., 103–5.
29. "Throughout this region": ibid., 176.
30. "Early in the morning": Hammond and Rey, 242.
30. "I can assure you": ibid., 170.
30. "God knows": ibid., 174.
32. "It seemed as if there was a curse": Weddle, 181.
32. "No one tells him anything": ibid., 159.
36. "If an obscurity . . . make the most of it": DeConde, 174.
39. "The business of volunteering . . . enterprise of our citizens": Warren, 35–36.
40. "They are a rascally set": ibid., 42.
40. "the People of the Province of Texas": ibid., 52.
41. "decidedly the best looking . . . dangerous statesmen": Calderón de la Barca, 65.
43. "All this is due": Callcot, 16.

3. The People of the Horse

44. "Two bands were living": Wallace and Hoebel, 9–10.
46. "anyone who wants to fight me": ibid., 4.
47. "He makes but an awkward figure . . . fleet and furious": ibid., 47–49.
48. "Thus many lives were saved": ibid., 61.
49. "For days together": ibid., 45.
49. "Each year at [a] certain time": Kavanagh, 66–67.
50. "copious number of souls": Castañeda, 3:341.
51. "And then began a cruel attack": Simpson, 88.
51. "When we reached the mission": ibid., 55–56.
53. "We found about twenty tents . . . to punish stealing": Flores, 66–72, 79–80.

4. Don Estevan

57. "I hope and pray": *AP,* 1:93–95.
57. "exemplary and praiseworthy manner": ibid., 171.
58. "This is one of the worst eddies": ibid., 205–7.
58. "Sheet lead will sell": ibid., 216.
59. "I have taken possession": ibid., 300.
60. "add another most important item": ibid., 291.
60. "My opinion of mankind . . . my family by living": ibid., 359.
60. "When the day arrives": ibid., 335.
61. "He is not rich . . . pay all off": ibid., 374.
61. "I now can go forward": ibid., 393.
61. "our intercourse has resulted . . . requires them": ibid., 397–98.
64. "The land lies on the Colorado": ibid., 399.
65. "This part of the country": ibid., 450.
65. "Started from Camp Ripley . . . very black and deep": S. Austin, "Journal," 288–96.
67. "The Spaniards": ibid., 296.
68. to give each family 320 acres of crop land and 640 acres of grazing land: Cantrell, 94.
68. "They must be governed by": Wooten, 1:472.

68. "The land adjoining the river . . . beautifully rolling": S. Austin,
    "Journal," 297–306.

71. "On my arrival here": *AP*, 1:419.

72. "They are to assist": ibid., 432–33.

73. "He was an European": ibid., 814.

73. Austin estimated fifty settlers: ibid., 511.

74. "One night's deliberation": ibid., 814.

74. "Fifty Comanches charged . . . going on tomorrow": ibid., 487.

75. "The country from the River Medina": ibid.

75. "the fountain head . . . perfect harmony prevails": ibid., 504–5.

76. "I make a tender of my services": ibid., 519.

76. "There has been and still is": ibid., 561.

77. "Comrades!": Callcott, 25.

78. "avenge themselves": ibid., 21.

78. "Veracruz!": ibid., 26.

78. "I cannot restrain my excessive joy": ibid., 34.

79. "without extending to me . . . to my nation its freedom": Santa Anna,
    Eagle, 16.

80. "Go and put Veracruz": ibid., 257 n. 8.

80. "Long live Anthony the First!": Wharton, 20–21.

80. "the spark of liberty": *AP*, 1:588.

81. "Don Estevan F. Austin": ibid., 590.

81. "with all my business . . . its being permanent": ibid., 631.

5. The Three Hundred

82. "On this river . . . this wandering mode of life": Dewees, 9–16, 21–23.

84. "We were several months . . . expenses had been paid": ibid., 23–27,
    29–36.

89. "I have just had the pleasure . . . on the Brazos River": ibid., 42.

91. "Since my return from Mexico": *AP*, 1:695.

92. "There have been a great many . . . down their pale cheeks": Dewees,
    43–44.

93. "They are an exceedingly fierce . . . curdle in my veins": ibid., 39–41.

95. "all the settlers able to bear arms . . . or on the river": *AP*, 1:715.

95. "Found at this encampment . . . Cannibal Creek": ibid., 886.

96. "It is not our wish . . . suspicion on either part": ibid., 930–31; also Cantrell, 138.

96. "To prevent such outrages . . . compelled to resort": *AP,* 1:702.

97. "We must be vigilant": ibid., 682.

97. "I expect to spend my life": ibid., 728.

98. "happy experience of many years . . . direction to the Federal party": ibid., 657, 668–69. Cantrell, 128–29, discusses Austin's influence.

98. "On my arrival in the colony . . . this part of the Province": *AP,* 1:727–28.

100. "The most unequivocal evidence . . . *no black sheep in our flock*": ibid., 716–17.

101. "I will receive any kind": ibid., 680.

102. "I was one of the first men . . . apply to that authority": ibid., 1076–7.

102. "I came to this colony . . . as any other man": ibid., 1094.

103. "You should listen with attention and confidence": ibid., 754.

103. The fee for a league was reduced to $192: ibid., 795; also Barker, *Life of Austin,* 101; Cantrell, 154.

103. "Look at the difficulties . . . motives of self-interest": *AP,* 1:811–24.

105. "A report has been in circulation": ibid., 872.

105. "I have done everything in my power": ibid., 901.

106. "I am sorry to hear": ibid., 868.

106. "You ask how I am getting on": ibid., 869.

107. "If they do not do this": Barker, *Life of Austin,* 152.

108. "Independence, Liberty, and Justice": ibid., 168.

108. "The Americans in this end of the Province": *AP,* 1:1550.

109. "I am a Mexican citizen": ibid., 1540.

109. "When I knew him in Missouri": ibid., 1528.

110. "Great God": ibid., 1539.

110. "They can send 3000 men": ibid., 1557.

110. "I know that the Cherokees": ibid., 1565–66.

110. "It is a duty which every good man": ibid., 1588.

111. "tranquility is fully and firmly established . . . it ever did before": ibid., 1610–11.

Part Two: Ravenous Democracy (1828—1834)

6. Love and War

118. "the wild liberty of the Red Men": Lester, 22.
120. "Shoot him! Shoot him!": Remini, 1:211.
121. "It is impossible to conceive": ibid., 1:214.
121. "many of the enemy's balls": ibid., 215.
126. "Our candidates for President": *AP*, 1:848.
127. "So you see the *Judas* of the West": James, 442.
127. "I never saw such a mixture . . . what a pity": Remini, 2:177—78.
131. "The canker worms": *WSH*, 1:13—14.
132. "The Greeks are struggling": ibid., 21—22.
132. "My own confident opinion": ibid., 25.
132. "The individual who was manifestly": ibid., 27.
133. "literary bureau": James, 56.
133. "I am charged": *WSH*, 1:106.
133. "Your friends here": ibid., 1:72.
133. "I have not in my life": ibid., 74.
133. "My firm and undeviating attachment": James, 64.
134. "General, you have killed me . . . injured no worse": ibid., 66—67.
134. "Houston stood six feet six": ibid., 68.
135. "I will not court": *WSH*, 1:5.
135. "I am making myself": James, 28.
136. "overwhelmed by sudden calamities": ibid., 79.
136. "publish in the Nashville papers": ibid., 84.
137. "About one o'clock": Haley, 59—60.

7. To Defend the Revolution

139. "General Santa Anna acted without instructions": Callcott, 55.
140. "My beloved friend and companion": ibid., 69.
141. "I am going to send him": ibid., 76.
143. "The buildings, though many are of stone": Sánchez, 257—58.
143. "Ciudad de Béxar": Berlandier, *Journey*, 2:290—91.
143. "The character of the people": Sánchez, 258.

144. "For months, and even years": ibid.

144. "I have witnessed": Berlandier, *Journey*, 2:291.

144. "The beauty of this country": Téran, 45.

144. "On the eastern bank . . . to come inside": ibid., 45–46.

145. "He is quite urbane . . . they seem happy": ibid., 53–54, 217.

146. the colony's annual corn crop . . . the cotton crop at 240,000 pounds: ibid., 56–58, 218.

146. "The reason for the emigration . . . in the ports": ibid., 56.

147. "I will remember for a long time . . . oozing lymph": ibid., 62, 70.

147. "There is a crudely built cabin": ibid., 74.

147. "A great number of the foreigners . . . to escape punishment": ibid., 79.

148. "As one travels . . . their abject condition": ibid., 97–98.

148. "the only one where they try . . . to bring his family": ibid., 133–35.

149. he currently had 30,000 pounds: ibid., 144.

149. "This settler, despite the vast assets . . . they enjoy abundance": ibid., 144–45.

149. "well-behaved people . . . is spent traveling": ibid., 149–50.

151. "Nature tells them . . . unless measures are taken soon": ibid., 32.

151. "On the frontier . . . just a few years": ibid., 38–39.

153. "The department of Texas . . . many humiliations": ibid., 178–79.

8. What Will Become of Texas?

156. "A more impolitic measure": *AP,* 2:405.

157. "They were becoming": ibid., 405.

157. "They are well calculated": ibid., 383.

158. "The idea of seeing . . . always be so": ibid., 415.

158. "My objects in coming to Texas . . . To be destroyed!!!": ibid., 380–81.

159. "No embarrassments . . . government on earth": ibid., 417–18.

160. "I will die . . . strength this fall": ibid., 416.

161. "Thou Shalt Not Muzzle the Ox": McDonald, 48.

163. "my personal acquaintance with Mr. T.": *AP,* 2:711.

165. "At some of these houses": *Visit to Texas*, 210.

166. A witness recalled him shouting: Davis, 270.

167. "Mexicans have learned . . . prosperous duration": ibid., 273–74.

169. "He was young . . . ride alligators": Bowie, 380.

170. "We continued to follow": ibid., 381.

172. "Had Wright not been rescued": ibid.

173. "twisted it to cut": Davis, 215.

176. His balance sheet was impressive: ibid., 293–94.

177. They had nearly reached: This account of the San Sabá fight follows ibid., 299–304.

180. "I write to inform": *AP*, 2:832–33.

181. "I find myself": Callcott, 84.

181. "Should I obtain a majority": ibid., 87–88.

182. "I would not be a lover": *AP*, 2:811.

182. "On my arrival . . . liberty of the nation": ibid., 825–26.

182. "The colony and all Texas": ibid., 2:821.

183. "indulgence with mistakes . . . of the people": Callcott, 96.

184. "I am not engaged": Morton, 171.

184. "I have come to be": ibid., 174.

184. "A great and respectable . . . What God wills": ibid., 182–83.

186. he fell forward and took his life: Some contemporaries (and later some historians) suspected murder, probably at the behest of Santa Anna. Morton, 179–81, weighs this possibility and persuasively finds it wanting.

9. A Conspiracy of Volunteers

188. "Liberty and Union": Peterson, 178.

188. "The Union of the States . . . I can reach": Remini, 2:235–37.

189. "Those who told you . . . the first victims": ibid., 3:23.

190. "The next pretext": ibid., 43.

190. "I have with much pride . . . Sam Houston": *WSH*, 1:274–76.

193. "the most unhappy man . . . supply nature's wants!!": ibid., 132–33.

194. "I am very feeble": ibid., 140.

195. "Peace would cost": ibid., 135.

195. "I will predict": ibid., 138.

196. "My honest belief": ibid., 151.

196. "Know all men": ibid., 196.

196. "conquer Mexico or Texas": memo by Andrew Jackson (citing a letter from Duff Green), May 21, 1829, Jackson Papers.

196. "It has been communicated": Jackson to Houston, June 21, 1829, ibid. (This letter in the Jackson Papers is a transcript, which includes the phrase "Your pledge of honor to the country . . ." Jackson presumably wrote—or at least meant—"Your pledge of honor to the contrary." And so it has been rendered here.)

198. "struck him elsewhere": James, 164.

198. "It's not you . . . some privileges": Terrell, 126.

198. "When he came": ibid.

199. "I seek no sympathies . . . eternity's waves": WSH, 1:208, 224.

199. "Houston, take my laurels!": James, 170.

200. "I was dying out": ibid., 172.

200. "So soon as matters": WSH, 1:204.

200. "It is important": ibid., 231.

201. "The land which . . . for moving about": ibid., 235.

201. "The more conflict": ibid., 237.

201. "The field is now open": ibid., 261.

201. "I have seen . . . citizens of Texas": ibid., 263–64.

202. "all the Tribes": James, 185.

202. "It has been my first . . . of that place": WSH, 1:267–70.

203. "He said he had been fired at": "Mr. Ham's Recollections of Col. Bowie," in unpublished memoirs of John S. Ford, p. 110, Ford Papers; Haley, 93.

204. "I found them": WSH, 1:272.

205. "Can Mexico ever": Washington Daniel Miller Papers.

206. "Colonel Crockett": Papers of Clay, 6:1098.

206. "if some skulking": Davis, 79.

207. "I was, without disguise": Crockett, 205.

207. "Fellow citizens": Davis, 166–67.

207. "His friends admit": ibid., 170.

207. "To return from the capitol . . . Lions of the West": Heale, 406.

208. "Two years ago": Tocqueville, 254.

208. "Rely upon it": *Correspondence of Polk*, 1:230.

208. "To General Jackson": Davis, 175. Shackford, 126, suggests that this letter was ghostwritten. Perhaps, but it nonetheless captures Crockett's feelings.

209. "I have not left": Shackford, 130.

209. "I have not got": ibid., 118–19.

209. "I would rather be beaten": ibid., 133.

210. "I think Crockett": *Correspondence of Polk*, 1:414.

211. "obscure as I am . . . hypocritically immortalized": Crockett, 1, 7, 10, 118, 135, 139, 163–64, 206.

10. The General Is Friendly

214. "They were all bound . . . begin life anew in Texas": Holley, *Texas*, 21–22, 29–30, 37–39, 123–25, 127–31.

218. "She is a very superior woman": *AP*, 2:725.

219. "Brazos Boat Song": Lee, 232.

219. "Mrs. H. is a *divine* woman": *AP*, 2:726.

219. "There is a pleasure . . . we can have": ibid., 727–29.

220. "I had a wretched trip": ibid., 992.

220. "There were 43,000 sick": ibid., 1006.

220. "I explained at large . . . serious reflection": ibid., 990.

221. "I told the vice president . . . he was reconciled": ibid., 1008.

221. "I believe that Texas . . . inexpedient and ruinous": ibid., 990–91.

222. "I have had a hard trip": ibid., 997.

222. "And in my opinion . . . God and Texas": ibid., 1007–8; Cantrell, 271.

223. "Texas matters are all right . . . at home soon": *AP*, 2:1016.

223. "All I can be accused of . . . in the colony": *AP*, 2:1024–25.

224. "Time drags on heavily . . . impatience and imprudence": S. Austin, "Prison Journal," 196–97.

226. "What a system . . . or common sense": ibid., 209–10.

226. "I am in such a condition": Callcott, 98.

227. "I swear to you": ibid., 102.

227. "Say to Mr. Poinsett": Wharton, 64.

228. "When I returned to the capital": Santa Anna, *Eagle*, 48.

228. "We were perishing": Callcott, 112.
229. "Our doors are now open": *AP*, 2:1051.
229. "I have no doubt": ibid., 1085.
229. "President Santa Anna is friendly": ibid., 1077.

Part Three: Blood on the Sand (1835—1836)
11. The Sword Is Drawn

233. "It awakened": *WSH*, 1:294.
233. "I have even been told": *AP*, 2:1077.
235. "As to Texas . . . so to remain": *WSH*, 1:289–90.
235. "General Houston was here. . . . I was a spy": Featherstonhaugh, 2:161.
237. "The plans of the revolutionists": Wooten, 1:173.
238. "Chingaba una mujer": Travis, 15.
238. "No pudiera": ibid., 129.
238. "Pagaba un peso . . . malo": ibid., 144.
238. "Venereo mala": ibid., 145. Davis, 687, suggests alternative interpretations of Travis's phrase. In light of Travis's traffic record, venereal disease seems the most likely.
238. "Proposals &c agreeably received": Travis, 128.
238. "Spent day pleasantly": ibid., 143.
238. "Started to Mill Creek": ibid., 139.
239. "Reception cold": ibid., 151.
239. "a simple understanding": ibid., 151.
240. "I landed at this place": McDonald, 110.
241. "In a very short time": ibid., 114.
241. "As it is impossible": ibid., 120–21.
242. "I discharged . . . I glory in it": ibid., 122–23.
242. "Strong man that he was": Smithwick, 137.
243. "Why, Jim . . . plenty of them": ibid., 138.
243. title to more than a half million acres: Davis, 423.
244. "You must look upon me . . . at liberty": *AP*, 3:2–4.
245. out-of-pocket expenses at ten thousand dollars: ibid., 48.

245. "I have been much more faithful": ibid., 6.

245. "If that change gives Santa Anna": ibid., 8.

246. "Santa Anna leaves": ibid., 63.

246. "All the rest of the country": ibid., 48.

246. "I do not understand": ibid., 68.

246. "I believe that the most of them": ibid., 90.

247. "It is well known . . . for the worst": ibid., 102–3.

249. "A grand dinner . . . such enthusiasm": ibid., 120.

250. "His arrival unites all parties": ibid., 119–20.

250. "My efforts to serve Texas . . . in the future": ibid., 116–19.

252. "Things have come on us": ibid., 128.

252. "The substance of this information . . . without effect": ibid., 128–29.

252. "War is upon us. . . . War is inevitable": ibid., 129–30.

253. "There must now be no half way measures": ibid., 130.

12. Lexington on the Guadalupe

254. "The glowing terms . . . lazy man's paradise": Smithwick, 17–18.

255. "I had a strong aversion": ibid., 19.

255. "A league of land . . . shot him dead": ibid., 37.

256. "Padre Muldoon was a bigoted . . . swallowing his medicine": ibid., 66–67.

257. "I have seen him sit . . . any other hypothesis": ibid., 67–68.

257. "gamblers' heaven . . . Declaration of Independence": ibid., 75.

257. "I told him": ibid., 84.

258. "an overbearing man . . . this iniquitous town": ibid., 84–86.

258. "just at the time": ibid., 99.

259. "Some were for independence": ibid., 102.

259. "Our whole available force . . . being necessary": ibid., 104–6.

261. "The Mexican commander": Wooten, 537.

263. "Your Lordship's orders": *PTR*, 2:36; Hardin, 12.

263. "It was our Lexington": Smithwick, 101.

264. "The same blood": Hardin, 9.

265. "No more doubts . . . not all at one jump": *AP*, 3:160–61.

266. "It is not in the nature . . . control its destiny?": Smithwick, 106.

268. "200 stands of muskets": *AP*, 3:181.

269. *"War in defense of our rights . . . down with the Usurper!!!"*: *WSH*, 1:302.

270. "with full powers": ibid., 303.

270. "The time has arrived": ibid., 304.

271. "committee of vigilance and safety . . . of a Jackson": ibid., 299–300.

272. "It certainly bore little resemblance": Smithwick, 109–10.

273. "all spoiling for a fight": ibid., 112.

274. "A large number of the citizens . . . *starved* out": *AP*, 3:202.

274. "Permit us to again suggest": ibid., 206–7.

275. "When the fog lifted . . . by all the furies": Smithwick, 114–15.

277. "The overwhelming superiority of force": *AP*, 3:217.

13. Behind Ben Milam

278. "He made a speech to us . . . touched the ground": Smithwick, 111.

280. it lost by a vote of fifteen to thirty-three: Wooten, 190.

280. "My health has been very bad . . . *to require rest*": *AP*, 3:262–63.

281. "It is an office": ibid., 247.

281. "He made the best speech": ibid., 238.

282. "Of these I think": Briscoe to Austin, c. November 21, 1835, Austin Papers.

282. "We are all captains": Hardin, 8.

283. "While we were busy": Dewees, 156.

283. "The army at present . . . or the people": *WSH*, 1:305–6.

284. "By express . . . the head knocked out": *AP*, 3:241.

284. "An immediate organization . . . defending the country": *WSH*, 1:311–13.

285. "Citizens of Texas": ibid., 317–18.

286. "I have at various times . . . such a service": *AP*, 3:263.

287. "Would it not be best . . . an eligible position": *WSH*, 1:305–6.

287. "the insidious attempts . . . command of the next": *PTR*, 2:248.

290. "All day we get more": Maverick, 44.

291. "Reports of the events . . . appalling blackness": Ehrenberg, 1–35.

296. "Colonel Milam is a native . . . all my sufferings": *PTR*, 2:194–95.

296. "Ben Milam and Frank Johnson": Taylor, 62–63.

297. "Remain like men": ibid., 63.

297. "The hollow roar": Ehrenberg, 71.

298. "Not a word . . . unable to reach it": ibid., 71–77.

301. "But she laughed . . . unfortunate woman": ibid., 81.

301. "The enemy's fire increased . . . another dead Mexican": Taylor, 67.

302. "At daylight of the 6th": *PTR*, 3:161.

303. "Yet our labors": Ehrenberg, 84.

303. "Boys, load your guns . . . at his heels": ibid., 69–71.

304. "It appeared we were to be swept off": *Papers of Lamar*, 5:97.

305. "The reaction of those": Huson, 196.

305. "The fact that many": Filisola, *Memoirs*, 2:93.

305. "We entered the town . . . has never surrendered": Huson, 190–93.

306. "We were surrounded": ibid., 194.

307. "retire with their arms . . . price of the country": *PTR*, 3:156–57.

14. The Army of Operations

308. "Some journalists had tried": Santa Anna, "Manifesto," 7.

309. "Our country found itself": ibid., 17.

309. "The foreigners who are making": *PTR*, 3:114.

310. "I have been unable . . . provisions and supplies?": Martínez Caro, 100.

311. "In an immense . . . part of another": de la Peña, 6–9.

312. "The great problem . . . to my genius": Santa Anna, "Manifesto," 12.

313. "I propose placing . . . spring will open": *WSH*, 1:319–20.

314. "It will give me . . . state of defence": ibid., 321.

314. "The brave men . . . for God's sake!": ibid., 332–33.

317. "In the event you can obtain . . . Copano is important": ibid., 1:322–23.

318. "Matamoros rage . . . abandon the place": ibid., 339–40.

319. "Our party now mustered . . . difficult to achieve": Ehrenberg, 120, 124–25.

320. "must not be wasted . . . that very day": ibid., 126–28. Crisp, "Sam Houston's Speechwriters," dissects the problematic nature of the various accounts of Houston's speech. The present author agrees with

Crisp's principal conclusions; for this reason the anti-Mexican and anti-Indian (Houston anti-Indian?!) remarks attributed to Houston by some authors have been omitted here.

321. "agents of the people . . . offensive and defensive": *PTR*, 3:123–24.
322. "From the papers": ibid., 18–19.
323. "A change of the basis": *AP*, 3:283.
323. "When I left Texas": ibid., 298–99.
324. "There is a Louisiana Battalion": ibid., 301.
325. "We have effected": ibid., 305.
325. "The universal wish": ibid., 299.
325. "Resolved: That the proud dictator": *PTR*, 3:165.
325. "I have never been": *AP*, 3:314.
325. "I had no idea . . . in their independence": ibid., 314.
326. "*a principle* . . . omnipotent God": Holley (1836 ed.), 260–80.
327. "This reminds me": Shackford, 202.
328. "You look tired . . . no use trying to": Davis, 392.
329. "I am not certain . . . this will be": Shackford, 173–74.
329. "wicked plan": *Correspondence of Polk*, 3:182.
329. "How is it": ibid., 190–91.
329. "If his vocabulary . . . carry such a skin": Davis, 405.
330. "I have him bad plagued": Shackford, 204.
330. "The great *Hunter*": *Correspondence of Polk*, 3:261.
330. "We have killed": ibid., 286.
331. "I am on the eve . . . before I return": *PTR*, 2:274.
331. "I am told": Davis, 413.
332. "It is the garden spot . . . among friends": Shackford, 214–16.

15. Victory or . . .

333. "We had set out . . . inside their fortifications": de la Peña, 26–37.
338. "Fortress Alamo . . . are all aiming": *PTR*, 4:58–61.
339. "All I can say . . . to the enemy": ibid., 237–38.
340. "*Relief* at this post . . . against thousands": ibid.
340. "I must beg": ibid., 4:185.
341. "I shall march today . . . few men I have": *PTR*, 4:176–77.

342. "My situation . . . in the colonies": ibid., 327–28.

343. "By the 15th of March": ibid., 328.

343. "all the measures in his power . . . any way responsible": ibid., 180.

343. "This country . . . to the British minister)": ibid., 251–52.

345. "Comrades in arms!": ibid., 373–74.

347. "The enemy in large force": ibid., 420.

348. "Commander of the invading forces . . . the volunteers of Bexar": ibid., 4:414.

348. "As the Aide-de-camp": ibid., 415.

349. "the certainty that Travis": de la Peña, 41.

350. "At the time . . . with laughter": Swisher, 19.

351. "Let us dance": Menchaca, 23.

352. "We have removed . . . for assistance": *PTR*, 4:419.

352. "To the People of Texas": ibid., 423.

354. "Today at 10 o'clock . . . Victory or Death!": ibid., 433–34.

355. "'Who is Dr. Grant?'" . . . resist them as such": *WSH*, 1:348–53.

356. "From the hurry . . . Texian liberty": *PTR*, 4:424–25.

357. "We have less than 350 . . . done our duty": ibid., 427.

358. "Not a particle . . . complete the fortifications": ibid., 443–44.

360. "In the present confusion . . . Victory or Death": ibid., 502–4.

361. "Let the Convention": ibid., 504–5.

362. "Take care of my little boy": ibid., 501.

362. "With the speed . . . Sabine River": ibid., 448.

363. "The night was very raw . . . munitions, and horses": Urrea, 214–16.

364. "Foreigners invading the republic . . . suffer as traitors": *PTR*, 4:501.

365. "Twelve days had passed . . . arguments were fruitless": de la Peña, 42–44.

365. "The time has come . . . Army of Operations": *PTR*, 4:518–19.

367. "a lady from Bejar . . . cover of darkness": de la Peña, 44.

368. "He wanted to cause": ibid., 44–45.

368. "The moon was up . . . shots and bayonets": ibid., 46–51.

16. At Discretion

374. "Among them was one": ibid., 53.

375. "As I was surveying . . . misrepresent the facts": Labadie, 174.

376. "Santa Anna sent one": Ruiz, 357.

377. a fourth eyewitness account: Martínez Caro, 103–4.

377. The details of Crockett's death: For a discussion of the various accounts and arguments, see Kilgore.

379. "their negroes, God damn them": Lack, 244.

380. "We, therefore": Texas Declaration of Independence, March 2, 1836, *Documents of Texas History*, 98–99.

382. "commander in chief of the land forces": *WSH*, 1:361.

382. The convention went on to write a constitution: Yoakum, 238.

383. "Goliad had been taken . . . in their commander": Barnard, 608–16.

387. "I have about 420 men . . . sluggards forever": *PTR*, 4:454.

388. "We are in hourly expectation . . . will not murmur": ibid., 508–10.

389. "Previous to abandoning . . . highly important": *WSH*, 1:365.

390. "As the affair . . . cheerfulness prevailed": Barnard, 619.

390. "The country around us . . . all our equipment": Ehrenberg, 169–70.

390. "His former experience": Barnard, 622.

391. "Our army now waited . . . cavalry squadrons": Ehrenberg, 171–72.

392. "We heaped, around our small camp . . . drop of water": ibid., 179.

393. "I immediately ordered . . . terms I proposed": Urrea, 228–29.

394. "After a long debate . . . almost every year": Ehrenberg, 182.

394. "After some parley . . . liberty and home' ": Barnard, 623–24.

395. "Art. 1st . . . José Urrea": Santa Anna, "Manifesto," 60–62; *PTR*, 5:147–48.

396. "They doubtless surrendered": Urrea, 235.

397. "the bravery and daring . . . all in my power": Santa Anna, "Manifesto," 58–59.

398. "Law commands . . . that wields it?": ibid., 18.

399. "I am informed": *PTR*, 5:175.

399. "At seven in the evening . . . restless night": Urrea, 236n.

400. "Their indignation . . . on the ground": Ehrenberg, 183–85.

400. Ehrenberg concluded: ibid., 185.

401. "I am now prepared . . . to indulge in": Barnard, 624–26.
402. "Several of my comrades . . . : we were Texans": Ehrenberg, 190–95.
403. "Grey clouds hung . . . in this direction": ibid., 198–201.
404. "He was very serious . . . that bloody day": Barnard, 626–28.
406. "A command to halt . . . my dying friends": Ehrenberg, 201–7.

17. Runaway

408. "It is said that Santa Anna": *PTR*, 5:40.
408. "The inhabitants of this country": ibid., 40.
409. "I am convinced . . . from Mexican territory": Santa Anna, "Manifesto," 65–66.
409. "We reached home . . . announce their arrival": Taylor, 118.
410. "There was not a soul": Swisher, 30–31.
411. "We could have met . . . of the drill": *WSH*, 1:374.
411. "Troops pent up in forts": ibid., 367.
412. "By falling back": ibid., 374.
412. "Sam Houston had . . . not to run": John Warren Hunter Papers, "Literary Effort."
412. "The declaration of independence": *PTR*, 5:159.
413. "Then on a day . . . trudged along": Taylor, 117–23.
416. "The army of Santa Anna . . . reduced to ashes!": *WSH*, 1:374–75.
417. "The Mexican army . . . conquer our enemies": ibid., 378–79.
418. "I am not easily depressed . . . in the lines": ibid., 380.
418. "All would have been well": ibid.
419. "If what I have heard . . . ill-fated man": ibid., 381.
419. "The retreat of the government": ibid.
419. "Men are flocking": ibid., 382.
420. "The capture of the Alamo . . . what a misfortune!": Santa Anna, "Manifesto," 20.
421. "There was a great abundance": de la Peña, 99.
421. "At the Colorado . . . pick up the last grain": ibid., 114–15.
422. "I found one house . . . so many of these destroyed": ibid., 111.
423. "No one would disagree": ibid., 120.
425. "duties which derive . . . with profound respect": *PTR*, 5:233.

426. "News—good news . . . as neutral ground": ibid., 317.

426. "When to this fact . . . prepare for action": *PTR*, 5:373.

427. "to join them in the war . . . daily increasing danger": ibid., 375–76.

427. "and had with him . . . upon this subject": ibid., 468–69.

428. "It is not the wish . . . by this Government": *PTR*, 6:53.

18. A People in Arms

430. "The capture of the Alamo . . . full flight": Santa Anna, "Manifesto,"20–21.

431. "Through some of the colonists . . . afternoon of the 14th": ibid., 74.

432. "The panic has reached . . . should it be otherwise . . .": *PTR*, 5:317.

432. "Our friend the commander-in-chief . . . upon ourselves": ibid., 444–45.

433. "Sir: The enemy": *WSH*, 1:412n.

433. "Taunts and suggestions . . . perform impossibilities": ibid., 411–12.

434. "By your retreat . . . universal consternation seized the country": Baker, 276–77.

435. "He came to the tents . . . in agitation": Kuykendall, 301–2.

436. "Col. Sidney Sherman . . . the Liberty company": Labadie, 150–51.

437. "The blacksmith is there . . . call in an hour": Sparks, 66–67.

438. "I went to work and killed . . . double the punishment": ibid., 68–69.

439. "I entered Harrisburg": Santa Anna, "Manifesto," 74.

440. "Due to the reports . . . detain him many days": Santos, 98.

442. "General, I have brought . . . to the right": Labadie, 152–53.

443. "This morning . . . go to conquer": *WSH*, 1:413–14.

443. "At about eight o'clock . . . idea of fighting": Delgado, 7.

444. "All of the members of the division": Santa Anna, "Manifesto," 75–76.

444. "It was two o'clock": Delgado, 8.

445. "About one hundred": Santa Anna, "Manifesto," 76.

446. "Seeing him under . . . if he desired it": Billingsley Papers, letter to Galveston *News*, September 19, 1857.

447. "It would be difficult": Swisher, 40–41.

448. "We had the enemy . . . His Excellency's tent": Delgado, 9–10.

448. "I shut the enemy up": Santa Anna, "Manifesto," 31.

449. "Col. Wharton visited . . . 'Fight, and be damned!' ": Labadie, 162.

449. "Our situation is strong": Houston, "Houston's Speech," 323.

450. "Our troops paraded": *WSH*, 1:418.

450. "Our regiments were volunteers . . . enemies' eyes": Sparks, 70.

451. "Remember the Alamo!" *WSH*, 1:419.

451. "I was in a deep sleep": Santa Anna, "Extracts," 270.

451. "The utmost confusion . . . carnage took place": Delgado, 10–11.

452. "We charged with such fury": Sparks, 71.

452. "He led me to the entrance": Martínez Caro, 124–25.

452. "At this place": ibid.

452. "It was nothing but a slaughter": *PTR*, 6:36.

453. "I pursued a fresh trail . . . forbear to recount": Labadie, 163.

453. "The most awful slaughter": Tolbert, 150.

454. "I could hardly see anything": ibid., 151.

454. "I observed Gen. Houston": Labadie, 164.

455. "General Houston gave orders . . . laying there yet": Hunter, 23–24.

Part Four: Lone Star and Union (1836—1865)
19. Victors and Vanquished

460. "He said he presumed . . . El Presidente!": Kuykendall Family Papers, "Recollection of Joel W. Robison," 34–35.

461. "General Santa Anna . . . he will do it": Labadie, 167–68.

463. "Since I had . . . Santa Anna": Filisola, *Memoirs*, 2:235–36; *Documentos Inéditos*, 187.

464. "A few hours before . . . our vanguard": Urrea, 244–46.

464. "Most of the army . . . carry it out": de la Peña, 146–47.

466. "Should it become": Filisola, "Representation," 175.

466. "in his official character . . . of this compact": Foote, 2:318–20.

467. "I did promise . . . could nullify": Santa Anna, "Manifesto," 39–40.

468. "My Friends": Callcott, 143; *Documentos Inéditos*, 197.

468. "I immediately wrote . . . had been shot": Santa Anna, "Manifesto," 87.

469. "Desolation it seems": *AP*, 3:340.

469. "Much more now depends": Cantrell, 347.

469. "Stephen F. Austin": Santa Anna, "Manifesto," 87.

470. "in fulfillment of the duties . . . upon their minds": *CAJ*, 5:411–12.

471. "Until the existing Government": ibid., 426.

471. "I have seen": ibid., 425.

472. "While Santa Anna": Tolbert, 186.

473. "Many of the old settlers": *AP*, 3:428.

473. "I once believed": ibid., 439.

473. "We must keep . . . blood and life": *WSH*, 1:450–52.

474. "A successful military chieftain": *AP*, 2:729; Cantrell, 356.

474. "Since my return": *AP*, 3:452.

474. "This has mortified . . . colonize this country": ibid., 443.

475. "*Suppose* that Santa Anna . . . more sacrifices": ibid., 450.

476. "General Santa Anna": *DCRT*, 2:427.

476. "pleasant of countenance": Callcott, 146–47.

476. "General Andrew Jackson . . . decide that question": Santa Anna, *The Eagle*, 57.

477. "fair consideration . . . suspend hostilities": Remini, 3:365.

477. "He said he was satisfied . . . apparent candour throughout": *DCRT*, 1:188–89.

478. "He placed at my disposal": Santa Anna, *The Eagle*, 57.

479. "The Father of Texas . . . illustrious deceased": *WSH*, 1:28–29.

20. *Slavery and Freedom*

481. "I *could not* be present": Nagel, 343.

481. "To withstand multitudes": ibid., 346.

482. "a covenant with death": Potter, 48.

483. "A device better calculated . . . a civil war": *Register of Debates in Congress*, 24th Congress, 1st session (1836), 4041–47.

485. "inevitably DISSOLVE THE UNION . . . PERMIT IT?": Lundy, 33, 64.

486. "I have at length": *DCRT*, 1:201.

487. "Bastrop county suffered . . . to their camp": Smithwick, 153, 173.

488. "After the fight": ibid., 175.

489. "They were the most peaceable . . . strike a woman": ibid., 181–83.

489. "I had many . . . not molest them": ibid., 188–89.

490. "If I could build": ibid., 194.

492. "Probably this will be": Callcott, 159.

21. Andrew Jackson Dies Happy

494. "Horses were generally considered": Smithwick, 234.

495. "Some were engaged . . . to total abandonment": Muir, 35.

495. "When the first issue": Smithwick, 269.

496. "While I hesitate . . . the same time": Muir, 34–35.

497. "Some of the disturbances": ibid., 36.

498. "God has said": Hogan, 260–61.

499. "A general gloom": ibid., 291.

501. "would be a subject": Smith, 77–78.

501. "intense anxiety for peace": *WSH*, 3:191.

502. "If England produces . . . politic indifference": ibid., 385–87.

503. "I am determined . . . sanctioned by wisdom": ibid., 4:260–65.

503. "all important to the security": *CAJ*, 6:272.

504. "I hope this golden moment . . . with Great Britain": ibid., 272.

504. "Houston and the people": ibid., 278.

504. "The United States . . . I answer no": ibid., 283–84.

505. "Eight years have elapsed . . . future danger": ibid., 290–91.

505. "The subject has carried": ibid., 278.

506. "Extraordinary": Bemis, 408.

506. "Yet my conscience": Adams diary, March 29, 1841, Adams Papers.

506. "bold, dashing, and utterly baseless . . . of posterity": Bemis, 474.

507. "If slavery were totally abolished . . . prospect is deathlike": Adams,
12:128, 152, 171; also *Congressional Globe*, January 24–25, 1845.

508. "I congratulate you . . . Union is secured": Remini, 3:511.

22. The Trial of Sam Houston

510. "Supposing a charming lady . . . [Laughter and cheers.]": *WSH*, 6:12.

510. "Mexicans!": Callcott, 219.

511. "Mexicans! You have a religion": ibid., 257.

513. "This task is done": Crane, 256.

514. "My son": James, 357.

514. "I suppose that not less": *PCSH*, 3:69.

515. "The Congress of the United States . . . glorious Union": *WSH*, 5:119–44.

517. "an eminently perilous measure . . . Give us peace!": ibid., 513, 522.

517. "All agree that if Sam Houston": James, 382.

518. "Upward of forty-seven . . . gazing on its ruin!": *WSH*, 8:145–60.

521. "The people are always right": Tocqueville, *Journey*, 156.

522. "Fellow citizens . . . of human freedom": *WSH*, 8:277.

Bibliography

Archival Collections

Adams, Henry Alexander, Papers, Center for American History (CAH), University of Texas at Austin.

Adams, John Quincy (and family), Papers, Massachusetts Historical Society, Boston.

Alamán, Lucas, Papers, Benson Latin American Collection (BLAC), University of Texas at Austin.

Allen, Samuel T., Papers, CAH.

Almonte, Juan N., Papers, CAH.

Ames, Harriet A., Papers, CAH.

Ampudia, Pedro de, Papers, CAH.

Archivo de México, Texas State Library (TSL), Austin.

Archivo General de Indias, TSL.

Archivo General de México, CAH.

Aury, Louis, Papers, CAH.

Austin, Moses and Stephen, Papers, CAH.

Austin, William T., Papers, CAH.

Austin Colony Census, 1826, CAH.

Baker, Mosely, Papers, CAH.

Béxar Archives, CAH.

Billingsley, Jesse, Papers, CAH.

Bowie, James, Papers, CAH.

Bryan, Guy M., Papers, CAH.

Bryan, Moses Austin, Papers, CAH.

Burnet, David G., Papers, CAH.

Butler, Anthony, Papers, CAH.

Crusemann, Paul C., Papers, CAH.

Davenport, Harbert, Papers, TSL.

Documentos Relativos a Coahuila, Coahuila y Tejas, y Nuevo León y Coahuila;
        Bancroft Library, University of California, Berkeley.

Documents Relating to Texas, Bancroft Library.

Edwards, Haden, Papers, CAH.

Felloseby, John, Papers, CAH.

Ford, John Salmon, Papers, CAH.

Hearne, Madge Williams, Papers, CAH.

Hearne, Sam Houston, Papers, CAH.

Houston, Andrew Jackson, Papers, TSL.

Houston, Sam, Papers, CAH.

Hunter, John Warren, Papers ("Literary Effort"), TSL.

Iturbide, Augustín de, Papers, BLAC.

Jackson, Andrew, Papers, Library of Congress.

Kuykendall Family Papers, CAH.

Lamar, Mirabeau B., Papers, TSL.

Lindsey Family Papers, TSL.

Mexia Family Papers, Bancroft Library.

Miller, Washington Daniel, Papers, TSL.

Nacogdoches Archive, TSL.

Peebles, Robert U., Papers, CAH.

Perry, James Franklin and Stephen Samuel, Papers, CAH.

Prather, Ben Caldwell, Papers, CAH.

Rusk, Thomas J., Papers, CAH.

Santa Anna, Antonio López de, Papers, BLAC.

Seguín, Juan N., Papers, CAH.

Stewart, Charles B., Papers, TSL.

Travis, William Barret, Papers, CAH.

Walker, Samuel Hamilton, Papers, TSL.

Yoakum, Henderson, Papers, TSL.

Zavala, Lorenzo de, Papers, CAH.

Published Works

Adams, John Quincy. *Memoirs of John Quincy Adams, Comprising Portions of His Diary from 1795 to 1848*. Edited by Charles Francis Adams. 12 volumes. Freeport, N.Y.: Books for Libraries Press, 1969.

Almonte, Juan Nepomuceno. "The Private Journal of Juan Nepomuceno Almonte: February 1–April 16, 1836," introduced by Samuel E. Asbury, *SWHQ* 48 (1944), 10–32.

Ashford, Gerald. *Spanish Texas: Yesterday and Today*. Austin: Jenkins Publishing Co., 1971.

Austin, Moses. "A Memorandum of M. Austin's Journey from the Lead Mines in the County of Wythe in the State of Virginia to the Lead Mines in the Province of Louisiana West of the Mississippi, 1796–1797." Edited by George P. Garrison. *American Historical Review*, vol. 5 (1900), 518–42.

Austin, Stephen Fuller. "Journal of Stephen F. Austin on His First Trip to Texas, 1821." *Texas Historical Association Quarterly*, vol. 7 (1904), 286–307.

——. "The 'Prison Journal' of Stephen F. Austin," *The Quarterly of the Texas State Historical Association*, vol. 2 (1899), 183–210.

Austin, Stephen Fuller, and Moses Austin. *The Austin Papers*. Edited by Eugene C. Barker. 3 volumes. Washington: Government Printing Office, 1924–1928 (volumes 1–2); Austin: University of Texas Press, 1927 (volume 3). By far the most valuable primary source on early Texas. Compiled and edited by the dean of Texas historians.

Baker, Mosely. "Extracts from Mosely Baker's Letter to Houston," in Barker, "The San Jacinto Campaign," 272–87.

Barker, Eugene C. *The Life of Stephen F. Austin, Founder of Texas, 1793–1836*. Austin: University of Texas Press, 1969. An admiring portrait that remains essential.

——. "The San Jacinto Campaign," *SWHQ* 4 (1901), 237–345. The view from several perspectives, not all edited equally well.

Barnard, J. H. "Fannin at Goliad—Battle of the Coleta—The Massacre of Fannin's Command," in Wooten, ed., 608–36.

Barr, Alwyn. *Texans in Revolt: The Battle for San Antonio, 1835*. Austin: University of Texas Press, 1990.

Bazant, Jan. *A Concise History of Mexico from Hidalgo to Cárdenas, 1805–1940*. Cambridge, England: Cambridge University Press, 1977.

Bean, Ellis P. *Memoir of Col. Ellis P. Bean, Written by Himself, about the Year 1816*. Edited by W.P. Yoakum. N.p.: Book Club of Texas, 1930.

Bemis, Samuel Flagg. *John Quincy Adams and the Union*. New York: Alfred A. Knopf, 1965.

Berlandier, Jean Louis. *The Indians of Texas in 1830*. Edited by John C. Ewers. Translated by Patricia Reading Leclercq. Washington: Smithsonian Institution Press, 1969.

———. *Journey to Mexico During the Years 1826 to 1834*. 2 volumes. Translated by Sheila M. Ohlendorf, Josette M. Bigelow, and Mary M. Standifer. Austin: Texas State Historical Association, 1980.

Bolton, Herbert Eugene. *Texas in the Middle Eighteenth Century: Studies in Spanish Colonial History and Administration*. 1915. New York: Russell & Russell, 1962. What eventually led to the decision to let the Americans in.

Bowie, John. "Early Life in the Southwest—The Bowies," *De Bow's Southern and Western Review* 13 (October 1852), 378–83.

Cabeza de Vaca, Álvar Núñez. *Relation*. 1542. Translated by Buckingham Smith. New York: n.p., 1871. One of the epic tales of the American Southwest.

Calderón de la Barca, Fanny. *Life in Mexico: The Letters of Fanny Calderón de la Barca*. Edited by Howard T. Fisher and Marion Hall Fisher. Garden City, N.Y.: Doubleday & Co., 1966. Although related only tangentially to Texas, worth reading simply for the shrewd insights of the author.

Callcott, Wilfrid Hardy. *Santa Anna: The Story of an Enigma Who Once Was Mexico*. Norman: University of Oklahoma Press, 1936. The most reliable life, in any language.

Campbell, Randolph B. *An Empire for Slavery: The Peculiar Institution in Texas, 1821–1865*. Baton Rouge: Louisiana State University Press, 1989.

Cantrell, Gregg. *Stephen F. Austin: Empresario of Texas*. New Haven, Conn.: Yale University Press, 1999. Updates Barker, asks harder questions of Austin, and is the current starting point for the study of Texas's founding father.

Castañeda, Carlos E., ed. *The Mexican Side of the Texan Revolution*. Dallas:

P. L. Turner Company, 1928. Invaluable for understanding the actions and motivations of Mexico's leading figures in the war for Texas. Written after the fact (that is, after the Mexican defeat), it contains much reciprocal finger-pointing, but is more interesting for that.

Castañeda, Carlos E. *Our Catholic Heritage in Texas, 1519–1936*. 7 volumes. Austin: Von Boeckmann-Jones Co., 1936–58.

Clay, Henry. *The Papers of Henry Clay*. Edited by James F. Hopkins et al. 10 volumes and supplement. Lexington: University Press of Kentucky, 1959–92.

Crane, William Carey. *Life and Select Literary Remains of Sam Houston of Texas*. Dallas: William G. Scarff & Co., 1884.

Crisp, James E. "Sam Houston's Speechwriters: The Grad Student, the Teenager, the Editors, and the Historians." *SWHQ* 97 (1993), 203–37.

Crockett, David. *A Narrative of the Life of David Crockett of the State of Tennessee*. 1834. Edited by James A. Shackford and Stanley J. Folmsbee. Knoxville: University of Tennessee Press, 1973.

Davis, William C. *Three Roads to the Alamo: The Lives and Fortunes of David Crockett, James Bowie, and William Barret Travis*. New York: HarperCollins, 1998. A wonderful work of investigation and narration. Especially valuable on Bowie.

Day, James M., comp. *The Texas Almanac, 1857–1873: A Compendium of Texas History*. Waco: Texian Press, 1967. A grab bag from grab bags, containing gems among much else.

De la Peña, José Enrique. *With Santa Anna in Texas: A Personal Narrative of the Revolution*. Translated and edited by Carmen Perry. College Station: Texas A&M University Press, 1975. The subject of far more controversy than it should have evoked. An essential component of the first-person literature on the Texas Revolution.

De León, Arnoldo. *The Tejano Community, 1836–1900*. Albuquerque: University of New Mexico Press, 1982.

DeConde, Alexander. *The Affair of Louisiana*. Baton Rouge: Louisiana State University Press, 1976.

Delgado, Pedro. *Mexican Account of the Battle of San Jacinto*. Deepwater, Tex.: W. C. Day, [1919].

Dewees, W. B. *Letters from an Early Settler of Texas*. 1852. Waco: Texian Press,

1968. Some historians have questioned the authenticity of certain of the letters in this book, suggesting that they were written after the dates assigned to them therein. This may well be so, and the "letters" may be in part a literary device. But no one disputes that Dewees was in Texas during the period covered by the book, or that it is at least a memoir if not always an account contemporary with the events it describes. The distinction is unimportant for the present purpose.

Documentos Inéditos o Muy Raros para la Historia de México. Mexico City: Editorial Porrúa, 1974 ed.

Documents of Texas History. Edited by Ernest Wallace, David M. Vigness, and George B. Ward. Austin: State House Press, 1994.

Ehrenberg, Herman. *With Milam and Fannin: Adventures of a German Boy in Texas' Revolution.* Originally published as *Texas und Seine Revolution;* Leipzig, 1843. Translated by Charlotte Churchill. Dallas: Tardy Publishing Co., 1935. Something has been lost in the translation and editing, but very much of value remains.

Featherstonhaugh, G. W. *Excursion Through the Slave States from Washington on the Potomac to the Frontier of Mexico.* 2 volumes. London: John Murray, 1844.

Fehrenbach, T. R. *Comanches: The Destruction of a People.* New York: Alfred A. Knopf, 1979.

Field, Joseph E. *Three Years in Texas, Including a View of the Texan Revolution and an Account of the Principal Battles.* 1836. Austin: Steck Company, 1935.

Filisola, Vicente. *Memoirs for the History of the War in Texas.* 2 volumes. 1848. Translated by Wallace Woolsey. Austin, Tex.: Eakin Press, 1985.

———. "Representation Addressed to the Supreme Government," in Castañeda, ed., *The Mexican Side of the Texan Revolution.*

Flores, Dan L., ed. *Journal of an Indian Trader: Anthony Glass and the Texas Frontier, 1790–1810.* College Station: Texas A&M University Press, 1985.

Foote, Henry Stuart. *Texas and the Texans, or, Advance of the Anglo-Americans to the South-west.* 2 volumes. 1841. Austin: Steck Company, 1935. A standard source, still very useful.

Fuentes Mares, José. *Santa Anna, el Hombre.* Mexico City: Editorial Grijalbo, 1982 ed.

Garrison, George P., ed. *Diplomatic Correspondence of the Republic of Texas*. 2 volumes. Washington: Government Printing Office, 1908–11.

Gonzalez Pedrero, Enrique. *Pals de un Solo Hombre: El México de Santa Anna*. 2 volumes to date. Mexico City: Fondo de Cultura Esconómica, 1993–2003.

Gracy, David B., II. *Moses Austin: His Life*. San Antonio, Tex.: Trinity University Press, 1987. The only good work on Moses Austin.

Gregory, Jack, and Rennard Strickland. *Sam Houston with the Cherokees, 1829–1833*. Austin: University of Texas Press, 1967.

Haley, James L. *Sam Houston*. Norman: University of Oklahoma Press, 2002. Less literary than James's biography, but more thorough and reliable. The current standard.

Hammond, George P., and Agapito Rey. *Narratives of the Coronado Expedition, 1540–1542*. Albuquerque: University of New Mexico Press, 1940.

Hardin, Stephen L. *Texian Iliad: A Military History of the Texas Revolution, 1835–1836*. Austin: University of Texas Press, 1994. Succinct and solid, the best account of the rebel campaign. The renderings of uniforms and arms are a delightful bonus.

Hatcher, Mattie Austin. *The Opening of Texas to Foreign Settlement, 1801–1821*. Austin: University of Texas, 1927. (University of Texas *Bulletin*, no. 2714: April 8, 1927.)

Heale, M. J. "The Role of the Frontier in Jacksonian Politics: David Crockett and the Myth of the Self-Made Man." *Western Historical Quarterly*, volume 4 (1973), 405–23.

Herring, Patricia Roche. *General José Cosme Urrea: His Life and Times, 1797–1849*. Spokane, Wash.: Arthur H. Clark Co., 1995.

Hogan, William Ransom. *The Texas Republic: A Social and Economic History*. Norman: University of Oklahoma Press, 1946. Life under the Lone Star.

Holley, Mary Austin. *Texas: Observations Historical, Geographic and Descriptive*. 1833. New York: Arno Press, 1973. Also the 1836 edition, subtitled *Original Narratives of Texas History and Adventure*, reprinted Austin: Steck Company, 1935.

———. *The Texas Diary, 1835–1838*. Edited by J. P. Bryan. Austin: University of Texas Press, 1965.

Houston, Sam. "Houston's Speech in the United States Senate," in Barker, "The San Jacinto Campaign."

———. *The Personal Correspondence of Sam Houston*. Edited by Madge Thornall Roberts. 4 volumes. Denton: University of North Texas Press, 1996–2001.

———. *The Writings of Sam Houston*. Edited by Amelia W. Williams and Eugene C. Barker. 8 volumes. Austin: University of Texas Press, 1938–43. Indispensable but uneven.

Howren, Alleine. "Causes and Origin of the Decree of April 6, 1830," *SWHQ* 16 (April 1913), 378–422.

Hunter, Robert Hancock. *Narrative of Robert Hancock Hunter, 1813–1902*. Austin: Cook Printing Co., 1936.

Huson, Hobart. *Captain Phillip Dimmitt's Commandancy of Goliad, 1835–1836: An Episode of the Mexican Federalist War in Texas, Usually Referred to as the Texian Revolution*. Austin: Von Boeckmann-Jones Co., 1974.

Jackson, Andrew. *Correspondence of Andrew Jackson*. Edited by John Spencer Bassett. 7 volumes. Washington: Carnegie Institution, 1926–35.

James, Marquis. *The Raven: The Life Story of Sam Houston*. New York: Grosset & Dunlap, 1929. Written with the flair James brought to all his writings. The book that made Houston a national hero.

Jefferson, Thomas. *Notes on the State of Virginia*. Edited by Merrill D. Peterson. New York: Library of America, 1984.

Jenkins, John H., ed. *The Papers of the Texas Revolution*. 10 volumes. Austin: Presidial Press, 1973. A work more of love than of scholarship, but one that no serious student of the Texas Revolution can do without.

Jenkins, John Holland. *Recollections of Early Texas: The Memoirs of John Holland Jenkins*. Edited by John Holmes Jenkins III. Austin: University of Texas Press, 1958.

Johnson, Frank W. *A History of Texas and Texans*. Edited by Eugene C. Barker. Chicago: American Historical Society, 1914. By a Texas revolutionary turned historian.

Jones, Oakah L., Jr. *Santa Anna*. New York: Twayne Publishers, 1968.

Kavanagh, Thomas W. *Comanche Political History: An Ethnohistorical Perspective, 1706–1875*. Lincoln: University of Nebraska Press, 1996.

Kuykendall, J. H. "Kuykendall's Recollections of the Campaign," in Barker, "The San Jacinto Campaign," 291–306.

Kilgore, Dan. *How Did Davy Die?* College Station: Texas A&M University Press,

1978. Dissects the controversy that makes sense only to Texans, and not to all of them.

Labadie, N. D. "San Jacinto Campaign," in Day, 142–77.

Lack, Paul D. *The Texas Revolutionary Experience: A Political and Social History, 1835–1836*. College Station: Texas A&M University Press, 1992. The complement to Hardin.

Lamar, Howard, ed. *The New Encyclopedia of the American West*. New Haven, Conn.: Yale University Press, 1998.

Lamar, Mirabeau Buonaparte. *The Papers of Mirabeau Buonaparte Lamar*. Edited by C. A. Gulick et al. 6 volumes. Austin: A. C. Baldwin Printers and Von Boeckmann-Jones Co., 1921–27.

Lee, Rebecca Smith. *Mary Austin Holley: A Biography*. Austin: University of Texas Press, 1962.

Lester, C. Edwards. *The Life of Sam Houston: The Only Authentic Memoir of Him Ever Published*. New York: J. C. Derby, 1855. Although Houston collaborated closely in the writing of this book, Marquis James errs in calling it a "virtual autobiography" (James, 437). Houston may have supplied the facts, but the voice is Lester's.

Lundy, Benjamin ["By a Citizen of the United States"]. *The War in Texas . . .* Philadelphia: Merrihew and Gunn, 1837.

Martínez, Antonio. *The Letters of Antonio Martínez, Last Spanish Governor of Texas, 1877–1822*. Edited by Virginia H. Taylor. Austin: Texas State Library, 1957.

Martínez Caro, Ramón. "A True Account of the First Texas Campaign, and the Events Subsequent to the Battle of San Jacinto," in Castañeda, ed., *Mexican Side of the Texan Revolution*, 90–159.

Matovina, Timothy N. *The Alamo Remembered: Tejano Accounts and Perspectives*. Austin: University of Texas Press, 1995.

Maverick, Samuel. *Samuel Maverick, Texan: 1803–1870: A Collection of Letters, Journals and Memoirs*. Edited by Rena Maverick Green. San Antonio: privately printed, 1952.

McDonald, Archie P. *Travis*. Austin: Jenkins Publishing Co., 1976. Not great, but the best devoted solely to its subject. Superseded in many respects by Davis, *Three Roads to the Alamo*.

McLean, Malcolm D. *Papers Concerning Robertson's Colony in Texas*. Compiled and edited by Malcolm D. McLean. 18 volumes. Arlington: University of Texas at Arlington Press, 1974–93.

Menchaca, Antonio. *Memoirs*. San Antonio: Yanaguana Society, 1937.

Moorhead, Max L. *The Apache Frontier: Jacobo Ugarte and Spanish-Indian Relations in Northern New Spain, 1769–1791*. Norman: University of Oklahoma Press, 1968.

Morton, Ohland. *Terán and Texas: A Chapter in Texas-Mexican Relations*. Austin: Texas State Historical Association, 1948.

Muir, Andrew Forest, ed. *Texas in 1837: An Anonymous, Contemporary Narrative*. Austin: University of Texas Press, 1958.

Nagel, Paul C. *John Quincy Adams: A Public Life, a Private Life*. New York: Alfred A. Knopf, 1997.

Newell, Chester. *History of the Revolution in Texas, Particularly of the War of 1835 & '36*. 1838. New York: Arno Press, 1973.

Noyes, Stanley. *Los Comanches: The Horse People, 1751–1845*. Albuquerque: University of New Mexico Press, 1993.

Peterson, Merrill D. *The Great Triumvirate: Webster, Clay, and Calhoun*. New York: Oxford University Press, 1987.

Polk, James K. *Correspondence of James K. Polk*. Edited by Herbert Weaver et al. 9 volumes to date. Nashville, Tenn.: Vanderbilt University Press, 1969–.

Potter, David M. *The Impending Crisis, 1848–1861*. Completed and edited by Don E. Fehrenbacher. New York: Harper & Row, 1976.

Remini, Robert V. *Andrew Jackson*. 3 volumes. New York: Harper & Row, 1977–84. The most thorough and reliable of the lives of Old Hickory.

Roberts, Randy, and James S. Olson. *A Line in the Sand: The Alamo in Blood and Memory*, New York: Free Press, 2001. The history and the history of the history.

Robertson, William Spence. *Iturbide of Mexico*. Durham, N.C.: Duke University Press, 1952.

Ruiz, Francisco Antonio. "Fall of the Alamo, and Massacre of Travis and His Brave Associates." Translated by J. A. Quintero. *Texas Almanac*, 1860. Reprinted in *The Texas Almanac, 1857–1873: A Compendium of Texas History*. Compiled by James M. Day. Waco: Texian Press, 1967.

Sánchez, José María. "A Trip to Texas in 1828." Translated by Carlos E. Castañeda. *SWHQ* 29 (April 1926), 249–88.

Santa Anna, Antonio López de. *The Eagle: The Autobiography of Santa Anna*. Edited by Ann Fears Crawford. Austin: Pemberton Press, 1967. Should be handled with even greater care than that accorded most memoirs. But does reveal the mind of the man who, more than anyone else, lost Texas.

——. "Extracts from Santa Anna's Report," in Barker, "The San Jacinto Campaign."

——. "Manifesto which General Antonio López de Santa Anna Addresses to IIis Fellow-Citizens Relative to His Operations During the Texas Campaign and His Capture of 10 of May 1837," in Castañeda, ed., *The Mexican Side of the Texan Revolution*, 2–89.

Santos, Richard G. *Santa Anna's Campaign Against Texas, 1835–1836: Featuring the Field Commands Issued to Major General Vicente Filisola*. Salisbury, N.C.: Texian Press, 1968.

Seguín, Juan N. *A Revolution Remembered: The Memoirs and Selected Correspondence of Juan N. Seguín*. Edited by Jesús F. de la Teja. Austin: State House Press, 1991.

Shackford, James Atkins. *David Crockett: The Man and the Legend*. Edited by John B. Shackford. Chapel Hill: University of North Carolina Press, 1956. The point of departure on Crockett.

Sibley, Marilyn McAdams. *Travelers in Texas, 1761–1860*. Austin: University of Texas Press, 1967.

Siegel, Stanley. *A Political History of the Texas Republic, 1836–1845*. Austin: University of Texas Press, 1956.

Simmons, Marc, ed. *Border Comanches: Seven Spanish Colonial Documents, 1785–1819*. Santa Fe, N.M.: Stagecoach Press, 1967.

Simpson, Lesley Byrd, ed. *The San Saba Papers: A Documentary Account of the Founding and Destruction of San Saba Mission*. Translated by Paul D. Nathan. San Francisco: John Howell Books, 1959.

Smith, Justin H. *The Annexation of Texas*. 1911. New York: Barnes & Noble, 1941.

Smithwick, Noah. *The Evolution of a State, or Recollections of Old Texas Days*. Compiled by Nanna Smithwick Donaldson. Austin: Gammel Book

Company, 1900. Facsimile reprint: Austin: Steck Company, n.d. Even after allowing for the passage of time between the doing and the telling, and for Smithwick's skills as a raconteur, it remains one of the most informative eyewitness accounts of the Texas revolution.

Sparks, S. F. "Recollections of S. F. Sparks," *SWHQ* 12 (1908), 61–79.

Stevens, Donald Fithian. *Origins of Instability in Early Republican Mexico*. Durham, N.C.: Duke University Press, 1991.

Swisher, John M. *The Swisher Memoirs*. Edited by Rena Maverick Green. San Antonio: Sigmund Press, 1932.

Taylor, Creed. *Tall Men with Long Rifles*. As told to James T. DeShields. San Antonio: Naylor Company, 1935, 1971. Shows the hand of the ghostwriter but retains the voice of the rebel.

Terán, Manuel de Mier y. *Texas by Terán: The Diary Kept by General Manuel de Mier y Terán on His 1828 Inspection of Texas*. Edited by Jack Jackson. Austin: University of Texas Press, 2000. The contemporary account by the man who struggled to save Texas for Mexico, and ended as a victim to despair.

Terrell, A. W. "Recollections of General Sam Houston," *SWHQ* 14 (October 1912), 113–36.

Tijerina, Andrés. *Tejanos and Texas Under the Mexican Flag, 1821–1836*. College Station: Texas A&M University Press, 1994.

Tocqueville, Alexis de. *Journey to America*. Translated by George Lawrence. Edited by J. P. Mayer. London: Faber and Faber, 1959.

Tolbert, Frank X. *The Day of San Jacinto*. New York: McGraw-Hill, 1959.

Travis, William Barret. *The Diary of William Barret Travis: August 30, 1833–June 26, 1834*. Edited by Robert E. Davis. Waco: Texian Press, 1966. Revealing rather than uplifting.

Tyler, Ron, et al., eds. *The New Handbook of Texas*. 6 volumes. Austin: Texas State Historical Association, 1996. The finest fruit of Texas nationalism. Indispensable. The online version is even better.

Urrea, José. "Diary of the Military Operations of the Division which under the Command of General José Urrea Campaigned in Texas," in Castañeda, ed., *The Mexican Side of the Texan Revolution*, 204–83.

Valadés, José C. *Mexico, Santa Anna, y la Guerra de Texas*. 1936. Mexico City: Editores Mexicanos Unidos, 1965.

Visit to Texas: Being the Journal of a Traveler Through Those Parts Most Interesting to American Settlers. New York: Goodrich & Wiley, 1834; Ann Arbor, Mich.: University Microfilms, 1966.

Wallace, Ernest, and E. Adamson Hoebel. *The Comanches: Lords of the South Plains*. Norman: University of Oklahoma Press, 1952. The most useful survey of the people who controlled most of Texas for most of the period discussed in the present book.

Warren, Harris Gaylord. *The Sword Was Their Passport: A History of American Filibustering in the Mexican Revolution*. Baton Rouge: Louisiana State University Press, 1943.

Weber, David J. *The Mexican Frontier, 1821–1846: The American Southwest Under Mexico*. Albuquerque: University of New Mexico Press, 1982. Texas in the context of Mexico's northern frontier.

Weddle, Robert S. *The Wreck of the* Belle, *the Ruin of La Salle*. College Station: Texas A&M University Press, 2001.

Wharton, Clarence R. *El Presidente: A Sketch of the Life of General Santa Anna*. Austin: Gammel's Book Store, 1926.

Wooten, Dudley G., ed. *A Comprehensive History of Texas, 1685 to 1897*. 2 volumes. Dallas: William G. Scarff, 1898. Reprint edition: Austin: Texas State Historical Association, 1986. Combines first- and second-hand accounts. Unwieldy but indispensable.

Yoakum, Henderson. "History of Texas, 1685–1845," in Wooten, ed., *A Comprehensive History of Texas*, 1–434. With Foote, one of the first serious studies.

Zuber, William Physick. *My Eighty Years in Texas*. Edited by Janis Boyle Mayfield. Austin: University of Texas Press, 1971.

Illustration Credits

Acknowledgments

The author would like to thank the many archivists and librarians who made the research for this book possible, rewarding, and nearly always pleasant. The staffs at the Center for American History and the Benson Latin American Collection at the University of Texas at Austin, the Texas State Library, the Bancroft Library at the University of California at Berkeley, the Library of Congress, the Massachusetts Historical Society, and the Cushing and Sterling Evans Libraries at Texas A&M University were most helpful and professional.

The author would also like to thank Roger Scholl and William Thomas of Doubleday and James Hornfischer of Hornfischer Literary Management.

Index

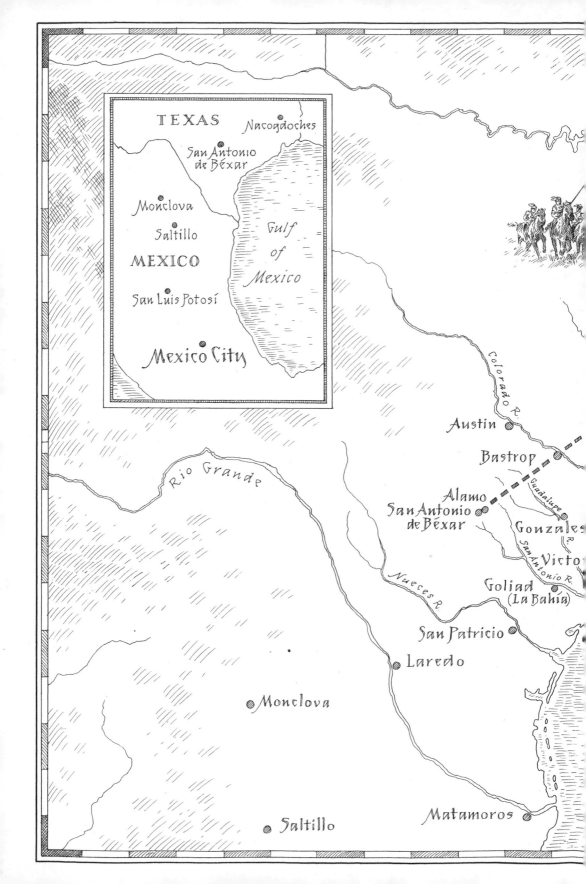

TEXAS

Nacogdoches

San Antonio
de Béxar

Monclova

Saltillo

MEXICO

San Luis Potosí

Gulf
of
Mexico

Mexico City

Colorado R.

Austin

Bastrop

Guadalupe R.

Alamo
San Antonio
de Béxar

Gonzales

San Antonio R.

Victo

Rio Grande

Nueces R.

Goliad
(La Bahía)

San Patricio

Laredo

Monclova

Saltillo

Matamoros